Economic Effects of the Government Budget

Economic Effects of the Government Budget

edited by Elhanan Helpman, Assaf Razin, and Efraim Sadka

The MIT Press
Cambridge, Massachusetts
London, England

This book was set in Times Roman by Asco Trade Typesetting Ltd. in Hong Kong, and printed and bound by Halliday Lithograph in the United States of America.

Library of Congress Cataloging-in-Publication Data

Economic effects of the government budget.

  Proceedings of the Fourth Pinhas Sapir Conference on Development, held in Dec. 1986 and sponsored by the Pinhas Sapir Center for Development at Tel-Aviv University.
  Includes bibliographies and index.
  1. Budget deficits—Congresses. 2. Finance, Public—Congresses. 3. Economic policy—Congresses. 4. Economic stabilization—Congresses. I. Helpman, Elhanan. II. Razin, Assaf. III. Sadka, Efraim. IV. Pinhas Sapir Conference on Development (4th: 1986: Tel-Aviv University). V. Merkaz le-fituaḥ ʻal-shem P. Sapir.
HJ2005.E25   1988   338.9   87-26187
ISBN 0-262-08172-5
ISBN 0-262-58090-X (pbk.)

Contents

List of Participants

Andrew B. Abel
Wharton School
University of Pennsylvania

Alan J. Auerbach
Department of Economics
University of Pennsylvania

Simon Benninga
Business School
Hebrew University of Jerusalem, Israel

Benjamin Bental
Department of Economics
Technion, Israel

Eitan Berglas
Department of Economics
Tel-Aviv University, Israel

Jagdish N. Bhagwati
Department of Economics
Columbia University

Guillermo A. Calvo
Department of Economics
University of Pennsylvania

Richard H. Clarida
Department of Economics
Yale University
and the Council of Economic Advisers

Alex Cukierman
Department of Economics
Tel-Aviv University, Israel

Allan Drazen
Department of Economics
Tel-Aviv University, Israel

Zvi Eckstein
Department of Economics
Tel-Aviv University, Israel

Jacob A. Frenkel
Department of Economics
University of Chicago
and the International Monetary Fund

Arnold C. Harberger
Department of Economics
University of Chicago

Elhanan Helpman
Department of Economics
Tel-Aviv University, Israel

Ephraim Kleiman
Department of Economics
Hebrew University of Jerusalem, Israel

Leonardo Leiderman
Department of Economics
Tel-Aviv University, Israel

David Levhari
Department of Economics
Hebrew University of Jerusalem, Israel

Yoram Mayshar
Department of Economics
Hebrew University of Jerusalem, Israel

Allan H. Meltzer
Department of Economics
Carnegie-Mellon University

Maurice Obstfeld
Department of Economics
University of Pennsylvania

Torsten Persson
Institute for International Economic Studies
University of Stockholm, Sweden

Assaf Razin
Department of Economics
Tel-Aviv University, Israel

Efraim Sadka
Department of Economics
Tel-Aviv University, Israel

Thomas J. Sargent
Hoover Institution
Stanford University

Eytan Sheshinski
Department of Economics
Hebrew University of Jerusalem, Israel

Lars E. O. Svensson
Institute for International Economic Studies
University of Stockholm, Sweden

Eli Talmor
Faculty of Management
Tel-Aviv University, Israel

Sweder van Wijnbergen
The World Bank, Washington DC

Charles Wyplosz
Department of Economics
Institute European d'Administration des Affairs, France

Joseph Zeira
Department of Economics
Hebrew University of Jerusalem, Israel

Preface

The role of government in the modern economy has been a focus of interest for economists in academia, in government, and in the private sector. A major instrument through which governments influence the economy is the budget. In December 1986, the Pinhas Sapir Center for Development at Tel-Aviv University sponsored an international conference on the economic effects of the government budget. This volume contains the proceedings of that conference.

This conference is the fourth in a series of international conferences of the Pinhas Sapir Center for Development.[1] The center is concerned with all aspects of development. Pinhas Sapir (1907–1975), Israel's seventh Minister of Trade and Industry (1955–1963) and third Minister of Finance (1963–1974), had been deeply concerned about development in Israel. Many consider him as the architect of Israel's remarkably rapid growth during the 1960s.

Partial financial support from the Bank of Israel is gratefully acknowledged.

1. The first conference, held in June 1979, was "Development in an Inflationary World." The proceedings were published in M. June Flanders and Assaf Razin (eds.), *Development in an Inflationary World* (Academic Press: New York, 1981). The second conference, held in December 1980, was "Social Policy Evaluation: Health, Education and Welfare." The proceedings were published in (1) Elhanan Helpman, Assaf Razin, and Efraim Sadka (eds.), *Social Policy Evaluation: An Economic Perspective* (Academic Press: New York, 1983) and (2) Shimon Spiro and Ephraim Yuchtman-Ya'ar (eds.), *Evaluating the Welfare State: Social and Political Perspectives* (Academic Press: New York, 1983). The third conference, held in May 1984, was "Economic Policy in Theory and Practice." The proceedings were published in Assaf Razin and Efraim Sadka (eds.), *Economic Policy in Theory and Practice* (Macmillan Press: London, 1987).

Introduction

Elhanan Helpman, Assaf Razin, and Efraim Sadka

The government budget affects the economy via a multitude of channels. This volume is concerned with effects that stem from the tax structure, the pattern of expenditures, the magnitude of the deficit, and the composition of its finance. Since other policies, such as monetary and exchange-rate policies, are inherently related to the budget, it is necessary to deal with them in conjunction with the budgetary stance. This volume contains studies that treat these issues also.

We chose to concentrate on budgetary problems that are related to macroeconomic performance, emphasizing recent thinking on a number of issues that have been at the forefront of research. This choice determines the topical bias of this volume.

Part I deals with the revenue side of the government budget, namely, taxation. The first chapter, by Jagdish Bhagwati, surveys recent developments in the literature on income taxation in an open economy (that is, with international mobility of people). The early literature focused on the question of income distribution between emigrants and the nonmigrants ("those left behind," or TLBs). The TLBs generally lose from migration. But it is usually possible to levy a tax on the emigrants in order to compensate the TLBs and still leave the emigrants better off than they were without migration ("taxing the brain drain").

More recent writings study the properties of the optimal income tax under two alternative systems: the schedular system, which does not extend the income tax to citizens living abroad, and the global system, which does. Most of the theorists have adopted the "nationalist" view, according to which the home country designs the optimal tax in order to maximize a social welfare function that depends on the utilities of its nationals only, ignoring the welfare of the host country. The range of social welfare functions adopted extends from counting nationals abroad equally with resident nationals to attaching zero value to the former.

Intuition suggests that opening an initially closed economy and allowing for outmigration (and loss of tax revenue) should lower the optimal tax rates and make the optimal tax structure loss egalitarian under the schedular system. However, a common implication of quite a few studies is that this intuition is not always valid. Nevertheless, low-income workers remaining in the home country are always worse off when borders are opened to migration. The global system, which allows the taxation of citizens abroad, provides the domestic government with a larger opportunity set and is therefore definitely superior to the schedular system. This conclusion may well be valid even when the domestic country is governed by malign politicians, acting to garner rewards for themselves rather than for the populace.

The next two chapters, by Alan Auerbach and James Poterba and by Simon Benninga and Eli Talmor, focus on various aspects of capital income taxation. U.S. corporate income tax revenues have declines sharply in the last two decades: from an average of about 3.9% of GNP in the period 1961–1965 to an average of only about 1.4% of GNP during the period 1981–1985. The prevailing view is that legislative changes are largely responsible for the sharp decline in corporate tax revenues. Alan Auerbach and James Poterba challenge this viewpoint. (Their study is confined to the U.S. nonfinancial corporate sector.) They maintain that while legislative changes that lowered the effective corporate tax rate have indeed been important contributors to the decline in corporate tax revenue, a much more important contributor has been the decline in corporate profitability. The average effective tax rate has indeed declined from an annual average of 42.5% during the period 1961–1965 to an annual average of 30.8% during the period 1981–1985. But the decline in the economic profit rate on corporate capital has been much sharper: from an average of 10.96% during 1961–1965 to an average of 4.91% in 1981–1985, with a postwar record low of 2.88% in 1982.

Auerbach and Poterba do not try to explain why corporate profitability has declined, but they do attempt to find the causes for the decline in the effective tax rate. A small role was played by the decline in the statutory tax rate from 52% to 46%, but the most important cause has been the increasingly generous capital recovery provisions. The latter refer to the investment tax credit and the differences between tax depreciation and true economic depreciation. During the period 1981–1985, these provisions caused a decrease of 22 percentage points in the effective tax rate below the statutory rate (compared to only 8.2 percentage points during the period 1961–1965).

They present also the path of corporate tax revenues over the next five years (under the new Tax Reform Act), based on estimates of the Congressional Budget Office (1986). Notably, the effective tax rate (34.9–35.7%) is going to be for the first time above the statutory rate (which is only 34%).

This reversal of the relation between the effective and the statutory tax rate is due mainly to tougher capital recovery provisions.

Simon Benninga and Eli Talmor examine the effects of changes in the capital income tax rates on investment, interest rates, and the degree of income inequality. They extend the framework employed by Miller (1977) to include a government's budget constraint, thus allowing a general equilibrium analysis of the effects of taxes. Benninga and Talmor consider two types of individuals with low and high personal income tax rates, a corporate sector with a corporate tax rate, which is intermediate between the low and the high personal tax rates, and a government, which levies taxes and issues tax-exempt bonds. Income from corporate equity is not subject to the personal income tax. As expected, their model gives rise to the following general equilibrium features: (1) the net (after corporate tax) cost of interest on corporate bonds is equal to the (tax-exempt) rate of interest on government bonds; (2) low-tax individuals hold the entire stock of corporate bonds; (3) high-tax individuals hold the entire stocks of corporate equity and government bonds.

Employing time-separable, power utility functions, they examine the general equilibrium effects of changes in tax rates and government consumption. They first consider an increase in the corporate tax rate that is offset by a change in the personal income tax rate imposed on the holders of equity (i.e., the high-tax individuals) in order to maintain a balanced government budget. They show that such a change increases investment, reduces the interest on government bonds, increases the interest on corporate bonds, decreases the welfare of the high-tax individuals, and increases the welfare of the low-tax individuals. Next, they consider an increase in government expenditure that is financed by an increase in the high personal tax rate. They show that such a change lowers investment and raises the interest rates on government bonds and corporate bonds.

Joseph Zeira's chapter deals with insurance aspects of tax policies. In the absence of full-contingent markets, he shows by means of two examples how the government shares risk with investors through income taxes and transfers, thereby raising investment. In the first example the source of stochastic demand fluctuations is specified as taste shifts between two consumption goods. In this case a specific excise-tax policy is shown to eliminate risk completely. The policy shifts the economy to the riskless equilibrium, thereby raising the stock of capital. The second example specifies an economy with stochastic productivity shocks to human capital.

Here a progressive income tax system is shown to raise the equilibrium stocks of human and physical capital. The more general message of these examples is that tax policies that provide an insurance could plausibly raise investment.

Part II deals with intertemporal consumption decisions and the "Ricardian Equivalence Theorem." Eytan Sheshinski's chapter employs an overlapping generations model with earnings uncertainty. Each generation lives two periods: earnings are obtained in the first period, while second-period consumption is financed by savings and transfers (social security system). Individuals are altruistic; that is, they care about the welfare of their offspring and provide bequests for them. A nonnegativity constraint on bequests, if one exists, is assumed to be not binding. The earnings of future generations (and the social security benefits financed by these earnings) are not known to the members of the current generation when they make their consumption and savings plans. A common utility function that is time separable and exhibits constant absolute risk aversion is assumed for all individuals.

Sheshinski considers first the case of homogeneous generations. In this case the "Law of Large Numbers" does not apply and the earnings uncertainty is perceived in the aggregate. The social security system cannot provide any insurance for altruistic individuals and the Ricardian Equivalence holds. In particular, he shows that a balanced-budget change in future social security taxes and benefits, which is announced today, has no effect on the equilibrium allocation. However, when generations are heterogeneous and it is assumed that by the "Law of Large Numbers" uncertainty is eliminated in the aggregate, the Equivalence Theorem breaks down: a pay-as-you-go social security system may provide both insurance against future earnings uncertainty and redistribution of income. The expected lifetime utility may rise for some individuals and fall for others. Obviously, the equivalence result does not hold also when an altruistic motive for bequests does not exist.

As was mentioned above, Sheshinski implicitly assumed that the nonnegativity constraint on bequests is not binding. Andrew Abel's chapter refers to this case as that of an operative bequest motive. He derives conditions under which the bequest motive is indeed operative and conditions under which the bequest motive is inoperative (that is, the nonnegativity constraint on bequests is binding). His model is fairly similar to that of Sheshinski, except that he has variable marginal products of labor and capital (according to a constant returns-to-scale Cobb-Douglas technology); a time-separable, log-linear utility function; and the uncertainty is with respect to both earned (labor) income and unearned (capital) income (through a random coefficient multiplying the production function).

Abel shows that the bequest motive is operative when the weight that one attaches to her heirs' utility relative to her own utility is larger than some critical value; the bequest motive is inoperative when this weight is smaller than some other critical value. For each individual, these two critical values depend on the ratio of her capital stock relative to the total capital stock, but they do not depend (explicitly) on time. Abel also shows that the initial (cross-sectional) distribution of the individual shares in the total stock of capital is preserved forever, if the bequest motive is operative for all consumers. When it is inoperative for all consumers, any cross-sectional inequality in the distribution of wealth is eliminated after one period. It then follows that in a one-consumer economy the bequest motive is either always (i.e., at all times) operative or always inoperative.

Obviously, the Ricardian Equivalence result does not hold when the bequest motive is inoperative. Abel notes that a pay-as-you-go social security system plays essentially the role of a negative bequest. Thus, an inoperative bequest motive may become operative when social security taxes (and benefits) increase. When this happens, Ricardian Equivalence starts to hold again with respect to further increases in social security taxes.

The last two chapters of this part provide empirical studies of the effects of taxes on private consumption and savings. Leonardo Leiderman and Assaf Razin develop and estimate a stochastic-intertemporal model of consumption behavior and use it to test the Ricardian Equivalence proposition with time series data. They allow for two channels that may give rise to deviations from Ricardian neutrality: finite horizons and liquidity constraints. Their model incorporates explicitly the role of taxes, substitution between public and private consumption, and different degrees of consumer-good durability. The evidence, based on data for Israel in the first half of the 1980s, supports the Ricardian neutrality specification against the unrestricted and the liquidity-constraints' specifications. It also yields plausible estimates for key parameters of the model such as the degree of consumer-good durability and the degree of relative risk aversion.

John Campbell and Richard Clarida apply a novel idea based on the permanent-income theory of household saving. The theory implies that savings should be the best available predictor of future changes in disposable labor income. Accordingly, they find for aggregate data in Canada and the United Kingdom that the correlation between saving and the unrestricted vector-autoregressive forecast of future changes in disposable labor income is extremely high in both countries. These results therefore suggest that the permanent-income theory provides a useful description of the dynamic behavior of household saving in Canada and Britain. However, using an elaborate econometric approach, they reject the theory as the single underlying mechanism of household saving behavior. This saving theory and its empirical tests have important implications for the effect of taxes on private saving and for the links between a country's current account and the intertemporal savings and investment choices of its households, firms, and governments.

Part III deals with budget deficits and optimal policies. Jacob Frenkel and Assaf Razin's chapter deals with the international effects of budget deficits arising from tax and transfer policies in a distortionary tax system. The analysis demonstrates that the consequences of tax policies and the characteristics of the international transmission mechanism depend critically on the precise composition of taxes. Specifically, the international effects of budget deficits of the same size differ sharply according to the types of taxes used to generate the deficits. They show that in determining the effects of taxes it is useful to divide the various taxes into two groups: those that stimulate current external borrowing (national dissaving) and those that stimulate current external lending (national saving). A pro-borrowing tax policy (such as a deficit generated by a cut in consumption taxes) raises the world rate of interest, while a prolending tax policy (such as a deficit generated by a cut in labor, or capital, income tax) lowers it. The resulting change in the rate of interest is the channel through which the effects of budget deficits are transmitted to the rest of the world, thereby redistributing current account imbalances.

Guillermo Calvo and Maurice Obstfeld's chapter deals with the theory of optimal fiscal policy for an overlapping-generations economy where heterogeneous generations coexist. They examine the dynamic resource-allocation path, chosen by a utilitarian planner, who weights the welfare of both existing and future generations symmetrically. They show how to reduce the aggregate planning problem to a standard problem of optimal allocation over time with a single representative infinitely lived individual by distributing consumption optimally, on each date, among the different generations alive then. Some plausible social welfare functions can lead, however, to time inconsistency. The authors' first aim is to characterize those social welfare functions that do not lead to such inconsistency. Using time-consistent welfare functions, the optimal allocation can be realized in a market economy if time-varying and age-dependent lump-sum transfers can be made by the government. But if the government cannot distinguish among different individuals in making lump-sum transfers, a time inconsistency problem may reemerge. The second aim of the analysis is then to identify the number of fiscal policy tools needed to attain the time-consistent optimum in such circumstances.

The last chapter of this part, by Torsten Persson and Lars Svensson, analyzes the time consistency problem of government policy. They point out that there exist two separate sources of inconsistency: preferences and constraints. The former arises when one government is expected to be replaced by another government with different preferences over private welfare and the size of government (its spending level). The latter arises when second-best taxation is used, and the optimal second-best policy in period t depends on private choices in period $t - 1$. They analyze both types of inconsistency and evaluate possible biases in public spending and public debt that arise when policies are required to be time consistent. Inconsistent constraints lead in this case to third-best solutions. Although no clear-cut results emerge from their analysis, it does shed light on the issues at hand, and in particular on the role of outstanding public debt as a precommitment variable and a constraint on future government actions. Public debt can be manipulated by a government in power in order to precommit its successor.

Part IV deals with episodes that occur during high inflations. Arnold Harberger's chapter considers different types of inflationary episodes: "acute" inflation, "chronic" inflation, and devaluation-crisis-induced inflation. Taking for granted that monetary expansion was an essential ingredient of the inflation process, his main focus is on the question why such expansions took place. In answering this question Harberger develops measures of the "pressure" that is put on the banking system by the need to finance government deficits. He makes a distinction between domestic credit, the largest single asset-side item on the banking system's consolidated balance sheet, and money, the largest single item on the liability side. Accordingly, the volume of credit as a policy variable is assumed to have a significant influence on inflation even when, as in a pegged-exchange rate system, the quantity of money is beyond the control of the central bank. He provides statistical links between policy actions and their inflationary consequences using nonparametric methods. The main conclusion is that running a modest fiscal deficit does not generate a significant inflation "disease," but that running big deficits, either financed by the banking system or by allowing total bank credit to expand rapidly, gives rise to "chronic" or "acute" inflation.

Benjamin Bental and Zvi Eckstein's chapter observes that in the hyperinflations of the 1920s and in some recent high-inflation episodes the rate of inflation was accelerating in the last period just before the stabilization policy took place. This accelerating pattern is inconsistent with the predictions of the standard models in which the rate of inflation converges with a decelerating pace toward a (stable) steady state. In the perfect-foresight model specified by the authors, in which the private-sector behavior during the inflationary stage crucially depends on the size of the post-stabilization government deficit and its financing, inflation accelerates before it is stopped. They observe that many other stylized facts, including those associated with the recent Israeli stabilization experience, are consistent with the predictions of their model.

Part V deals with stabilization in open economies. Barry Eichengreen and Charles Wyplosz's chapter considers in detail a historical episode— France in the 1920s. Their work challenges the conventional view that France's resistance of the Great Depression was mainly due to export-led growth that was orchestrated by monetary and exchange rate policies, and to confidence in Poincaré's policies that led to capital inflow. It is suggested that investment expansion rather than export-led growth was the major driving force, and that the investment boom was to a large extent the result of a standard crowding in consequence of Poincaré's fiscal contraction. Substantial evidence, as well as plausible theoretical arguments, is brought to bear on these issues, thereby illuminating important aspects of France's economic success during that period. This historically oriented chapter, as well as the two succeeding theoretical chapters, attributes a central role to fiscal discipline.

The chapter by Sweder van Wijnbergen deals with exchange-rate policy in a disinflation program. It explores the restrictions on exchange-rate management that are imposed by the government budget and solvency of public debt. Here, exchange-rate policy is potent and its success depends on fiscal variables as well as on accompanying financial policies. There are two possible restrictions: on gross government debt or on the cumulative loss of reserves. Either one brings to an abrupt end an exchange-rate freeze that is designed to disinflate the economy. Which one is binding first depends on the domestic credit policy. It is demonstrated that in each case there might be a collapse of the exchange-rate policy that will come with a run on reserves of the nature described by Krugman (1979). Moreover, in each case the accumulation of *net* government interest bearing debt brings about higher inflation than in the steady state preceding the exchange rate freeze. This, it is argued, explains the surge in inflation following the collapse of exchange-rate management in several well-known episodes.

Similar issues are taken up in the chapter by Allan Drazen and Elhanan Helpman. They consider the effects of an exchange-rate freeze that will be followed by a second-stage adjustment that may consist of the abandoning of exchange-rate management, an increase in taxes, an expenditure cut on nontraded goods, or an expenditure cut on traded goods. These possibilities are analyzed for the case of a known policy-switch date as well as for the case in which there is uncertainty about the policy-switch date. It is shown that balance of payments developments, such as the existence of deficits or surpluses in the current account, depend on the public's expectations concerning the instrument that will be used in the second stage of the program. In addition, in some cases there will be a run on reserves, while no run takes place in other cases. While discussing uncertainty about the policy-switch date, it is shown that real interest rates may be high during an exchange-rate freeze. If the Central Bank is forced to end the exchange-rate freeze, there will typically be a discrete devaluation. It is claimed that this explains certain empirical phenomena.

The last chapter, by Thomas Sargent and Bruce Smith, deals with conditions under which government foreign exchange operations are irrelevant, in the sense that they do not affect the real allocation and prices. The chapter does not deal directly with stabilization. However, since exchange-rate management is often an integral part of stabilization packages, these results have a bearing on the main issues with which we were concerned in this part of the volume.

The fact that exchange-rate policy does not affect the real allocation when money is used only as a store of value has been shown in Helpman and Razin (1979) and in Kareken and Wallace (1981). In the former contribution the economy was modeled as a representative individual economy, while in the latter an overlapping generations framework was used. In both cases unrestricted arbitrage across assets ensured the absence of rate of return domination.

Real neutrality of exchange-rate policies was also demonstrated by Helpman (1981) and Lucas (1982) for models with cash-in-advance constraints and with representative consumers. In both cases there were no distortions.

Sargent and Smith take up this analysis from the point left by Kareken and Wallace. They introduce restrictions on asset holdings of one group of individuals (the "poor"), who can use only money for store of volume purposes. Other individuals (the "rich") may use in addition other financial assets. They show that Modigliani-Miller type theorems in the area of exchange-rate policies apply to broader environments then initially conceived. But this extension is restricted to economies in which money is used only for store-of-value purposes. It is now well known, however, that in economies with cash-in-advance constraints the presence of distortions makes exchange-rate policies affect real allocations (see, for example, Aschauer and Greenwood, 1983, and Calvo, 1987).

References

Aschauer, David, and Greenwood, Jeremy (1983). "A Further Exploration in the Theory of Exchange Rate Regimes," *Journal of Political Economy*, October, 91, 868–875.

Calvo, Guillermo A. (1987). "Balance-of-Payments Crises in a Cash-in-Advance Economy," *Journal of Money, Credit, and Banking*, February, 19, 19–32.

Congressional Budget Office (1986). *The Economic and Budget Outlook: An Update*, Washington: Government Printing Office.

Helpman, Elhanan (1981). "An Exploration in the Theory of Exchange Rate Regimes," *Journal of Political Economy*, October, 89, 865–890.

Helpman, Elhanan, and Razin, Assaf (1979). "Towards a Consistent Comparison of Alternative Exchange Rate Regimes," *Canadian Journal of Economics*, August, 12, 394–409.

Kareken, John, and Wallace, Neil (1981). "On the Indeterminacy of Equilibrium Exchange Rates," *Quarterly Journal of Economics*, May, 96, 207–222.

Krugman, Paul R. (1979). "A Model of Balance-of-Payments Crises," *Journal of Money, Credit, and Banking*, August, 11, 311–325.

Lucas, Robert E., Jr. (1982). "Interest Rates and Currency Prices in a Two-Country World," *Journal of Monetary Economics*, November, 10, 335–360.

Miller, Merton, H. (1977). "Debt and Taxes," *Journal of Finance*, 32, 261–275.

I TAXATION

1 International Migration and Income Taxation

Jagdish N. Bhagwati

This chapter provides an overview of recent developments in analysis of the question raised by international mobility of people of the appropriate exercise of income tax jurisdiction over them by the different nation-states between which this international mobility is defined.

1.1. Evolution of the Problem

The question itself is novel in the concerns of public finance theorists, having generally been neglected because *either*, as with the celebrated Meade Commission in the United Kingdom, it was simply assumed implicitly in the policy realm that the income tax jurisdiction must exclude nonresident nationals (this being the so-called "schedular" system in Anglo-Saxon legal jargon), as was the historically received U.K. practice, *or* the theoretical analyses of optimal income taxation were generally "closed" on the dimension of the people over whom the social welfare function was defined.[1]

Where did the problem, which has now attracted the analytical skills of many of the best public-finance theorists and of distinguished professors of law, and the attention of policymakers in national and international forums, then come from?

1. *"Taxing the Brain Drain" and Thereafter:* The major impetus came paradoxically from the analytical work on the "brain drain," or (less emotively) the outmigration of skilled people, that engaged the attention of theorists of international trade and development during the 1960s. In particular, the focus of this literature, especially the early writings of Johnson (1965, 1967) and Grubel and Scott (1966), was to address the policy concerns that this phenomenon was harmful to the developing countries.

The chief contribution of this literature on international personal mobility was to focus attention on the distinction between migrants and

This chapter was written while the author was on leave as Consultant to The World Bank during 1986–1987. The World Bank does not accept responsibility for the views expressed herein, which are those of the author and should not be attributed to the World Bank or its affiliated organizations. The chapter was presented as a paper at the Tel-Aviv Conference on Public Finance, organized by the Pinhas Sapir Center for Development, December 22–25, 1986. Thanks are due to John Wilson for his extensive collaboration on the substance of the latter parts of this paper. The research underlying this chapter was originally supported by a grant from the German Marshall Fund of the United States.

nonmigrants (or TLBS, "those left behind," a term that itself prejudged the nature of the brain drain phenomenon in a world of immigration restrictions). These authors introduced the notion that the welfare effect of outmigration on the source country must be considered in light of its effect on TLBs, rather than on indices such as overall GNP or per capita GNP. Thus, in a model with diminishing returns operative, a *finite* outflow of migrants would lose for TLBs the "surplus" that they enjoyed from the presence of the migrants: outmigration was therefore a source of loss to TLBs. But for infinitesimal changes in the size of the labor force, TLBs would be simply unaffected (though the per capita GNP would fall).[2]

The controversy was then focused exclusively on the question whether TLBs would be harmed or helped by the outmigration, and had reached rapidly diminishing returns by the late 1960s.

i. *Refocusing Issue, New Perspective—Rationale I:* I happened then to refocus the issue (Bhagwati, 1972; Bhagwati and Dellalfar, 1973) in an altogether different direction by essentially introducing a fiscal policy instrument that could be used in conjunction with free outmigration. Thus, the question was not just a welfare comparison between no-migration and outmigration. Rather, outmigration with deployment of tax policy instruments would be compared with no-migration. This was an important shift of focus because, from the viewpoint of policy, permitting outmigration must be regarded as a human right and therefore, even if it imposes costs on TLBs, emigration restrictions are not a feasible response in civilized societies. But other policy instruments may well be.

In considering therefore tax policy as such an instrument, I proposed that it would make sense to tax the outmigrants to compensate the TLBs and that, if outmigration was Pareto-better, it should be possible to compensate the TLBs and still leave the migrants better off than they were without migration.

The essential idea behind such a "tax on the brain drain," as the proposal came to be known in the literature, can be set forth with reference to figure 1.1. Assuming that there are no externalities or distortions, the MP (marginal product) is both PMP (private) and SMP (social), and exhibits diminishing returns for the LDC (less developed country) and the DC (developed country). The premigration supply of labor in each country is $O_{DC}F$ and $O_{LDC}F$, respectively, adding up to $O_{DC}O_{LDC}$. This leads to initial

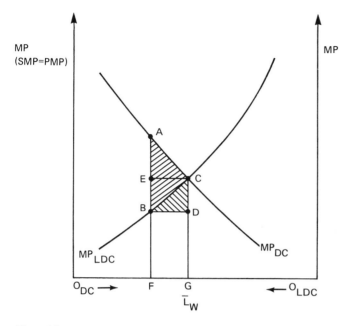

Figure 1.1
1. LDC: Migrants' *Gain* = ECDB = EBC + BCD.
2. LDC: TLBs' *Loss* = BCD.
3. LDC: Migrants + TLBs Together: *Gain* = EBC.
4. DC: Monmigrants' *Gain* = AEC.
5. WORLD *Gain* = ABC = EBC + AEC.
                      (3)   (4)

wages being AF and BF in the DC and the LDC, respectively. Hence, wage-equalizing migration will result in migration of GF labor to the DC and an equalized wage CG.

Now, it is evident that the gains and losses came out as follows:

LDC: (1) Migrants' *Gain* = ECDB ≡ EBC + BCD.
           (2) TLBs' *Loss* = BCD.
           (3) (Migrants + TLBs) *Gain* = EBC.

DC: (4) Native Nonmigrants' *Gain* = AEC.

WORLD: [LDC (Migrants + TLBs) *Gain* (3)
           +
           DC *Gain* (4)] *Gain* = ABC.

Therefore it is clear that if a tax can be levied on the LDC migrants to compensate the TLBs, the TLBs come out as well off as, and the other two groups better off than, under nonmigration, making the outcome Pareto-better *actually* (and not just in the potential-compensation sense).

Once the problem is then cast in this format, it is also immediately clear that international personal mobility, which has often been treated in traditional trade theory as symmetric to the case of international capital mobility, is really asymmetric to it in an essential way. For, if in figure 1.1, we were considering capital mobility instead of labor mobility, it *would* make sense to treat impact on LDC welfare as simply EBC. But when people move out of a society, TLBs are likely to think of national welfare as defined for themselves alone. The income-distributional problem between TLBs and the outmigrants has no real counterpart in the analysis of international capital flows.

ii. *Further Refocus and Novel Questions in Public Finance Theory—Rationale II:* But, in turn, this leads one to reexamine the notion that international mobility, and indeed tax policy in regard thereto, can be thought of exclusively in terms of a sharp focus on the welfare impact on TLBs alone, even though "national advantage" is the objective.

The Johnson-Grubel-Scott focus on TLBs is strictly relevant only if the outmigration is considered permanent; and even then, it may not be. Certainly, however, in the world of modern communications, frequent journeys back and forth between home and host countries, retention of ethnic ties, and increased tolerance for ethnic diversity in host countries such as the United States, migration is no longer thought of as removing one's population out of the set over which social welfare is defined. Especially if citizenship is retained, as a mark of one's societal affiliation to the home country, it seems perfectly appropriate to extend income taxation on the principle of "ability to pay" to citizens who reside abroad, quite regardless of the "compensatory" type of redistributive argument advanced under *Rationale I* above.

To put it somewhat vividly, if the early Americans thought that "taxation without representation" was not a good idea, "representation without taxation" would be equally inappropriate and would be the case if the "schedular" system of income tax jurisdiction was adopted *à la* the practice of European countries and their excolonies. This was the rationale, in fact, behind my original proposal to "tax the brain drain" with an income tax surcharge on what LDC migrants paid to their host countries: prosperous migrants from LDCs would make a contribution, reflecting their ability to pay, toward the revenue needs of their home countries. In the early formulations of my ideas, the citizenship nexus was implicit; the nexus became clearer as discussions with lawyers and policymakers made manifest the fact that citizenship alone would provide the basis, as it does in the United States, for income taxation of migrants by their home countries.

iii. *Rents and Rationale III:* I had also suggested that, given the extensive nature of immigration restrictions, migrants typically enjoyed rents. If so, the oldest argument for taxation in economics suggested that these rents be taxed for social use such as redistribution to the LDCs for development! This is a cute idea; but, as you discover when you work on public policy issues, cuteness in economics does not translate into feasibility in politics. If the United States taxed its immigrants for such a purpose, levying, say, an income tax surcharge on Bhagwati (I hold a U.S. green card and an Indian passport) but not on Obstfeld, there would be an immediate threat of the U.S. Supreme Court declaring the practice *ultra vires* the Constitution in being discriminatory. In the United Kingdom, since immigrants are typically from the Commonwealth countries of darker pigmentation, the outcry could also invoke notions of racism.[3]

In the end, therefore, the strongest and clearest rationale for considering the exercise of income tax jurisdiction over nationals residing abroad, i.e., of adopting the so-called "global" system of income taxation, seemed to be the argument that citizenship provides the nexus for income taxation by the home country according to "ability to pay," regardless of where you reside. Thus, while the original idea of exploring the issue had come from examining the policy implications of the brain drain from LDCs to DCs, this served only as a scaffolding that was discarded, whereas the analytical problem became a more general, and specifically defined one: that of examining the question of the appropriate design of income taxation on nationals residing abroad. This also shifted attention, from the earlier examination within the context of models of brain drain, as in McCulloch and Yellen (1976), to analysis of the question within the context of the modern theory of optimal income taxation, as in Hamada (1975) and Bhagwati and Hamada (1982).

2. *Extending Optimal Income Tax Models:* While therefore the central thrust to this new branch of income tax theory was provided by these policy interests, the desire to extend the closed-economy optimal-income-tax model of Mirrlees to an open-economy context (where people can move abroad and not be taxed) appears to have motivated John Wilson in his

dissertation at MIT in the late 1970s to explore independently (but not without, in the end, input down the road from the policy-induced literature, since I wound up as a member of his dissertation committee, with Peter Diamond as his principal advisor) some of the consequences of international migration for the Mirrlees conclusions on optimal income taxation.

3. *The U.S. Policy Debate:* Finally, as the policy-induced literature grew out of the original "brain-drain-taxation" format into the more general question of the appropriate exercise of income tax jurisdiction when citizens are internationally mobile, it became evident that the *actual practice* on this question was radically different between the few practitioners of the "global" system—the United States, the Philippines and, in principle, Mexico—and the many practitioners of the "schedular" system (predominantly led by the European countries). I stumbled into this discovery as, together with distinguished tax and human-rights lawyers such as Oliver Oldman, Richard Pomp, and Frank Newman, I was examining the feasibility of my taxing-the-brain-drain proposal at a conference in Bellagio (February 15–19, 1975).[4] In turn, this led to the realization that, in the U.S. tax policy discussions, the global system of taxation had been the subject of intense lobbying and congressional debates for decades: with equity-oriented congressmen embracing it with vigor while U.S. citizens resident abroad and U.S. corporations competing for construction jobs abroad were opposing it with equal passion. Some of the issues that I discuss below in regard to the income tax jurisdiction question have emerged from reflection on this policy debate altogether different from the brain-drain policy debate—in particular, the question of the coexistence of global and schedular income tax systems in the world economy and its implications for the global system's economic efficiency.[5]

These three strands of influence, in descending order of importance, converged to provide the impetus for a substantial examination of the theory and practices of optimal income taxation for "open" economies, i.e, for economies with citizens who are internationally mobile, at a 1981 conference on the subject in New Delhi. The main theoretical papers from this conference were published in a symposium issue of the *Journal of Public Economics* (1982), the contributions being by Baumol, Bhagwati and Hamada, Mirrlees, and Wilson.

I and Wilson have also just completed editing a volume (1988) that brings together these plus several other papers on the subject, and have written a substantial "Overview" of the issues for that volume, on which I shall now draw intensively for the rest of this chapter.

1.2. Two Key Questions

In evaluating the merits and demerits of the global and the schedular income tax systems, the analysts have approached the question at two levels of analysis:[6]

i. If the schedular system is adopted, thus exempting citizens resident abroad from taxation, then we are evidently in a "second-best" situation vis-à-vis the optimal income tax solutions in, say, the Mirrlees and Atkinson models; how does the optimal choice of the tax rates, for instance, modify in this case?

ii. If the global tax system is adopted, permitting taxation of citizens abroad, how should the tax rates be set on them vis-à-vis the citizens who are domestic residents?

Before reviewing the nature of the analytical contributions to these two questions, however, it is useful to consider the various criteria that different authors in the BW (Bhagwati and Wilson, 1988) volume have used to evaluate the different income tax regimes.

1.3. Social Welfare Criteria

If a government is to choose among alternative tax systems, it must have a criterion for evaluating the relative desirability of these tax systems. Two separate and well-known approaches to tax design can be used to justify the proposal that citizens living abroad continue to pay domestic income taxes.

According to the "benefit approach," each citizen's tax burden should reflect the benefits that he receives from the goods and services provided by the government. An important benefit often received by LDC citizens before they emigrate is state-subsidized educational services. Some proponents of a tax on the "brain drain" have therefore argued that such a tax could be imposed to compensate LDCs for the loss of human capital that they experience as a result of emigration. Interestingly, opponents of home-country income taxes on emigrants have also used the benefit approach partially to justify their stand. Thus, Hufbauer argues in the BW volume against such taxes by noting that "... the assertion of these taxes amounts to assertion of a quasi-property claim by the state, a claim not balanced by public goods or cultural associations offered by the state to the citizen living abroad." [7] Clearly, the difference of opinion here involves critically a matter of timing: should tax payments be received only when the benefits are received, or should we take a wider view that "lifetime benefits," appropriately discounted over time, should equal discounted lifetime payments?

A proponent of the "ability-to-pay approach," such as myself, would argue that this controversy is largely irrelevant because it ignores equity considerations. According to this approach, everyone's tax burden should in some sense reflect his ability to pay. It can then be argued that most LDC emigrants should pay taxes to the home government because their level of economic well-being is generally significantly higher than that of those citizens remaining in the home country.

Both approaches represent only partial guides to tax policy, however, because they ignore efficiency considerations. Taxes that are both administratively feasible and equitable invariably distort economic decision-making, and some taxes are better than others simply because the efficiency losses that they create are less severe.

The theoretical papers in the BW volume explicitly attempt to incorporate the trade-off between efficiency and equity into the design of income tax systems for open economies. They do so by taking the "social welfare approach." This approach treats tax policy as a problem in applied welfare economics, thereby allowing the modern tools of economic theory to be brought to bear on tax policy issues.

Under the social welfare approach, the objective of a tax planner is to maximize a social welfare function that has as arguments the utilities of individuals.[8] Assumptions must be made about both the form of this function and the cardinal properties of utility functions, and these assumptions essentially represent value judgments about the relative desirability of different distributions of economic well-being.

For closed economies, a popular value judgment seems to be that all individuals should be treated equally in the measurement of social welfare. That is, any two individuals with identical utilities should count equally in the measurement of social welfare. However, once different national boundaries are admitted, the economist has two problems: (i) should nationals abroad count equally with resident nationals, and (ii) should nonnationals count equally with one's own nationals? The latter question is one of "world welfare" and arises even if people never cross national boundaries; treatment of the issue divides the "cosmopolitans" from the "nationalists." The former question, on the other hand, is central even to the "nationalist" approach; and, as I have noted, the treatment of this extends from counting nationals abroad equally to attaching zero value to them (as when the focus is on nonmigrants, the TLBs, exclusively).

Most of the theorists who have recently explored the question of the appropriate exercise of income tax jurisdiction in open societies have focused on the nationalist criterion, ignoring the cosmopolitan or host-country perspective. The only exception is Wilson (1982b), whose analysis adopts a world-welfare, cosmopolitan view, maximizing the utilities of the world population where social welfare is a function of the utilities of individual members of the world population and this function is increasing in each utility.[9] Since it is unlikely that national governments will take a cosmopolitan view, especially as the world economy is not blessed with mechanisms to ensure that potential Pareto-superiority translates via transfers into actual Pareto-superiority, the economic analysts have typically taken the nationalist criterion for analyzing the problem at hand.

It is important to note, however, especially in the year of James Buchanan's Nobel award, that all economists do not share the view that governments will follow what I call the "puppeteer" model of political economy, where politicians simply pursue the objectives, with optimal policy formulations worked out with reference thereto, that the economist defines. Thus, governments may have their own "autonomous" objectives, which may well be malign or simply different from the economists' conventional, often utilitarian objectives. Thus, for instance, Niskanen (1971) models government decision-making as the outcome of the expenditure-maximizing behavior of government bureaucrats, while Brennan and Buchanan (1980) assume that the government attempts to maximize its surplus, defined as the excess of tax revenue over public expenditures. Again, even if governments are largely concerned with the welfare of the populace, they may be greatly constrained by the "directly unproductive profit-seeking" (DUP) activities of political pressure groups (see Bhagwati, 1982).

Hufbauer's argument in the BW volume against citizenship-based tax systems clearly reflects his fear that governments will abuse the power to tax citizens abroad. Although this is certainly a legitimate concern, it may be (as I discuss below) that the possible government abuses of their ability to tax emigrants are outweighed by the potential efficiency and equity gains.

1.4. The Schedular System: Income Tax Not Extended to Citizens Abroad

In light of the foregoing discussion, consider now the problems that a schedular income tax system would create in the optimal-income-tax framework. This system amounts to saying that a country faces potential emigration but cannot tax its citizens abroad.

This may not be a problem that needs analysis simply because countries on the schedular system need to know what their choice of income tax regime entails. It may also be that a schedular tax regime may be the only *feasible* policy option.

This may be because politically it may be impossible to shift to a global regime because of DUP-theoretic lobbying by current and potential emigrants. I have found, for example, that my continued advocacy of the global tax regime in LDCs typically arouses hostility from fairly well-placed and politically influential groups, since, with current migration patterns, nearly each member of most of these groups has *someone* abroad and hence they see a stake in international migration and an immediate personal loss from the adoption of the global tax regime. Equally, the expatriate LDC community, often radical in its aspirations and vociferous in its demands for foreign aid and in its slogans of "self-reliance," finds it impossible to embrace the notion that it must make its own tax contribution to the revenues of the LDCs.

But the objection to the shift may also be because of problems with feasibility at an administrative level. Pomp, a well-known Professor of Tax Law and formerly Director of the International Tax Program at Harvard, has examined the Filipino experience with its collection of tax revenues from citizens abroad in his contribution to the BW volume, and finds that there are serious difficulties because of the difficulty of devising suitable tax rolls and because of inadequate capacity for tax audits. Due to the current absence of bilateral tax treaties that permit sharing of tax information between the host countries and the Philippines, these difficulties cannot be obviated, even though the Filipino system is simple and consists essentially in piggybacking with surcharges of 1, 2, and 3% on foreign tax payments (and therefore, in principle, requires only knowing accurately the host-country tax returns of the Filipinos being assessed). If the global system is to be adopted widely, it will require entertaining reform in bilateral tax-information-sharing procedures, much as federal nations are beginning to see movement in that direction between constituent states. Of course, progress in reaching such bilateral arrangements will depend partly on the perceived desirability of the global tax system and the drawbacks of the schedular system.

Consider then the schedular tax system and how the nontaxation of citizens abroad will affect national well-being. Thus, consider the use of an income tax to raise national welfare by redistributing income between people with different productivities in work. Intuitively, the existence of a high propensity to migrate, if appropriately defined, should imply that the income tax creates a sizable distortion of migration decisions. Thus, a high propensity should significantly reduce the extent to which it is desirable to use income taxation as a tool for income redistribution. Surprisingly, a common implication of the papers in the BW volume is that this intuition is not always valid.

Thus Mirrlees (1982) constructs a simple model where the income tax distorts only migration decisions. The migration propensity of a given type of worker is defined as the elasticity of the supply of nonmigrants with respect to after-tax income in the home country. The main implication of the model is that "rather high tax rates are justifiable even if the propensity to migrate is quite large."

Bhagwati and Hamada (1982) and Wilson (1980, 1982a) take the standard closed-economy optimal income tax models, where education decisions or labor-leisure decisions are the focus, and extend them by including migration decisions. Unlike Mirrlees, they constrain the tax system to be linear, in which case the tax schedule can be completely described by two parameters, a constant marginal tax on income and a uniform poll subsidy. The particular way in which these papers characterize the impact of potential emigration on the optimal income tax is to ask how the optimal marginal tax depends on whether the home country is "open" or "closed" to migration. Intuitively, opening the country should lower the optimal marginal tax by introducing an additional cost associated with income redistribution, namely, the distortion of migration decisions. In Bhagwati and Hamada's (BH) model, where only high-income individuals are potential emigrants, the marginal migration distortion is measured by the revenue loss that occurs when these individuals emigrate in response to a rise in the marginal tax. Yet BH demonstrate that opening the borders to migration may actually raise the optimal marginal tax (see their Proposition 3). Wilson (1982a) explains this possibility in terms of the "income effects" created by opening the borders, and then he shows that it depends on BH's particular definition of a "closed country." Under the alternative definition introduced by Wilson (1980), closing the country must raise the optimal marginal tax.[10] In any case, an important message of BH's result is that one cannot unambiguously state that the existence of potential emigration makes the optimal tax structure less egalitarian.

This message appears in a different form in Wilson (1980). By not restricting the innate "ability" levels possessed by potential emigrants, he is able to demonstrate that the effect of potential emigration on the optimal income tax depends on the distribution of ability levels among potential emigrants. Closing the country to migration will raise the optimal marginal tax if the people who migrate in response to a tax change possess sufficiently high or low ability levels. However, if these potential emigrants possess ability levels in some intermediate range, then closing the country will lower the optimal marginal tax. The basic argument is that these potential emigrants are individuals who bear a positive tax burden while residing in the home country, but will desire to emigrate if the marginal tax is reduced. Consequently, the marginal tax should be raised to encourage them to remain in the home country, where they pay taxes.

The issue of how *tax rates* differ between closed and open regimes should be distinguished from the issue of how *welfare* differs between these regimes. Whereas BH find that a country's marginal tax may rise or fall when the borders are opened to migration, they conclude unambiguously that national welfare, which is determined in their model by the utilities of the low-income workers remaining in the home country, must fall (see their Proposition 1). The basic reasoning is that opening the borders allows high-income individuals to escape taxation and thereby worsens the trade-off between equity and efficiency as viewed by the home country.

1.5. The Global System and the Taxation of Citizens Abroad

Taxing the incomes of citizens abroad clearly provides a domestic government both efficiency and equity gains. The global system is definitely superior. But it is not clear how much of a tax burden emigrants should bear relative to residents.

Bhagwati and Hamada (1982) investigate this issue using a model where the decisions facing an individual are how much education to obtain and whether to emigrate. They prove that emigrants and residents should both be taxed nearly 100%, with educational expenses being subsidized nearly 100%. Their analysis does not indicate, however, how emigrants should be taxed relative to residents in more realistic models where (nearly) 100% taxation is undesirable. On the other hand, the significant contribution of Mirrlees (1982) is to investigate a model where incomes should be taxed significantly less than 100% because individuals are able to engage in tax avoidance activities.

1.6. Extensions

There are several directions in which the theoretical research discussed in the previous sections could be usefully extended.

a. *Evasion:* One important extension would be to model explicitly some of the more important mechanisms, both legal and illegal, by which residents and emigrants avoid paying taxes. Doing so should provide a better understanding of the relative magnitudes of the "taxable work elasticities" that are central to the relative rates at which emigrants and residents should be taxed in the Mirrlees model.

Furthermore, it would then be possible to model the enforcement methods that the home government might use to reduce illegal tax evasion among both residents and emigrants. Presumably, such methods would be more effective at reducing tax evasion by residents rather than by emigrants.[11] If so, the implementation of an optimal enforcement program might tend to raise the optimal rates at which residents should be taxed relative to emigrants.

Even for closed economies, there has been almost no research on optimal taxation in the presence of illegal tax evasion (see Sandmo, 1981, for an exception). One problem with modeling tax evasion is that it is inherently a problem involving intertemporal decision-making. An individual's present and future probabilities of getting caught, along with the various penalties, will normally depend on his past history of tax evasion. Consequently, his present decision to evade taxes will partially depend on his expectations about future work or leisure activities; and this decision will also influence his future choices among these activities.

These intertemporal aspects are especially evident in the open-economy context, as is nicely illustrated by Pomp (1985) in his discussion of the "tax clearance system" used by the Philippines prior to 1973 to enforce its income tax on emigrant incomes. Without a "tax clearance certificate," a citizen could not leave the Philippines or, if already abroad, could be prevented from renewing his or her Philippines passport. Pomp observes that the tax clearance system was not viewed as a satisfactory device for dealing with tax delinquents. One problem is that it reduced the number of times the emigrants returned to the Philippines for visits, thereby diminishing the amount of revenue and foreign exchange generated by these visits. Furthermore, it may have induced a sizable number of emigrants to obtain DC citizenship, in which case their tax liability to the Philippines was entirely eliminated. To analyze appropriately the problems created by the tax clearance program, it is clear therefore that we would need a model that recognized the possibility that emigrants could return to the home country either permanently or for temporary visits.

The absence of intertemporal considerations is an important limitation of the models. The model presented by Bhagwati and Hamada (1982) does contain an intertemporal utility maximization problem where individuals must choose how many years of education to receive before they start earning income. But each individual earns all of his or her other lifetime income in only one location, at home or abroad. This limitation, which is shared by the other theoretical models in the BW volume, prevents consideration of many important legal and illegal tax avoidance methods.

One particularly important legal method by which an emigrant may avoid paying taxes to the home government is to change citizenship.[12] Presumably, the emigrant's ability and willingness to do so are positively related to the number of years spent abroad. This relation would appear to provide a pure efficiency argument for a tax system where the total tax burden faced by an emigrant declines with the number of years spent abroad.

b. *Remittances:* Another issue not addressed in existing theoretical models concerns the remittances that migrants make to friends and relatives remaining in the home country. If an emigrant's willingness to make these remittances is negatively related to his or her tax payments to the home country, a significant "remittance elasticity" may provide a justification for taxing emigrants at relatively low rates.

Such empirical estimates as are available, however, suggest that remittances are an important characteristic of low-income rather than of high-income emigrants. If so, this may moderate in turn the remittance-led justification for taxing emigrants at relatively low rates, since most remittances may then be from emigrants who are below the tax-exemption limit and because the propensity to remit may be declining with taxable income.

1.7.   Political Economy: DUP Activities and Malign Governments

A major characteristic that all the theoretical contributions here share is that they assume, with conventional economics, the assumption of a *benign* government. Such a government simply exists with a view to implementing the optimal or suboptimal tax policy whose consequences we analyze.

But a powerful new trend in economic theory rejects this view of the government and permits what are described variously as directly unproductive profit-seeking DUP (Bhagwati, 1982) activities. In this view, lobbying activities are addressed to enacting policies that improve one's income or are triggered by such policies. For example, a tariff may be enacted by tariff seeking; and the revenues from the tariff may trigger revenue seeking by lobbies. Again, the bureaucrats or politicians who are cogs in the governmental machine may act as a malign force, utilizing policies to garner rewards for themselves rather than for the populace. They may divert revenues to personal use to buy gold beds or to fatten their Swiss numbered accounts.

This latter viewpoint is expounded by Hufbauer in the BW volume. He claims that "malign states are far more commonplace than benign states." He goes on to argue that emigration may serve the important function of limiting the degree to which a government is able to exploit its citizens. To support his argument, he recalls Tiebout's (1956) famous insight that local public goods could be efficiently provided by communities within a country if people could costlessly migrate between communities until they obtained their most preferred tax-expenditure packages.

Extensive research in recent years has uncovered many reasons why decentralized decision-making by local governments is likely to be inefficient, even if there are no impediments to labor mobility (see Bewley, 1981, for a survey). These negative results would seem to be applicable to the uncoordinated decision-making by national governments in the world economy. However, just as Tiebout's argument certainly contains an important grain of truth, so does the assertion that emigration opportunities between countries serve to make national governments more responsive to the preferences of the populace.

Presumably, a malign LDC government could use its ability to tax citizens working abroad to further its own objectives at the expense of the populace. Consequently, a DC government could appeal to the malign nature of most governments to justify not aiding LDCs in the collection of taxes on emigrant incomes. However, the case against taxing emigrants is far less clear-cut than it may appear at first, even if the assertion that governments are malign is accepted at face value. Thus, Bhagwati and Wilson (BW, 1988, "Overview") have constructed a model that demonstrates the utility of the global tax system even when governments are malign. The statement that governments are generally "malign" simply does not constitute a compelling argument against the global tax system.

Finally, it should be noted that under commonly accepted international law the income tax jurisdiction of the home country may be exercised by a malign government but simply cannot be enforced in the host-country courts. It is always open for citizens escaping malign countries to refuse to pay without legal harassment by the host country. The disturbing notion that somehow Picasso would have had to pay income taxes to Franco of Spain or that Idi Amin would chase Ugandans through the courts in New York is occasionally aired. But it has simply no foundation whatsoever.

1.8. Concluding Observations: The Harmonization Question

Evidently, the research reported here starts us on the road to an extension of the usual income tax theory to an open economy (where the openness implies international personal mobility). But it is only a beginning, and many problems, such as those that were already sketched above, will need to be modeled in turn.

I may conclude, however, by remarking on one further problem that is particularly important if only one country or subset of countries in the world economy proceeds to exercise tax jurisdiction on citizens abroad.

This is the problem of harmonization implied by the coexistence of different income tax systems. It is best illustrated by reference to the questions raised in the concrete case of the United States. Recall that in the United States (and the Philippines) the global income tax system that extends the income tax to citizens abroad is practiced. Other countries are on the "schedular" income tax system that does not.[13] For the United States, this has meant a twofold problem, with consequent opposition to its global system from political lobbies preferring the schedular system.

1. Private U.S. citizens abroad, who are taxed on the basis of the global system, allege that they are unfairly taxed because nationals of other countries abroad (e.g., Frenchmen in Bangkok, alongside Americans) are not so taxed by their own governments and because nationals of the countries where they reside (e.g., Thais in Bangkok) are subject only to domestic taxes (e.g., the Thai income tax) that are equally borne by the U.S. citizens on top of such U.S. income tax as becomes applicable. Hence the intranational (*horizontal*) *equity* of the global system runs afoul of the international (*horizontal*) *equity* claims.

2. Also, once trade in goods and services is considered, the harmonization issue becomes one of otherwise distorting comparative advantage, and hence efficiency, in turn. If U.S. firms have to pay the U.S. income tax on U.S. citizens they employ abroad, whereas French firms employing Frenchmen abroad do not have to pay the French income tax, distortion of comparative advantage could easily follow. That is to say, French firms having to pay certain net-of-tax salaries for, say, Saudi construction contracts would then have a smaller real cost, *ceteris paribus*, than would U.S. firms competing for the same contracts. Of course, this model, unlike the models of personal income taxation in this volume, which are in the tradition of the classic papers of Mirrlees (1971) and Atkinson (1973), assumes that the incidence of the global tax system does not fall on the taxed individuals. It also assumes, in the stark version outlined above, that the French firms must hire Frenchmen and the U.S. firms must hire Americans: if the two were total substitutes, as they almost certainly are not for different reasons, the harmonization issue would disappear. This problem needs formal analysis but has certainly played a major role in the political economy of American income taxation. People such as Senator Proxmire, who accept the equity underlying the global system and argue that the café-crawling Americans in Paris ought to pay their share of American taxes instead of leaving the burden to be borne by the workers in Detroit, have traditionally been pitted against pressure groups such as corporations handling construction works abroad.[14]

Notes

1. The escape of some from the income tax net, through outmigration and the use of the schedular system, was thus not modeled. "Closed" models nonetheless could have explored analytically similar issues by permitting nontaxability of a subset through evasion or avoidance. Alternatively, similar questions may arise in exploring federal models with local income tax jurisdictions.

2. For a synthesis and extension of the substantial literature on the welfare effects of (skilled) outmigration, see Bhagwati and Rodriguez (1976).

3. These and other difficulties emerged at the 1975 Bellagio Conference, where my tax proposal was discussed; cf. Bhagwati and Partington (1976).

4. The proceedings of that conference resulted in two companion volumes, one edited by me and the other jointly with a Professor of Law at the University of London, Martin Partington: Bhagwati (1976) and Bhagwati and Partington (1976). Also see the article by Oliver Oldman, the Learned Hand Professor of Law at Harvard, and Richard Pomp in the *Harvard International Law Journal* (winter 1979) and Pomp's later article in the *Journal of International Law and Politics*, New York University (winter 1985).

5. Eventually, as I note below, we have a "harmonization" issue here that the optimal-income-taxation type of modeling does not address.

6. The two systems are being treated here as "idealized" pure systems whereas, in practice, each tends to be compromised somewhat in the other's direction. Thus, Section 911 of the U.S. tax law now permits exemptions that constitute currently a noticeable leak from the global approach.

7. Citizenship does provide assurance of having access to these benefits at will, so that Hufbauer's argument is certainly overstated even if its premises are not challenged.

8. Utilitarianism may not be accepted, of course, as a decisive choice criterion by all. Thus, within international trade theory, since the early work of Harry Johnson (1965) and Bhagwati and Srinivasan (1969), for instance, it has long been customary to put "noneconomic" objectives alongside goods and services into the social utility function as arguments. Recently, nonutilitarian approaches have become even more fashionable, thanks to the impetus provided by Nozick's theory of rights.

9. Wilson notes, however, he means that if a country's income tax system maximizes national welfare, then it is likely to be inefficient from the viewpoint of world welfare. By "inefficient," he means that there exists a change in the tax system, accompanied by lump sum transfers of income between countries, which raises every country's national welfare. The problem here is that it is difficult to imagine the correct international income transfers being implemented in the actual world economy.

10. Bhagwati and Hamada close the economy by allowing no individual to emigrate. Wilson (1980, 1982a), on the other hand, considers a closed economy to be formed by taking an open economy where emigration occurs freely, with its tax set optimally, and then imposing the constraint that no individual may change his residence in response to changes in the tax. This means, of course, that individuals who are emigrants (residents) in the optimal open economy remain so in the closed economy.

11. This need not be so, paradoxically, if bilateral cooperation on tax information makes evasion more difficult for emigrants while domestic tax enforcement continues for political and administrative reasons to be difficult.

12. Renunciation of citizenship and refusal to pay (thus making it extremely risky to return to one's home country in any way) are other alternatives to change of citizenship.

13. As noted earlier, these contrasts are not wholly pure. Thus, for example, the United States does not extend several exemptions (other than double-tax avoidance) to citizens abroad, and there are certainly restrictions in European systems on the definition of foreign residence that justifies exclusion from tax liability. The central thrust, and principles, of the two tax systems are very clear and different, however, in both cases.

14. For a historical review of this tussle, see Bhagwati and Wilson in the BW volume (1988, chapter 1).

References

Atkinson, A. B., 1973, "How progressive should income tax be?" in M. Parkin (ed.), *Essays in Modern Economics* (Longmans: London).

Baumol, W. J., 1982, "The income distribution frontier and taxation of migrants," *Journal of Public Economics* 18, 343–362, reprinted in Jagdish Bhagwati and John Wilson (eds.), 1987, *Income Taxation and International Mobility* (North Holland: Amsterdam) (forthcoming).

Berry, R., and R. Soligo, 1969, "Some welfare aspects of international migration," *Journal of Political Economy* 77.

Bewley, T., 1981, "A critique of Tiebout's theory of local public expenditures," *Econometrica* 49, 713–740.

Bhagwati, Jagdish N., 1972, "The loss of innocence: U.S. in the Nixon era," *The Daedalus* (American Academy of Arts and Sciences: Cambridge, MA).

Bhagwati, Jagdish N. (ed.), 1976, *The Brain Drain and Taxation II: Theory and Empirical Analysis* (North Holland: Amsterdam).

Bhagwati, Jagdish N., 1977. "The brain drain: international flow accounting, compensation, taxation and related proposals," paper for the Intergovernmental Group of Experts Meeting, UNCTAD, Geneva, printed as chapter 19 in J. Bhagwati (ed.), 1985, *Essays in Development Economics*, vol. 1: *Dependence and Interdependence* (Basil Blackwell: Oxford).

Bhagwati, Jagdish N., 1980, "North-South dialogue: an interview," *Third World Quarterly*, April.

Bhagwati, Jagdish N., 1982, "Directly unproductive, profit-seeking (DUP) activities," *Journal of Political Economy* 90, 988–1002.

Bhagwati, J., and W. Dellalfar, 1973, "The brain drain and income taxation," *World Development* 1, no. 1.

Bhagwati, J., and K. Hamada, 1974, "The brain drain, international integration of markets for professionals and unemployment: a theoretical analysis," *Journal of Development Economics* 1, no. 1, reprinted as chapter 6 in J. N. Bhagwati (ed.), 1976, *The Brain Drain and Taxation II: Theory and Empirical Analysis* (North Holland: Amsterdam).

Bhagwati, J., and K. Hamada, 1982, "Tax policy in the presence of emigration," *Journal of Public Economics* 18, 291–318, reprinted in Jagdish Bhagwati and John Wilson (eds.), 1987, *Income Taxation and International Mobility* (North Holland: Amsterdam) (forthcoming).

Bhagwati, J., and Martin Partington (eds.), 1976, *Taxing the Brain Drain, vol. I: A Proposal* (North Holland: Amsterdam).

Bhagwati, J., and Carlos Rodriguez, 1976, "Welfare-theoretical analyses of the brain drain," printed as chapter 5 in J. N. Bhagwati (ed.), 1976, *The Brain Drain and Taxation II: Theory and Empirical Analysis* (North Holland: Amsterdam).

Bhagwati, Jagdish, and T. N. Srinivasan, 1969, "Optimal policy intervention to achieve non-economic objectives," *Review of Economic Studies*, October.

Bhagwati, Jagdish, and John Wilson (eds.), 1988, *Income Taxation and International Mobility* (MIT Press: Cambridge, MA).

Brennan, G., and J. M. Buchanan, 1980. *The Power to Tax* (Cambridge University Press: Cambridge).

Grubel, Herbert, and A. Scott, 1966, "The international flow of human capital," *American Economic Review*, May.

Hamada, K., 1975, "Efficiency, equity, income taxation, and the brain drain: a second best argument," *Journal of Development Economics* 2, 281–287—argument reprinted as chapter 10 in J. N. Bhagwati (ed.), 1976, *The Brain Drain and Taxation II: Theory and Empirical Analysis* (North Holland: Amsterdam).

Hufbauer, G. C., 1984, "The state, the individual and the taxation of economic migration," in Jagdish Bhagwati and John Wilson (eds.), 1987, *Income Taxation and International Mobility* (North Holland: Amsterdam) (forthcoming).

Johnson, H. G., 1965. "The economics of the 'brain drain': the Canadian case," *Minerva*.

Johnson, H. G., 1967. "Some economic aspects of brain drain," *Pakistan Development Reivew* 3.

McCulloch, Rachel, and Janet L. Yellen, 1976, "Consequences of a tax on the brain drain for unemployment and income inequality in the less developed countries," printed as chapter 8 in J. N. Bhagwati (ed.), 1976, *The Brain Drain and Taxation II: Theory and Empirical Analysis* (North Holland: Amsterdam).

Mirrlees, J. A., 1971, "An exploration in the theory of optimal income taxation," *Review of Economic Studies* 38, 175–208.

Mirrlees, J. A., 1982, "Migration and optimal income taxes," *Journal of Public Economics* 18, 319–342, reprinted in Jagdish Bhagwati and John Wilson (eds.), 1988, *Income Taxation and International Mobility* (North Holland: Amsterdam) (forthcoming).

Niskanen, W., 1971, *Bureaucracy and Representative Government* (Aldine-Atherton: Chicago).

Oldman, Oliver, and Richard Pomp, 1975, "The Brain Drain: a tax analysis of the Bhagwati proposal," *World Development* 3.

Oldman, Oliver, and Richard Pomp, 1979, "Tax measures in response to the Brain Drain," *Harvard International Law Journal* 20(1).

Pomp, Richard D., 1985, "The experience of the Philippines in taxing its nonresident citizens," *Journal of International Law and Politics* 17, no. 2, 245–286, reprinted in Jagdish Bhagwati and John Wilson (eds.), 1988, *Income Taxation and International Mobility* (MIT Press: Cambridge, MA).

Sandmo, A., 1981, "Income tax evasion, labor supply, and the equity-efficiency tradeoff," *Journal of Public Economics*, 265–288.

Tiebout, C. M., 1956, "A pure theory of local expenditures," *Journal of Political Economy* 64, 416–424.

Tobin, J., 1974, "Notes on the economic theory of expulsion and expropriation," *Journal of Development Economics* 1, no. 1.

Wilson, J. D., 1980, "The effect of potential emigration on the optimal linear income tax," *Journal of Public Economics* 14, 339–353.

Wilson, J. D., 1982a, "Optimal linear income taxation in the presence of emigration," *Journal of Public Economics* 18, 363–380, reprinted in Jagdish Bhagwati and John Wilson (eds.), 1988, *Income Taxation and International Mobility* (MIT Press: Cambridge, MA).

Wilson, J. D., 1982b, "Optimal income taxation and migration: a world welfare point of view," *Journal of Public Economics* 18, 381–398, reprinted in Jagdish Bhagwati and John Wilson (eds.), 1988, *Income Taxation and International Mobility* (MIT Press: Cambridge, MA).

2 Why Have Corporate Tax Revenues Declined?

Alan J. Auerbach and James M. Poterba

Corporate income tax revenues have declined dramatically during the last two decades. The corporate tax accounted for almost 20% of federal receipts during the 1960s, compared with only 7% of federal receipts in the last five years. Federal corporate taxes averaged 3.9% of GNP during the first five years of the 1960s, 2.7% of GNP for the first five years of the 1970s, and only 1.4% of GNP for the first five years of the 1980s. In 1985, the ratio of tax to GNP was less than half what it was ten years ago, and only one-quarter as large as in 1955. In 1982, real corporate tax payments were lower than in any year since 1940. Although corporate taxes in each of the last three years were substantially greater than in 1982, the average level of tax receipts remains at its postwar low.

The erosion of corporate tax revenues is widely regarded as the result of legislative changes. For example, McIntyre's frequently cited study (1984) argues, "The decline of the corporate tax began with the adoption of the investment tax credit in the 1960s, and continued into the 1970s as Congress adopted one loophole after another in response to corporate lobbyists ... the largest single blow to the corporate tax came in 1981 with the passage of ... the Accelerated Cost Recovery System, which opened up massive new possibilities for corporate tax avoidance" (p. 1). This viewpoint clearly influenced the architects of the recently enacted Tax Reform Act of 1986. The new law's stringent corporate minimum tax of 20%, coupled with significant reductions in capital recovery allowances, will raise corporate taxes by $120 billion during the next five years.

This chapter examines why corporate taxes have declined. It decomposes movements in federal tax receipts into components attributable to changes in tax rates, changes in tax preferences, changes in corporate profitability, and other factors. The results suggest that while legislative changes have been important contributors to the decline of corporate tax revenues, they account for less than half of the change since the mid-1960s. Reduced profit-

This chapter is an abridged version of a paper published in Lawrence H. Summers, ed., *Tax Policy and the Economy* (Cambridge, MA: MIT Press). *The 1987 NBER Tax Policy Annual.* We thank William Gentry for research assistance, Sandra Byberg (IRS), Ken Petrick (BEA), Len Smith (Joint Tax Committee), William States (IRS), John Voight (IRS), and Teresa Weadock (BEA) for data assistance, Jane Gravelle and Lawrence Summers for helpful comments, and the NSF, NBER, and the University of Pennsylvania Institute for Law and Economics for financial support. This research was completed while the second author was a Batterymarch Fellow. It is part of the NBER Program on Taxation.

ability, which has shrunk the corporate tax base, is the most important cause of declining corporate taxes.

The chapter is divided into four sections. The first presents a simple division of changes in corporate taxes into components due to changes in tax rules and changes in the corporate tax base. It shows that during the last twenty years, while the average tax rate has fallen by nearly one-third, corporate profitability has declined by a factor of two. The second examines the factors that have been most important in reducing average corporate tax rates. It focuses on changes in capital recovery, inflation-induced misstatement of corporate profits, and various legislative changes. The third section examines the expected revenue gains under the Tax Reform Act of 1986, and presents preliminary evidence on how the bill will alter average tax rates. There is a brief conclusion.

2.1. Declining Tax Rates versus Declining Tax Base

The decline in corporate taxes can be divided into two components: a decline in the rate at which corporate profits are taxed and a decline in corporate profits themselves. The first component is the average tax rate, which has attracted widespread attention in the tax policy debate of the last five years (see Joint Committee on Taxation, 1984, or Spooner, 1986, for example). Many analyses of the corporate tax focus exclusively on the average rate, however, and imply the misleading conclusion that its movements are the sole cause of recent reductions in corporate tax revenues. This section demonstrates that while average tax rates have in fact declined, changes in corporate profits, the base of the corporate income tax, are an equally important factor in explaining the change in corporate taxes.

2.1.1. Effective Tax Rates and the Tax-to-Asset Ratio

The tax-to-asset ratio is the product of the average tax rate and the corporate profit rate:

$$\text{TAXES}/\text{ASSETS} = (\text{TAXES}/\text{PROFITS}) \cdot (\text{PROFITS}/\text{ASSETS}). \qquad (1)$$

PROFITS denote the real economic profits earned by corporate equity-holders,[1] TAXES/PROFITS is the average effective tax rate, and PROFITS/ASSETS defines the real economic profit rate. PROFITS excludes foreign source income of U.S. corporations, since our asset measure includes only domestic capital. A detailed description of our measure of economic profits, and of our calculations more generally, is found in Auerbach and Poterba (1987).

Table 2.1 presents data on the tax-to-asset ratio, the average tax rate, and the profit rate for each year since 1959, the year when some IRS data used in our calculations first became available. The data clearly indicate that both falling average tax rates and a decline in profitability have contributed to lower corporate taxes. The average effective tax rate is 41.8% during the 1960s, compared with 30.8% during the last five years, a decline of more than one-quarter. Average tax rates declined throughout the 1970s, averaging 43.4% for the 1971–1975 period and 40.1% for the 1976–1980 period. The average effective tax rate for the 1981–1985 period was 9% lower than its value for the 1976–1980 period. This decline is twice as large as the drop between the first and second halves of the 1970s.

The third column of table 2.1 reports the economic profit rate on nonfinancial corporate capital. The profit rate trends down throughout our sample period, but drops particularly sharply in the 1980s. From an average of 10.9% during the 1960s, the profit rate fell to 7.2% during the 1970s and 4.9% during the last five years. In 1982, when corporate taxes reached their postwar low, the corporate profit rate was also at its lowest level (2.9%). Although profits accruing to equity holders have rebounded since then, averaging 6.3% in the last two years, they are still well below their level in the previous two decades.

This dramatic decline in corporate profits is an important source of lower corporate tax receipts. The last column of table 2.1 shows that the tax-to-asset ratio at the beginning of the 1960s, for example, was 3.1 times that at the beginning of the 1980s. The average effective tax rate was 1.35 times its level in recent years, while the profit rate was 2.2 times its recent value. Declining profitability is therefore substantially more important than changes in the average tax rate in accounting for the reduction in corporate taxes.

The relative importance of changes in tax rates and the tax base can be illustrated by calculating what corporate tax receipts in the early 1980s would have been if either of the average tax rate or the profit rate had remained at its earlier level while the other changed over time. Actual corporate tax receipts averaged $49.6 billion 1986 dollars in the 1981–1985 period. If the profitability of corporate assets had been the same as in the 1960s, tax receipts would have more than doubled to $110.4 billion. Even setting the profit rate equal to its value for the 1976–1980 period would have increased annual revenues by over $20 billion, to $72.5 billion. Fixing

Table 2.1
The average tax rate and corporate profitability, 1959–1985[a]

Year	Average tax rate	Corporate profit rate	Ratio of taxes to NFC net assets
1959	0.50	9.55	4.74
1960	0.51	8.30	4.25
1961	0.48	8.79	4.22
1962	0.42	10.09	4.24
1963	0.44	10.70	4.65
1964	0.41	11.69	4.74
1965	0.38	13.55	5.17
1966	0.38	13.70	5.16
1967	0.38	11.52	4.38
1968	0.41	11.93	4.88
1969	0.43	10.17	4.42
1970	0.45	7.07	3.21
1971	0.41	7.94	3.29
1972	0.41	8.38	3.41
1973	0.43	8.67	3.69
1974	0.50	6.20	3.12
1975	0.42	5.95	2.53
1976	0.43	6.83	2.96
1977	0.38	7.98	3.04
1978	0.38	7.92	3.01
1979	0.40	6.59	2.66
1980	0.41	5.27	2.14
1981	0.36	4.62	1.68
1982	0.34	2.88	0.98
1983	0.32	4.40	1.39
1984	0.28	6.24	1.76
1985	0.24	6.40	1.51
Five-year averages			
1961–1965	0.42	10.96	4.60
1966–1970	0.41	10.88	4.41
1971–1975	0.44	7.43	3.21
1976–1980	0.40	6.92	2.76
1981–1985	0.31	4.91	1.47

a. The last three columns correspond to TAXES/PROFITS, PROFITS/ASSETS, and TAXES/ASSETS as described in the text. The last column is the product of the first two.

the average effective tax rate at its earlier level would also have raised taxes, though not by as much as the return to earlier profit levels. If the tax rate during the last five years had returned to its level in the early 1960s, taxes would have averaged $68.4 billion per year. Replacing the actual tax rate with its average value for the late 1970s would raise tax receipts by $13 billion to $62.5 billion per year.

2.1.2.   Interpreting the Average Tax Rate

Although our division of the tax-to-asset ratio into average tax rate and profit rate components may provide some insight into the source of declining tax revenues, the two components are not independent. The nature of the corporate income tax makes the average tax rate critically dependent upon the level of corporate profits. For taxable firms, many corporate tax deductions, such as depreciation allowances and tax credits, may be claimed regardless of the level of profits. A 1% increase in profits therefore raises the firm's taxable corporate income by more than 1%, increasing the average tax rate.

An offsetting effect arises for nontaxable firms. For firms with negative taxable income and no capacity to carry losses back against prior taxes, current tax payments will be zero regardless of how negative their real economic income is. An increase in profitability will not affect their taxes. It will, however, increase their economic profits, which enter the denominator of the average tax rate calculation for the entire corporate sector. These links between profitability and tax rates make it impossible to interpret changes in the average tax rate solely as the result of legislation.

The sensitivity of average tax rates to economic conditions is only one of their many shortcomings as a measure of corporate tax burdens. It is well known (see Auerbach, 1983, or Fullerton, 1984) that average tax rates may provide little information on the pattern of marginal tax incentives facing new investments. In addition, aggregate average tax rates may conceal important differences in tax burdens across different assets and different firms. Average corporate tax rates also provide an incomplete account of the tax burden on corporate income by ignoring the taxes paid by shareholders.

There are also measurement problems associated with average tax rates. They fail to consider "implicit taxes," such as the reduced returns received by banks that invest in municipal debt, as part of the total tax burden. Likewise, many sources of true economic income are ignored, since certain accounting practices that misstate economic income are not corrected. This problem even applies to the National Income Accounts. An example of such a misstatement is the inappropriate timing of expenses under the completed contract accounting method. Accounting differences accentuate the problem of comparing industry average tax rates.

2.2. Why Have Average Tax Rates Declined?

Despite numerous shortcomings, average tax rates do prove useful in analyzing changes in corporate tax revenues. They have also played an important part in the recent corporate tax reform debate. This section therefore extends our previous analysis by investigating the proximate causes of declining average tax rates.

2.2.1. Statutory Tax Rates versus Average Tax Rates

Movements in average tax rates may be traced to changes in capital recovery provisions, the increased prevalence of firms with tax losses, increased use of investment tax credits, and other factors. Each of these factors causes the average tax rate to differ from the statutory maximum rate, as shown in table 2.2. The second column in table 2.2 shows the maximum statutory tax rate for each year from 1959 to 1985. The entries in columns 3–8 describe how various factors have caused the average tax rate to differ from the statutory rate. Negative entries indicate factors that caused the average tax rate to be less than the statutory rate, while positive entries correspond to factors that increased the tax burden above the statutory rate. The average tax rate, TAXES/PROFITS, is reported in the last column. It is the sum of the maximum statutory tax rate plus the six adjustment factors in columns 3–8.

The first source of differences between statutory and average tax rates is increasingly generous capital recovery, as shown in the third column of table 2.2. This term includes both the tax reduction from use of the investment tax credit, as well as that due to differences between tax depreciation and true economic depreciation. During the most recent five-year period, capital recovery provisions accounted for a 22% differential between the statutory and the average tax rate. This is a substantial increase from the late 1970s, when these provisions explained a 9.5% difference between the two tax rates, or the 1960s, when these factors reduced the average tax rate by 8.9%.[2] Because generous capital recovery provisions have been one

Table 2.2
Causes of changing average tax rates, 1959–1985[a]

Year	Statutory rate	Capital recovery	Other inflation effects	Tax losses	Foreign tax effects	Progres- sivity	Other factors	Average tax rate
1959	52.0	−3.1	−1.2	2.6	1.0	−3.4	1.7	49.7
1960	52.0	−4.2	−0.8	4.9	1.2	−3.4	1.5	51.1
1961	52.0	−4.4	−1.5	3.6	0.5	−3.8	1.7	48.0
1962	52.0	−9.5	−2.0	3.3	0.4	−3.6	1.4	42.1
1963	52.0	−9.3	−1.0	3.2	0.5	−3.5	1.7	43.5
1964	50.0	−9.2	−0.8	2.5	0.4	−3.7	1.3	40.5
1965	48.0	−8.6	−1.3	1.8	0.3	−3.2	1.1	38.2
1966	48.0	−8.5	−1.6	1.6	0.3	−3.2	1.0	37.7
1967	48.0	−9.5	−1.0	2.2	0.4	−3.3	1.3	38.0
1968	52.8	−9.6	−2.4	2.4	0.6	−3.9	1.0	40.9
1969	52.8	−10.0	−1.5	4.1	0.7	−4.2	1.5	43.4
1970	49.2	−9.7	−1.5	7.8	0.7	−3.2	2.1	45.4
1971	48.0	−8.5	−4.1	6.4	0.5	−2.9	2.1	41.5
1972	48.0	−10.5	−1.1	4.0	1.1	−2.9	2.0	40.6
1973	48.0	−11.1	1.5	3.1	1.8	−2.6	1.9	42.6
1974	48.0	−13.9	10.2	5.1	1.0	−2.1	1.9	50.2
1975	48.0	−8.0	−4.6	4.8	3.5	−2.9	1.7	42.4
1976	48.0	−7.9	0.9	3.6	−0.2	−2.6	1.6	43.4
1977	48.0	−8.3	−0.6	3.2	−1.2	−2.7	−0.3	38.2
1978	48.0	−8.5	0.3	3.0	−0.5	−3.1	−1.1	38.0
1979	46.0	−10.4	3.8	4.3	−0.9	−3.1	0.6	40.4
1980	46.0	−12.2	2.1	6.6	0.2	−3.3	1.3	40.6
1981	46.0	−17.3	−2.1	10.5	0.9	−2.5	0.9	36.4
1982	46.0	−26.3	−5.5	22.2	0.3	−3.8	1.2	34.2
1983	46.0	−21.8	−2.7	10.8	0.2	−3.7	2.9	31.7
1984	46.0	−21.2	−2.9	7.7	0.2	−3.7	2.1	28.2
1985	46.0	−24.2	−4.3	7.6	0.2	−3.7	1.9	23.6
Five-year averages								
1961–65	50.8	−8.2	−1.3	2.9	0.4	−3.5	1.4	42.5
1966–70	50.2	−9.5	−1.6	3.6	0.5	−3.6	1.5	41.1
1971–75	48.0	−9.5	0.4	4.7	1.6	−2.7	1.9	43.5
1976–80	47.2	−9.5	1.3	4.1	−0.5	−3.0	0.4	40.1
1981–85	46.0	−22.1	−3.5	11.8	0.4	−3.5	1.8	30.8

a. All entries for 1984 and 1985 are based on preliminary data and extrapolations. The average tax rate (column 9) equals the statutory rate (column 2) plus the adjustment factors in columns 3–8.

of the popular villains behind the recent decline in corporate taxes, we shall return below to provide a more detailed breakdown of these effects.

The fourth column in table 2.2 reports the effect of inflation on average tax rates. This column combines two separate influences. First, inflation leads to spurious inventory profits that raise corporate tax payments and the average tax rate. (Inflation's positive impact through a related channel, the failure to index depreciation allowances for inflation, is subsumed in the capital recovery term above.) Inflation also exerts a countervailing effect on the average tax rate by reducing the real value of corporate debt, generating capital gains for equity holders. These gains are untaxed, so inflation raises economic income but does not affect taxes. The two effects roughly cancel, resulting in a small net effect of inflation on the average tax rate. Inflation raised the average tax rate by less than 1% during the 1970s, and it has reduced the average tax rate by 3.5% during the 1980s.

The fifth column in table 2.2 indicates the impact of imperfect loss-offset provisions on the average tax rate. The principal effect of imperfect loss offset is to raise the average tax rate when firms experience losses, since firms with negative income cannot claim tax refunds. Tax receipts are therefore higher than they would be in a system with proportional taxation of economic income. This effect is somewhat attenuated by the availability of loss carrybacks and net operating loss carryforwards. Carrybacks allow some loss offset in the year when losses occur. Loss carryforwards, in contrast, reduce a firm's current tax liability as a result of previous losses.

Imperfect loss offset provisions may raise or lower the average tax rate, depending on whether net operating loss deductions exceed the value of losses not carried back. The entries in column 5 of table 2.2 show that throughout the 1959–1985 period imperfect loss offsets generated a substantial net increase in the average tax rate. For the most recent five years, the provisions regarding losses *increased* the average tax rate by 11.8%. This is much larger than the impact of losses in any previous period. Imperfect loss offsets accounted for a 4.4% increase in the average tax rate in the 1970s, and a 3.2% increase during the 1960s. This result deserves emphasis: the increased incidence of tax losses during the 1980s has increased, not reduced, the average corporate tax rate.

The sixth column of table 2.2 describes how foreign tax provisions affect the average tax rate. This term consists of two parts. The first measures the increase in taxes that would have resulted if foreign source income were taxable at the U.S. statutory rate, while the second reduces taxes by the amount of foreign tax credits claimed. If the statutory tax rates in all other countries equaled that in the United States and all firms could utilize foreign tax credits in full, then the net foreign tax effect in our table would equal zero. If foreign countries levied taxes at rates below the domestic rate, the foreign tax effect would be positive since the domestic taxes on foreign source income would exceed the foreign tax credit. In our data, the net effect of foreign tax provisions is a small increase in the average tax rate. This effect averages 0.4% in the last five years, compared with 0.45% during the 1970s and 1960s.

The seventh and eighth columns of table 2.2 indicate the influence of two other factors, tax progressivity and an "other" category, which includes posttabulation revisions and miscellaneous tax credits on the average tax rate. Neither factor has a large effect. Tax progressivity, which accounts for the fact that some corporate income is taxed at rates below the statutory maximum, lowers the average tax rate by roughly 3.5% with little variation over time. The "other" category usually raises the average corporate tax rate, since the results of tax audits are included in this category and they outweigh the other tax credits.

2.2.2.   Changes in Capital Recovery Provisions

Table 2.2 clearly suggests that the most important factor causing average tax rates to fall below the statutory rate is capital recovery provisions. For the last five years, capital recovery provisions depressed the average tax rate by 14% more than they did during the 1960s and by 13% more than during the late 1970s. We now consider a more detailed breakdown of changes in capital recovery provisions.

The capital consumption adjustment is the difference between tax depreciation and real economic depreciation. It has two components: Accelerated Depreciation and Basis Misstatement. Accelerated Depreciation is the difference between tax depreciation and economic depreciation at historic cost. Tax depreciation is based on tax service lives and depreciation schedules. It usually provides larger depreciation allowances than would application of realistic economic lifetimes and decay patterns to the historic costs of corporate assets. Taxable income therefore understates economic income, reducing the average tax rate. The second term, Basis Misstatement, measures the difference between straight-line depreciation using economic asset lives but historic asset costs and that using the same decay profiles but revaluing assets each year to their current replacement cost.

Failure to index the basis of depreciable assets raises taxable income above economic income and therefore increases the average tax rate.

During the last five years, accelerated depreciation reduced the average tax rate by 35%, the ITC lowered it by 13%, and inflationary misstatement of asset basis raised it by 26%. These large offsetting effects correspond to the net effect of -22% that is reported in the fourth column of table 2.2. All three factors have become larger in absolute value during our sample period. In the 1960s, for example, accelerated depreciation lowered the average rate by 11.9%, inflation effects raised it by 5.4%, and the ITC lowered it by another 2.3%.

These results naturally raise the question of whether movements in the capital recovery factor are primarily the result of legislative changes or have been caused by other forces, such as a shift in the composition of investment toward equipment rather than structures. Although separating average tax rate movements into components due to legislative and other changes is a treacherous exercise, some illustrative calculations are nonetheless possible. Ziemer (1985) estimates the change in federal corporate tax revenues due to the passage of ERTA and TEFRA, and presents a separate calculation for the impact of accelerated depreciation and other provisions. Using his revenue estimates, we calculate that the average tax rate would have been about 7% higher during the last four years if ACRS had not been adopted. This corresponds to increased revenues of $20 billion per year, on average, since 1982. The effect would have been largest in 1985, the year with the largest stock of assets receiving generous ACRS depreciation.

Although ACRS has lowered corporate taxes in the past four years, focusing only on the immediate postenactment effects of tax legislation can be misleading. Passage of a bill such as the Economic Recovery Tax Act depresses corporate taxes by more in the period immediately after enactment than it does in the steady state. Immediately after enactment, revenues are reduced both because new assets are given substantial depreciation benefits immediately after installation and because some relatively old prereform assets are still eligible for depreciation benefits under the prior, less generous depreciation rules. In the steady state, only the generous depreciation for new assets reduces revenues. This partially explains why, even without the 1986 Tax Reform Act, corporate tax revenues were expected to rise during the late 1980s. An opposite effect arises with the recent legislation, which lengthens asset lives. It will collect more revenue in the short run than in the steady state, because some aging pre-TRA assets are paying higher taxes than they would had they been depreciated under the new rules.[3]

2.3. Corporate Taxes under the 1986 Tax Reform Act

The recently enacted Tax Reform Act of 1986 shifts $120 billion of federal tax liability from households to corporations over the 1987–1991 period. The TRA will therefore affect both the average tax rate and the tax-to-asset ratio for nonfinancial corporations. This section uses revenue projections from the Congressional Budget Office (1986) to estimate the course of average tax rates over the next five years. It compares the tax trajectory without the Tax Reform Act with the trajectory under the new legislation, and places the increased corporate tax burden in historical perspective.

Table 2.3 compares the paths of corporate tax payments under old law and the Tax Reform Act of 1986. The first two rows show the level of corporate tax payments by NFCs in 1986 dollars under the two regimes. Even under old law, corporate taxes are projected to rise. By 1990, for example, they will be 77% higher than in the first five years of the 1980s. Rising corporate tax payments can be traced to two sources. First, corporate profits are forecast to rise in the late 1980s. Our CBO-based projections imply a profit rate of 8.2% for the period 1987–1991, compared with 4.9% in the early 1980s. In addition, the front-loading of depreciation under ACRS implies that the average tax rate on projects undertaken since 1981 is low early in the project's life and high later on. As more projects reach the high-tax stage of their life cycle, corporate taxes also rise.

Under the Tax Reform Act, revenues rise even more rapidly than under old law. By 1990 corporate taxes from the NFCs exceed $100 billion (1986 dollars), more than double the level of the past five years. For the 1987–1991 period, corporate taxes are 22% greater under the TRA than under current law. The new bill's revenue impact is largest in 1987, when it raises over 30% more revenue than the current law. This is because rates remain high, but most tax preferences have been eliminated.

The next four rows of table 2.3 show corporate taxes relative to GNP and corporate assets. Under current law the tax-to-GNP ratio would rise from 1.2% in 1985 to 1.8% in 1991, while the Tax Reform Act raises this ratio to 2.2%. The new law therefore returns the tax-to-GNP ratio to its level during the late 1970s, but not to the level (3.2% on average) of the

Table 2.3
Projected tax payments and average tax rates, 1986–1991[a]

	Year					
	1986	1987	1988	1989	1990	1991
NFC federal tax payments						
Old law (1986 $billion)	56.0	69.9	79.2	83.6	87.7	90.3
New law (1986 $billion)	61.5	90.9	96.9	99.4	103.6	107.8
NFC federal taxes/GNP						
Old law (%)	1.3	1.6	1.8	1.8	1.8	1.8
New law (%)	1.5	2.1	2.2	2.1	2.2	2.2
NFC federal taxes/NFC assets						
Old law (%)	1.7	2.1	2.3	2.4	2.5	2.6
New law (%)	1.9	2.7	2.9	2.9	3.0	3.1
Average tax rate						
Old law	22.9	26.8	29.0	29.7	30.2	29.9
New law	25.1	34.9	35.5	35.3	35.7	35.7
Tax rate differential						
New law − old law	2.2	8.1	6.5	5.6	5.5	5.8
Differential due to						
Statutory rate	0.0	−6.0	−12.0	−12.0	−12.0	−12.0
Capital recovery	1.5	5.6	6.5	8.4	9.6	11.0
Accounting rules	1.0	4.1	4.9	4.3	3.5	2.4
Other factors	−0.3	4.4	7.1	4.9	4.4	4.4

a. Calculations are based on CBO (1986) projections of corporate profits and tax revenues under pre-1986 law, combined with Joint Committee on Taxation forecasts of revenue changes from the Tax Reform Act of 1986.

1960s. A similar statement applies to the ratio of tax payments to net NFC assets, which is plotted in figure 2.1. From an average of 1.5% in the 1981–1985 period, this tax measure rises to 2.6% under old law and to 3.1% under new law by 1991. The new law will double the ratio of taxes to corporate assets, although this ratio will still be lower than it was during the 1960s.

Although part of the change in tax revenues is due to anticipated increases in corporate profits, the average tax rate will also change significantly during the next five years. This is shown in the seventh and eighth rows of table 2.3, which report the tax rates under old law and under the Tax Reform Act for the 1986–1991 period. Without any legislative change, the average tax rate would have increased from 0.24 in 1985 to 0.30 by 1990. This is higher than in the first five years of the 1980s, but still below the level of the late 1970s. Under new law, by comparison, the average tax rate

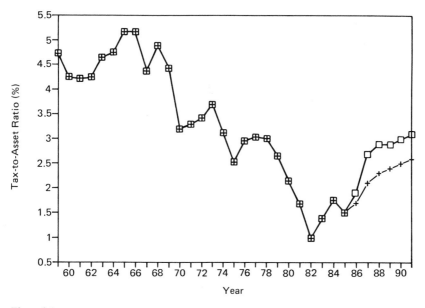

Figure 2.1
Tax-to-asset ratio, 1959–1991. Key: square, new law; cross, old law.

rises to 0.36 by the end of the decade, almost returning to its level of the late 1970s. The Tax Reform Act has its largest impact on the tax rate in the transition period, 1987 and 1988, when the ratio of taxes to economic profits rises by 8.1% and 6.5%, respectively. Figure 2.2 plots the movements in average tax rates both for the 1959–1985 period as well as for the next five years under both old law and new law.

The Tax Reform Act of 1986 changes numerous provisions in the corporate income tax. The Joint Committee on Taxation's revenue estimates (House of Representatives, 1986) for example, include seventeen major categories, and hundreds of minor categories, through which revenue changes occur. A detailed analysis of why the average tax rate will differ from the statutory rate is impossible because many of the required data series are unavailable. We can, however, provide a rough sketch of why the average tax rate changes under the new law. The last four rows in table 2.3 disaggregate changes in the effective tax rate between old law and the Tax Reform Act into four categories.

The change in the statutory rate reduces the average rate. There are no rate changes for 1986. In 1987, the statutory rate falls by 6% to the 40%

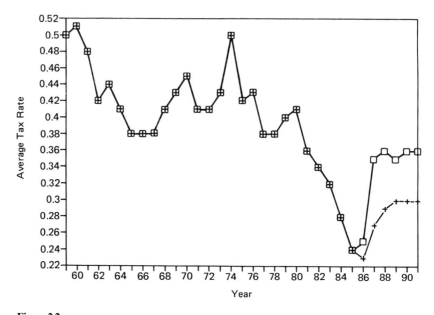

Figure 2.2
Average tax rate, 1959–1991. Key: square, new law; cross, old law.

"blended" rate for a company whose fiscal year coincides with the calendar year. Beginning in calendar 1988, the top statutory rate is 34%. Several provisions offset the statutory rate reduction and raise the average tax rate. Changes in capital recovery provisions, principally the repeal of the Investment Tax Credit and the extension of tax depreciation lives, account for an 11% increase in the average tax rate in 1991. In the earlier years these changes are somewhat less important, principally because transition rules allow a substantial share of the investment undertaken prior to 1988 to obtain favorable tax treatment.[4]

The penultimate row in table 2.3 shows how changes in accounting rules affect the average tax rate. There are a number of important provisions in this category, including changes affecting long-term contracts, the capitalization of construction and development costs, and the treatment of capital gains on installment obligations. These accounting changes raise the average tax rate by nearly 5% in 1988, and by an average of 3.8% during the 1987–1991 period.[5] The final row of table 2.3 shows how various other factors cause the average tax rate under the new law to differ from that under previous law. These provisions include the strengthened minimum tax, changes in foreign tax credit provisions, and revenues from increased tax compliance. These miscellaneous provisions increase the average tax rate by 4.4% in 1991.

Although our calculations of the factors behind changes in average tax rates are necessarily uncertain, they do underscore two important features of the 1986 Tax Reform Act. First, changes in capital recovery provisions will significantly raise corporate taxes. By the late 1980s, the differential between the statutory and the average tax rate that will be attributable to capital recovery rules will return to its level in the 1960s and 1970s. The Tax Reform Act therefore reverses the changes of the early 1980s, when the combination of accelerated depreciation and investment credits lowered average tax rates by as much as 25%. Second, many of the important revenue-raising provisions in the new law are excluded from the usual economic analysis of corporate tax incentives. Marginal effective tax rate calculations, such as those in King and Fullerton (1984), do not usually incorporate particular accounting rules, minimum taxes, or many of the other provisions that have an important effect on corporate investment incentives.

2.4. Conclusions

This chapter explores why corporate tax revenues have declined for the last thirty years. Contrary to many claims, legislative changes explain less than half of the decline in revenues since the mid-1960s. The decline in corporate profits, which averaged nearly 11% of the value of net corporate assets during the 1960s as compared with just under 5% in the 1980s, is a more important factor.

Declining corporate tax revenues have been accompanied by a decline in the average tax rate, the ratio of corporate taxes to economic profits. While this average tax rate is of limited value for analyzing the incentive effects of the corporate tax, it has attracted widespread attention in the recent tax reform discussion. Changes in both the tax law and the rate of corporate profits affect the average tax rate. The change in depreciation provisions between the late 1970s and the early 1980s reduced the average tax rate by roughly 13%.

The Tax Reform Act of 1986, which raises $120 billion in corporate taxes over the next five years, accelerates the trend toward rising average tax rates that would have occurred under old law. Reduced capital recovery allowances and other changes in the 1986 Act will combine to raise average effective tax rates to 36% by 1990, compared with 31% in the first five years of the 1980s. Corporate taxes as a share of GNP and relative to corporate assets will also rise significantly. By 1990, federal tax payments will equal 3% of net corporate assets, well above their level in the early 1980s and approximately equal to their asset share in the late 1970s. Taxes will still remain a smaller fraction of assets than they were in the 1960s, however, in part because corporate profitability is projected to be well below its level two decades ago. Although we focus on the Tax Reform Act's revenue impact over the next five years, this is a potentially misleading indicator of a tax bill's revenue effects. By lengthening the depreciation lives of many assets, the new law raises corporate tax revenues in the short run at the expense of some reduction in future years. The inherent uncertainty in long-range forecasts, however, makes it difficult to quantify these effects.

Much of our analysis implicitly divorces the average tax rate from the corporate profit rate, although such a separation is in fact impossible. Because corporate taxes do not rise proportionally with corporate profits, changes in the profit rate have a direct influence on the average tax rate. Over longer horizons, the average tax rate may also affect the profit rate, at least if average and marginal tax rates move in tandem. Higher tax burdens will induce offsetting reductions in capital investment that should increase pretax profitability.

Finally, our analysis of revenue changes in the 1986 Tax Reform Act suggests that a wide range of corporate tax provisions that have important revenue effects are typically ignored in the economic analysis of the corporate income tax. These provisions affect both the average and marginal tax rates on new investment, and deserve to be incorporated in future work.

Notes

1. Alternative views of what constitutes the corporate tax base are also possible. Feldstein and Summers (1979) and Feldstein, Dicks-Mireaux, and Poterba (1983) consider the total earnings of the corporate sector, including those paid to debt-holders, as the tax base. Because interest payments are taxed less heavily than equity earnings, measuring the average tax rate relative to this base would lower the average tax rate but not affect its decline over time.

2. Our calculations may overstate the importance of capital recovery provisions in lowering the average tax rate, because we assume that all changes in the difference between tax and economic depreciation were actually claimed by firms. For firms that are carrying losses forward, this will overstate the importance of depreciation provisions, and overstate the importance of losses as well.

3. Although revenues will be lower immediately after a tax reform like ERTA than in the steady state, it does not follow that tax revenues two years after the reform are higher than those in the year after the reform. There is a countervailing revenue-reducing effect: as the stock of assets being depreciated under the generous new rules rises, tax receipts may decline.

4. Our measure of the average tax rate change due to capital recovery may understate the actual impact of the new law because of the interaction between depreciation provisions and the strengthened minimum tax. For firms with substantial depreciation deductions, the new minimum tax may raise tax payments. We classify this as an effect of the minimum tax, not depreciation rules.

5. An important caveat applies to the accounting-induced change in average tax rates. Table 2.3 reports the accounting-induced change in taxes divided by our measure of economic income. Each accounting change, however, also affects the measured value of economic income. Repeal of the completed contract method of accounting, for example, will change the IRS measure of receipts less deductions that forms the basis for our profits variable. Average tax rates computed relative to measured economic income under the new tax regime would therefore be slightly lower than those we report since income will be higher as a result of these accounting changes. Average tax rates in all previous years, computed relative to an economic income measure that did not allow for deferred accrual under the completed contract method, would be lower than those reported in table 2.1. The change in average rates over time is not affected by the choice of convention for economic income, however, even though the level of the average rate is.

References

Auerbach, Alan J. 1983. "Corporate Taxation in the United States," *Brookings Papers on Economic Activity* 2: 451–513.

Auerbach, Alan J., and James M. Poterba. 1987. "Why Have Corporate Taxes Declined?" in Lawrence H. Summers, ed., *NBER Tax Policy Annual* 1, 1–29.

Congressional Budget Office (CBO). 1986. *The Economic and Budget Outlook: An Update.* Washington: Government Printing Office.

Feldstein, Martin S., and Lawrence H. Summers. 1979. "Inflation and the Taxation of Capital in the Corporate Sector," *National Tax Journal* 32 (December): 445–470.

Feldstein, Martin S., Louis Dicks-Mireaux, and James Poterba. 1983. "The Effective Tax Rate and the Pretax Rate of Return," *Journal of Public Economics* 21 (July): 129–158.

Fullerton, Don. 1984. "Which Effective Tax Rate?" *National Tax Journal* 37: 23–41.

Joint Committee on Taxation. 1984. *Study of 1983 Effective Tax Rates of Selected Large U.S. Corporations.* Washington: Government Printing Office.

King, Mervyn A., and Don Fullerton. 1984. *The Taxation of Income From Capital.* Chicago: University of Chicago Press.

McIntyre, Robert S. 1984. *Corporate Income Taxes in the Reagan Years: A Study of Three Years of Legalized Tax Avoidance.* Washington: Citizens for Tax Justice.

Spooner, Gillian. 1986. "Effective Tax Rates from Financial Statements," *National Tax Journal* 39: 293–306.

U.S. House of Representatives. 1986. *Tax Reform Act of 1986: Conference Report to Accompany H.R. 3838.* Report 99-841. Washington: Government Printing Office.

Ziemer, Richard C. 1985. "Impact of Recent Tax Law Changes," *Survey of Current Business* 65 (April): 28–31.

3 Revenue-Neutral Changes in Corporate and Personal Income Taxes and Government Debt

Simon Benninga and Eli Talmor

We examine the equilibrium effects of financing the government budget with various combinations of debt and differential taxes on the incomes of firms and consumers. Raising the corporate income tax rate increases investment and lowers real interest rates, but raises the interest rate paid to corporate bondholders. Raising government expenditures lowers investment and raises real interest rates.

3.1. Introduction

In this chapter we examine the general equilibrium effects of changes in the corporate tax rate on investment, production, and interest rates in an economy in which different kinds of income are taxed differentially. The framework we use is that of Miller (1977), a model in which an equilibrium in the private sector is determined, given differential taxation.

The Miller framework is needed because of the problematic nature of the general equilibrium in the presence of corporate taxation. Modigliani and Miller (1958) showed that in the absence of taxation, debt and equity financing are perfect substitutes. When a corporate tax is introduced into their 1958 model, Modigliani and Miller (1963) argued that since interest is a tax-deductible expense for the corporation, issuing debt increases shareholder wealth.

The Modigliani-Miller (1963) model explains the incremental value of debt at the corporate level, but leaves open the question of how equilibrium is determined when corporate interest expenses are tax-deductible while outflows to shareholders are not. The solution proposed in Miller (1977) recognizes that the tax asymmetry between debt and equity is a two-edged sword. The advantage of debt over equity financing at the corporate level is reversed at the investor's personal level, at which interest is taxed as ordinary income while equity income is taxed at an effectively much lower rate. Once both corporate and personal taxes are considered in a capital market equilibrium, the pretax interest on corporate debt is grossed up, yielding capital structure irrelevance for the individual firm. Facing differential pretax rates of return between debt and equity, investors cluster

We acknowledge the helpful comments of Alan Auerbach, Jeffrey Callen, Joram Mayshar, and participants in the Sapir Conference on the Economic Effects of the Government Budget. The usual disclaimer applies.

into two tax clienteles: Investors at a personal tax bracket below the corporate tax rate find it desirable to invest in taxable bonds, while investors at a higher personal tax bracket than the corporate rate buy equity and tax-exempt municipal bonds.[1]

The Miller framework does not include a government sector that uses the proceeds of the taxation to finance the government budget, nor does it include explicit modeling of production in the private sector. In this chapter, we add these sectors to the model. This allows a full, general equilibrium, examination of the effects of changing the corporate tax rate.[2]

The structure of the chapter is as follows: In section 3.2 we set out the chapter's model. Section 3.3 solves the consumer and firm maximization problems and extends Miller's main results to our framework. In section 3.4 we employ these results to integrate the government and consumer budget constraints. In Sections 3.5 and 3.6 we solve the equilibrium and derive the model's comparative statics.

3.2. The Model

We assume a nonmonetary economy in which there are two representative consumers and one representative firm. There are two dates, labeled 0 and 1, and perfect certainty. In each period the government levies income taxes on personal and corporate incomes; tax revenue is used to finance the government's consumption G of the economy's single good at date 0 and to pay the principal and interest on the government bonds at date 1.[3] The government bonds issued at date 0, denoted by B, bear an interest rate of r.

The Tax System: In the model we examine a simple system of income taxation whose features are designed to reflect some of the salient features of most Western income tax systems. Corporate income is taxed at rate t_c, with interest on corporate bonds and the cost of inputs to the firm's production being recognized expenses for tax purposes at the corporate level.

Personal tax rates depend on both the consumer and the type of income being taxed. The general rule is that endowments and interest income from corporate bonds are subject to the consumer's personal income tax, whereas income from corporate equity and from government bonds is not taxed.[4] Denote the personal income tax rates of the two consumers by t_{p1}

and t_{p2}, respectively. We shall assume that $t_{p1} > t_c > t_{p2}$; this assumption is critical to the model's results.[5]

The Firm: The single representative firm in the model is endowed with a production technology that transforms inputs z purchased by the firm at date 0 into output $f(z)$ at date 1. We assume that $f'(z) > 1$, $f''(z) < 0$, and that $f'(z) \to \infty$ as $z \to 0$; these assumptions guarantee that the real interest rate will always be positive (in the absence of this assumption theorem 1 below breaks down) and that there will always be some investment. At date 0 the firm has output of F from inputs purchased one period previously. At date 0 the firm sells D bonds at interest rate i, so that purchasers of the bonds will receive $D(1 + i)$ at date 1. The firm acts competitively, taking the interest rate i as given.

The firm's income is taxed at the corporate income tax rate t_c. Inputs purchased by the firm at date 0 are immediately expensible for income tax purposes.[6] Thus the firm's date 0 cash flow is

$$(1 - t_c)[F - z] + D, \tag{1}$$

and its date 1 cash flow is

$$(1 - t_c)f(z) - D(1 + i(1 - t_c)). \tag{2}$$

Initial shareholders of the firm at date 0 receive $(1 - t_c)F$ as a dividend from the firm at date 0. At date 0, new shareholders decide on inputs z and debt D; given the expensibility of the inputs, the net cost of the shares to these shareholders is $[P + z(1 - t_c) - D]$, where P denotes the market value of the firm's equity at date 0. At date 1 the firm pays as a dividend to shareholders its net cash receipts: $(1 - t_c)f(z) - D(1 + i(1 - t_c))$. The firm selects z and D in order to maximize its market value P.[7]

Consumers: Each consumer i is endowed with w_{ih} of labor income at date h, $h = 1, 2$. At date 0 each consumer i decides what proportion q_i of the corporate equity to purchase and how much corporate debt D_i and government debt B_i to purchase. Initially consumer 1 is the firm's sole shareholder.[8] At date 0, consumer 1 sells his shareholding in the firm and each consumer purchases a proportion q_i of the firm's equity. We denote the market price of the equity at date 0 by P.

Denote the consumption of consumer i at date h by c_{ih}, $i = 1, 2, h = 0, 1$. We assume that consumer 1 chooses (c_{10}, c_{11}) to maximize a concave, differentiable, and increasing utility function $U(c_{10}, c_{11})$. Consumer 2 is assumed to choose (c_{20}, c_{21}) to maximize a utility function $V(c_{20}, c_{21})$. The consumers' budget constraints are given by

Consumer 1:

$$c_{10} = (1 - t_{p1})w_{10} + (1 - t_c)F + P - q_1[P + z(1 - t_c) - D]$$

$$- D_1 - B_1,$$

$$c_{11} = (1 - t_{p1})w_{11} + q_1[(1 - t_c)f(z) - D(1 + i(1 - t_c))]$$

$$+ D_1(1 + i(1 - t_{p1})) + B_1(1 + r);$$

(3)

Consumer 2:

$$c_{20} = (1 - t_{p2})w_{20} - q_2[P + z(1 - t_c) - D] - D_2 - B_2,$$

$$c_{21} = (1 - t_{p2})w_{21} + q_2[(1 - t_c)f(z) - D(1 + i(1 - t_c))]$$

$$+ D_2(1 + i(1 - t_{p2})) + B_2(1 + r).$$

(4)

Throughout we impose constraints on borrowing and short-selling: q_i, D_i, and $B_i \geqslant 0$ for $i = 1, 2$.

Government: The government consumes G of the model's single good at date 0. At date 0, the government must collect enough taxes and sell enough bonds to finance its consumption G of the good. At date 1 the government must collect enough taxes to repay the bonds and the interest. This gives the following budget constraints:

$$G = t_{p1}w_{10} + t_{p2}w_{20} + t_c[F - z] + B,$$

$$B(1 + r) = t_{p1}w_{11} + t_{p2}[w_{21} + iD] + t_c[f(z) - iD].$$

(5)

3.3. Solving the Consumer and Firm Problems: The Miller Equilibrium

The first-order conditions for the consumers' maximization problems are

$$\frac{V_1}{V_0} \geqslant \frac{1}{1 + i(1 - t_{p2})}, \qquad \text{with equality if } D_2 > 0,$$

(6)

$$\frac{V_1}{V_0} \geqslant \frac{1}{1 + r}, \qquad \text{with equality if } B_2 > 0,$$

(7)

$$\frac{U_1}{U_0} \geqslant \frac{1}{1+r}, \qquad \text{with equality if } B_1 > 0, \tag{8}$$

$$\frac{U_1}{U_0} \geqslant \frac{1}{1+i(1-t_{p1})}, \qquad \text{with equality if } D_1 > 0, \tag{9}$$

$$P \geqslant \frac{U_1}{U_0}[(1-t_c)f(z) - D(1+i(1-t_c))] - [z(1-t_c) - D], \tag{10}$$

with equality if $q_1 > 0$,

$$P \geqslant \frac{V_1}{V_0}[(1-t_c)f(z) - D(1+i(1-t_c))] - (z(1-t_c) - D), \tag{11}$$

with equality if $q_2 > 0$.

It is evident from the first-order conditions that not all the consumer choice variables can be positive in equilibrium. In particular, as we shall show in theorem 1, equilibrium requires that $q_2 = D_1 = 0$. Furthermore, it is clear that in equilibrium the amount government and corporate debt issued must equal the amounts purchased by consumers:

$$D_1 + D_2 = D,$$
$$B_1 + B_2 = B. \tag{12}$$

THEOREM 1   Suppose $t_{p1} > t_c > t_{p2}$ and suppose that in equilibrium $f'(z) > 1$. Then in a competitive equilibrium

1.1. $q_1 = 1, \qquad q_2 = 0.$

1.2. $f'(z) = 1 + r.$

1.3. $i = r/(1 - t_c).$

1.4. $B_1 = B.$

1.5. $D_2 = D.$

Proof   First we note that if in equilibrium there is a positive amount of corporate debt and of government debt (i.e., $D > 0$ and $B > 0$), then $i(1 - t_{p2}) \geqslant r \geqslant i(1 - t_{p1})$. To see this, suppose that $i(1 - t_{p2}) < r$. Then it follows that $i(1 - t_{p1}) < r$, since $t_{p1} > t_{p2}$. It thus follows that neither consumer would be willing to buy the corporate debt in equilibrium, which is a contradiction. Similarly, if $i(1 - t_{p1}) > r$, it follows that in equilibrium both consumers would prefer corporate debt to government debt, which is also a contradiction.

Thus in equilibrium consumer 1 will buy the government debt and not the corporate debt, and consumer 2 will buy the corporate debt and not the government debt. This proves (1.4) and (1.5) of the theorem.

To prove (1.1), note that the shares in the firm are perfect substitutes for government debt (i.e., their returns are both certain are not taxed at the personal level). It thus follows that consumer 2 will not desire to purchase shares in equilibrium. This proves (1.1) of the theorem.

It remains to prove (1.2) and (1.3). The firm's shares are owned, by the above argument, by consumer 1 only. This consumer has a marginal rate of substitution between periods of $1 + r$, and the firm will therefore use this rate to determine its optimal investment and bond policy (i.e., the firm will try to maximize the net present value accruing to its shareholders). Maximizing

$$\frac{f(z)(1 - t_c) - D(1 + i(1 - t_c))}{1 + r} - z(1 - t_c) + D$$

with respect to z gives $f'(z) = 1 + r$. Finally since the firm behaves competitively it will act to maximize the net present value of its debt to its shareholders given the market interest rate i. This net present value is

$$D\left\{1 - \frac{1 + i(1 - t_c)}{1 + r}\right\}.$$

As long as $i < r/(1 - t_c)$, the firm will find it profitable to continue to issue more debt. But this debt issuance will in itself push up the market interest rate i. In the resulting equilibrium the relative interest rates are given by $i = r/(1 - t_c)$.   QED

Theorem 1 is a slight generalization of Miller's (1977) result, since our theorem also includes the utility-maximizing conditions for the firm's production decision [(1.2) of theorem 1]. As Miller showed, when capital gains and ordinary income are taxed differentially, ownership of financial assets will be segmented. High-tax consumers will specialize in assets that are accorded favorable tax treatment, and that pay a relatively low before-tax return. Low-tax consumers will purchase financial assets that pay a relatively higher before-tax return but that are accorded less favorable tax treatment (corporate bonds).

3.4. Integrating the Government and Consumers' Budget Constraints

It follows from theorem 1 that consumer 1's budget constraints may be written as

$$c_{10} = (1 - t_{p1})w_{10} + (1 - t_c)F - z - B,$$
$$c_{11} = (1 - t_{p1})w_{11} + [(1 - t_c)f(z) - D(1 + i(1 - t_c))] + B(1 + r). \tag{13}$$

We may obtain a simple representation of the economy's equilibrium by substituting the government's budget constraints into those of consumer 1. Doing this, and using the results of theorem 1 to simplify consumer 2's maximization problem, gives the following conditions for an equilibrium:

Consumer 1:

(M.1.)
$$\max U(c_{10}, c_{11}) \qquad \text{subject to}$$
$$c_{10} = w_{10} + F - z + D - G + t_{p2}w_{20},$$
$$c_{11} = w_{11} + f(z) - D(1 + i) + t_{p2}[w_{21} + iD];$$

Consumer 2:

(M.2.)
$$\max V(c_{20}, c_{21}) \qquad \text{subject to}$$
$$c_{20} = (1 - t_{p2})w_{20} - D,$$
$$c_{21} = (1 - t_{p2})w_{21} + D(1 + i(1 - t_{p2}));$$

The firm:

(M.3.)   choose z so that $f'(z) = 1 + r$.

DEFINITION   A *general equilibrium* in an economy with differential income taxation (t_{p1}, t_{p2}, t_c) is a vector $e^* = \{z, r, i, D, B\}$ such that (c_{10}, c_{11}) as defined in (M.1) maximizes $U(c_{10}, c_{11})$, (c_{20}, c_{21}) as defined in (M.2) maximizes $V(c_{20}, c_{21})$, (M.3) holds, and the government budget constraints (5) are fulfilled at e^*.

3.5. Solving the General Equilibrium

In order to solve the general equilibrium problem, we assume that both consumers have separable power utility functions with exponents γ and ζ, respectively. Thus consumer 1 is assumed to maximize

$$U(c_{10}, c_{11}) = h_1(c_{10}) + \delta h_1(c_{11}),$$

and consumer 2 is assumed to maximize

$$V(c_{20}, c_{21}) = h_2(c_{20}) + \delta h_2(c_{21}),$$

where

$$h_1(c) = \frac{c^{1-\gamma}}{1-\gamma} \quad \text{and} \quad h_2(c) = \frac{c^{1-\zeta}}{1-\zeta}.$$

The assumption that both consumers have the same pure time-preference factor δ does not detract from the generality of the argument.

Given i, the optimal D for the consumer 2 is

$$D = \begin{cases} \dfrac{(1 - t_{p2})\{w_{20}[\delta A]^{1/\zeta} - w_{21}\}}{A + (A\delta)^{1/\zeta}} & \text{if this expression is } > 0 \\ 0 & \text{otherwise,} \end{cases} \tag{14}$$

where

$$A = \frac{f'(z)(1 - t_{p2}) + (t_{p2} - t_c)}{(1 - t_c)}. \tag{15}$$

Rearranging (15), by using $i = r/(1 - t_c)$, gives

$$A = 1 + i(1 - t_{p2}), \tag{15'}$$

which is the marginal rate of time substitution of consumer 2.

The equilibrium condition for the optimal z is

$$\frac{U'(c_{11})}{U'(c_{10})} = \frac{1}{\delta f'(z)}.$$

When specialized to the power utility functions, this gives

$$\frac{c_{11}}{c_{10}} = [\delta f'(z)]^{1/\gamma} \equiv \alpha.$$

Substituting into (14) the expression for c_{11} gives

$$w_{11} + t_{p2} w_{21} = \phi(z), \tag{16}$$

where

$$\phi(z) = DA - f(z) + \alpha c_{10}.$$

Note that (16) is a function only of the initial endowments, government expenditures G, production inputs z, and the two tax rates t_c and t_{p2}. Since in our economy government expenditures and the tax rates are taken as

given, this suggests the following way of viewing an equilibrium: Given the
two tax rates t_{p2} and t_c and given firm inputs z, we know that $r = f'(z) - 1$,
$i = r/(1 - t_c)$. Since i and t_{p2} determine the demand for corporate bonds D,
it follows that the equilibrium is wholly determined by two out of the three
income tax rates. If we assume that the utility functions of the consumers
are strictly concave, it follows that a unique equilibrium corresponds to
each pair of tax rates t_{p2} and t_c. The tax rate t_{p1} will be determined by the
government budget constraints (5).[9]

The following proposition shows that if the demand for D by consumer
2 is upward sloping in i, then the right-hand side of (16) is downward sloping
in z:

LEMMA   Suppose that $\partial D/\partial i \geqslant 0$. Then in the neighborhood of an equilibrium $\partial \phi/\partial z < 0$.

Proof   Differentiation ϕ with respect to z gives

$$\frac{\partial \phi}{\partial z} = \frac{\partial D}{\partial z} A + \frac{\partial A}{\partial z} D - \frac{df}{dz} + \frac{\partial \alpha}{\partial z} c_{10} + \alpha \frac{\partial c_{10}}{\partial z}. \tag{16}$$

We first note that our assumption on the demand for D implies that
$\partial D/\partial z \leq 0$. To see this, note that we assume that the production function
$f(z)$ is concave, $f'' < 0$. Then this assumption, coupled with results (1.2) and
(1.3) of theorem 1, implies that when z increases, i decreases. By our
assumption that the demand for bonds is upward sloping in their yield, this
implies that D decreases.

Now

$$\frac{\partial \alpha}{\partial z} = \delta(1/\gamma) f''(z) [\partial f'(z)]^{1/\gamma - 1} < 0,$$

$$\frac{\partial A}{\partial z} = \frac{\partial i}{\partial z}(1 - t_{p2}) < 0,$$

$$\frac{\partial c_{10}}{\partial z} = -1 + \frac{\partial D}{\partial z} < 0.$$

To complete the proof, note that at an equilibrium $c_{10} > 0$.   QED

The interpretation of this result is that an equilibrium in our economy
lends itself to a simple graphical exposition. It follows from the lemma that
the graph of expression (16) in a neighborhood of an equilibrium is as
shown in figure 3.1. As we shall now show, the comparative statics of the

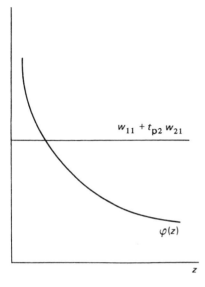

Figure 3.1

equilibrium with respect to t_c and to G may be derived from this graphical exposition.

3.6. Comparative Statics

We now use the result of the previous section to explore the ramifications of changes in corporate tax rate and government expenditure on equilibrium investment and interest rates. All of the results are revenue-neutral, in the sense that a change in any single tax rate implies changes in at least one other tax rate that will maintain a balanced government budget.[10] Throughout this section we shall assume that $\partial D/\partial i > 0$. This implies, as noted in section 3.5, that $\partial D/\partial z < 0$.

THEOREM 2   An increase in the corporate tax rate t_c that is offset only by a change in t_{p1} and B will lead to an increase in investment z; that is, $\partial z/\partial t_c \geqslant 0$.

Proof   We hold z constant and take the derivative of ϕ with respect to t_c:

$$\frac{\partial \phi}{\partial t_c} = \left\{ A\frac{\partial D}{\partial i} + D\frac{\partial A}{\partial i} + \alpha\frac{\partial c_{10}}{\partial i} \right\} \frac{\partial i}{\partial t_c}.$$

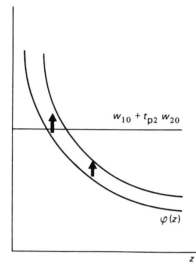

Figure 3.2

By our assumption on the demand for D, the first and the third terms in curly brackets are strictly positive. Next, note that by (1.2) of theorem 1

$$i = \frac{r}{1 - t_c} = \frac{f'(z) - 1}{1 - t_c}. \tag{17}$$

Hence the sign of $\partial i / \partial t_c$ is positive. Since the second term is also positive, it follows that when we increase t_c, the right-hand side of (16) moves up while the left-hand side stays the same. This proves the claim (see figure 3.2).   QED

The intuition behind theorem 2 is the following: When t_c rises, the interest rate paid to low-tax consumers, i, rises, causing low-tax consumers to demand more corporate debt. But this demand for corporate debt, which shifts more of the consumption of low-tax consumers from the present into the future, can be accommodated only if the high-tax consumer (the owner of the firm) invests more in productive inputs z. This is what, in fact, happens in our model. Effectively, in the economy as a whole the only way of transferring consumption from one period to the next is through the production function.

The result seems counterintuitive, since it might be anticipated that an increase in corporate taxation will make corporations less profitable, thus decreasing corporate investment. The increase in investment does, indeed, lead to a decrease in welfare for the high-tax consumer (the owner of the firm) and an increase in the low-tax consumer's welfare:

COROLLARY 1   If the low-tax consumer's demand curve for D is upward sloping in i, then an increase in the corporate tax rate t_c that is offset by a change in t_{p1} leads to a decrease in consumer 1's welfare and an increase in consumer 2's welfare.

Proof   Differentiating the high-tax consumer's utility function with respect to t_c yields

$$\frac{\partial U}{\partial t_c} = U'(c_{10})\frac{\partial c_{10}}{\partial t_c} + U'(c_{11})\frac{\partial c_{11}}{\partial t_c}$$

$$= U'(c_{10})\left(\frac{\partial c_{10}}{\partial t_c} + \frac{1}{1+r}\frac{\partial c_{11}}{\partial t_c}\right).$$

For the remainder of the proof we ignore $U'(c_{10})$, which is in any case positive. The above expression is proportional to

$$-\frac{\partial z}{\partial t_c} + \frac{\partial D}{\partial t_c} + \frac{1}{1+r}\left\{f'(z)\frac{\partial z}{\partial t_c} - \frac{\partial D}{\partial t_c}(1+i(1-t_{p2})\right.$$

$$\left. - D\left[\frac{\partial i}{\partial t_c}(1-t_{p2})\right]\right\} \tag{18}$$

$$= \frac{\partial z}{\partial t_c}\left[\frac{f'(z)}{1+r}-1\right] + \frac{\partial D}{\partial t_c}\left[1 - \frac{(1+i(1-t_{p2})}{1+r}\right]$$

$$- \frac{D}{1+r}\frac{di}{dt_c}(1-t_{p2}).$$

The first term of the last expression is zero, since the first-order condition for maximization implies that $f'(z) = 1 + r$. The second term of this expression is negative except for the case where $t_{p2} = t_c$. The third term represents the change in the taxable interest rate i. Unlike the case in the proof of theorem 2, the change in i now does not assume a fixed z. From (17),

$$\frac{di}{dt_c} = \frac{z'f''(z)(1-t_c) + f'(z) - 1}{(1-t_c)^2},$$

where we write $z' = \partial z/\partial t_c$. Using a first-order Taylor series expansion, we get $z'f''(z) = f'(z + z') - f'(z)$, and substituting this in the above expression gives a numerator of

$$t_c(f'(z) - f'(z + z')) + f'(z + z') - 1.$$

Since $z' > 0$ and since f is concave, it follows that

$$1 < f'(z + z') < f'(z),$$

so that $di/dt_c > 0$. This proves that an increase in t_c decreases consumer 1's welfare. Since the economy modeled here is a zero-sum game (the government consumption G does not change), it follows that a decrease in consumer 1's welfare implies an increase in consumer 2's welfare. This completes the proof.   QED

The welfare of the owner of the firm (the high-tax consumer) decreases when t_c is increased due to two factors, represented by the last two terms in (18). The middle term of (18) represents the net present value of the so-called "bondholder's surplus," the excess return over the marginal product of capital paid by the firm to its bondholders. This is clearly a burden on the shareholders of the firm except in the case where $t_{p2} = t_c$. This is usually considered to be the source of the welfare burden on shareholders in the segmented Miller equilibrium.[11]

A second corollary to theorem 2 relates to the changes in r and i when the corporate income tax rate t_c is raised:

COROLLARY 2   An increase in the corporate tax rate t_c that is offset by a change in t_{p1} and B will lead to a fall in the real interest rate r and a rise in interest rate i paid on corporate bonds.

Proof The first part of the corollary follows immediately from theorem 2 and the fact that $r = f'(z) - 1$. The statement about i was proved in the last part of the previous corollary and is restated here for completeness.   QED

A final result relates to increases in the government budget financed by the high-tax consumer through his personal income tax rate:

THEOREM 3   Suppose an increase in government consumption G is financed through an increase in the tax rate t_{p1}. If consumers' utility is additive in the public good, this increase will lead to a decline in z and a consequent rise in r and i.

Proof   When the utility functions are additive in the public good, if neither tax rate t_c nor t_{p2} is changed, then $\partial\phi/\partial G = -\alpha$. Thus, for a given z, the right-hand side of (16) moves down. This proves the contention.   QED

3.7. Conclusion

We have considered a simple general equilibrium model in which personal income is taxed differentially, depending upon its source. Corporate income is subject to a tax, though interest expenses are deductible for corporations. As shown by Miller (1977), such a framework can account for a unique, noncorner, solution to the corporate debt/equity problem.

In this chapter we extend the Miller framework to include a government sector, thus closing the equilibrium. We simplify the complex redistributional problems among consumers by considering only two representative consumers, one of whom is taxed at a high income tax rate, and the other of whom is taxed at a low income tax rate.

When financial markets are segmented because of the differential treatment of personal income depending upon its source (equity versus debt), the comparative statics of the equilibrium are relatively straightforward. As long as the demand curve for corporate debt is upward sloping in the interest paid on the debt, an increase in the corporate tax rate will produce an increase in equilibrium investment, and an increase in the low income tax rate will produce a decrease in equilibrium investment.

Notes

1. In this chapter we employ the simplest possible Miller framework, in which there are only two representative consumers and there is no uncertainty. For extensions to the Miller model, see DeAngelo and Masulis (1980), Auerbach and King (1983), Ross (1985), Park and Williams (1985), Taggart (1980), Talmor, Haugen, and Barnea (1985), and Aivazian and Callen (1987). For a survey of the literature, see Auerbach (1983).

2. Previous studies of this problem have either not included a government sector (e.g., Taggart, 1984) or have been in an explicitly partial equilibrium framework (e.g., McDonald, 1983).

3. For simplicity we assume that there is no government consumption at date 1. This does not affect any of the results of the paper.

4. This is meant to reflect the common distinction between ordinary income taxes and capital gains taxes, and the fact that in many countries the income from certain kinds of government securities is not subject to any income tax. In the United States, for example, interest on municipal bonds is untaxed.

5. The tax assumptions follow closely those made by Miller (1977).

6. The immediate expensibility of the firm's inputs at date 0 makes the optimal level of z independent of t_c, which simplifies the analysis but does not materially affect it.

7. The interest rates r and i, and the firm value, P, are determined so as to equilibrate the three asset markets. The government has to select total government debt B and tax rates t_{p1}, t_{p2}, and t_c to balance its budget constraints [see equations (5) below].

8. This assumption is consistent with the results of theorem 1 below, which states that consumer 1 will be the sole owner of the firm after trading at date 0. The equilibrium results still hold, however, if we relax the assumption to allow initial ownership of equity by consumer 2.

9. The role of t_{p2} and t_c is not unique. It can be seen from (5) that any two of the three tax rates determine the equilibrium, given G and the initial endowments of the consumer.

10. Since, as we noted in section 3.5, the equilibrium is uniquely determined by any two of the three tax rates, this is always possible.

11. If shareholders of the firm operated in a noncompetitive environment, they would issue only that amount of debt that would maximize their profits from debt issuance. Since the demand curve for debt is downward sloping, the total debt issuance would be *less* than in our model, and the differential between i and r would be smaller.

References

Aivazian, V. A., and J. L. Callen (1987). "Miller's Irrelevance Theorem: A Note," *Journal of Finance*, 42, 169–180.

Auerbach, A. J. (1983). "Taxation, Corporate Financial Policy and the Cost of Capital," *Journal of Economic Literature* 21, 905–940.

Auerbach, A. J., and M. King (1983). "Taxation, Portfolio Choice, and Debt-Equity Ratios: A General Equilibrium Model," *Quarterly Journal of Economics* 98, 587–609.

DeAngelo, H., and R. W. Masulis (1980). "Optimal Capital Structure under Corporate and Personal Taxation," *Journal of Financial Economics* 8, 3–29.

McDonald, R. (1983). "Government Debt and Private Leverage," *Journal of Public Economics* 22, 303–325.

Miller, M. H. (1977). "Debt and Taxes," *Journal of Finance* 32, 261–275.

Modigliani, F., and M. H. Miller (1958). "The Cost of Capital Corporation Finance and the Theory of Investment," *American Economic Review* 48, 261–297.

Modigliani, F., and M. H. Miller (1963). "Taxes and the Cost of Capital: A Correction," *American Economic Review* 53, 433–443.

Park, S. Y., and J. Williams (1985). "Taxes, Capital Structure, and Bondholder Clienteles," *Journal of Business* 58, 203–224.

Ross, S. A. (1985). "Debt and Taxes and Uncertainty," *Journal of Finance* 40, 637–657.

Taggart, R. A. (1980). "Taxes and Corporate Capital Structure in an Incomplete Market," *Journal of Finance* 35, 645–659.

Taggart, R. A. (1984). "Secular Patterns in the Financing of U.S. Corporations," in B. Friedman (ed.), *Corporate Capital Structure in the United States*, The University of Chicago Press, pp. 13–80.

Talmor, E., R. A. Haugen, and A. Barnea (1985). "The Value of the Tax Subsidy on Risky Debt," *Journal of Business* 58, 191–202.

4 Risk Reducing Fiscal Policies and Economic Growth

Joseph Zeira

4.1. Introduction

This chapter emphasizes an aspect of government economic activities that has been somewhat overlooked by economists. A variety of economic policies causes among other things a reduction in the risk of capital, whether it is physical or human capital. By doing so, either by intention or as a by-product of other goals, these policies increase capital accumulation in the economy, if investors are risk averse, and may even raise the level of welfare as well. The market failure in these cases is the inexistence of a full set of Arrow-Debreu contingent securities. The fiscal authorities therefore supply investors with insurance, which for various reasons cannot be created by the market system.

This point is demonstrated in this chapter by the use of two simple models, one of demand fluctuations and the other of investment in human capital. In both models no private insurance for investors exists, and hence there is a place for government intervention that reduces risk. It is shown that traditional policies, which were originally motivated by other motives, also reduce investors' risk. Such is the countercyclical fiscal policy, which was originally intended to secure full employment or price stability but stabilizes profits and investors' returns as well. Such is the progressive tax system that reduces the personal risk of investing in human capital. And such is the policy of subsidizing education and investment in human capital. It is shown in this chapter that these policies increase capital accumulation and may even raise welfare.

This idea is related to a series of papers that were initiated by Domar and Musgrave (1944), continued by Stiglitz (1969), Mayshar (1977), and Gordon (1985), and deal with government as sharing risk with investors through income taxes and thus raising investment. This chapter extends this line of investigation by considering the ability of government not only to share risk passively but also to offset it by active policies. This chapter therefore presents government as a producer of insurance services, which are a remedy to a severe market failure.

The chapter is organized as follows. The first example is presented in

I wish to thank Benjamin Bental, Joram Mayshar, and Oren Sussman for helpful comments on earlier drafts. Remaining errors are all mine.

section 4.2, which constructs a general equilibrium model of an economy where a fiscal stabilizing policy contributes to economic growth. Section 4.3 presents the second model, which deals with investment in human capital, and section 4.4 summarizes the chapter.

4.2. Stabilization Policy

In the following example the effect of a stabilizing fiscal policy on economic growth is analyzed within a general equilibrium model that is as simple as possible. Real business cycles are modeled within this framework as a series of independent shocks to preferences, with (for the sake of simplicity) neither persistence nor momentum. In addition to capital there is a government bond, which is a riskless asset, and thus risk, portfolio considerations, and investment decisions become interrelated in this model.

4.2.1. The Model

Consider a closed economy that produces two goods: good a, which is used for both consumption and investment, and good b, which is used for consumption only. Good a is produced by labor and the quantity produced is

$$Y_t^a = AL_t^a, \tag{1}$$

where L_t^a is the labor input in the production of a, and $A > 0$. Good b is produced by labor L_t^b and capital K_t, where production is described by the following Cobb-Douglas function:

$$Y_t^b = F(K_t, L_t^b) = BK_t^\alpha (L_t^b)^{1-\alpha}, \tag{2}$$

where $B > 0$ and $0 < \alpha < 1$. There is no capital depreciation and there are no adjustment costs to investment.

This is an overlapping generations economy where individuals live two periods each, and supply one unit of labor in the first period of life and none when old. No population growth is assumed and the number of individuals in each generation is normalized to one. The lifetime utility of the young in period t is described by

$$U_t = \gamma_t \log C_t^{1,b} + (1 - \gamma_t) \log C_t^{1,a} + \beta \log C_{t+1}^{2,a}, \tag{3}$$

where $C_t^{1,b}$ and $C_t^{1,a}$ are consumption of b and a in first period of life, etc.

The parameters are $\beta > 0$, the subjective rate of time preference, and $0 < \gamma_t < 1$, the share of consumption of b in aggregate consumption by the young. It is assumed that γ_t is different for each generation, and $\{\gamma_t\}$ is a series of independent, identically distributed random variables. Utility of the old is the same as implied by equation (3). Let γ denote the expectation of γ_t: $\gamma = E(\gamma_t)$.

Government bonds are real consols that pay one unit of good a in each period. The outstanding amount of bonds is B_0 and interest payments are financed by a tax of T_0 units of a on the young, where $T_0 = B_0$.

Let good a be the numeraire in our economy. Let P_t denote the price of good b and let Q_t be the price of the consol bond in period t. We further assume that expectations are formed rationally.

4.2.2. Equilibrium and Capital

Clearing of all markets, including those for labor and for the good a, determines the equilibrium wage rate at A. Maximized profits of the b producing firms are

$$K_t \pi(P_t) = K_t \alpha B \left(\frac{1 - \alpha}{A} \right)^{(1-\alpha)/\alpha} P_t^{1/\alpha},$$

and production is

$$Y_t^b = K_t y(P_t) = \frac{1}{\alpha} \frac{1}{P_t} K_t \pi(P_t).$$

The young maximize their expected lifetime utility $E_t U_t$. If savings are denoted S_t and the share of capital in savings x_t, then it can be shown that expected utility maximization is equivalent to

$$\max_{S_t, x_t} \{ \log(A - T_0 - S_t) + \beta \log S_t + \beta E_t \log [x_t \pi(P_{t+1}) + x_t \tag{4}$$

$$+ (1 - x_t) \frac{1 + Q_{t+1}}{Q_t}] \}.$$

The equilibrium in the market for the good b is therefore described by

$$K_t y(P_t) = \frac{\gamma_t}{1 + \beta} (A - T_0) \frac{1}{P_t}, \tag{5}$$

and hence the equilibrium rate of profit is

$$\pi(P_t) = \frac{\alpha}{K_t} \frac{\gamma_t}{1 + \beta} (A - T_0).$$

$$(6)$$

The equilibrium conditions for the asset markets are

$$\frac{\beta}{1 + \beta} (A - T_0) x_t = K_{t+1},$$

$$(7)$$

where x_t is the optimal share given by (4) and

$$\frac{\beta}{1 + \beta} (A - T_0) = K_{t+1} + Q_t B_0.$$

$$(8)$$

It is clear from the optimization and from these equilibrium conditions that K_{t+1} and Q_t do not depend on γ_t and are therefore nonstochastic, and so is Q_{t+1}. The rate of profit in the next period $\pi(P_{t+1})$, which depends on K_{t+1} and γ_{t+1}, as can be seen from (6), can therefore be substituted in the optimization problem (4) to yield

$$x_t = x(K_{t+1}, Q_t, Q_{t+1}).$$

$$(9)$$

Equations (7)–(9) determine the equilibrium values of K_{t+1} and Q_t as dependent on the expected value of Q_{t+1}. Let Q^* and K^* be the steady state of the economy. It can be shown that the steady state is the unique stable rational expectations solution to the model. Hence this is a stationary economy that instantaneously converges to the steady state (K^*, Q^*).

It can also be shown that if risk is reduced—that is, if the uncertainty of γ_t is lowered while keeping the mean γ unchanged—then x is higher. Hence Q^* falls while K^* increases. Reducing the uncertainty of demand therefore leads both to a higher rate of interest and to a higher amount of capital.[1] This is a result of a change in portfolio allocation. In the case of riskless demand, where $\gamma_t \equiv \gamma$, the equilibrium values of capital and the price of bonds are $\bar{K}$ and $\bar{Q}$. In this case the riskless rate of interest $1/\bar{Q}$ is equal to the rate of profit $\pi(\bar{P})$, where $\bar{P}$ is the riskless price.

4.2.3. Stabilization Policy

The source of demand fluctuations in this economy is taste shifts between two consumption goods. Hence it is reasonable to consider a policy that stabilizes these demand fluctuations by using a subsidy for one good that is financed by an excise tax on the other good, according to the size and sign of the shock. Such a policy can lead the economy even to the riskless equilibrium $(\bar{K}, \bar{Q})$ by making producers' price of good b equal to $\bar{P}$ in all situations. Since the equilibrium condition in the market for good b must be

$$\bar{K} y(\bar{P}) = \frac{\gamma_t}{P_t} \frac{1}{1 + \beta} (A - T_0),$$

it follows that $\gamma_t/\gamma - 1$ should be the rate of excise tax on the consumption of good b. If we assume that the subsidy for good a is for consumption only, then it can be shown that this policy rule shifts the economy to the riskless equilibrium $(\bar{K}, \bar{Q})$, and it raises the amounts of capital and of output in the economy. Notice that this policy stabilizes the quantities produced of the two goods but increases the variability of consumer prices.

It is interesting to examine the effect of this stabilization policy on individual utility in addition to its effect on output and capital. It can be shown that the second-period expected utility of each generation increases while the effect on average first-period utility is ambiguous. On the one hand the young consume more of b on average, but on the other hand consumption of the two goods is less responsive to changes in tastes, which reduces average utility.

An issue worth consideration is why private insurance for losses incurred by business cycles does not emerge. The answer is that such insurance would not be able to break even in each period of time, but only inter-temporally, since risks in all firms are perfectly correlated. Hence such insurance only shifts risk from production companies to insurance companies with no real change in the economy. Only the government, due to its ability to affect demands, can finance and supply such insurance by conducting a stabilization policy.

4.3. Investment in Human Capital

The following model presents an economy where individuals invest in human capital in order to increase future productivity and thus future wages, but the outcome of this investment is uncertain in advance and is revealed to each individual only later in life.[2] It is shown that fiscal policies that reduce this risk increase investment in human capital and in physical capital as well. It is also shown that due to moral hazard no private insurance exists for this risk and therefore the government has a role as a supplier of such insurance.

4.3.1. The Model

Consider a small open economy in a world with only one physical good and with perfect capital markets, in which the rate of interest is equal to r. The single good is produced in this economy by capital and labor. Output is equal to

$$Y = F(K, E), \tag{10}$$

where K is the amount of capital, E is the amount of productive labor input—labor multiplied by productivity—and F is a concave production function with constant returns to scale. For simplicity assume that capital does not depreciate and that there are no adjustment costs to investment.

It is an overlapping generations economy where individuals live for two periods each. They work and invest in human capital in the first period and work in the second period, in which their productivity is higher.[3] There is no population growth in the economy and there is a continuum of individuals in each generation; hence their amount can be normalized to one.

An individual with no human capital at all has productivity P_0. If the individual invests i units of time in acquiring human capital in the first period of life, productivity in the next period rises to

$$P = P_0[1 + \theta f(i)], \tag{11}$$

where f is a concave nondecreasing function with $f(0) = 0$ and θ differs among individuals with a distribution of $\theta = 1$ in probability q and $\theta = 0$ in probability $1 - q$. θ is unknown in advance and since all individuals are a priori the same, the first-period individual probabilities for θ are also q and $1 - q$.

Each individual has a time resource of one unit in each period of life. The cost of investment in human capital is only lost labor income. The individual's lifetime utility is given by

$$U = u(C_1) + \beta u(C_2), \tag{12}$$

where C_i is consumption in the ith period of life, u is a concave atemporal utility function, and $\beta > 0$ is the subjective rate of time preference. Every individual maximizes expected lifetime utility EU.

4.3.2. Equilibrium and Impossibility of Private Insurance

Notice that in this economy only individual productivities are uncertain but not the overall productive labor input. Hence, the following condition,

$$F_K(K, E) = r, \tag{13}$$

holds in every period (time subscripts are deleted for the sake of simplicity since the economy is stationary). Hence the equilibrium wage rate of an individual with productivity P is equal to PF_E, where F_E depends on r only, due to the constant returns to scale technology. Let W_0 denote the non-human-capital wage rate: $W_0 = P_0 F_E$.

Let B denote the amount an individual borrows in first period of life. The expected lifetime utility maximization is therefore described by

$$\max_{B, 0 < i < 1} \{u[B + W_0(1 - i)] + \beta q u[W_0 + W_0 f(i) - B(1 + r)] \tag{14}$$

$$+ \beta(1 - q)u[W_0 - B(1 + r)]\}.$$

The optimal amount of investment in human capital i determines the aggregate amount of productive labor input:

$$E = 2P_0 + P_0[qf(i) - i], \tag{15}$$

and E determines the amount of capital K, according to equation (13). From the first-order conditions to (14) we get

$$qf'(i) > 1 + r.$$

Hence if investment in human capital i is raised, both E and K increase.

Let us now discuss why there is no private insurance in this economy for losses incurred by unsuccessful investments in human capital, even though such insurance raises the expected utility of individuals. The explanation builds on the assumption that success of an individual is private information that can be either revealed or not revealed through work by choice. Thus when income is fully insured, even successful individuals can declare themselves as $\theta = 0$ individuals in order not to implement their higher skills.

The formal proof that no private insurance equilibrium exists in this economy goes as follows. If there is an insurance contract it should be of the following type: the individual pays x in the first period and gets paid y in the second period if investment in human capital has failed. If we assume that aggregate profits are zero for the insurance company, then the insurance contract breaks even at

$$y = (1 + r)\frac{1}{1 - q}x. \tag{16}$$

It is easy to verify that optimal utility is an increasing function of x. Thus for each contract, as long as human capital is implemented, there is a preferred contract with the same price but higher x, and hence it cannot be an equilibrium contract. The only contract that maximizes individual utility is the one that fully insures income. But when such a contract is offered part of the winners may avoid the effort and declare themselves losers, since they become indifferent between the two states. Thus (16) can no longer hold, which leads to a contradiction. A private insurance equilibrium therefore cannot exist in this economy, because a competitive insurance market cannot maintain an income incentive, which is necessary for the implementation of successful human capital.[4]

4.3.3. Fiscal Policies

First consider a policy that sets a progressive system of an income tax and a subsidy and aims at higher equality between the ex-post incomes of investors in human capital. Imagine that the government taxes each successful individual by an amount t and that this tax finances a subsidy of size s given to those who failed. A balanced government budget calls for $s = t \cdot q/(1 - q)$, and if the government wishes to encourage implementation of human capital t should satisfy

$$W_0 f(i) - t > \frac{q}{1 - q}t. \tag{17}$$

Under such tax and subsidy the maximization of expected lifetime utility by the young looks as follows:

$$\max_{B, 0 < i < 1} \left\{ u[B + W_0(1 - i)] + \beta q u[W_0 + W_0 f(i) - t - B(1 + r)] \right.$$
$$\left. + \beta(1 - q)u\left[W_0 + \frac{q}{1 - q}t - B(1 + r) \right] \right\}. \tag{18}$$

It can be shown that the optimal investment in human capital i satisfies

$$\frac{di}{dt} > 0,$$

and hence a progressive system of taxes and subsidies raises i and thus increases human and physical capital K as well. That is correct as long as (17) holds and guarantees incentive to raise productivity by implementing formerly acquired human capital.

This result therefore sheds a new light on the effect of a progressive tax system as reducing the risk involved in investment in human capital and thus inducing more accumulation of both human and physical capital. As for the welfare effects of this policy, although it lowers the ex-post utility of some of the inhabitants in the economy in their second period of life, it raises the ex-ante expected utility, as can be realized from equation (18). Hence we can view the policy as welfare improving in the Rawlsian sense.

A policy with a similar effect is to subsidize investment in human capital by the young, i.e., to subsidize education, and to finance this subsidy by a tax on income of workers in the second period of life. If the subsidy is of size s and is paid by a tax on the successful ($\theta = 1$) of size $(1/q)(1 + r)s$, its effect is precisely the same as that of the policy described above.

In addition to reducing risk, subsidizing education may be recommended due to capital market imperfections as well.[5] Investors in human capital, for example, are one-time borrowers who may not care about their reputation as future borrowers, and hence tend to default more.

4.4. Summary and Conclusions

Many discussions on fiscal policy focus on how public expenditures are financed—by tax, debt, or issue of money—rather than on how these expenditures themselves are determined. This chapter is instead part of an effort to examine specific effects of various government activities on capital accumulation and on the economy, and not to view all G as a monolithic mass of expenditures. By the use of two examples, demand fluctuations and risky investment in human capital, this chapter demonstrates that the government can affect the level of risk by supplying insurance where a private insurance equilibrium cannot exist. By providing such services the government increases capital accumulation and may even raise welfare in the economy.

Notes

1. This result, which is obtained in a general equilibrium framework with risk averse individuals, differs from the partial equilibrium results of Hartman (1972) and Abel (1985).

2. The importance of investment in human capital for the understanding of economic development has been emphasized lately by Lucas (1985).

3. A third period of life can be added in order to account for the existence of lenders in this world without any change in the results.

4. Another possible argument for the inexistence of such insurance can be that individuals have different prior talents that are known to them only. This explanation follows Rothschild and Stiglitz (1976).

5. See Mankiw (1986).

References

Abel, Andrew B., "Stochastic Model of Investment, Marginal q and the Market Value of the Firm," *International Economic Review* 26 (1985), 305–320.

Domar, Evsey D., and Richard Musgrave, "Proportional Income Taxation and Risk Taking," *Quarterly Journal of Economics* 58 (1944), 382–422.

Gordon, Roger H., "Taxation of Corporate Capital Income: Tax Revenues versus Tax Distortions," *Quarterly Journal of Economics* 100 (1985), 1–27.

Hartman, Richard, "The Effects of Price and Cost Uncertainty on Investment," *Journal of Economic Theory* 5 (1972), 258–266.

Lucas, Robert E., Jr., "On the Mechanism of Economic Development," Memo (1985).

Mankiw, Gregory N., "The Allocation of Credit and Financial Collapse," *Quarterly Journal of Economics* 101 (1986), 445–470.

Mayshar, Joram, " Should Government Subsidize Risky Private Projects?" *American Economic Review* 67 (1977), 20–28.

Rothschild, Michael, and Joseph Stiglitz, "Equilibrium in Competitive Insurance Markets: An Essay on the Economics of Imperfect Information," *Quarterly Journal of Economics* 90 (1976), 629–649.

Stiglitz, Joseph E., "Effects of Wealth, Income and Capital Gains Taxation on Risk Taking," *Quarterly Journal of Economics* 83 (1969), 263–283.

II CONSUMPTION AND RICARDIAN EQUIVALENCE

5 Earnings Uncertainty and Intergenerational Transfers

Eytan Sheshinski

5.1. Introduction

An extensive literature has studied the effects of intergenerational transfer systems on intertemporal consumption and wealth equilibrium paths (for example, Feldstein, 1974, Kotlikoff and Summers, 1981, Abel, 1985, and the references therein). A balanced pay-as-you-go transfer system levies taxes on the earnings of workers and uses the tax revenue to pay benefits to retirees. Much of the analysis has focused on the underlying assumptions concerning the effects of such a system on voluntary bequests based on altruistic motives. When descendants' utility is incorporated into one's own utility, individuals internalize the effects of taxes and transfers on future generations. Consequently, bequests are adjusted so as to neutralize these effects. The so-called *Ricardian Equivalence Theorem* has been shown to hold under quite general conditions (e.g., Barro, 1974, and Bernheim and Bagwell, 1984).

One line of analysis has focused on the effects of uncertainty in overlapping generations models. Most commonly, uncertainty is associated with the length of lifetime during which the transfer system has an annuity characteristic (Sheshinski and Weiss, 1981). It has been shown that if uncertainty of this type is eliminated in the aggregate (*Law of Large Numbers*) and if cohorts (generations) can be treated as homogeneous, then the neutrality result is preserved. However, with heterogeneous cohorts (due, say, to different "dynastic" mortality rates), the transfer system has distributional effects and neutrality does not hold (Abel, 1985).

In this chapter I analyze the effects of a different type of uncertainty, that of *earnings uncertainty*. I focus on the interaction between the characteristics of the stochastic process that generates earnings and those of the transfer system. Specifically, I assume that earnings follow a *Markov*, or first-order autoregressive, process. For constant absolute risk aversion utility functions, I solve explicitly for the optimal consumption path under alternative assumptions concerning the nature of the transfer system and the diversity within generations.

With homogeneous generations, earnings uncertainty is preserved in

Support from NSF grant SES-8105184 is gratefully acknowledged. I would like to thank Andy Abel for useful comments.

the aggregate. Altruistic individuals, however, internalize this uncertainty about future taxes and transfers and the equivalence result is shown to be preserved.

With heterogeneous generations, i.e., different individual paths of earnings' realizations, uncertainty is assumed to be eliminated in the aggregate. Since wealth varies across individuals, the transfer system may then have distributional effects. This depends on the relation between the retirement benefits schedule and the correlation of earnings over time. It is shown that *the system is distributionally neutral only if the progressivity of the benefits schedule coincides with this intertemporal correlation.*

I also analyze the effects of the transfer system in the absence of bequests (section 5.6). Obviously, transfers are not neutral and affect the optimal consumption path. There are two types of efficiency effects: one due to the difference between the rate of return and the growth rate and the other due to the provision of insurance. With heterogeneous generations, it is always desirable to provide benefits as lump-sums, independent of the income of recipients. The desirability of such transfers cannot be established without further specification of the parameters. However, the optimal level of transfers always decreases as the correlation of earnings increases, since the insurance ("averaging") aspect diminishes.

5.2. An Altruistic Overlapping Generations Model

Individuals live two periods, denoted 0 and 1. Consumption of an individual born at the beginning of time t ("generation t") is C_{0t} in the first period and C_{1t+1} in the second period. Generations overlap so that at time t generations $t - 1$ and t coexist. It is assumed that population grows at a fixed rate of $g - 1$ (≥ 0).

Individuals can freely borrow and lend at a constant (and known) interest rate of $r - 1$ (≥ 0). Earnings, y_t, are obtained by individuals in their first period, while second-period consumption is financed by savings and transfers. Earnings are random over time but are known to each generation when it plans its lifetime consumption.

Individuals are *altruistic*; that is, they care for the welfare of their next-generation descendants and provide for them through bequests. This concern and the presence of an intergenerational transfer system that provides benefits to retirees financed by taxes on earnings introduce uncertainty into individual planning. Specifically, earnings of generation $t + 1$, y_{t+1}, and transfers are not known to members of generation t when they make their consumption and savings plans.

We assume that earnings, $\{y_t\}$, are generated by a stationary first-order *Markov Process*. A fraction, θ, of each generation's earnings is transferred to members of the previous generation.

Denote by W_t ($\geqslant 0$) the wealth inherited by a member of generation t. Wealth in successive periods is linked by the following equation:

$$gW_{t+1} = r[(1 - \theta)y_t + W_t - C_{0t}] + \mu_{t+1} - C_{1t+1}, \tag{1}$$

where the μ_{t+1} are the transfers to a member of generation t in period $t + 1$. These transfers may also be random over time depending on the specifications of the social security system. Let us write in general form

$$\mu_{t+1} = f(y_t, y_{t+1}); \tag{2}$$

that is, transfers may depend on the recipient's and on his/her descendant's earnings.

Assume that the *conditional distribution* of y_{t+1} is given by

$$y_{t+1} \sim N(\alpha + \beta y_t, \sigma^2) \tag{3}$$

where α (> 0), β ($1 > \beta \geqslant 0$) and σ^2 ($\geqslant 0$) are constants. Thus, the unconditional expectation and variance of y_{t+1} are

$$\frac{\alpha}{1 - \beta} \quad \text{and} \quad \frac{\sigma^2}{1 - \beta^2},$$

respectively. We are particularly interested in exploring the implications of dynastic earnings correlation, i.e., $\beta > 0$, on the dynamics of consumption and wealth in the presence of a transfer system.

The optimization problem solved by an individual of generation t can be written in the familiar recursive form

$$V(W_t, y_t) = \max_{C_{0t}} \{U(C_{0t}) + \delta E[U(C_{1t+1}^*) + mgV(W_{t+1}, y_{t+1})|y_t]\} \tag{4}$$

given (1), (2), and (3), where V is the maximum expected discounted lifetime utility; δ ($0 < \delta < 1$) is a constant discount rate; $u(\cdot)$ is utility from consumption ($U' > 0$ and $U'' < 0$); and m (> 0) is a constant reflecting the degree of altruism. It is assumed that C_{1t+1} is determined *after* the uncertainty about y_{t+1} and μ_{t+1} is resolved. Thus, C_{1t+1} satisfies the first-order condition (F.O.C.)

$$U'(C_{1t+1}) - mV_1(W_{t+1}, y_{t+1}) = 0, \tag{5}$$

where V_1 is the partial derivative of V with respect to its first argument. The solution of (5), C^*_{1t+1}, is the argument in (4).

The F.O.C. with respect to C_{0t} is

$$U'(C_{0t}) = r\delta m E[V_1(W_{t+1}, y_{t+1})| Y_t] = 0. \tag{6}$$

Substituting from (5), (6) can be written

$$U'(C_{0t}) = r\delta E[U'(C^*_{1t+1})| Y_t] = 0, \tag{7}$$

which is the expression derived by Hall (1978), implying that, along the optimal path, marginal utility follows a random walk with a trend. It should be noted that, without further assumptions about the form of U, equation (7) does not provide a characterization of the optimal *consumption function*.[1]

In order to provide such a characterization, we specialize to a family of utility functions with constant absolute risk aversion

$$U(C) = -e^{-RC}, \tag{8}$$

where R (>0) is a constant. We now specify two alternative assumptions concerning the intergenerational transfer system.

5.3. Homogeneous Generations

If the members of each generation can all be regarded as identical, then a pay-as-you-go transfer (social security) system collects θy_{t+1} in taxes from the earnings of each member of generation $t + 1$. Since the ratio of successive generations' sizes is g, the transfer to each member of generation t is given by

$$\mu_{t+1} = f(y_{t'}, y_{t+1}) = g\theta y_{t+1}. \tag{9}$$

Substituting (9) in (1), the method of solution for (4)–(6) is as follows. Assume that V inherits the form of U, i.e.,

$$V(W_t, Y_t) = -ke^{-R[a+bW_t+cy_t]}, \tag{10}$$

where k, a, b, and c are constant parameters. Solving (5) and (6), we look for those parameters that are consistent with (4).

Assuming that $r - g > 0$, it is shown in appendix A that (1) is indeed the solution to (4)–(6), and that the unique parameters, denoted by *, are

$$k^* = [(rg^{1+gr/(1+r)}m^g]^{1/(r-g)}\left(\frac{1+r}{r-g}\right),$$

$$a^* = \frac{gr}{(1-r)(r-\beta g)}\left[\alpha - \frac{1}{2}\frac{Rg\sigma^2}{(1+g)(r-\beta g)}\right],$$

$$b^* = \frac{r-g}{1+r},$$

(11)

$$c^* = \left(\frac{(1-\theta)r + \theta\beta g}{r-\beta g}\right)\frac{(r-g)}{(1+r)}.$$

The functions C_{0t}^* and C_{1t+1}^* are also shown to be linear in W_t and Y_t.

As could be expected, the *Ricardian Equivalence Theorem* is seen to hold in this case.

PROPOSITION 1   For a given initial net wealth, $(1-\theta)y_t + W_t$, a change in θ does not affect expected utility, V^*, and the optimal consumption levels C_{0t}^* and C_{1t+1}^*.

Proof   The argument that appears in V^* is

$$a^* + b^*W_t + c^*y_t = a^* + b^*((1-\theta)y_t + W_t) + \frac{\beta g b^*}{r-\beta g}y_t.$$

(12)

Since a^* and b^* are independent of θ, expression (12) depends only on initial net wealth, $(1-\theta)y_t + W_t$, and on y_t. Hence, since k^* is also independent of θ, it is seen from (10) that a compensated change in θ that leaves $(1-\theta)y_t + W_t$ unchanged does not affect V^*. The result concerning C_{0t}^* and C_{1t+1}^* is verified in appendix A.   QED

5.4.   Heterogeneous Generations

Now suppose that members of each generation have different y_t and W_t, but that descendants of each member follow the same conditional distribution of earnings, (3).

In contrast to the case where generations are homogeneous, and hence uncertainty about descendants' earnings being preserved in the aggregate, it is here assumed that, by the *Law of Large Numbers*, uncertainty is eliminated in the aggregate. That is, total taxes and benefits (per capita) are constant over time. Specifically, let (2) be

$$\mu_{t+1} = f(y_t, y_{t+1}) = g\theta(\hat{\alpha} + \hat{\beta}y_t), \tag{13}$$

where $\hat{\alpha}$ and $\hat{\beta}$ are constants. Thus, transfers may be conditioned on each recipient's past earnings ($\hat{\beta} \neq 0$). Aggregatively, the transfer system must satisfy the budget constraint

$$E(\mu_{t+1}) = g\theta E(y_{t+1}) = \frac{g\theta\alpha}{1 - \beta}.$$

This implies, by (13), that $\hat{\alpha}$ and $\hat{\beta}$ must satisfy the constraint

$$\frac{\hat{\alpha}}{1 - \hat{\beta}} = \frac{\alpha}{1 - \beta}. \tag{14}$$

As shown in appendix A, the solution to (4) again has the form (10), with unique parameters, denoted by **, given by

$$k^{**} = k^*,$$

$$b^{**} = b^*,$$

$$a^{**} = \frac{g}{(1 + r)(r - \beta g)}\left[\left(r + \frac{\theta(r - g)(\hat{\beta} - \beta)}{1 - \beta}\right)\alpha \right.$$

$$\left. - \frac{1}{2}\frac{Rg(r - g)((1 - \theta)r + \theta g\hat{\beta})^2\sigma^2}{(r - \beta g)(1 + g)r}\right], \tag{15}$$

$$c^{**} = \left(\frac{(1 - \theta)r + \theta\hat{\beta}g}{r - \beta g}\right)\left(\frac{r - g}{1 + r}\right).$$

As before, the optimal consumption functions, C_{0t}^{**} and C_{1t+1}^{**}, are linear in W_t and y_t. The variable that appears in expected utility, V^{**}, can now be written

$$a^{**} + b^{**}W_t + c^{**}y_t = a^{**} + b^{**}((1 - \theta)y_t + W_t)$$

$$+ \left(\frac{\beta g - \theta g(\beta - \hat{\beta})}{r - \beta g}\right)b^{**}y_t. \tag{16}$$

Clearly, for a fixed y_t and initial wealth, a change in θ changes (16). The direction of change depends on the level of y_t and on the relation between the parameters $(\hat{\alpha}, \hat{\beta})$ and (α, β). Two special cases of interest are when $\beta - \hat{\beta} = 0$ and when $\beta - \hat{\beta} > 0$.

a. $\beta - \hat{\beta} = 0$: In this case, a change in θ affects (16) only through a^{**} and therefore the effects of such a change are unambiguous. This is the case in which the transfer system has no distributional effects and, by providing *insurance* against future earnings uncertainty, always increases expected utility. We may regard this as a case in which the transfer system is *distributionally neutral*.

b. $\beta - \hat{\beta} > 0$: Benefits to each member of generation t may depend on his/her own earnings ($\hat{\beta} \neq 0$), but *marginal* benefits are lower than the correlation between expected earnings of successive generations in each dynasty. The system is *distributionally progressive*, in the sense that for large y_t, with a corresponding high expected level of y_{t+1}, it implies a negative redistributive effect, and the opposite holds for small y_t. The overall effect on expected utility of an increase in θ, holding initial net wealth unchanged, is therefore ambiguous: for small y_t the effect is to raise V^{**}, while the opposite holds for large y_t.

The distribution of y_t generates, through successive generations, distributions of W_t. We want to explore the implications of the transfer system on these distributions over time.

5.5. Wealth Distributions

Denote initial wealth at time t by $x_t = (1 - \theta)y_t + W_t$. Consider first the homogeneous generations case. By (1), (A8), (A11), and (11), initial wealth at time $t + 1$ can be expressed by the recursive formula

$$
\begin{aligned}
x_{t+1} = x_t &+ \frac{1 - r}{R(r - g)} \ln(r\delta m) \\
&- \frac{g(1 + r)}{(r - \beta g)(1 + g)}\left[\alpha - \frac{1}{2}\frac{\beta g(r - g)\sigma^2}{(r - \beta g)(1 + g)}\right] \\
&- \frac{\beta g(r - g)}{(r - \beta g)(1 + g)}y_t + \frac{g(1 + r) - \beta g(1 + g)}{(r - \beta g)(1 + g)}y_{t+1}.
\end{aligned}
\tag{17}
$$

Thus, x_t is a *random walk* with an infinite assymptotic variance. The familiarity of this result becomes clear when we set $\sigma^2 = \beta = 0$, i.e., the certainty case where $y_t = \alpha$ for all t. In this case, (17) becomes

$$x_{t+1} = x_t + \frac{1+r}{R(r-g)} \ln(r\delta m),$$

which is the familiar result that $x_{t+1} - x_t \gtrless 0$ as $r\delta m \gtrless 1$.
From (17),

$$E(x_{t+1}|x_t, y_t) = x_t + \frac{1+r}{R(r-g)} \ln(r\delta m) + \frac{1}{2} \frac{Rg^2(1+r)(r-g)\sigma^2}{(r-\beta g)^2(1+g)^2}$$

$$- \frac{\beta g}{r - \beta g}(\alpha - (1-\beta)y_t). \tag{18}$$

Since $E(y_t) = \alpha/(1-\beta)$, whether x_t has a positive or negative trend depends on whether the *sum* of the second and third terms in (18) is larger or smaller than unity, which is the *certainty-equivalent* analogue to the certainty case.

Clearly, to discuss asymptotic wealth distributions, one has to imbed the constant rate of return, $r-1$, case in a flexible macroproduction model, where this rate depends negatively on aggregate wealth. For our purpose, however, it suffices to notice that *the distribution of wealth is independent of the transfer system, θ*. This result is implied by the *Ricardian Equivalence Theorem*.

When generations are heterogeneous, consider the progressive case $\hat{\beta} = 0$; i.e., benefits for all recipients are equal. By (1), (A15), and (B1), we obtain after some manipulations

$$x_{t+1} = x_t + \frac{1-r}{R(r-g)} \ln(r\delta m) + \frac{1}{2} \frac{Rg^2(r-g)(1+r)(1-\theta)^2\sigma^2}{2(r-\beta g)^2(1+g)^2}$$

$$- \frac{(1-\theta)}{r-\beta g}\alpha + (1-\theta)\frac{(g(1+r) - \beta g(1+g))}{(r(-\beta g)(1+g)}y_{t+1} \tag{19}$$

$$- \frac{(1-\theta)g(r-g)}{(r-\beta g)(1+g)}(\alpha + \beta y_t).$$

It follows that

$$E(x_{t+1}|w_t, y_t) = x_t + \frac{1+r}{R(r-g)} \ln(r\delta) + \frac{1}{2} \frac{Rg^2(1+r)(r-g)(1-\theta)^2\sigma^2}{(r-\beta g)^2(1+g)^2}$$

$$- \frac{g(r(1-\beta) + \theta(r-g)\beta)}{(r-\beta g)r(1-\beta)}\alpha + \frac{(1-\theta)g(1-\beta)}{r-\beta g}(\alpha + \beta y_t). \tag{20}$$

Since $E(y_t) = \alpha/(1 - \beta)$, when taking the expectation of (20) over y_t, the last two terms cancel. The remaining terms are similar to (18); only the third (variance) term is smaller by $(1 - \theta)^2$.

5.6. Overlapping Generations without Bequests

Consider now the previous economy without bequests ($m = 0$). The budget constraint for a member of generation t is given by

$$C_{1t+1} = r[(1 - \theta)y_t - C_{0t}] + \mu_{t+1}. \tag{21}$$

Lifetime utility, V, is

$$V(y_t) = \max\{U(C_{0t}) + \delta E[u(C_{1t+1})]\}. \tag{22}$$

where C_{1t+1} is given by (21). The F.O.C. is

$$U'(C_{0t}) - r\delta E[U'(C_{1t+1})|y_t] = 0. \tag{23}$$

As before, we distinguish between two alternative assumptions concerning the transfer system:

a. *Homogeneous Generations:* $\mu_{t+1} = g\theta y_{t+1}$. The transfer system introduces (aggregate) uncertainty into the individual's optimization, (22). One can distinguish between two effects. Since $r - g > 0$, the system has a negative effect because the unconditional expected transfers per paid taxes are smaller than the return on savings. There is, however, a positive insurance aspect since transfers imply an "averaging" of two earnings' realizations y_t and y_{t+1}. The overall outcome of these two effects is, in general, ambiguous. Calculating the ex-ante expected utility of a typical generation (see appendix B),

$$E[V] = -\left(\frac{1 + r}{r}\right)(r\delta)^{1/(1+r)}\exp\left[-\frac{R(r(1 - \theta) + g\hat{\beta}\theta)\alpha}{(1 + r)(1 - \beta)}\right]$$
$$\times \frac{R^2(r(1 - \theta) + g\hat{\beta}\theta)^2\sigma^2}{e^{2(1+r)^2(1-\beta^2)}} + \frac{R^2g^2\theta^2\sigma^2}{2(1 + r)}. \tag{24}$$

The sign of $dE[V]/d\theta$ is, in general, indeterminate. However, if $dE[V]/d\theta = 0$ has an interior solution, $1 > \theta^* > 0$, then it is easy to show that $d\theta^*/d\beta < 0$, i.e., a higher correlation of earnings reduces the desirability of intergenerational transfers.

b. *Heterogeneous Generations:* $\mu_{t+1} = g\theta(\hat{\alpha} + \hat{\beta}y_y)$. The parameters $(\hat{\alpha}, \hat{\beta})$ satisfy the constraint

$$\frac{\hat{\alpha}}{1 - \hat{\beta}} = \frac{\alpha}{1 - \beta}.$$

Expected lifetime utility of a typical generation is now given by (see appendix B)

$$E[V] = -\left(\frac{1+r}{r}\right)(r\delta)^{1/(1+r)} \exp\left[-\frac{R}{1+r}\left(\frac{r(1-\theta)+g\theta}{1-\beta}\right)\alpha \right.$$

$$\left. + \frac{1}{2}\frac{R^2(r(1-\theta)+g\hat{\beta}\theta)^2\sigma^2}{(1+r)^2(1-\beta^2)}\right]. \tag{25}$$

Observe that for a given θ, the value of $\hat{\beta}$ that maximizes $E[V]$ is given by

$$\hat{\beta}_{\text{opt}} = -\frac{r}{g}\left(\frac{1-\theta}{\theta}\right). \tag{26}$$

This value of $\hat{\beta}_{\text{opt}}$, eliminates the effect of uncertainty on expected utility. Furthermore, when $\hat{\beta}$ is adjusted optimally, by (26), to any level of θ, then by (25)

$$\left.\frac{dE[V]}{d\theta}\right|_{\beta_{\text{opt}}} < 0.$$

That is, transfers always decrease expected utility.

The effect of transfers on expected savings, $E[(1-\theta)y_t - C_{0t}^{**}]$, can be seen from equation (B8) in appendix B to be *always negative.*

Appendix A

Consider the recursive equation (4),

$$V(W_t, y_t) = \max_{C_{0t}}\{U(C_{0t}) + \delta E[U(C_{1t+1}^*) + mgV(W_{t+1}, y_{t+1})|y_t]\}, \tag{A1}$$

where

$$gW_{t+1} = r[(1-\theta)y_t + W_t = C_{0t}] + \mu_{t+1} - C_{1t+1}, \tag{A2}$$

and C_{1t+1}^* satisfies the F.O.C. (5),

$$U'(C_{1t+1}^*) - mV_1(W_{t+1}, y_{t+1}) = 0. \tag{A3}$$

Equation (A3) reflects the assumption that C_{1t+1} is determined *after* the resolution of uncertainty about y_{t+1} (and μ_{t+1}).

The F.O.C. with respect to C_{0t}, (4), is

$$U'(C_{0t}) - r\delta m E[V_1(W_{t+1}, y_{t+1})|y_t] = 0. \tag{A4}$$

We assume that

$$U(C) = -e^{-RC}, \tag{A5}$$

where $R > 0$ is a constant. Since U in (A5) is strictly concave, the solution to (A1) is unique. We try a solution where V inherits the form of U:

$$V(W, y) = -ke^{-r[a+bW+cy]}, \tag{A6}$$

with k, a, b, and c constants. Condition (A3) now becomes

$$\exp[-RC_{1t+1}] = mbk \exp\left[-R\left[a + \frac{br}{g}((1-\theta)y_t - C_{0t}) + \frac{b(\mu_{t+1} - C_{1t+1})}{g} + cy_{t+1}\right]\right]. \tag{A7}$$

Solving for C_{1t+1},

$$C_{1t+1}^* = \frac{g}{R(g+b)}\ln(mbk) + \frac{g}{g+b}\left[a + \frac{br}{g}((1-\theta)y_t + W_t - C_{0t})\right.$$
$$\left. + \frac{b\mu_{t+1}}{g} + cy_{t+1}\right]. \tag{A8}$$

By (A2), (A6), and (A8),

$$U(C_{1t+1}^*) + mgV(W_{t+1}, y_{t+1})$$

$$= -\left(\frac{g+b}{b}\right)(mbk)^{g/(g+b)}\exp\left[-\frac{Rg}{g+b}\left[a + \frac{br}{g}((1-\theta)y_t + W_t - C_{0t})\right.\right.$$
$$\left.\left. + \frac{b\mu_{t+1}}{g} + cy_{t+1}\right] \right] \tag{A9}$$

$$= -\left(\frac{g-b}{b}\right)\exp[-RC_{1t+1}].$$

Assume that $y_{t+1} \sim N(\alpha + \beta y_t, \sigma^2)$. We shall use the fact that if $x \sim N(x, \sigma^2)$, then $E(e^{sx}) = \exp[sx + \frac{1}{2}s^2\sigma^2]$. With respect to μ_{t+1} we make two alternative assumptions:

I. $\mu_{t+1} = g\theta y_{t+1}$.

We now have, from (A9),

$$E[U(C_{1t+1}^*) + mgV(W_{t+1}, y_{t+1})|y_t]$$

$$= -\left(\frac{g+b}{b}\right)(mbK)^{g/(g+b)}\exp\left[-\frac{Rg}{g+b}\left[a + \frac{br}{g}((1-\theta)y_t + W_t - C_{0t})\right.\right.$$
$$\left.\left. + (b\theta + c)(\alpha + \beta y_t)\right] \times \exp\left[\frac{1}{2}\frac{R^2 g^2(b\theta+c)^2\sigma}{(g+b)^2}\right]. \right. \tag{A10}$$

From (A4) and (A10), the solution C_{0t}^* is

$$C_{0t}^* = -\frac{g+b}{R((g+b(1+r))}\ln(r\delta(mbk)^{g/(g+b)})$$

$$+\frac{g}{g+b(1+r)}\left[a+\frac{br}{g}((1-\theta)y_t + W_t) + (b\theta + c)(\alpha + \beta y_t)\right] \qquad (A11)$$

$$-\frac{1}{2}\frac{Rg^2(b\theta+c)^2\sigma^2}{(g+b)(g+b(1+r))}.$$

Substituting (A11) into (A10), equation (A1) becomes

$$k\exp[-R[a+bW_t + cy_t]]$$

$$= (r\delta(mbk)^{g/(g+b)})^{(g+b)/[g+b(1+r)]}\left(\frac{g+b(1+r)}{rb}\right)$$

$$\times \exp\left[-\frac{rg}{g+b(1+r)}\left[a+\frac{br}{g}((1-\theta)y_t + W_t) + (b\theta + c)(\alpha + \beta y_t)\right]\right] \qquad (A12)$$

$$\times \exp\left[\frac{1}{2}\frac{R^2g^2(b\theta+c)^2\sigma^2}{(g+b)(g+b)(1+r)}\right].$$

Equating coefficients for the corresponding variables on the left-hand side and on the right-hand side of (A12), we finally obtain, after some manipulation, the necessary identities for the undetermined coefficients. For $r - g > 0$, the solutions k^*, a^*, b^*, and c^* are given in equation (11). The corresponding value of V, denoted V^*, is

$$V^*(w, y) = k^* e^{-R[a^* + b^*W + c^*y]}. \qquad (A13)$$

II. $\mu_{t+1} = g\theta(\hat{\alpha} + \hat{\beta}y_t)$.
The constants $\hat{\alpha} > 0$ and $\hat{\beta}$ $(1 > \hat{\beta} \geqslant 0)$ satisfy the relation

$$\frac{\hat{\alpha}}{1-\hat{\beta}} = \frac{\alpha}{1-\beta}.$$

Using the same method as above, the analogous solution to (A8), denoted C_{1t+1}^{**}, is

$$C_{1t+1}^{**} = -\frac{g}{R(g+b)}\ln(mbk) + \frac{g}{g+b}\left[a + \frac{br}{g}((1-\theta)y_t + W_t - C_{0t})\right.$$

$$\left. + b\theta(\hat{\alpha} + \hat{\beta}y_t) + cy_{t+1}\right]. \qquad (A14)$$

Similarly, solving for the optimal C_{0t},

$$C_{0t}^{**} = -\frac{b}{R(g+b(1+r))}\ln(r\delta(mbk)^{g/(g+b)}) + \frac{g}{g+b(1+r)}\left[a + \frac{br}{g}((1-\theta)y_t + W_t)\right.$$

$$\left. + b\theta(\hat{\alpha} + \hat{\beta}y_t) + c(\alpha + \beta y_t)\right] - \frac{1}{2}\frac{Rg^2c^2\sigma^2}{(g+b)(g+b(1+r))}. \qquad (A15)$$

The undetermined coefficients consistent with the F.O.C. are given in equation (15).

Appendix B

With no bequests ($m = 0$), the budget constraint for a member of generation t is given by

$$C_{1t+1} = r[(1 - \theta)y_t - C_{0t}] + \mu_t. \tag{B1}$$

Lifetime utility is

$$V(y_t) = \max\{U(C_{0t}) + \delta E[U(C_{1t+1})|y_t]\} \tag{B2}$$

such that (B1) holds. The F.O.C. is

$$U'(C_{0t}) - r\delta E[U'(C_{1t+1})|y_t] = 0. \tag{B3}$$

Following the previous analysis, we distinguish between two alternative assumptions concerning the transfer system:

a. *Homogeneous Generations:* $\mu_{t+1} = g\theta y_{t+1}$. Solving from (B3), optimal consumption and utility are

$$C_{0t}^* = -\frac{1}{R(1 + r)}\ln r\delta + \left(\frac{r(1 - \theta) + g\beta\theta}{1 + r}\right)y_t + \frac{g\theta\alpha}{1 + r} - \frac{1}{2}\frac{Rg^2\theta^2\sigma^2}{1 + r}, \tag{B4}$$

$$C_{1t+1}^* = \frac{r}{R(1 + r)}\ln r\delta + \left(\frac{r(1 - \theta) - g\beta\theta}{1 + r}\right)y_t - \frac{g\theta\alpha}{1 + r} + \frac{Rrg^2\theta^2\sigma^2}{2(1 + r)} + g\theta y_{t+1}, \tag{B5}$$

and

$$V = -\left(\frac{1 + r}{r}\right)(r\delta)^{1/(1+r)}\exp\left[-\frac{R}{1 + r}[(r(1 - \theta) + g\beta\theta)y_t + g\theta\alpha]\right] \times \exp\left[\frac{R^2g^2\theta^2\sigma^2}{2(1 + r)}\right]. \tag{B6}$$

The unconditional distribution of y_t is $N(\alpha/(1 - \beta), \sigma^2/(1 - \beta^2))$. Hence, expected utility of generation t, $E[V]$, is given by

$$E[V] = -\left(\frac{1 + r}{r}\right)(r\delta)^{1/(1+r)}\exp\left[-\frac{R(r(1 - \theta) + g\beta\theta)\alpha}{(1 + r)(1 + \beta)}\right]$$
$$\times \exp\left[-\frac{R^2(r(1 - \theta) + g\beta\theta)^2\sigma^2}{2(1 + r)^2(1 - \beta^2)} + \frac{R^2g^2\theta^2\sigma^2}{2(1 + r)}\right]. \tag{B7}$$

b. *Heterogeneous Generations:* $\mu_{t+1} = g\theta(\hat{\alpha} + \hat{\beta}y_t)$. The coefficients (α, β) satisfy the aggregate constraint

$$\frac{\alpha}{1 - \beta} = \frac{\alpha}{1 - \beta}.$$

The solutions to (B2) are now

$$C_{0t}^{**} = -\frac{1}{R(1 + r)}\ln r\delta + \left(\frac{r(1 - \theta) + g\hat{\beta}\theta}{1 + r}\right)y_t + \frac{g\theta\hat{\alpha}}{1 + r}, \tag{B8}$$

$$C_{0t}^{**} = \frac{1}{R(1 + r)}\ln r\delta + \left(\frac{r(1 - \theta) + g\hat{\beta}\theta}{1 + r}\right)y_t + \frac{g\theta\hat{\alpha}}{1 + r}, \tag{B9}$$

and

$$V = -\left(\frac{1+r}{r}\right)(r\delta)^{1+r}\exp\left[-\frac{r}{1+r}[(r(1-\theta)+g\hat{\beta}\theta)y_t+g\theta\hat{\alpha}]\right].\tag{B10}$$

Hence,

$$E[V] = -\left(\frac{1+r}{r}\right)(r\delta)^{1/(1+r)}\exp\left[-\frac{R}{1+r}\left(\frac{r(1-\theta+g\theta)}{1-\beta}\right)\alpha+\frac{1}{2}\frac{R^2(r(1-\theta)+g\hat{\beta}\theta)^2\sigma^2}{(1+r)^2(1-\beta^2)}\right].\tag{B11}$$

Notes

1. It follows that if marginal utility is linear, then consumption itself follows a random walk. This is the hypothesis tested in a number of recent works (Hayashi, 1986, Flavin, 1981). But as Hey (1980) correctly points out, in general, condition (7) is an implication of the optimal policy but, in itself, not a *characterization* of this policy.

References

Abel, Andrew B. (1985), "Capital Accumulation with Adverse Selection and Uncertain Lifetimes," *Econometrica* (forthcoming).

Barro, Robert, J. (1974), "Are Government Bonds Net Wealth?" *Journal of Political Economy* 82, 1095–1117.

Bernheim, Douglas B., and Kyle Bagwell (1984), "Is Everything Neutral?: The Implications of Intergenerational Altruism in an Overlapping Generations Model," Mimeo.

Feldstein, Martin S. (1974), "Social Security, Induced Retirement and Aggregate Capital Accumulation," *Journal of Political Economy* 89, 1020–1037.

Flavin, Margorie, A. (1981), "The Adjustment of Consumption to Changing Expectation about Future Income," *Journal of Political Economy* 89, 1020–1037.

Hall, Robert, E. (1978), "Stochastic Implications of the Lifecycle-Permanent Income Hypothesis: Theory and Evidence," *Journal of Political Economy* 86, 971–987.

Hayashi, Fumio (1986), "The Permanent Income Hypothesis and Consumption Durability: Analysis Based on Japanese Panel Data," *Quarterly Journal of Economics*.

Hey, John D. (1980), "Optimal Consumption under Income Uncertainty," *Economic Letters* 5, 129–133.

Kotlikoff, Lawrence J., and Lawrence Summers (1981), "The Role of Intergenerational Transfers in Aggregate Capital Accumulation," *Journal of Political Economy* 89, 706–732.

Sheshinski, Eytan, and Yoram Weiss (1981), "Uncertainty and Optimal Social Security Systems," *Quarterly Journal of Economics*, 86, 189–206.

6 An Analysis of Fiscal Policy under Operative and Inoperative Bequest Motives

Andrew B. Abel

It is well-known that if a consumer has an infinite horizon, then his consumption and saving behavior is invariant to changes in the timing of lump-sum taxes that leave the present value of his taxes unchanged. Barro (1974) argued that if consumers have operative altruistic bequest motives, then they behave as if they have infinite horizons. This important insight implies that the Ricardian Equivalence Theorem, which is the proposition that changes in the timing of lump-sum taxes have no effect, can hold even in an economy in which consumers have finite lifetimes. Since the appearance of Barro's seminal paper, there have been several challenges to the Ricardian Equivalence Theorem that have shown that even with an operative altruistic bequest motive, lump-sum tax changes can have an effect. Such effects arise if there are not complete insurance markets for stochastic fluctuations in labor income (Barsky, Mankiw, and Zeldes, 1986), if there are preexisting nonlinear taxes on wealth or property income (Abel, 1986), or if new consumers who do not receive bequests from current domestic consumers enter the economy (Weil, 1986).

This chapter also analyzes a reason for departure from Ricardian Equivalence but focuses on a different channel than the research cited above. The assumption that the altruistic bequest motive is operative, which is a hypothesis maintained in the work mentioned above, will be critically examined in this chapter. Specifically, I shall assume that individual consumers are indeed altruistic with respect to their heirs, and I shall then determine, in a specific model, how strong the bequest motive must be in order to be operative. I shall then show that lump-sum fiscal policy affects whether the bequest motive is operative, and I shall analyze the effects of fiscal policy when the bequest motive is not operative.

The question of whether the bequest motive is operative has received some attention in the literature. Drazen (1978) presented conditions on equilibrium marginal rates of substitution that must hold for the bequest motive to be operative, but in his general nonseparable formulation of altruism, there is no single parameter, or set of parameters, that measures the strength of the bequest motive. In an elegantly simple analysis, Weil

This chapter was prepared for the Pinhas Sapir Conference on the Economic Effects of the Government's Budget, Tel-Aviv University, December 22–24, 1986. Research support from the National Science Foundation and the Sloan Foundation is gratefully acknowledged. I thank Allan Drazen and Philippe Weil for helpful comments.

(1987) derived a lower bound for the strength of the bequest motive in order for there to be positive bequests in the steady state. This lower bound is not stated directly in terms of preferences and technology, but rather is expressed in terms of the steady state marginal product of capital in an economy without bequests. Weil's analysis is extended in Abel (1987) to determine conditions under which the gift motive (from child to parent) or the bequest motive (from parent to child) or neither will be operative. However, Weil's analysis and the extension are both confined largely to steady states. Weil did explore bequest behavior outside of the steady state but did not find a clean set of conditions that guarantee that the bequest motive would be operative for every generation, even for specific examples of preferences and technology. It must be emphasized, as noted by Weil, that the Ricardian Equivalence Theorem in general requires that the bequest motive be operative for every generation. Therefore, the determination of conditions under which the Ricardian Equivalence Theorem holds along the transition path remains an important open question.

In this chapter I derive conditions for operative bequests everywhere along the transition path for a specific structure of preferences and technology. In particular, I restrict attention to a logarithmic utility function and a Cobb-Douglas production function and present conditions under which the bequest motive will always be operative, regardless of the initial level of capital intensity. It should be recalled that Weil also considered the case with a logarithmic utility function and a Cobb-Douglas production function but was able to show that the bequest motive is always operative only under the assumption that the initial capital stock was above a certain critical level. The difference between Weil's example and the model in this chapter is that, unlike Weil's specification, my specification of the Cobb-Douglas production function essentially assumes complete depreciation of capital in one period. The importance of this assumption is simply technical: it implies that in equilibrium the logarithm of the capital stock follows a linear (stochastic) difference equation, whereas in Weil's specification the evolution of the capital stock is not log-linear. This log-linearity permits the derivation of simple conditions for operative bequests.

Recently, Cukierman (1986) and Feldstein (1986) have each analyzed binding nonnegativity constraints on bequests when individual consumers face uncertainty. In Cukierman (1986), young consumers are uncertain about their state of health in old age (modeled formally as uncertainty about tastes) and thus are uncertain about whether they will ultimately want to leave a positive bequest. In Feldstein (1986) young consumers are also uncertain about whether they will ultimately want to leave a positive bequest but this uncertainty arises from uncertainty about income in old age. The prospect that each young consumer may ultimately face a strictly binding constraint on bequests leads to a violation of the Ricardian Equivalence Theorem because consumers who are constrained would prefer shifting taxes onto future generations.

In this chapter I introduce uncertainty by making the production function subject to random shocks. It turns out that with the specification of preferences and technology in this chapter, each young consumer knows whether his bequest motive will be operative in old age. Although this formulation ignores an interesting aspect of the individual decision problem that is emphasized in the partial equilibrium analyses of Cukierman and Feldstein, it permits aggregation across consumers with heterogeneous wealth. I exploit the easy aggregation in the model to analyze the general equilibrium effects of policy on endogenous factor prices as well as on the individual's decision problem.

In addition to introducing uncertainty, this analysis departs from the now standard representative consumer framework by allowing for a non-degenerate cross-sectional distribution of capital holdings. In this simple model, I can study the evolution of the distribution of wealth. In addition, I can determine how much variation in wealth is compatible with the requirement that all consumers have operative bequest motives.

In section 6.1 I present a model with a stochastic production function and with altruistic consumers. I then derive the optimal saving and consumption rules for an artificial decision problem in which the old consumer is given control over the wage income of his children. This artificial decision problem ignores the nonnegativity constraint on bequests. In section 6.2 I analyze conditions under which bequests will in fact be nonnegative and present restrictions that are sufficient to guarantee that the bequest motive will be operative in every period. In section 6.3 I analyze individual and aggregate behavior when the bequest motive is not operative and in section 6.4 I present restrictions that guarantee that the bequest motive will never be operative. The relation between dynamic efficiency and the possibility of operative bequests is analyzed in section 6.5. Section 6.6 examines a laissez-faire economy without taxes or transfers and analyzes bequest behavior in the presence of cross-sectional variation in wealth. In section 6.7, I confine attention to a representative consumer economy and examine the effects of changes in the tax and transfer system on the stochastic evolution of the capital stock. Section 6.8 concludes the chapter.

6.1.   Consumption and Capital Accumulation in the Absence of Nonnegativity Constraints

Consider an overlapping generations economy in which each consumer lives for two periods and gives birth to n heirs at the beginning of the second period. Each consumer inelastically supplies one unit of labor when young and does not work when old. A consumer born at the beginning of period t receives a competitive wage W_t and consumes an amount c_t^y in period t when he is young and consumes c_{t+1}^0 in period $t + 1$ when he is old. Let k_t be the stock of capital (per worker) held by an individual family at the beginning of period t. This capital is actually owned by the old consumers in the family and represents their saving from the previous period. Let R_t be the gross rate of return on capital held from period $t - 1$ to period t. Therefore the capital stock held by the family evolves according to

$$nk_{t+1} = R_t k_t + W_t - c_t^y - c_t^0/n. \tag{1}$$

Equation (1) states that the amount of capital carried into period $t + 1$ is equal to the family's total income in period t, $R_t k_t + W_t$, minus the consumption of the young and old consumers. Let K_t, C_t^y, and C_t^0, denote the economy-wide average values of k_t, c_t^y, and c_t^0, respectively. With competitive factor markets, all families face the same wage rate, W_t, and the same return to capital R_t. Therefore, since (1) is linear in k_t, c_t^y, and c_t^0,

$$nK_{t+1} = R_t K_t + W_t - C_t^y - C_t^0/n. \tag{2}$$

Suppose that consumers have altruistic bequest motives. Letting U_t be the utility of a consumer born at the beginning of period t, we specify the utility function to be

$$U_t = E_t\{u(c_t^y, c_{t+1}^0) + \delta U_{t+1}\}, \qquad 0 \leqslant \delta < 1, \tag{3}$$

where $E_t\{\ \}$ denotes the expectation conditional on information available at the beginning of period t. The parameter δ, which is assumed to be nonnegative and less than one, measures the strength of the bequest motive. One goal of this analysis is to determine how large δ must be in order for the bequest motive to be operative.

Now suppose that the utility function is logarithmic,

$$u(c_t^y, c_{t+1}^0) = \beta \ln c_t^y + (1 - \beta) \ln c_{t+1}^0, \qquad 0 < \beta < 1, \tag{4}$$

and that the production function is Cobb-Douglas,

$$Y_t = \psi_t K_t^\alpha, \qquad 0 < \alpha < 1, \tag{5}$$

where Y_t is output per worker and ψ_t is a positive random variable. With the Cobb-Douglas production function in (5) the competitive wage rate is

$$W_t = (1 - \alpha)\psi_t K_t^\alpha \tag{6}$$

and the competitive rate of return on capital is

$$R_t = \alpha \psi_t K_t^{\alpha - 1}. \tag{7}$$

It is useful first to consider the artificial decision problem in which the old consumer maximizes his altruistic utility function (3) subject to the family's budget constraint in (1). This problem is artificial in that the old consumer is allowed to consume some or all of the wage income of his children. This decision problem can be solved using the value function

$$V(k_t, \psi_t, K_t) = \max[(1 - \beta)\ln c_t^0 + \delta\beta \ln c_t^y + \delta E_t\{V(k_{t+1}, \psi_{t+1}, K_{t+1})\}], \tag{8}$$

where the maximization in (8) is with respect to c_t^0, c_t^y, and k_{t+1} and is subject to the family and aggregate capital accumulation constraints in (1) and (2).

The value function is the expected present value of utility from the old consumer's own consumption when old plus the utility the old consumer obtains from his heirs' utility. The value function is a solution to the functional equation in (8). I have used the method of undetermined coefficients to solve (8). Because the solution procedure is neither novel nor instructive, and because the solution is easily verified, I shall simply present a solution to the functional equation

$$V(k_t, \psi_t, K_t) = [(1 - \beta + \delta\beta)/(1 - \delta)]\ln[(1 - \alpha)K_t + (1 - \delta)\alpha k_t]$$
$$+ \phi \ln K_t + J(\psi_t) + D, \tag{9}$$

where

$$\phi = -(1 - \beta + \delta\beta)(1 - \alpha)/[(1 - \delta)(1 - \delta\alpha)]$$

and

$$J(\psi_t) = [(1 - \beta + \delta\beta)/(1 - \delta\alpha)] \ln \psi_t + \delta E_t\{J(\psi_{t+1})\}$$

and D is an unimportant constant.

Using equation (9) it is straightforward but tedious to derive the optimal consumption and capital accumulation for the artificial decision problem and to derive the behavior of aggregate consumption and capital accumulation. The behavior of an individual family is given by

$$c_t^y = [\delta\beta/(1 - \beta + \delta\beta)]\psi_t K_t^{\alpha-1}\{(1 - \alpha)K_t + (1 - \delta)\alpha k_t\]\}, \tag{10}$$

$$c_t^0/n = [(1 - \beta)/(1 - \beta + \delta\beta)]\psi_t K_t^{\alpha-1}\{(1 - \alpha)K_t + (1 - \delta)\alpha k_t\]\}, \tag{11}$$

$$nk_{t+1} = \alpha\delta\psi_t K_t^{\alpha-1}k_t. \tag{12}$$

To illustrate the "artificial" nature of this problem, observe that if $\delta = 0$, then (10)–(12) imply that $c_t^y = 0$, $c_t^0 = n(W_t + R_t k_t)$, and $k_{t+1} = 0$. That is, if the consumer does not care about the utility of his children, then he will consume the family's entire income, including his children's wages. He would neither save nor allocate any current consumption to his children. Clearly, this allocation would imply a negative bequest. As shown in section 6.2, the consumer will make a positive bequest if δ is sufficiently large.

Because the optimal consumption and capital accumulation decision rules are linear in k_t, it is easy to aggregate these rules to obtain

$$C_t^y = [\delta\beta(1 - \delta\alpha)/(1 - \beta + \delta\beta)]\psi_t K_t^\alpha, \tag{13}$$

$$C_t^0/n = [(1 - \beta)(1 - \delta\alpha)/(1 - \beta + \delta\beta)]\psi_t K_t^\alpha, \tag{14}$$

$$nK_{t+1} = \alpha\delta\psi_t K_t^\alpha. \tag{15}$$

By distinguishing an individual family's holding of capital, k_t, from average capital per worker, K_t, I have allowed for cross-sectional variation in k_t. Observe that with the assumed specification of preferences and technology, the cross-sectional distribution of capital remains fixed over time. More precisely, dividing (12) by (15) yields $k_{t+1}/K_{t+1} = k_t/K_t$, so that any initial inequality in the distribution of capital is preserved forever.

6.2. The Nonnegativity Constraint on Bequests: Nonbinding

The formal analysis to this point has ignored any nonnegativity constraint on bequests. In this section we determine how strong the bequest motive must be in order to be operative, i.e., for the nonnegativity constraint to be nonbinding. Let y_t^0 be the disposable resources available to an old consumer in period t and let b_t be the bequest left by this consumer, so that

$$b_t \equiv y_t^0 - c_t^0. \tag{16}$$

Suppose that there is a permanent tax and transfer system that taxes wage income at rate τ and uses the tax revenues τW_t to finance a lump-sum transfer of $n\tau W_t$ to each old consumer in period t. If τ is positive, then the tax and transfer scheme is a pay-as-you-go social security system. Because labor supply is inelastic, the tax is nondistortionary. Furthermore, since the taxes paid by the young consumers in each family are equal to the transfers received by the old consumers in that family, this scheme has no effect on the present value of taxes paid by any family. Therefore, if the bequest motive is always operative, then the path of consumption and capital accumulation is invariant with respect to τ. The optimal consumption and capital accumulation rules presented for the artificial decision problem in section 6.1 continue to hold in the presence of this tax and transfer scheme.

The disposable resources of an old consumer consist of the gross return on his capital as well as the fiscal subsidy he receives, so that

$$y_t^0 = n\psi_t K_t^{\alpha-1}\{(1-\alpha)\tau K_t + \alpha k_t\}. \tag{17}$$

Substituting (11) and (17) into (16) yields an expression for the bequest that an old consumer in period t would like to leave:

$$b_t = (1 - \beta + \delta\beta)^{-1} n\psi_t K_t^{\alpha}\{(1-\alpha)[\tau\delta\beta - (1-\beta)(1-\tau)] + \alpha\delta(k_t/K_t)\}. \tag{18}$$

The desired bequest will be positive if and only if the term in curly brackets on the right-hand side of (18) is positive. Recall that in an equilibrium in which all families have operative bequests, each family's k_t/K_t is constant over time, so that the condition that the right-hand side of (18) be positive is time-invariant.

It is convenient to express the condition that the bequest motive be operative in terms of how strong the bequest motive must be as measured by δ. Define $\delta^0 = \delta^0(\tau, k_t/K_t)$, where

$$\delta^0(\tau, k_t/K_t) \equiv (1-\alpha)(1-\beta)(1-\tau)/[\alpha k_t/K_t + (1-\alpha)\tau\beta]. \tag{19}$$

Observe that $\delta > \delta^0$ is a necessary and sufficient condition for the right-hand side of (18) to be positive. Therefore, if $\delta > \delta^0(\tau, k_t/K_t)$ for all relevant values of k_t/K_t, then the bequest motive is operative for all families.

6.3. Inoperative Bequests

In this section I analyze the dynamic behavior of an economy in which the bequest motive is not operative. It might appear that to analyze an economy with an inoperative bequest motive, one can simply analyze the behavior of a standard Diamond (1965) model. However, in general, this strategy would not be appropriate because even if the bequest motive is currently inoperative, it may become operative at some date in the future. Therefore, to describe the dynamics of an economy with a currently in-operative bequest motive, I must use a procedure that allows for the possibility that the bequest motive will be operative at some future date(s). It turns out that for the particular preferences and technology assumed in this chapter, the bequest motive will always be operative or will always be inoperative in a representative consumer economy, but this is a result to be derived from studying the model and should not be assumed at the outset.

The decision problem facing an old consumer in period t can be solved using the value function. Indeed, the functional equation (8) applies to consumers with inoperative bequest motives. However, because the constraint $b_t \geqslant 0$ is binding, the solution to the functional equation $V(k_t, \psi_t, K_t)$ differs from that in (9). It can be verified that the value function in this case is

$$V(k_t, \psi_t, K_t) = (1 - \beta)\ln[(1 - \alpha)\tau K_t + \alpha k_t] + d\ln K_t + H(\psi_t) + E, \quad (20)$$

where

$$d = [\delta\alpha - (1 - \alpha)(1 - \beta)]/(1 - \alpha\delta),$$

$$H(\psi_t) = [1 - \beta + \delta + \delta d]\ln\psi_t + \delta E_t\{H(\psi_{t+1})\},$$

and E is an unimportant constant that depends on the parameters of preferences and technology as well as on the tax rate τ.

Using the value function in (20) it is straightforward to derive the optimal consumption and capital accumulation for an individual family with capital per worker k_t:

$$c_t^y = \beta(1 - \alpha)(1 - \tau)[(\alpha + (1 - \alpha)\tau)/(\alpha + (1 - \alpha)\beta\tau)]\psi_t K_t^\alpha, \tag{21}$$

$$c_t^0/n = y_t^0/n = \psi_t K_t^{\alpha-1}[\alpha k_t + (1 - \alpha)\tau K_t], \tag{22}$$

$$nk_{t+1} = [\alpha(1 - \alpha)(1 - \beta)(1 - \tau)/(\alpha + (1 - \alpha)\beta\tau)]\psi_t K_t^\alpha. \tag{23}$$

With a binding constraint on bequests, the consumption of each old consumer is equal to his disposable income y_t^0. If there is cross-sectional variation in y_t^0, and if all consumers face binding nonnegativity constraints on bequests, then there will of course be cross-sectional variation in c_t^0; however, there will be no cross-sectional variation in the consumption of young consumers or in the accumulation of capital for the next period. Any cross-sectional variation in wealth is eliminated in one period. The reason for this strong result is that the only source of cross-sectional variation is the variation in the initial holdings of capital. If all consumers leave zero bequests, then this inequality in the distribution of wealth is not transmitted to subsequent generations. It should be noted that this result contrasts sharply with the result that under operative bequests any inequality in the distribution of wealth is preserved forever.

Aggregate consumption and capital accumulation are easily calculated from (21)–(23) to be

$$C_t^y = \beta(1 - \alpha)(1 - \tau)[(\alpha + (1 - \alpha)\tau)/(\alpha + (1 - \alpha)\beta\tau)]\psi_t K_t^\alpha, \tag{24}$$

$$C_t^0/n = \psi_t K_t^\alpha[\alpha + (1 - \alpha)\tau], \tag{25}$$

$$nK_{t+1} = [\alpha(1 - \alpha)(1 - \beta)(1 - \tau)/(\alpha + (1 - \alpha)\beta\tau)]\psi_t K_t^\alpha. \tag{26}$$

6.4. The Nonnegativity Constraint on Bequests: Binding

I now determine under what conditions the nonnegativity constraint on bequests will be binding. Formally, I could derive the optimal consumption and capital accumulation rules by substituting (1) and (2) into (20) and then performing the indicated maximization in the functional equation (8). Letting θ_t be the Lagrange multiplier associated with the constraint $b_t \equiv y_t^0 - c_t^0 \geqslant 0$, the Kuhn-Tucker conditions are

$$\delta\beta/c_t^y = \delta\alpha(1 - \beta)/\{[(1 - \alpha)\tau K_{t+1} + \alpha k_{t+1}]n\}, \tag{27}$$

$$(1 - \beta)/c_t^0 = \delta\alpha(1 - \beta)/\{[(1 - \alpha)\tau K_{t+1} + \alpha k_{t+1}]n^2\} + \theta_t, \tag{28}$$

$$\theta_t(y_t^0 - c_t^0) = 0, \tag{29}$$

$$\theta_t \geq 0. \tag{30}$$

Conditions (27) and (28) are obtained by differentiating with respect to c_t^y and c_t^0, respectively. Substituting (27) into (28) yields the simpler expression

$$(1 - \beta)/c_t^0 = \delta\beta/(nc_t^y) + \theta_t. \tag{31}$$

When the nonnegativity constraint is strictly binding, the Lagrange multiplier θ_t is positive. In this case, (31) indicates that the appropriately weighted marginal utility of the old consumer's consumption exceeds the appropriately weighted marginal utility of the young consumer's current consumption. Thus, the appropriately weighted sum of utilities could be increased if some consumption could be shifted from the young consumer to the old consumer by a negative bequest. However, because the nonnegativity constraint is binding, this reallocation is not possible.

When the nonnegativity constraint binds, $c_t^0 = y_t^0$ and $\theta_t > 0$, so that (31) implies that

$$(1 - \beta)c_t^y > \delta\beta y_t^0/n. \tag{32}$$

Substituting (17) and (21) into (32) motivates the definition of δ^c, the critical value of the bequest motive parameter, as $\delta^c = \delta^c(\tau, k_t/K_t)$, where

$$\delta^c(\tau, k_t/K_t) \equiv [(1 - \beta)(1 - \alpha)(1 - \tau)/(\alpha + (1 - \alpha)\beta\tau)]$$
$$\times [(\alpha + (1 - \alpha)\tau)/(\alpha k_t/K_t + (1 - \alpha)\tau)]. \tag{33}$$

Observe that $\delta < \delta^c(\tau, k_t/K_t)$ is a necessary and sufficient condition for (32) to hold. This condition is applicable in an equilibrium in which all old consumers face binding nonnegativity constraints.

6.5. Dynamic Efficiency

Abel et al. (1986) have shown that if, in a competitive stochastic economy, the rate of return on some asset is always less than the growth rate of the aggregate capital stock, then the economy is dynamically inefficient in the sense that it suffers from an inefficient overaccumulation of capital. If the rate of return on some asset always exceeds the growth rate of the aggregate capital stock, then the economy is dynamically efficient.

To determine whether the economy is dynamically efficient, observe from (7) and (15) that the growth rate of the aggregate capital stock in the economy with operative bequests, G_t^0, is

$$G_t^0 \equiv (nK_{t+1}/K_t)^{\circ} = \delta R_t^0 \tag{34}$$

where the superscript o denotes the equilibrium value of a variable in the economy with operative bequests. Under the assumption that δ is less than 1, it follows immediately from (34) that $R_t^0 > G_t^0$ for all t, and hence the economy with operative bequests is dynamically efficient. Of course, the dynamic efficiency of the economy in which the bequest motive is always operative is to be expected because the consumers behave as if they have infinite horizons.

The growth rate of the aggregate capital stock in the economy without bequests, G_t^c, can be calculated from (7), (19), and (26) to be

$$G_t^c \equiv (nK_{t+1}/K_t)^c = \delta^0(\tau, 1)R_t^c, \tag{35}$$

where the superscript c denotes the equilibrium value of a variable in the economy with constrained bequests. Equation (35) implies that the ratio G_t^c/R_t^c is constant and equal to $\delta^0(\tau, 1)$. If $\delta^0(\tau, 1)$ is less than or equal to one, then the economy without operative bequests is efficient; if $\delta^0(\tau, 1)$ is greater than one, the economy is inefficient. Because in this model dynamic inefficiency implies $\delta^0(\tau, 1) > 1$ and because a positive bequest requires $\delta > \delta^0(\tau, 1)$, there is no admissible value of δ for which bequests will be positive if the no-bequest economy is inefficient. This result was originally derived by Weil (1987). Weil's result is more general in that it is not restricted to logarithmic utility and Cobb-Douglas production functions; however, his result is less general in that he did not consider stochastic economies, and more important, his result could not be applied everywhere along the transition path.

6.6. Bequests in the Absence of Fiscal Transfers

In this section I examine bequest behavior in the competitive economy without fiscal transfers ($\tau = 0$). Observe from (19) and (33) that when $\tau = 0$

$$\delta^0(0, k_t/K_t) = \delta^c(0, k_t/K_t) = (1 - \alpha)(1 - \beta)K_t/(\alpha k_t). \tag{36}$$

Although the critical values $\delta^0(\tau, k_t/K_t)$ and $\delta^c(\tau, k_t/K_t)$ are not, in general, equal to each other, equation (36) states that in the absence of taxes, these critical values are equal for all values of k_t/K_t. The critical value is a declining function of k_t/K_t, which illustrates that a stronger bequest motive is required in order to induce a poorer consumer to leave a positive bequest.

The critical values of the bequest parameter were derived under the alternative assumptions that all consumers have operative bequest motives or that all consumers face binding nonnegativity constraints on their bequests. However, if there is a nondegenerate cross-sectional distribution of capital holding, then there is a range of values of δ for which neither of these assumptions is satisfied. This range depends on the range of values of k_t/K_t in the population as illustrated in figure 6.1. If δ is greater than $(1 - \alpha)(1 - \beta)K_t/\alpha k_t^{min}$, where k_t^{min} is the minimum value of k_t, then the bequest is operative for all families and hence the Ricardian Equivalence Theorem holds. This range of values of δ and the corresponding values of k_t/K_t are shown in the shaded region of figure 6.1 labeled Ricardian Equivalence. Alternatively, if the bequest motive is sufficiently weak so that δ is less than $(1 - \alpha)(1 - \beta)K_t/\alpha k_t^{max}$, not even the richest families in the economy will leave positive bequests. In this case, there will be no bequests. As discussed earlier, if there are no positive bequests, then any inequality in the distribution of capital is eradicated completely after one period and k_t/K_t equals one for all families in subsequent periods.

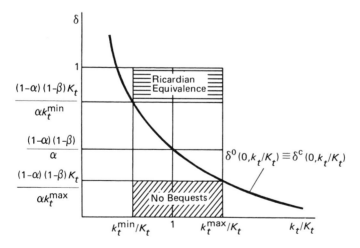

Figure 6.1

6.7.   The Effects of Taxes and Transfers in a Representative Consumer Economy

In this section we analyze the effects of permanent changes in τ, the tax rate on labor income that finances pay-as-you-go social security. For simplicity I consider only representative consumer economies, i.e., economies in which the cross-sectional distribution of wealth is degenerate so that $k_t/K_t \equiv 1$ for all families. It follows immediately from (19) and (33) that if $k_t/K_t = 1$, the critical values of the bequest parameter, δ^0 and δ^c, are equal to each other.

To derive the stochastic process governing the evolution of the capital stock in the economy with operative bequests, substitute (7) into (34) and take logarithms to obtain

$$\ln K^0_{t+1} = \ln \delta + \ln(\alpha/n) + \alpha \ln K^0_t + \ln \psi_t. \tag{37}$$

The unconditional mean of the log of the aggregate capital stock per worker, $E\{\ln K^0\}$, is equal to $[\ln \delta + \ln(\alpha/n) + E\{\ln \psi\}]/(1 - \alpha)$, where $E\{\ln \psi\}$ is the unconditional mean of $\ln \psi$.

If the bequest motive is not operative, then it follows from (7) and (35) that

$$\ln K^c_{t+1} = \ln \delta^0(\tau, 1) + \ln(\alpha/n) + \alpha \ln K^c_t + \ln \psi_t. \tag{38}$$

The stochastic process followed by the capital stock in the absence of bequests, (38), is identical to the stochastic process followed by the capital stock the presence of bequests, (37), except that the unconditional mean, $E\{\ln K^c\}$, is equal to $[\ln \delta^0(\tau, 1) + \ln(\alpha/n) + E\{\ln \psi\}]/(1 - \alpha)$ rather than to $[\ln \delta + \ln(\alpha/n) + E\{\ln \psi\}]/(1 - \alpha)$.

Now consider the effects of permanent changes in τ on the stochastic process for capital. According to (37), if the bequest motive is operative, then the stochastic process for capital is invariant with respect to τ, as predicted by the Ricardian Equivalence Theorem. If the bequest motive is inoperative, then according to (38) all autocovariances of the stochastic process for capital are invariant with respect to τ. However, since $\delta^0(\tau, 1)$ is a decreasing function of τ, the unconditional mean of $\ln K_t$ is a decreasing function of τ. Thus, if the bequest motive is inoperative, then a permanent increase in pay-as-you-go social security reduces the long-run expected value of $\ln K_t$. However, if the tax rate τ becomes sufficiently large, then eventually old consumers will have sufficiently large disposable resources

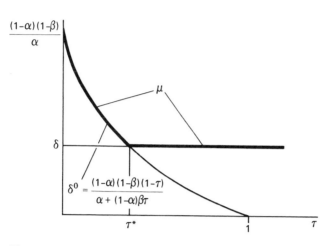

Figure 6.2

that the bequest motive becomes operative. At this point, further increases in τ would have no effect. The effects of changes in τ are illustrated in figure 6.2.

Define μ as

$$\mu \equiv \exp[(1 - \alpha)E\{\ln K\} - \ln(\alpha/n) - E\{\ln \psi\}] \tag{39}$$

and observe that μ is an increasing function of the unconditional expectation of $\ln K$. If the bequest motive is operative, then, as discussed above, μ is equal to δ and $\delta > \delta^0(\tau, 1)$. Alternatively, if the bequest motive is not operative, then μ is equal to $\delta^0(\tau, 1)$ and $\delta < \delta^0(\tau, 1)$. Therefore, we have

$$\mu = \max[\delta, \delta^0(\tau, 1)]. \tag{40}$$

The heavy line in the figure shows the value of μ as a function of the tax rate τ. This figure is drawn under the assumption that in the absence of taxes, the bequest motive is inoperative. This assumption is illustrated in the figure by the fact that $\delta^0(0, 1) > \delta$. As the tax rate τ is increased from zero, the value of μ, and hence the expected long-run capital stock, falls monotonically as predicted from previous analyses of the Diamond model. Eventually when τ reaches τ^*, the old consumers are receiving large enough transfers that the bequest motive now becomes operative. Any increases in τ beyond τ^* will have no effect on the stochastic behavior of the capital stock.

6.8.   Conclusion

Barro's (1974) formulation of intergenerationally altruistic consumers has become the basis for a widely used framework to study competitive economies with overlapping generations of consumers. Much of the subsequent work in this tradition has been conducted in deterministic models with a representative consumer in each generation, and the bequest motive is often simply assumed to be operative. The model in this chapter was developed to relax these three sets of restrictions with the goal of understanding channels by which lump-sum taxes and transfers can affect economic activity. I derived conditions for the bequest motive to be operative and expressed these conditions in two different ways: first, I expressed the conditions in terms of the parameters of preferences and technology; then, as in Weil (1987), I expressed these conditions in terms of the rate of return on capital and the growth rate of the capital stock in an economy without bequests.

After determining conditions under which the altruistic bequest motive will be operative, I then examined the effects of a pay-as-you-go social security system financed by a proportional tax on (exogenous) wage income. If the bequest motive is initially inoperative, then the introduction of social security increases the consumption of old consumers and reduces the unconditional capital stock. Further increases in social security will continue to reduce the unconditional capital stock until eventually old consumers receive a large enough transfer that the bequest motive becomes operative. Once this point is reached, further increases in social security have no effect on consumption or capital accumulation.

An additional feature of the model examined in this chapter is that we can examine an economy with cross-sectional variation in the distribution of capital holdings. If the bequest motive is operative for all families, then, in the particular model examined in this chapter, the initial inequality in the distribution of capital holdings is preserved forever. By contrast, if the bequest motive is inoperative, then any inequality in capital holdings is eradicated after one generation.

This chapter departs from the representative consumer framework and presents conditions that guarantee that the bequest motive will always be operative for all consumers or, alternatively, will always be inoperative for all consumers. An interesting extension of this research would be to analyze the behavior of an economy in which some consumers have operative bequest motives while other consumers face binding constraints on bequests. At this stage, we can say that the Ricardian Equivalence Theorem would not hold in such an economy, but the effects of fiscal policy in such an economy merit further study.

References

Abel, Andrew B., "The Failure of Ricardian Equivalence under Progressive Wealth Taxation," *Journal of Public Economics* 30:1 (June 1986), 117–128.

Abel, Andrew B., "Operative Gift and Bequest Motives," *American Economic Review*, 77:5 (December 1987), 1037–1047.

Abel, Andrew B., N. Gregory Mankiw, Lawrence H. Summers, and Richard J. Zeckhauser, "Assessing Dynamic Efficiency: Theory and Evidence," National Bureau of Economic Research Working Paper No. 2097 (December 1986).

Barro, Robert J., "Are Government Bonds Net Wealth?" *Journal of Political Economy* 82 (November/December 1974), 1095–1117.

Barsky, Robert, N. Gregory Mankiw, and Stephen Zeldes, "Ricardian Consumers with Keynesian Propensities," *American Economic Review* 76:4 (September 1986), 676–691.

Cukierman, Alex, "Uncertain Lifetimes and the Ricardian Equivalence Proposition," mimeo, Tel-Aviv University (1986).

Diamond, Peter A., "National Debt in a Neoclassical Growth Model," *American Economic Review* 55 (December 1965), 1126–1150.

Drazen, Allan, "Government Debt, Human Capital, and Bequests in a Lifecycle Model," *Journal of Political Economy* 86 (June 1978), 505–516.

Feldstein, Martin S., "The Effects of Fiscal Policies When Incomes Are Uncertain: A Contradiction of Ricardian Equivalence," National Bureau of Economic Research Working Paper No. 2062 (November 1986).

Weil, Philippe, "Overlapping Families of Infinitely Lived Agents," mimeo, Harvard University (1986).

Weil, Philippe, "Love Thy Children: Reflections on the Barro Debt Neutrality Theorem," *Journal of Monetary Economics* 19:3 (May 1987), 377–391.

7 Effects of Government Finance: Testing Ricardian Neutrality

Leonardo Leiderman and Assaf Razin

7.1. Introduction

The impact of government budget variables on private-sector consumption is a key issue in assessing the implications of fiscal and monetary policy on the real side of the economy. In fact there are sharp controversies on this topic, most of which center around the Ricardian Equivalence Proposition.[1]

The purpose of this chapter is to develop and estimate a stochastic-intertemporal model of consumption behavior and to use it for testing a version of the Ricardian Equivalence Proposition with time series data. Our framework allows for two channels that may give rise to deviations from Ricardian neutrality: finite horizons and liquidity constraints. In addition, it incorporates explicitly the roles of taxes, substitution between public and private consumption, and different degrees of consumption durability.

The standard approach in empirical studies of the neutrality hypothesis is based on directly specifying regression equations linking consumption to disposable income, measures of nonhuman wealth, government spending, taxes, government transfers, etc. (see, for example, Kochin, 1974, Tanner, 1979, Feldstein, 1982, Seater, 1979, Kormendi, 1983, and Reid 1985). While the results from applying this approach are informative, a limitation, which makes the interpretation of the results ambiguous, is that the connection between the estimated equations and the underlying theoretical model is not specified explicitly. Although the theoretical model typically specifies that current consumption is influenced by current and expected future changes in labor income, taxes, etc., most of the empirical applications focus mainly on current explanatory variables and ignore expected future ones. Therefore, the estimated coefficients of a given explanatory variable (such as current government spending or taxes) in a consumption equation may reflect not only direct effects of this variable but also its effects as a predictor of future relevant variables. Moreover, these results cannot be used to assess the effects of policy changes, as, for example, a change in taxation, on consumption (Lucas's 1976 critique).[2] In contrast, the present study

This chapter is an abridged version of our paper "Testing Ricardian Neutrality with an Intertemporal Stochastic Model," published in *Journal of Money, Credit, and Banking* 20,1 (February 1988). We thank Sweder van Wijnbergen for helpful comments on an earlier draft.

adopts an intertemporal optimizing framework whose implications, derived explicitly in the analysis, are the subject of empirical tests.

Since the seminal contribution of Hall (1978), numerous studies have applied the intertemporal optimizing approach to examine consumption behavior. However, almost none of these studies focus on the comovements of consumption and government-budget variables.[3] Moreover, these studies typically assume an infinite-horizon representative consumer. This assumption restricts the economic channels through which government-budget finance exerts its effects on consumption, resulting in an extreme case in which the model exhibits Ricardian properties. To move away from this case, Blanchard (1985) extended the intertemporal framework by relaxing the infinite-horizon assumption. His formulation allows for a richer set of interactions between government-budget-deficit variables and consumption, with Ricardian implications emerging only as a special case.[4] Another factor that may give rise to deviations from Ricardian neutrality is the existence of liquidity constraints that prevent some consumers from free access to capital markets (see the early work by Tobin and Dolde, 1971, and the more recent contributions by Hayashi, 1985, and Hubbard and Judd, 1986). In the present study, we develop a testable model that allows for deviations from neutrality through both these channels.

By virtue of the assumption of rational expectations, our framework results in a set of cross-equation restrictions. These restrictions are taken into account in the joint estimation of the consumption-behavior parameters and those of the stochastic processes governing the evolution of the forcing variables. We implement the model on monthly time series data for Israel covering the 1980–1985 period. This case is of particular interest in testing the Ricardian Equivalence Hypothesis because of the high volatility of movements in the budget deficit, taxes, and private consumption in an economy with an unusually high government budget deficit—the deficit amounting to 15% of aggregate output, on average, during this period. These characteristics differ from those of the more stable environments studied in previous empirical works. They, therefore, enable a potentially more powerful test of hypotheses related to the comovements of private-sector consumption and taxes and public-sector spending.

The chapter is organized as follows. Section 7.2 outlines the model. Empirical specifications and implementation of the model are presented in section 7.3. Section 7.4 extends the basic model to account for direct effects of public consumption on private consumption. Last, section 7.5 concludes the chapter.

7.2. Theoretical Framework

We assume that there are overlapping generations of rational agents that have finite horizons. Specifically, there is a probability γ, smaller than unity, that individuals living in the present period will survive to the next period. A small open economy is considered, one that takes as given the world interest rate. We begin by considering the choice problem of an individual consumer.

7.2.1. Individual Consumer

The consumer is assumed to face a given safe interest factor R (where $R = (1 + r)$ and r denotes the safe rate of interest), but due to lifetime uncertainty the effective (risk adjusted) interest factor is R/γ.[5] Disposable income is assumed to be stochastic and is denoted by y. Viewed from the standpoint of period t, consumer's utility from his stock of consumption goods during period $t + \tau$, $c_{t+\tau}$, is given by $\delta^\tau U(c_{t+\tau})$, where δ is the subjective discount factor. The probability of survival from period t through period $t + \tau$ is γ^τ, and therefore expected lifetime utility as of period t is

$$E_t \sum_{\tau=0}^{\infty} (\gamma\delta)^\tau U(c_{t+\tau}), \tag{1}$$

where E_t is the conditional expectations operator. Individuals are assumed to maximize (1) subject to

$$c_t = (1 - \phi)c_{t-1} + x_t, \tag{2a}$$

$$x_t = b_t + y_t - \left(\frac{R}{\gamma}\right)b_{t-1}, \tag{2b}$$

and the solvency condition $\lim_{t\to\infty} (\gamma/R)^t b_t = 0$. The variable x_t denotes the flow of consumption purchases, c_t denotes the stock of consumer goods, and ϕ denotes the rate of depreciation of this stock. The variable b_t is the one-period debt issued in period t. Consolidating equations (2a) and (2b), the expected value of the lifetime budget constraint is given by

$$\left[1 - \left(\frac{\gamma}{R}\right)(1 - \phi)\right] E_t \sum_{\tau=0}^{\infty} \left(\frac{\gamma}{R}\right)^{\tau} c_{t+\tau}$$

$$= E_t \sum_{\tau=0}^{\infty} \left(\frac{\gamma}{R}\right)^{\tau} y_{t+\tau} - \left(\frac{R}{\gamma}\right) b_{t-1} + (1 - \phi)c_{t-1}$$

$$\equiv E_t w_t,$$

where $E_t w_t$ is (a specific definition of) expected wealth. This consolidated budget constraint is implied by the equality of the expected value of the discounted sum of the flow of consumption purchases and the corresponding discounted sum of the flow of disposable income, minus initial debt commitment.

With a view toward empirical implementation, we specify the utility function to be quadratic. That is,

$$U(c_t) = \alpha c_t - \tfrac{1}{2}c_t^2, \tag{3}$$

where $\alpha > 0$ and $c_t < \alpha$.

It is shown in Leiderman and Razin (1988, appendix) that the solution to the optimization problem is

$$c_t = \beta_0 + \beta_1 E_t w_t, \tag{4}$$

where

$$\beta_0 = \gamma\alpha \frac{1 - \delta R}{\delta R(R - \gamma)}$$

and

$$\beta_1 = \left[1 - \frac{\gamma}{\delta R^2}\right]\left[1 - \left(\frac{\gamma}{R}\right)(1 - \phi)\right]^{-1}.$$

Equation (4) is a linear consumption function, relating the stock of consumer goods c_t to the expected value of wealth, where β_1 is the marginal propensity to consume wealth.

7.2.2. Aggregate Consumption

The economy consists of overlapping generations. The size of each cohort is normalized to 1, there are γ^a individuals of age a, and the size of population is constant at the level $1/(1 - \gamma)$.

From equation (4), the consumption of an individual of age a at time t is

$$c_{t,a} = \beta_0 + \beta_1 \left[E_t \sum_{\tau=0}^{\infty} \left(\frac{\gamma}{R}\right)^{\tau} y_{t+\tau} - \frac{R}{\gamma} b_{t-1,a-1} + (1 - \phi)c_{t-1,a-1} \right]. \tag{5}$$

Aggregating consumption over all cohorts and dividing by the size of population yields per capita aggregate consumption, C_t,

$$C_t = (1 - \gamma) \sum_{a=0}^{\infty} \gamma^a c_{t,a}$$

$$= \beta_0 + \beta_1 \left[E_t \sum_{\tau=0}^{\infty} \left(\frac{\gamma}{R}\right)^{\tau} y_{t+\tau} - RB_{t-1} + \gamma(1 - \phi)C_{t-1} \right], \tag{6}$$

where B_{t-1} is aggregate per capita debt issued in period $t - 1$.

Equation (6) can be rearranged as follows:

$$C_t = \gamma\alpha(R - 1)\frac{\delta R - 1}{\delta R(R - \gamma)} + (1 - \gamma)\left(1 - \frac{\gamma}{\delta R^2}\right)$$

$$\times \left[1 - \left(\frac{\gamma}{R}\right)(1 - \phi)\right]^{-1} E_{t-1} \sum_{\tau=0}^{\infty} \left(\frac{\gamma}{R}\right)^{\tau} (Y_{t+\tau} - T_{t+\tau}) \tag{7a}$$

$$+ \Gamma C_{t-1} + \varepsilon_t,$$

where

$$\Gamma = \left[\frac{\gamma}{\delta R} + \gamma(1 - \phi)\left[1 - \gamma\left(1 + \frac{1}{\delta R^2}\right)\right]\right]\left[1 - \left(\frac{\gamma}{R}\right)(1 - \phi)\right]^{-1},$$

Y is gross income, T is the level of taxes (both in per capita terms), and ε_t is a zero mean, finite variance, error term. In order to express the consumption equation in terms of observed consumer purchases, we use recursively the per capita aggregate version of equation (2a) applied to aggregate per capita consumption, and substitute it into (7a). This yields

$$X_t = \gamma\alpha(R - 1)\frac{\delta R - 1}{\delta R(R - \gamma)}$$

$$+ (1 - \gamma)\left(1 - \frac{\gamma}{\delta R^2}\right)\left[1 - \left(\frac{\gamma}{R}\right)(1 - \phi)\right]^{-1} E_{t-1} \sum_{\tau=0}^{\infty} \left(\frac{\gamma}{R}\right)^{\tau} \tag{7b}$$

$$\times (Y_{t+\tau} - T_{t+\tau}) + (\Gamma - \gamma(1 - \phi)) \sum_{\tau=0}^{\infty} \gamma^{\tau}(1 - \phi)^{\tau} X_{t-\tau-1} + \varepsilon_t.$$

where X_t is the aggregate per capita value of consumer purchases.

Equation (7b) is the focal relation for our empirical work. It expresses aggregate consumption purchases (per capita) as a function of a constant term, expected human wealth, lagged purchases, and an error term. The present formulation is general enough to encompass both Ricardian and non-Ricardian systems as special cases. The key parameter, in this context, is γ. When $\gamma = 1$ the system possesses Ricardian neutrality, and equation (7b) indicates that only lagged consumer purchases can be used to predict current purchases (similar to Hall, 1978). However, when $\gamma < 1$, expected human wealth affects current consumption purchases over and beyond the impact of lagged consumption purchases. For example, a current-period cut in taxes raises expected human wealth and thus results in an increase in consumption. The reason is that the future tax hike, needed in order to balance the intertemporal budget constraint of the government, is given a smaller weight, by finite-horizon consumers, than the weight attached by them to the current cut in taxes.

7.2.3. Liquidity-Constrained Consumers

The foregoing specifications hold under the assumption that all consumers have free access to the capital market and thus can borrow against future incomes. In that case, Ricardian neutrality breaks down due to finite horizons (as captured by $\gamma < 1$). In this subsection, we extend the model to allow for an additional channel through which nonequivalence results may arise: the existence of liquidity constraints. Accordingly, we allow here for the possibility that while a fraction π of aggregate consumption is due to consumers that have access to capital markets, a fraction $(1 - \pi)$ is due to consumers that are liquidity constrained in their consumption purchases. Formally,

$$X_t = \pi X_{ut} + (1 - \pi)X_{ct}, \tag{8}$$

where X_{ut} denotes consumption purchases of liquidity-unconstrained individuals, and X_{ct} denotes purchases of those that are subject to liquidity constraints. For X_{ut}, we use the specification in equation (7b), and for X_{ct} we use the following simple specification:

$$X_{ct} = Y_{t-1} + v_t. \tag{9}$$

That is, consumption purchases under liquidity constraints are modeled as the sum of two components: last period's net income and an error term.

It can be easily verified that in this augmented version of the model,

Ricardian equivalence holds only under the restriction that $\gamma = 1$ and $\pi = 1$. This restriction is tested in the next section.

7.3. Empirical Implementation

7.3.1. Specifications

To implement equation (7b) it is necessary to specify, under rational expectations, the stochastic processes that govern the evolution of gross income and taxes. Accordingly, we stipulate simple first-order autoregressive processes for these variables[6]

$$Y_t - Y_{t-1} = \rho_Y(Y_{t-1} - Y_{t-2}) + \eta_{Yt}, \tag{10}$$

$$T_t - T_{t-1} = \rho_T(T_{t-1} - T_{t-2}) + \eta_{Tt}, \tag{11}$$

where the ρ's are time-independent, and the η's are serially uncorrelated zero-mean stochastic terms that are orthogonal to variables dated $t - 1$ and earlier.[7]

Using equations (10) and (11) to calculate expected human wealth yields the following expression for consumption purchases:

$$X_t = d_0 + \sum_{i=1}^{n} d_{1i}X_{t-i} + d_2 Y_{t-1} + d_3 Y_{t-2} + d_4 T_{t-1} + d_5 T_{t-2} + \eta_{xt}, \tag{12}$$

where n is the number of lagged-purchases terms, and the d-coefficients satisfy the following restrictions:

$$d_0 = \frac{\gamma\alpha(R-1)(\delta R - 1)}{\delta R(R - \gamma)},$$

$$d_{1i} = [\Gamma - \gamma(1-\phi)]\gamma^{i-1}(1-\phi)^{i-1} \qquad \text{for } i = 1, \ldots, n,$$

$$d_{1,n+1} = \Gamma\gamma^n(1-\phi)^n,$$

$$d_2 = (1-\gamma)\left(1 - \frac{\gamma}{\delta R^2}\right)\left[1 - \frac{\gamma}{R}(1-\phi)\right]^{-1}\left[\left(\frac{R}{R-\gamma}\right)(1+\rho_y) + \frac{\rho_Y^2\gamma}{R}\right.$$

$$\left. + \frac{\gamma^2\rho_Y^2}{R(1-\rho_Y)(R-\gamma)} - \frac{\rho_Y^4\gamma^2}{(1-\rho_Y)R(R-\rho_Y\gamma)}\right],$$

$$d_3 = (1-\gamma)\left(1 - \frac{\gamma}{\delta R^2}\right)\left[1 - \frac{\gamma}{R}(1-\phi)\right]^{-1}\left(\frac{R}{R-\gamma}\right) - d_2,$$

$$d_4 = -(1-\gamma)\left(1-\frac{\gamma}{\delta R^2}\right)\left[1-\frac{\gamma}{R}(1-\phi)\right]^{-1}\left[\left(\frac{R}{R-\gamma}\right)(1+\rho_T)\right.$$

$$\left. +\frac{\rho_T^2\gamma}{R}+\frac{\gamma^2\rho_T^2}{R(1-\rho_T)(R-\gamma)}-\frac{\rho_T^4\gamma^2}{(1-\rho_T)R(R-\rho_T\gamma)}\right],$$

$$d_5 = (1-\gamma)\left(1-\frac{\gamma}{\delta R^2}\right)\left[1-\frac{\gamma}{R}(1-\phi)\right]^{-1}\left(\frac{R}{R-\gamma}\right)-d_4.$$

Equations (8)–(12) form the system to be empirically analyzed.

7.3.2. Findings

Several versions of the system consisting of equations (8)–(12) are estimated using Israeli monthly data covering the period 1980–1985. The use of monthly data clearly limits our choice of the actual time series that serve as counterparts for the variables in the model. For consumption purchases, X, we use an index of purchases within the organized retail trade.[8] The total wage bill is used for income. Y, and government tax receipts are used for T. The data source is Bank of Israel's publication *Main Economic Indicators* (various issues).

Estimation was performed by nonlinear least squares jointly applied to the system. Table 7.1 reports different versions of the estimated model, allowing for seven lags in the estimation of the durability parameter and setting the monthly risk-free real interest factor to 1.002.[9] Column (1) gives the parameter estimates of the model. The likelihood ratio test of the model against its unrestricted counterpart yields a χ^2 statistic of 12.3 (with 8 degrees of freedom), which is not significant at the 1% significance level. While this indicates that the data do not reject the model, some of the parameters obtain somewhat implausible estimated values. In particular, δ and π seem to be too high relative to what is commonly expected. The parameter γ is smaller but close to unity. Under Blanchard's formulation, this parameter stands for the survival probability. A monthly $\gamma = 0.989$ implies under this interpretation an expected life of $\gamma^{12}/[(1-\gamma^{12})]^{-2} = 58$ years. Although viewed from the time of birth this is a low life expectancy, it seems more plausible when viewed from the point of view of the average horizon for consumption decision-making of the mature population.

Columns (2) and (3) impose further restrictions on the estimated model. In column (2), we set consumer's time horizon to infinity ($\gamma = 1.0$) and the estimated model is not rejected when compared to the unrestricted model.

Table 7.1
Estimated versions of the model (Israel: 1980:9–1985:12)[a]

Parameter	Model's restrictions (1)	As in column (1) and $\gamma = 1.0$ (2)	As in column (1) and $\pi = 1.0$ (3)	As in columns (2) and (3) (4)
ρ_Y	−0.17 (0.05)	−0.23 (0.10)	−0.23 (0.10)	−0.24 (0.10)
ρ_T	−0.57 (0.09)	−0.58 (0.09)	−0.58 (0.09)	−0.58 (0.09)
δ	1.20 (0.06)	1.03 (0.02)	1.04 (0.02)	1.03 (0.02)
α	104.81 (105.89)	233.19 (112.11)	220.54 (110.03)	301.80 (62.79)
ϕ	0.24 (0.04)	0.20 (0.06)	0.20 (0.06)	0.21 (0.06)
γ	0.986 (0.01)	1.00[b]	0.999 (0.0002)	1.00[b]
π	2.09 (0.45)	0.99 (0.02)	1.00[b]	1.00[b]
L	−618.94	−622.27	−622.19	−622.45

a. The basic model consists of equations (8)–(12). Its parameter estimates are reported in column (1). L denotes the value of the log-likelihood function. Figures in parentheses are estimated standard errors. The value of L for the unrestricted system is 612.79 (free parameters).
b. Imposed value.

(The likelihood ratio is 18.96, with 9 degrees of freedom.) Interestingly, more plausible parameter estimates obtain in this column than in the previous one, including an estimated value for the fraction of liquidity-unconstrained consumption close to (and below) unity. Column (3) allows for estimation of γ, but sets the parameter π equal to unity. Again, this version of the model is not rejected using a likelihood ratio test (whose value is about the same as the one for column (2)). The parameter γ obtains a value of 0.999, which is larger than the one reported in column (1). Notice that in moving from column (1) to the next columns the estimated values of δ decline and become closer to unity.

The Ricardian Equivalence Proposition implies the $\gamma = \pi = 1.0$ restriction, which is tested in column (4). The likelihood ratio for testing this restriction against the unrestricted counterpart of the model is 19.32 (with 10 degrees of freedom). This is lower than the 1% χ^2 critical value of 23.2. Thus, Ricardian neutrality is not rejected by the data.[10]

Having established this result, we can now discuss the parameter estimates for the specification of the model that embodies the neutrality properties. The parameters generally attain the hypothesized signs and are significantly different from zero. The estimated first-order autoregressive parameters of the processes for $(Y_t - Y_{t-1})$ and $(T_t - T_{t-1})$ are negative, indicating that shocks to these variables tend to be reversed in subsequent months. Shocks to the gross income variable show a larger degree of persistence than shocks to the tax variable. The estimated monthly subjective discount factor is slightly above unity; however, we have tested for $\delta = 1.0$ and the test does not reject this hypothesis.[11] The utility function parameter α is positive and equal to 301.8. An important feature of this value is that it satisfies the assumption that marginal utility of consumption is positive, i.e., $\alpha > c$. Specifically, the maximal value of consumption purchases in the sample implies, using a durability parameter of 0.79, for seven lags, a maximal stock of consumption goods of about 85 (index units), which is smaller than the estimated α. Further, this estimated parameter can be used to calculate the implied degree of relative risk aversion $(C/(\alpha - C))$, which turns out to be equal to 0.3 (at the mean sample value of consumption purchases).[12] The parameter estimate for ϕ implies that 21% of the stock of consumer goods depreciates from month to month. Since, due to lack of more refined monthly data, our measure of consumption purchases includes goods with different degrees of durability, this parameter ϕ should be interpreted as an average depreciation rate.

7.4. Substitution between Public and Private Consumption

We now extend the model by allowing direct effects of government spending on private consumption. The model's specification in section 7.2 can be interpreted as one that incorporates public goods in the utility function in a separable way, implying that public goods have neutral effects on the consumption of private goods. The present extension differs from the foregoing specifications since it allows for substitutability between public and private consumption. When the degree of substitution approaches zero we are back to the original model.

Let the utility function be specified by

$$U(c_t, G_t) = \alpha(c_t + \theta G_t) - \tfrac{1}{2}(c_t + \theta G_t)^2, \tag{13a}$$

$$G_t = (1 - \phi)G_{t-1} + g_t, \tag{13b}$$

where G denotes the stock of public consumption, g denotes the flow of government purchases, and θ is a parameter that measures the weight of public consumption in total private effective consumption, $c_t + \theta G_t$, (see Aschauer, 1985). For tractability, the rates of depreciation of the shocks of private and public consumption goods are assumed to be identical and are denoted by ϕ. As shown in Leiderman and Razin (1988, appendix), the analogue of equation (6), expressing aggregate per capita consumption, is

$$
C_t = \beta_0 + \beta_1 \left[E_t \sum_{\tau=0}^{\infty} \left(\frac{\gamma}{R} \right)^{\tau} (y_{t+\tau} + \theta g_{t+\tau}) - R B_{t-1} \right.
$$

$$
\left. + \gamma(1 - \phi)(C_{t-1} + \theta g_{t-1}) \right] - \theta G_t.
$$

(14)

Similarly, the analogue of (7a) is

$$
C_t = \gamma \alpha (R - 1) \frac{\delta R - 1}{\delta R(R - \gamma)} + (1 - \gamma)\left(1 - \frac{\gamma}{\delta R^2}\right)\left[1 - \frac{\gamma}{R}(1 - \phi)\right]^{-1}
$$

$$
\times E_{t-1} \sum_{\tau=0}^{\infty} \left(\frac{\gamma}{R} \right)^{\tau} [Y_{t+\tau} - T_{t+\tau} + \theta g_{t+\tau}]
$$

(15)

$$
+ \Gamma(C_{t-1} + \theta G_{t-1}) - \theta G_t + \varepsilon_t.
$$

We assume that the expected flow of future public consumption evolves according to the simple process

$$
g_t - g_{t-1} = \rho_g(g_{t-1} - g_{t-2}) + \eta_{gt}.
$$

(16)

Equation (15) can then be rewritten as

$$
X_t = d_0 + \sum_{i=1}^{n} d_{1i}(X_{t-i} + \theta g_{t-i}) + d_2 Y_{t-1} + d_3 Y_{t-2} + d_4 T_{t-1}
$$

$$
+ d_5 T_{t-2} + d_6 g_{t-1} + d_7 g_{t-2} + \varepsilon_t,
$$

(17)

where d_1 through d_5 are as in equation (12) and

$$
d_6 = \theta(1 - \gamma)\left(1 - \frac{\gamma}{\delta R^2}\right)\left[1 - \frac{\gamma}{R}(1 - \phi)\right]^{-1}\left[\frac{R}{R - \gamma}(1 + \rho_g) + \frac{\rho_g^2 \gamma}{R}\right.
$$

$$
\left. + \frac{\gamma^2 \rho_g^2}{R(1 - \rho_g)(R - \gamma)} - \frac{\rho_g^4 \gamma^2}{(1 - \rho_g)R(R - \rho_g \gamma)}\right] - \theta(1 + \rho_g),
$$

$$
d_7 = \theta(1 - \gamma)\left(1 - \frac{\gamma}{\delta R^2}\right)\left[1 - \frac{\gamma}{R}(1 - \phi)\right]^{-1}\left(\frac{R}{R - \gamma}\right) + \theta \rho_g - d_6.
$$

Table 7.2
The model with public goods (Israel: 1980:9–1985:12)

Parameter	Model's restrictions (1)	As in column (1) and $\gamma = \pi = 1.0$ (2)
ρ_Y	−0.23 (0.08)	−0.22 (0.10)
ρ_T	−0.59 (0.07)	−0.59 (0.07)
ρ_g	−0.56 (0.08)	−0.55 (0.07)
δ	1.17 (0.12)	1.04 (0.04)
α	152.66 (218.47)	128.78 (36.64)
ϕ	0.41 (0.08)	0.39 (0.09)
γ	0.989 (0.02)	1.00[b]
π	1.37 (0.29)	1.00[b]
θ	−0.52 (0.20)	−0.47 (0.26)
L	−781.87	−782.52

a. The model consists of eqs. (8)–(11), (16)–(17). Its parameter estimates are reported in column (1). L denotes the value of the log-likelihood function. Figures in parentheses are estimated standard errors. The value of L for the unrestricted system is −774.61 (16 free parameters).
b. Imposed value.

Note that equation (17) holds for liquidity-unconstrained consumers. As in subsection (7.2.3) we embed this equation in a more general framework in which aggregate consumption includes also another component, which is due to liquidity-constrained individuals. Accordingly, (8)–(11), and (16)–(17) constitute the more general system to be implemented in this section.

Table 7.2 reports the results of estimating two versions of the system. To save degrees of freedom under this augmented version of the model, the number of lags used in estimating the durability parameter is set equal to 3. Column (1) gives the parameter estimates under the model's restrictions. These restrictions are not rejected against the unrestricted version of the model; the pertinent likelihood ratio is 14.52 (with 7 degrees of freedom), a value that is below the critical 1% value of 18.5. Column (2) can be used to test Ricardian neutrality, which implies the $\gamma = \pi = 1.0$ restriction. As before, this hypothesis is not rejected by the data. In extending the model and going from table 7.1 to table 7.2 it can be observed that most of the parameter estimates do not change noticeably. However, in contrast to the notion of government consumption yielding positive marginal utility, the estimated value of θ is negative.[13] Thus, although statistically the specification underlying column (2) is not rejected by the data, the public consumption variable has effects that do not conform with the theoretical model.

7.5. Conclusions

In this chapter, we have developed a stochastic framework in which the intertemporal implications of the Ricardian Equivalence Proposition can be tested with aggregate time series data. The framework allows for two types of deviations from Ricardian neutrality. The first is due to finite consumers' planning horizons, and is modeled as an extension of Blanchard (1985) to a stochastic environment. The second is due to the existence of liquidity constraints on consumption behavior. In addition, our framework allows for direct substitutability between private and public consumption, and treats explicitly the degree of durability of aggregate consumption.

The model was implemented on monthly data for Israel during the first half of the 1980s, a period of high and volatile government budget deficits. Our main findings are that the restrictions implied by the Ricardian neutrality hypothesis are not rejected by the sample information, and that the resulting parameter estimates generally conform with the theoretical model. These features held up when the model was extended to allow for public goods consumption, with the exception that the parameter capturing the direct effects of public consumption on private utility turned out to be implausible.

There are several interesting possible extensions of the present research. First, it would be important to allow for additional sources of deviations from Ricardian neutrality, such as the existence of distortionary taxes. In this context, it is desirable to decompose taxes into at least two categories, consumption and income taxes.[14] Second, another channel through which government policies can affect private consumption is related to monetary and exchange rate policies.[15] Third, the model's specifications can be modified to allow for different effects on private consumption of various components of government spending, potentially capturing substitutability as well as complementarity with private consumption. These extensions to the intertemporal framework of consumption determination could enhance the conformity of the theory to the data.

Notes

1. See Barro (1974).

2. For a recent survey of empirical tests of Ricardian equivalence, also Leiderman and Blejer (1988).

3. For an exception, see Aschauer (1985).

4. For analysis of effects of fiscal policy in open economies using this type of model, see Frenkel and Razin (June 1986). For an empirical implementation motivated by a model of this type, see van Wijnbergen (1985).

5. See Blanchard (1985). Throughout we use the assumption of a constant real rate. While this is a restrictive assumption, it need not be very unrealistic in an economy with widespread indexation in financial markets.

6. On the sensitivity of the empirical results with respect to alternative specifications see note 7.

7. Experimentation with univariate and multivariate autoregressive processes with longer lag structures for the forcing variables and with constant terms yielded results that do not reject the present first-difference univariate system (with no constants).

8. These monthly measures of consumption are closely correlated with the national-accounts series for consumption. Using quarterly moving averages of the monthly purchases data we obtain a correlation coefficient of 0.9 between our time series and the national-accounts quarterly consumption series. (See also Fisher, 1986.)

9. Experimenting with different lags as well as different realistic values of R did not yield noticeably different results from those reported in table 7.1. We a priori set the value of R in order to identify the other parameters.

10. This result is different from that in our NBER (September 1986) paper. It turns out that once we allow for some degree of durability in consumption (as in the present paper) the results become more favorable to Ricardian neutrality.

11. Interestingly, Hansen and Singleton (1983) also found that the point estimate of δ (with monthly U.S. data) is close to (and sometimes above) unity.

12. This estimate for the degree of relative risk aversion falls within the range of those reported in studies for the United States.

13. This may reflect improper measurement of public consumption in our data set. This measure is derived from cash-flow accounts of the Treasury, which partly include transfer payments such as consumption subsidies. In a study based on U.S. data, Aschauer (1985) reports estimated value for θ of 0.23.

14. As shown by Frenkel and Razin (December 1986), private spending responds differently to cuts in alternative types of taxes.

15. For a theoretical analysis, see Helpman and Razin (1987).

References

Aschauer, David A. "Fiscal Policy and Aggregate Demand," *American Economic Review* 75 (March 1985). 117–127.

Barro, Robert J. "Are Government Bonds Net Wealth?" *Journal of Political Economy* 82 (November/December 1974), 1095–1117.

Blanchard, Olivier J. "Debt, Deficits and Finite Horizons," *Journal of Political Economy* 93 (April 1985), 223–247.

Feldstein, Martin. "Government Deficits and Aggregate Demand," *Journal of Monetary Economics* 9 (January 1982), 1–20.

Fisher, Yaacov. "Economic Indicators in the Israeli Economy," *Bank of Israel Economic Quarterly* 61 (July 1986), 75–103. (Hebrew).

Frenkel, Jacob A., and Assaf Razin. "Fiscal Policies in the World Economy," *Journal of Political Economy* 94 (June 1986), 564–594.

Frenkel, Jacob A., and Assaf Razin. "Deficits with Distortionary Taxes: International Dimension," paper prepared for the 4th Sapir Conference, Tel-Aviv University (December 1986).

Hall, Robert E. "Stochastic Implications of the Life-Cycle Permanent Income Hypothesis: Theory and Evidence," *Journal of Political Economy* 86 (December 1978), 971–988.

Hansen, Lars P., and Kenneth J. Singleton. "Consumption, Risk Aversion and the Temporal Behavior of Asset Returns," *Journal of Political Economy* 91 (April 1983), 1269–1286.

Hayashi, F., "Tests for Liquidity Constraints: A Critical Survey," Working Paper 1720, NBER (October 1985).

Helpman, Elhanan and Assaf Razin. "Exchange Rate Management: Intertemporal Tradeoffs," *American Economic Review* 77 (March 1987), 107–123.

Hubbard, R. G., and K. L. Judd. "Liquidity Constraints, Fiscal Policy, and Consumption," *Brookings Papers on Economic Activity* 1 (1986), 1–50.

Kochin, Levis A. "Are Future Taxes Anticipated by Consumers?" *Journal of Money, Credit and Banking* 6 (August 1974), 385–394.

Kormendi, Roger C. "Government Debt, Government Spending and Private Sector Behavior," *American Economic Review* 73 (December 1983), 994–1010.

Leiderman, Leonardo and Mario Blejer. "Modelling and Testing Ricardian Equivalence: A Survey," IMF Staff Papers (March 1988).

Leiderman, Leonardo, and Assaf Razin, "Consumption and Government-Budget Finance in a High-Deficit Economy," Working Paper 2032, NBER (September 1986), 1–21.

Leiderman, Leonardo and Assaf Razin. "Testing Ricardian Neutrality with Intertemporal Stochastic Model," *Journal of Money, Credit and Banking* 20 (February 1988).

Lucas, Robert E., Jr., "Econometric Policy Evaluation: A Critique," in K. Brunner and A. H. Meltzer, *The Phillips Curve and Labor Markets* (Amsterdam: North-Holland, 1986).

Poterba, James M., and Lawrence H. Summers. "Finite Lifetimes and the Crowding Out Effects of Budget Deficits," Discussion Paper No. 1255 (August 1986), Harvard Institute of Economic Research.

Reid, Bradford G. "Aggregate Consumption and Deficit Financing: An Attempt to Separate Permanent from Transitory Effects," *Economic Inquiry* (1985).

Seater, John. "Are Future Taxes Discounted?" *Journal of Money, Credit and Banking* 11 (May 1979), 214–218.

Tanner, J. E. "An Empirical Investigation of Tax Discounting," *Journal of Money, Credit and Banking* 11 (May 1979), 214–218.

Tobin, J., and W. Dolde, "Wealth, Liquidity and Consumption," in *Consumer Spending and Monetary Policy: The Linkages* (Federal Reserve Bank of Boston, 1971). pp. 99–146.

van Wijnbergen, Sweder. "Interdependence Revisited: A Developing Countries' Perspective on Macroeconomic Management and Trade Policy in the Industrial World," *Economic Policy* 1 (September 1985).

8 Saving and Permanent Income in Canada and the United Kingdom

John Y. Campbell and Richard H. Clarida

8.1. Introduction

Recent theoretical research in open-economy macroeconomics has emphasized the connection between a country's current account and the intertemporal savings and investment choices of its households, firms, and governments (Buiter, 1981, Sachs, 1981, 1982, Dornbusch, 1983, Frenkel and Razin, 1985, Persson and Svensson, 1983). To the extent that national saving and investment patterns reflect forward looking behavior on the part of households and firms that optimize in the absence of liquidity constraints, expectations about future economic variables can significantly influence the magnitude and persistence of current account deficits and surpluses observed in the present.

The objective of this chapter is to assess the empirical relevance of the permanent income theory of household saving, a key building block of recent theoretical models of the current account. According to the permanent income hypothesis, consumption is proportional to permanent income; it thus tends to be above current income when current income is relatively low and expected to rise, and to be below current income when current income is relatively high and expected to fall. This intuitive observation has the striking and until recently ignored econometric implication that household saving should be the best available predictor of future changes in disposable labor income. Using the econometric methodology developed in Campbell (1987), we test this implication of the permanent income hypothesis on quarterly aggregate data for Canada and the United Kingdom and compare our findings to those obtained by Campbell for U.S. data.

Our approach is to test cross-equation restrictions on the coefficients of a bivariate vector autoregression (VAR) comprised of saving and changes in disposable labor income. Thus, by contrast with most of the recent literature, we do not directly test the consumption martingale property emphasized by Hall (1978).

This chapter was prepared for the Pinhas Sapir Conference on Economic Effects of the Government Budget, held in December 1986. We are grateful to Zvi Eckstein, our discussant, and to participants in the conference and at a Yale University seminar for helpful comments. We acknowledge financial support from the Olin Foundation (Campbell) and the National Science Foundation.

In both the Canadian and British data, we find that saving Granger causes changes in disposable labor income and that it is significantly negatively correlated with the subsequent change in disposable labor income. This is exactly what one would expect if the permanent income hypothesis is true, since saving occurs because labor income is expected to decline in the future. However, we are able to reject statistically the cross-equation restrictions implied by the permanent income hypothesis. In the case of Canada, the statistical rejection of the theory appears to result from the fact that the mean of the unrestricted forecast of future changes in labor income differs substantially from the mean of Canadian saving. In the case of the United Kingdom, violations of the cross-equation restrictions implied by the theory are more pervasive.

To assess the economic significance of these statistical rejections of the theory, we compare the behavior of saving in each country with that of the unrestricted VAR forecast of future changes in disposable income. If the permanent income hypothesis is true, saving and the unrestricted VAR forecast should have identical standard deviations and should be perfectly correlated. In fact, we find that the correlation between saving and the unrestricted VAR forecast of future changes in disposable labor income is extremely high in both countries, exceeding .89 in the British data and .99 in the Canadian data. While the sample standard deviation of saving is somewhat less than the standard deviation of the VAR forecast, time series plots of the two series for each country reinforce the impression conveyed by the correlation results that a substantial fraction of the forecastable variation in disposable labor income is incorporated in Canadian and British household saving behavior. Thus, even though it is possible to reject the permanent income hypothesis at conventional levels of statistical significance, our results suggest that the theory provides a useful description of the dynamic behavior of household saving in Canada and United Kingdom. Our findings correspond quite closely to those obtained by Campbell in his test of the permanent income hypothesis on U.S. data.

8.2. The Permanent Income Hypothesis

Following Flavin (1981), we write the permanent income model as

$$C_t = \gamma y_{Pt} = \gamma \left[y_{kt} + \left(\frac{r}{1+r} \right) \sum_{i=0}^{\infty} \left(\frac{1}{1+r} \right)^i E_t y_{l,t+i} \right], \tag{1}$$

where c_t is real per capita consumption, y_{Pt} is permanent income, y_{kt} is real per capita capital income, y_{lt} is real per capita labor income, r is the expected real interest rate, and γ is the propensity to consume out of permanent income. The model assumes that γ and r are constant and that $\gamma \leqslant 1$.

Permanent income is defined as the Hicksian income generated by nonhuman and human wealth. The Hicksian income from human wealth is r times the present discounted value of expected labor income. The Hicksian income from nonhuman wealth, W_t, is just $y_{kt} = rW_t$. Wealth evolves according to $W_t = (1 + r)W_{t-1} + yl_{t-1} - c_{t-1} + \eta_t$, so that capital income obeys

$$yk_t - (1 + r)yk_{t-1} - r[yl_{t-1} - c_{t-1}] = r\eta_t, \tag{2}$$

where η_t represents unanticipated capital gains and is unforecastable as of time $t - 1$. Note that in general the conditional variance of η_t will be positively related to the level of wealth W_{t-1}.

Our interest is in ascertaining and testing the restrictions that the permanent income hypothesis places on saving behavior. Define transitory income y_{Tt} as the difference between total disposable income, $y_t \equiv y_{kt} + y_{lt}$, and permanent income, y_{Pt}, which is defined in equation (1). Define saving, s_t, as the difference between total disposable income and consumption: $s_t \equiv y_t - c_t$. If $\gamma = 1$, so that consumption is equal to permanent income, equation (1) can be rearranged so that it becomes a statement about saving:

$$s_t = y_t - y_{Pt} = y_{Tt}$$

$$= -\left(\frac{r}{1 + r}\right) \sum_{i=0}^{\infty} \left(\frac{1}{1 + r}\right)^i [E_t y_{l,t+i} - y_{lt}] \tag{3}$$

$$= -\sum_{i=1}^{\infty} \left(\frac{1}{1 + r}\right)^i E_t \Delta y_{l,t+i},$$

where Δ denotes a standard backward difference.

Equation (3) says that saving equals transitory income, which in turn can be expressed as the expected present value of future declines in labor income. It follows from (3) that

$$s_t - \Delta y_{lt} - (1 + r)s_{t-1} = -r\varepsilon_t, \tag{4}$$

where $\varepsilon_t = [1/(1 + r)] \sum_{i=0}^{\infty} [1/(1 + r)]^i [E_t y_{l,t+i} - E_{t-1} y_{l,t+i}]$ is the unforecastable revision from $t - 1$ to t in the expected value of human wealth. Equation (4) is not immediately intuitive, stating that a linear combination of the change in labor income, current, and lagged saving is unforecastable. However, subtracting (4) from (2) and using the definition of s_t, we obtain Hall's (1978) celebrated result that consumption is a random walk:

$$c_t - c_{t-1} = r[\eta_t + \varepsilon_t]. \tag{5}$$

If $\gamma < 1$, the above analysis needs to be modified. We can define a new variable $\tilde{s}_t$ as $\tilde{s}_t \equiv y_t - c_t/\gamma$. Equations (3) and (4) now apply to $\tilde{s}_t$ rather than to s_t and we have

$$s_t = \tilde{s}_t + (1 - \gamma)y_{Pt} = y_{Tt} + (1 - \gamma)y_{Pt}. \tag{6}$$

Equation (6) says that people save their transitory income, and a fraction $(1 - \gamma)$ of their permanent income. Our approach is to evaluate the model by examining $\tilde{s}_t$.

Although tests of the permanent income hypothesis usually focus on the consumption martingale implication given by equation (5), we shall adopt the econometric methodology developed by Campbell (1987), which uses the restriction on savings behavior given by equations (3) and (4) to assess the empirical relevance of the theory. There are two main reasons for this choice.

First, the random walk behavior of consumption is only one implication of the permanent income hypothesis. A time series can follow a random walk and yet not be determined by permanent income (although such a series will not obey the intertemporal budget constraint). Equations (3) and (4) directly examine the relation between consumption and income.

Second, the restriction on household saving behavior given by equation (3) can be used to characterize the fit of the permanent income model. In the context of the recent theoretical work in open-economy macroeconomics, it is worthwhile to investigate the extent to which the movements of household saving incorporate forecastable variations in income, even—or perhaps especially—if the theory is statistically rejected.

8.3. Econometric Methodology

In this section we explain the econometric concepts and techniques that we use to evaluate the permanent income model. We begin by discussing the stationarity of the different variables in the model; then we show that the model implies an intuitive set of restrictions on a stationary VAR; and finally we discuss the estimation of nuisance parameters.

If the permanent income hypothesis holds with $\gamma = 1$ and changes in labor income are stationary, then equations (2), (3), and (5) imply that consumption and capital income are also stationary in first differences but that saving is stationary in its level. This is because the theory restricts saving to equal the discounted present value of expected changes in labor income; these changes are stationary and thus so is saving.

More formally, define the vector $x_t = [y_{kt}, y_{lt}, c_t]'$. Each of the elements of x_t is stationary in first differences but a linear combination of the elements $s_t = [1 \quad 1 \quad -1] x_t$ is stationary in its level. The vector x_t is said to be cointegrated.

DEFINITION (Engle and Granger, 1987)   A vector x_t is said to be cointegrated of order d,b, denoted x_t CI(d, b), if (i) all components of x_t are integrated of order d (stationary in dth differences) and (ii) there exists at least one vector α ($\neq 0$) such that $z_t = \alpha' x_t$ is integrated of order $d - b, b > 0$.

The vector α is called the cointegrating vector; it is unique up to a scalar normalization and, in the present example, is proportional to $[1 \quad 1 \quad -1]'$. Stock (1987) proves that if there is a single unknown element of α, a variety of methods provide estimates with a standard error that goes to zero at a rate proportional to the sample size T (rather than $\sqrt{T}$). Intuitively, all linear combinations of the elements of x_t other than $\alpha' x_t$ have infinite variance because variables in a CI(1, 1) vector share a common stochastic trend (a unit root) while exhibiting stationary deviations from one another in the short run. The practical implication of this result is that an unknown element of α may be estimated in a first-stage regression and then treated as known in second-stage procedures, whose asymptotic standard errors will still be correct.

If the propensity to consume is known—or assumed—to equal unity and the economically relevant measure of consumption is observable, all elements of α are known a priori. However, in the context of the permanent income hypothesis, the relevant measure of consumption is consumption of nondurables, services, and the services yielded by the existing stock of durable goods. The latter is unobservable, and in what follows we shall postulate that consumption, c_t, is proportional to the observed consumption of nondurables and services, c_{nt}, so that $c_t = \lambda c_{nt}$. In this case, the vector

$x_{nt} = [y_{kt} \quad y_{lt} \quad c_{nt}]'$ is CI(1, 1) and the scale factor λ can be estimated from the cointegrating vector $[1 \quad 1 \quad -\lambda]$ using Stock's theorem.

If the permanent income hypothesis holds with $\gamma < 1$, then from equations (2) and (5), both y_{kt} and c_t are explosive rather than stationary in first differences and the vector x_{nt} no longer satisfies the formal definition of cointegration. However, x_{nt} still exhibits the key property that a linear combination of its elements, $s_{nt} = [1 \quad 1 \quad -\lambda/\gamma]x_{nt}$, is stationary. This follows from equations (1) and (2) and the assumption that $c_t = \lambda c_{nt}$. The linear combination s_{nt} can still be estimated precisely in a first-stage regression since it is the only linear combination with asymptotically finite variance. Note, however, that with data only on c_{nt}, the cointegrating vector identifies only the ratio λ/γ. In the discussion that follows, we shall refer to $s_{nt} = y_t - (\lambda/\gamma)c_{nt}$ as saving. If in fact the theory holds with $\gamma < 1$, s_{nt} equals the difference between current saving and the fraction $(1 - \gamma)$ of permanent income; i.e., $s_{nt} = \tilde{s}_t = s_t - (1 - \gamma)y_{pt}$.

As we have seen the permanent income hypothesis implies that saving is equal to the discounted present value of expected future declines in labor income. Campbell (1987) shows that this can be tested as a set of cross-equation restrictions on a bivariate VAR comprised of saving and changes in disposable labor income. The test of restrictions on the VAR is, in fact, equivalent to a single-equation regression test of equation (4), but the VAR easily generates an optimal unrestricted forecast of future changes in labor income. Because the VAR includes saving as a variable, the unrestricted forecast should equal saving if the model is true; this can be used to characterize informally the fit of the permanent income hypothesis.

Consider the following VAR,

$$\begin{bmatrix} \Delta y_{lt} \\ s_{nt} \end{bmatrix} = \begin{bmatrix} a(L) & b(L) \\ c(L) & d(L) \end{bmatrix} \begin{bmatrix} \Delta y_{l,t-1} \\ s_{n,t-1} \end{bmatrix} + \begin{bmatrix} u_{1t} \\ u_{2t} \end{bmatrix}, \tag{7}$$

which can be rewritten in "companion" form as $z_t = Az_{t-1} + v_t$. Note that, for all i, $E[z_{t+1}|H_t] = A^i z_t$, where H_t is the information set $\{z_t, z_{t-1}, \ldots\}$, a proper subset of agents' information set I_t. As is common in empirical research, we take conditional expectations to be linear projections on information.

If the theory is correct, s_{nt} is an optimal forecast of future changes in income conditional on the full information set I_t. A weak implication is that s_{nt} will have incremental explanatory power for future labor income changes if agents have information useful for forecasting labor income beyond the history of that variable. s_{nt} must Granger cause Δy_{lt}, unless agents have no useful information beyond the history of labor income, in which case s_{nt} is an exact linear function of current and lagged changes in labor income.

Projecting equation (3) onto the information set H_t, and noting that the left-hand side is unchanged because s_{nt} is in H_t, we obtain the following set of cross-equation restrictions on the matrix A:

$$g' = -\sum_{i=1}^{\infty} [1/(1 + r)^i h' A^i], \tag{8}$$

where g' and h' are row vectors with $2p$ elements, all of which are zero except for the $(p + 1')$th element of g' and the first element of h'. These nonlinear cross-equation restrictions are in fact equivalent to the restriction that the linear combination of the change in disposable labor income, current, and lagged saving derived in equation (4) is orthogonal to lagged Δy_{lt} and s_{nt}.

To see this, note that the right-hand side of equation (8) can be expressed as $-h'[1/(1 + r)]A\{I - [1/(1 + r)]A\}^{-1}$. Postmultiplying equation (8) by $\{I - [1/(1 + r)]A\}$, we obtain

$$g'\{I - [1/(1 + r)]A\} = -h'[1/(1 + r)]A. \tag{9}$$

Using the structure of the A matrix, the cross-equation restrictions defined by equation (9) can be written as follows: $a_1 = c_1, \ldots, a_p = c_p, d_1 - b_1 = (1 + r), b_2 = d_2, \ldots, b_p = d_p$. Subtracting the Δy_{lt} equation of the VAR from the s_{nt} equation, we obtain

$$s_{nt} - \Delta y_{lt} = (c_1 - a_1)\Delta y_{l,t-1} + \cdots + (c_p - a_p)\Delta y_{l,t-p} + (d_1 - b_1)s_{n,t-1}$$
$$+ (d_2 - b_2)s_{n,t-2} + \cdots + (d_p - b_p)s_{n,t-p} + u_{1t} - u_{2t}.$$

Thus, if the theory is true, $s_{nt} - \Delta y_{lt} - (1 + r)s_{n,t-1}$ is orthogonal to lagged Δy_{lt} and s_{nt}. The implication is that a single-equation regression test of equation (4) is equivalent to a test of (9). However, the VAR can be used to generate optimal unrestricted forecasts (conditional on lagged Δy_{lt} and s_{nt}) of the discounted present value of future changes in labor income. These forecasts can be compared with s_{nt} to characterize the fit of the permanent income model, since the theory predicts that the unrestricted forecast and s_{nt} should have identical standard deviations and should be perfectly correlated.

A weaker version of the permanent income hypothesis that allows for a "transitory consumption" error in equation (2) can also be tested in this framework, provided that the error is assumed to be orthogonal to all lagged information. In this case, the theory restricts the conditional expectation of saving, one period ahead, to equal the discounted present value of expected future declines in labor income

$$E_t s_{n,t+1} = - \sum_{i=1}^{\infty} [1/(1 + r)]^i E_t \Delta y_{l,t+1+i}, \tag{3'}$$

since, by definition, the conditional expectation of next period's transitory consumption is zero. Equation (3') can be tested by regressing $s_{nt} - \Delta y_{lt} - (1 + r)s_{n,t-1}$ on twice-lagged Δy_{lt} and s_{nt}.

There are at least two methods available for estimating the cointegrating vector $[1 \quad 1 \quad -\lambda/\gamma]$. The first is a "levels regression" of total income y_t on nondurables and services consumption c_{nt}, while the second is an "error-correction regression" of Δy_t on lagged changes in and levels of y_t and c_{nt}. In the levels regression, the estimate of λ/γ is the coefficient on c_{nt}, while in the error-correction regression the estimate is given by the ratio of the coefficient on lagged consumption to that on lagged income. The residual from the levels regression can be used to test the hypothesis that c_{nt} and y_t are not cointegrated. In particular, Granger and Engle (1987) develop an "Augmented Dickey-Fuller" test in which the change in the residual is regressed on one lagged level of itself and at least one lagged change. Based upon the Monte Carlo work of Granger and Engle, a t-statistic on the coefficient of the lagged level exceeding 2.84 is sufficient to reject the hypothesis of no cointegration at the 10% level; a t-statistic exceeding 3.17 is sufficient to reject at the 5% level.

8.4. Data and Empirical Results

Quarterly data on real per capita consumption, disposable income, and disposable labor income in Canada and the United Kingdom are used in the empirical work. All data are seasonally adjusted quarterly series for the period 1955:1–1984:4. Canadian data are from *Statistics Canada*, while the British data are from the Central Statistical Office. Following Blinder and Deaton (1985), the disposable labor income series are constructed as follows. Proprietor's income and personal income taxes are attributed to labor and capital according to their overall factor shares;

Table 8.1
Univariate tests for unit roots[a]

Variable	Country/test statistic			
	Canada		United Kingdom	
	$Zt\tilde{\alpha}$	$Z\Phi_3$	$Zt\tilde{\alpha}$	$Z\Phi_3$
y_{lt}	-1.428	1.023	-2.827	4.005
y_t	-1.792	1.816	-3.561 (5%)	6.353 (5%)
c_{nt}	-1.506	1.411	-2.762	3.965
s_{nt}	-4.374 (1%)	9.579 (1%)	-6.749 (1%)	22.804 (1%)

a. These test statistics are from Phillips and Perron (1986) and Perron (1986). $Zt\tilde{\alpha}$ is formed from the t-statistic on α in the regression $\Delta X_t = \mu + \beta t + \alpha X_{t-1}$. $Z\Phi_3$ is formed from the F-statistic for H_0: ($\beta = 0$, $\alpha = 0$) in this regression. All statistics are corrected for serial correlation in the equation error using a fourth-order Newey-West (1987) correction. Asymptotic critical values, from Fuller (1976) and Dickey and Fuller (1981), are $Zt\tilde{\alpha}$: 1%, 3.96; 2.5%, 3.66; 5%, 3.41; 10%, 3.12; $Z\Phi_3$: 1%, 8.27; 2.5%, 7.16; 5%, 6.25; 10%, 5.34.

social insurance contributions are deducted from labor income; obviously, income from dividends, rent, and interest is not included in the disposable labor income series. Nominal, aggregate magnitudes are converted to a real, per capita basis by dividing by total population and the consumer spending deflator for each country. Annual population figures are from *International Financial Statistics*; quarterly population series are constructed by interpolation.

As a preliminary diagnostic, in table 8.1 we test for a unit root in the disposable labor income process in Canada and the United Kingdom. The VAR methodology described in the previous section relies on the presence of a unit root in labor income. We also test for unit roots in total income y_t, nondurables and services consumption c_{nt}, and "saving" $s_{nt} = y_t - (\lambda/\gamma)c_{nt}$, where the parameter λ/γ is estimated in table 8.2. We expect to be unable to reject the unit root hypothesis for y_t and c_{nt} (although strictly speaking these variables have explosive rather than unit roots if $\gamma < 1$), and to reject strongly for s_{nt} (in fact, the test in table 8.1 is biased toward rejection because it ignores the fact that λ/γ must be estimated— a test that takes this into account is presented in table 8.2).

The test statistics in table 8.1 have recently been proposed by Phillips (1986) and Phillips and Perron (1986). To test the null hypothesis that a series X_t has a unit root (perhaps with drift), against the alternative that it is stationary around a linear trend, one runs the regression $\Delta X_t = \mu + \beta t + \alpha X_{t-1} + \varepsilon_{xt}$. Fuller (1976) and Dickey and Fuller (1981) tabu-

Table 8.2
Estimation of λ/γ and cointegration tests[a]

Canada[b]	
(1) $y_t = -3.241 + 1.698c_{nt}$	$R^2 = 0.995$
$\quad\quad\ \ (0.223)\ \ (0.012)$	Estimate of $\lambda/\gamma = 1.698$
(2) $\Delta y_t = -0.758 + 0.764\,\Delta y_{t-1} - 0.455\,\Delta c_{n,t-1}$	$R^2 = 0.197$
$\quad\quad\quad\ \ (0.283)\ \ (0.301)\quad\quad\ \ (0.097)$	Estimate of $\lambda/\gamma = 1.720$
$\quad\quad\quad -0.263y_{t-1} + 0.452c_{n,t-1}$	
$\quad\quad\quad\ \ (0.072)\quad\quad\ \ (0.122)$	

United Kingdom[c]	
(1) $y_t = -2.107 + 1.801c_{nt}$	$R^2 = 0.991$
$\quad\quad\ \ (0.069)\ \ (0.016)$	Estimate of $\lambda/\gamma = 1.801$
(2) $\Delta y_t = -0.952 + 1.105\,\Delta y_t - 0.536\,\Delta c_{n,t-1}$	$R^2 = 0.249$
$\quad\quad\quad\ \ (0.221)\ \ (0.268)\quad\ \ (0.102)$	Estimate of $\lambda/\gamma = 1.802$
$\quad\quad\quad -0.463y_{t-1} + 0.835c_{n,t-1}$	
$\quad\quad\quad\ \ (0.101)\quad\quad\ \ (0.182)$	

a. The Granger and Engle (1987) critical values for the null hypothesis of no cointegration are 3.17 at the 5% level (*) and 2.84 at the 10% level (**).
b. Augmented Dickey-Fuller test with 1 lag 3.217*; with 5 lags 3.365*.
c. Augmented Dickey-Fuller test with 1 lag 3.812*; with 5 lags 2.073.

lated critical values for the t-statistic on α, $t\tilde{\alpha}$, and the F-statistic testing (H_0: $\alpha = 0, \beta = 0$), Φ_3, but these are correct only if ε_{Xt} is serially uncorrelated. We present Phillips and Perron's modified statistics, $Zt\tilde{\alpha}$ and $Z\Phi_3$, which make a nonparametric correction for serial correlation in ε_{Xt}.

The results in table 8.1 are generally consistent with our prior expectations. For Canada, there is no evidence at even the 10% level against the hypothesis that y_{lt}, y_t, and c_{nt} have unit roots; but the hypothesis that s_{nt} has a unit root is rejected at the 1% level. Results for the United Kingdom are similar except that the unit root hypothesis for y_t is rejected at the 5% level.

Table 8.2 presents estimates of λ/γ and the tests for no cointegration. In the Canadian data, the parameter λ/γ is estimated at 1.698 by the levels regression and 1.720 by the error-correction regression; in the British data, λ/γ is estimated at 1.801 by the levels regression and 1.802 in the error-correction regression. Recall that, since the consumption of services yielded by durables is unobservable, we postulate that $c_t = \lambda c_{nt}$. While the cointegrating regressions do not identify the λ parameter, we note that, if the propensity to consume out of permanent income is assumed to be unity, the estimates of λ/γ imply a share of nondurables and services in total consumption of 59% in Canada and 55% in the United Kingdom. These implied shares seem somewhat low, suggesting that the value of γ is less than unity. Evidence on the value of γ, along with an assessment of the robustness of our findings, is presented in the next section. Finally, we note that the hypothesis of no cointegration is rejected at the 5% level in the Canadian data, while in the British data it can only be rejected at the 10% level.

We next construct time series for saving, $s_{nt} = y_t - (\lambda/\gamma)c_{nt}$, in each country, estimate the bivariate VARS given by equation (7), and use the estimates to evaluate the permanent income hypothesis. The Akaike Information Criterion is used to select the VAR lag length: four lags are selected for the British VAR, and one lag is selected for the Canadian VAR. (The robustness of the results to alternative choices of lag length is discussed in the next section.) In computing standard errors, we allow for conditional heteroskedasticity by using White's (1984) heteroskedasticity-consistent estimate of the variance-covariance matrix of the VAR coefficient estimates. This is given by $(X'X)^{-1}X'VX(X'X)^{-1}$, where V is a diagonal matrix with squared residuals on the diagonal.

Table 8.3 and 8.4 present the empirical results for Canada and the United Kingdom, respectively. In each table there are four columns of regression coefficients (sums of coefficients in the British case, to reduce the complexity of the table). Column (1) reports the regression of Δy_{lt} on the lagged change in labor income and lagged saving. Column (2) reports the regression of s_{nt} on these variables. The two columns together make up the VAR system. Column (3) is the regression of $s_{nt} - \Delta y_{lt} - (1 + r)s_{n,t-1}$ on the VAR explanatory variables; recall that, if the permanent income hypothesis is true, all coefficients should be zero in this regression. Column (4) is the regression with $s_{n,t+1} - \Delta y_{l,t+1} - (1 + r)s_{nt}$ as the dependent variable; this tests the hypothesis that the permanent income model holds except for serially uncorrelated transitory consumption. A fifth column reports the coefficients of the optimal unrestricted VAR forecast of the present value of labor income declines, which we write $s'_{n,t-1}$. If the permanent income hypothesis is true, we should have $s'_{n,t-1} = s_{n,t-1}$.

In both Canada and the United Kingdom, the full set of restrictions of the permanent income hypothesis is strongly rejected. In each country, the coefficients in column (3) are jointly significant at the 0.004% level or better. For Canada, the strength of the rejection is due largely to the restriction that the mean of s_{nt} should equal $(-1/r)$ times the mean change

Table 8.3
Tests of the permanent income hypothesis—Canada[a]

	Regression coefficients of column variables on row variables				
	(1)	(2)	(3)	(4)	(5)
	Δy_{lt}	s_{nt}	$s_{nt} - \Delta y_{lt}$ $- (1 + r)s_{n,t-1}$	$s_{n,t+1} - \Delta y_{l,t+1}$ $- (1 + r)s_{nt}$	$s'_{n,t-1}$
Constant	—	—	−0.139 (0.158)	−0.044 (0.163)	
$\Delta y_{l,t-1}$	−0.207 (0.143)	−0.339 (0.143)	−0.132 (0.049)	−0.052 (0.054)	−0.135 (0.115)
$s_{n,t-1}$	−0.236 (0.064)	0.765 (0.070)	−0.008 (0.047)	0.024 (0.048)	1.096 (0.313)
R^2	0.196	0.565	0.042	0.005	

a. s_{nt} Granger causes Δy_{lt} at 0.02% level in column (1). Δy_{lt} Granger causes s_{nt} at 1.8% level in column (2).
  Coefficients are jointly significant at $1.6 \times 10^{-7}\%$ level in column (3). Coefficients, excluding the intercept, are jointly significant at 1.7% level in column (3).
  Coefficients are jointly significant at $2.9 \times 10^{-4}\%$ level in column (4). Coefficients, excluding the intercept, are jointly significant at 60.8% level in column (4).
  Summary statistics:

$\sigma(s_{nt}) = 0.619$,

$\sigma(s'_{nt})/\sigma(s_{nt}) = 1.079$,
    (0.302)

$\rho(s'_{nt}, s_{nt}) = 0.997$.
    (0.004)

in labor income, a result that follows immediately from equation (3). When $\gamma < 1$, $s_{nt} = s_t - (1 - \gamma)y_t^P$, so it is possible to have s_{nt} be negative even though s_t is positive; nevertheless, the mean of s_{nt} is too high to satisfy the model's restrictions. When the mean restriction is dropped, the other restrictions of the model are rejected at only the 1.7% level. In the United Kingdom, however, the dynamic restrictions of the model are rejected just as strongly as the mean restriction.

Allowing serially uncorrelated transitory consumption also helps the model fit the Canadian data; the coefficients in column (4), excluding the intercept, are not even significant at the 60% level for Canada. But for the United Kingdom, the model with transitory consumption is rejected as strongly as the model without.

As discussed in the introduction, our goal is to do more than simply conduct formal tests of the permanent income model. We are interested in characterizing the fit of the model, bringing out its strengths and its

Table 8.4
Tests of the permanent income hypothesis—United Kingdom[a]

	Sums of regression coefficients of column variables on row variables				
	(1)	(2)	(3) $s_{nt} - \Delta y_{lt}$ $- (1 + r)s_{n,t-1}$	(4) $s_{n,t+1} - \Delta y_{l,t+1}$ $- (1 + r)s_{nt}$	(5)
	Δy_{lt}	s_{nt}			$s'_{n,t-1}$
Constant	—	—	0.260 (0.148)	0.377 (0.178)	—
$\Delta y_{l,t-i}$ $i = 1, \ldots, 5$	0.256 (0.226)	0.445 (0.256)	0.189 (0.195)	−0.023 (0.235)	0.513 (0.555)
$s_{n,t-i}$ $i = 1, \ldots, 5$	−0.274 (0.097)	0.863 (0.097)	0.128 (0.070)	0.181 (0.085)	2.704 (0.898)
R^2	0.201	0.448	0.370	0.184	

a. s_{nt} Granger causes Δy_{lt} at 0.007% level in column (1). Δy_{lt} Granger causes s_{nt} at 4.9% level in column (2).
　Coefficients are jointly significant at 0.004% level in column (3). Coefficients, excluding the intercept, are jointly significant at 0.002% level in column (3).
　Coefficients are jointly significant at 4.5×10^{-4}% level in column (4). Coefficients, excluding the intercept, are jointly significant at $2.0\% \times 10^{-4}$% level in column (4).
　Summary statistics:

$\sigma(s_{nt}) = 0.105$,

$\sigma(s'_{nt})/\sigma(s_{nt}) = 2.114$,
　　　　(0.679)

$\rho(s'_{nt}, s_{nt}) = 0.896$.
　　　(0.023)

weaknesses. Tables 8.3 and 8.4 also present summary statistics for the VAR systems that help us to do this.

In both Canadian and British data, saving Granger causes changes in labor income at extremely high levels of statistical significance. Furthermore, the estimated coefficients on $s_{n,t-1}$ are negative in both countries and statistically significant. These findings are exactly those implied by the permanent income hypothesis since saving is forward looking and rises in anticipation of future declines in labor income. As shown in detail in section 8.3, the single-equation regression tests already discussed are equivalent to the test of the cross-equation restrictions on the VARs. In fact, the deviations of the estimated VAR coefficients from these restrictions are just the coefficients reported in the regressions of column (3).

We also report, for each country, the standard deviation of saving, the ratio of the standard deviation of the unrestricted VAR forecast of the discounted present value of future changes in labor income to the standard deviation of saving, and the correlation between saving and the unrestricted forecast. In the Canadian data, the correlation is .997 and the standard deviation ratio is 1.079. If the theory were exactly correct, the correlation and the standard deviation ratio would both equal one. We have seen that these differences are statistically significant, but Canadian household saving appears to incorporate virtually all of the forecastable variation in future labor income.

In the British data, the correlation between saving and the unrestricted forecast is also quite high at .896. However, s_{nt} is less than half as volatile as the unrestricted forecast of the present value of the future labor income declines. This may be taken as evidence of excess sensitivity of consumption to current income in the United Kingdom since, if consumption were in fact determined by current as opposed to permanent income, saving—the difference between income and consumption—would be expected to have substantially less volatility than the unrestricted optimal forecast. It should be noted, though, that the asymptotic standard error on the excess sensitivity statistic is high at 0.679.

We conclude this section by plotting s_{nt} and the unrestricted optimal forecast of labor income declines. These plots are given in figures 8.1 and 8.2. The figures convincingly support the inferences drawn from the summary statistics. In particular, the statistical rejection of the permanent income hypothesis in Canadian data does not appear to have substantial economic significance. Forecastable variations in the present value of future labor income declines are incorporated virtually one-for-one in Canadian household saving behavior (figure 8.1). The noteworthy feature of the British plot (figure 8.2) is that, while the magnitude of swings in saving does not in general match that of swings in forecastable labor income declines, the former tracks every turning point in the latter. Despite the statistical rejections of the present income hypothesis reported in table 8.2, the theory seems to be able to account for much of the variation in household saving in Canada and the United Kingdom.

8.5.   How Robust Are the Findings?

In this section we check to see whether our results are robust to changes in the econometric specification and the measure of consumption. We are

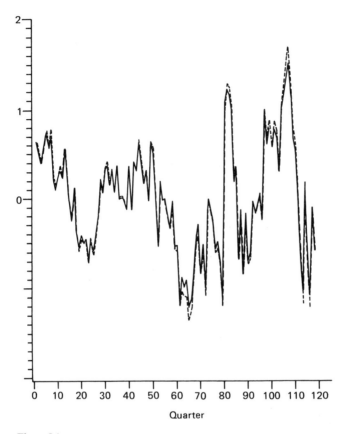

Figure 8.1
Saving (mean deviations) and VAR forecast: Canadian data, nondurables and services consumption. Key to variables: ---, forecast; ———, saving.

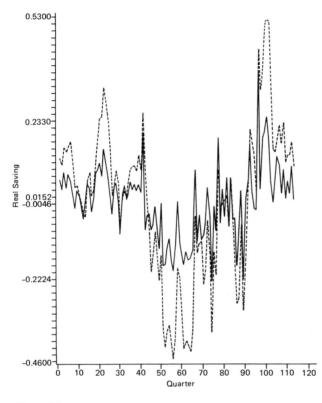

Figure 8.2
Saving (mean deviations) and VAR forecast: British data, nondurables and services consumption. Key to variables: ---, forecast; ———, saving.

particularly concerned with the possibility that our results are sensitive to lag length, since Campbell (1987) found this to be the case for U.S. data.

Fortunately, in British and Canadian data we obtain rather similar results to those reported for all lag lengths between 1 and 5. In Canadian data, the permanent income hypothesis (without transitory consumption) is rejected at the 2.1% level for lag length 2, the 1.1% level for lag length 3, the 0.3% level for lag length 4, and the 0.4% level for lag length 5. The correlation of s_{nt} and s'_{nt} falls slightly from 0.996 with lag length 1 to 0.908 with lag length 5, and the standard deviation ratio rises to 1.518 with lag length 5, but the standard errors on these numbers also rise, so that individually they remain insignificantly different from one. In British data the model is strongly rejected but the correlation of s_{nt} and s'_{nt} remains above 0.85 for all lag lengths. We find strong evidence of excess sensitivity only at the lag lengths above 3.

The assumption that the unobservable consumption of services yielded by the existing stock of durable goods is proportional to c_{nt}, the consumption of nondurables and services, involves a potential specification error. To evaluate the robustness of our findings, we test and evaluate the fit of the permanent income model using data on total consumption expenditures, c_t, to construct a series for saving $\tilde{s}_t = y_t - c_t/\gamma$ in each country.

In this case, the cointegrating regression of y_t on a constant and c_t uniquely identifies the parameter $1/\gamma$. The estimate of $1/\gamma$ for Canada is 1.289 with a standard error of .013; the estimate for Britain is 1.299 with a standard error of .012. The null hypothesis of no cointegration is rejected at the 10% level in the United Kingdom, and at the 5% level in Canada, as in table 8.2.

For the United Kingdom the results of the single equation regression tests are unchanged: the restriction that $\tilde{s}_t - \Delta y_{lt} - (1 + r)\tilde{s}_{t-1}$ or $\tilde{s}_{t+1} - \Delta y_{l,t+1} - (1 + r)\tilde{s}_t$ be orthogonal to lagged Δy_{lt} and $\tilde{s}_t$ is resoundingly rejected. However, for Canada, we cannot reject at the 5% level the hypothesis that the source of the rejection is solely a significant constant term in both the strict and transitory-consumption regression tests.

The only substantive differences in the VAR summary statistics relative to those reported in tables 8.3 and 8.4 are that the standard deviations of Canadian saving and the unrestricted forecast increase from .661 and .669, respectively, to .900 and 1.408. However, the correlation between Canadian saving and the unrestricted forecasts falls only slightly to .996 from .997. The corresponding British correlation rises to .913 (from .896), while the standard deviation of the unrestricted British forecast declines to .154 from .221.

Figures 8.3 and 8.4 give a visual impression of the results using total consumption expenditure. The conclusions drawn in section 8.4 are not weakened when total consumption is used. If anything, the British plots in figure 8.4 provide stronger support for the proposition that the permanent income hypothesis provides a parsimonious and empirically relevant account of the cyclical dynamics of household saving behavior.

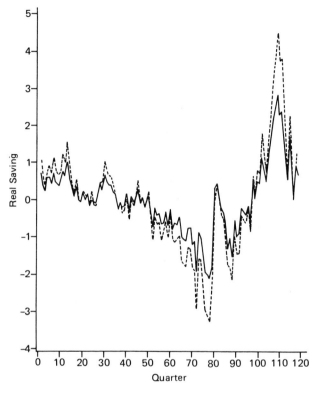

Figure 8.3
Saving and VAR forecast: Canadian data, total consumption. Key to variables: ---,
forecast; ———, saving.

8.6.   Concluding Remarks

In this chapter, we have found substantial support for the prediction of the
permanent income hypothesis that forecastable variations in disposable
labor income are incorporated in household saving behavior in Canada
and the United Kingdom. The tight formulation of the permanent income
hypothesis tested in this chapter can be statistically rejected, but we conclude that the theory has surprising empirical content. Because it abstracts
from the demographic considerations of the life-cycle hypothesis, the permanent income hypothesis is not successful at explaining average saving
rates, or differences in these rates across countries. However, the theory's

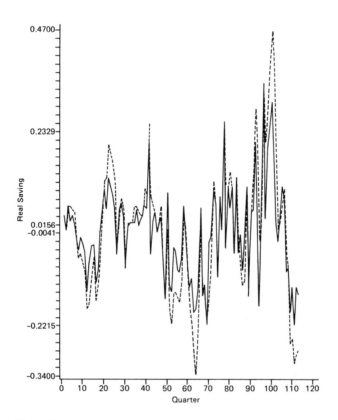

Figure 8.4
Saving and VAR forecast: British data, total consumption. Key to variables: ---, forecast;
————, saving.

predictions about the dynamics of saving and income appear to be worth
taking seriously.

References

Blinder, Alan S., and Angus S. Deaton, "The Time Series Consumption Function Revisited,"
Brookings Papers on Economic Activity 2 (1985): 465–511.

Buiter, Willem, "Time Preference and International Lending and Borrowing in an Overlapping-
Generations Model," *Journal of Political Economy* 89 (August 1981): 769–797.

Campbell, John Y., "Does Saving Anticipate Declining Labor Income? An Alternative Test
of the Permanent Income Hypothesis," *Econometrica* 55 (November 1987): 1249–1275.

Dickey, David A., and Wayne A. Fuller, "Likelihood Ratio Statistics for Auto-regressive Time
Series with a Unit Root," *Econometrica* 49 (1981): 1057–1072.

Dornbusch, Rudiger, "Real Interest Rates, Home Goods, and Optimal External Borrowing," *Journal of Political Economy* 91 (1983): 141–153.

Engle, Robert F., and Clive W. J. Granger, "Cointegration and Error-Correction: Representation, Estimation and Testing," *Econometrica* 55 (March 1987): 251–276.

Flavin, Marjorie A., "The Adjustment of Consumption to Changing Expectations about Future Income," *Journal of Political Economy* 89 (October 1981): 974–1009.

Frenkel, Jacob, and Assaf Razin, "Government Spending, Debt, and International Economic Interdependence," *Economic Journal* 95 (1985): 619–636.

Fuller, Wayne A., *Introduction to Statistical Time Series*, New York: Wiley (1976).

Hall, Robert E., "Stochastic Implications of the Life Cycle-Permanent Income Hypothesis: Theory and Evidence," *Journal of Political Economy* 86 (October 1978): 971–987.

Newey, Whitney K., and Kenneth D. West, "A Simple Positive Definite, Heteroskedasticity and Autocorrelation Consistent Covariance Matrix Estimator," *Econometrica* 55 (May 1987): 703–708.

Perron, Pierre, "Trends and Random Walks in Macroeconomic Time Series: Further Evidence from a New Approach," unpublished paper, Université de Montreal (1986).

Persson, Torsten, and Lars Svensson, "Current Account Dynamics and the Terms of Trade: Harberger-Laursen-Metzler Two Generations Later," *Journal of Political Economy* 93 (February 1985): 43–65.

Phillips, Peter C. B., "Time Series Regression with a Unit Root," *Econometrica* 55 (March 1987): 277–302.

Phillips, Peter C. B., and Pierre Perron, "Testing for Unit Roots in Time Series Regression," Cowles Foundation Discussion Paper (June 1986).

Sachs, Jeffrey, "The Current Account and Macroeconomic Adjustment in the 1970s," *Brookings Papers on Economic Activity* 1 (1981): 201–282.

Sachs, Jeffrey, "The Current Account in the Macroeconomic Adjustment Process," *Scandinavian Journal of Economics* 24 (1982): 147–164.

Stock, James H., "Asymptotic Properties of Least Squares Estimates of Cointegrating Vectors," *Econometrica* 55 (September 1987): 1035–1056.

White, Halbert, *Asymptotic Theory for Econometricians*, New York: Academic Press (1984).

III BUDGET DEFICITS AND OPTIMAL POLICIES

9 International Aspects of Budget Deficits with Distortionary Taxes

Jacob A. Frenkel and Assaf Razin

This chapter deals with the international effects of budget deficits arising from tax and transfer policies. In order to focus on issues of public finance we assume that the path of government spending is given and we examine the implications of alternative time profiles of taxes and of public-debt issue. To conduct a meaningful analysis of budget deficits we depart from the pure Ricardian model (in which the timing of taxes does not matter) by allowing for distortionary taxes, and examine the effects of budget deficits arising from tax policies under alternative tax systems. We consider deficit policies involving taxes of different types: consumption taxes, taxes on income from domestic investment, taxes on income from foreign lending, and taxes on labor income.

Throughout we assume that capital markets in the world economy are fully integrated and, therefore, that individuals and governments of different countries face the same world rate of interest. This feature provides the key channel through which the effects of policies undertaken in one country are transmitted to the rest of the world.

Much of the recent research in macroeconomics and public finance has been conducted in a closed-economy framework and has emphasized the intertemporal dimensions of tax policies and their effects on saving, investment, labor supply, and growth. In this context special attention has been given to the implications of budget deficits.[1] Our analysis extends the closed-economy framework to a two-country model of the world economy. This extension permits the treatment of questions that could not have been dealt with in a closed-economy framework. Furthermore, we show that open-economy considerations lead to modifications of propositions derived previously in a closed-economy model.[2]

The key result of this chapter is that the consequences of tax policies and the characteristics of the international transmission mechanism depend critically on the precise composition of taxes. Specifically, the international effects of a budget deficit of a given size differ sharply according to the types of taxes used to generate the deficit.[3]

In section 9.1 we develop a simple analytical framework suitable for the analysis of distortionary taxes. This framework is applied in the subsequent

We thank Thomas Krueger and Alan Auerbach for helpful comments.

three sections to an examination of the international effects of budget deficits arising from cuts in consumption taxes, income taxes, and taxes on international borrowing. The analytical framework is extended in section 9.5 to incorporate variable labor supply and to allow for the endogenous response of labor to income taxes. This framework is used in section 9.6, where we examine the effects of budget deficits arising from a cut in income taxes. The chapter concludes in section 9.7 with an integrated summary of the main results.

In what follows we examine the effects of budget deficits under alternative assumptions about the taxes that are reduced. We consider consumption taxes, taxes on income from foreign lending, taxes on income from domestic investment, and taxes on labor income. The analysis extends the closed-economy framework developed by Barro (1979) and exposited in Aschauer and Greenwood (1985). The extension to the open economy is based on Frenkel and Razin (1986b, 1987a).

9.1.   The Analytical Framework

To incorporate the effects of taxes consider a one-good stylized model. With taxes the private sector's periodic budget constraints are

$$(1 + \tau_{c0})C_0 = (1 - \tau_{y0})(\bar{Y}_0 - I_0) + (1 - \tau_{b0})B_0^p - (1 + r_{-1} - \tau_{b0})B_{-1}^p, \quad (1)$$

$$(1 + \tau_{c1})C_1 = (1 - \tau_{y1})(\bar{Y}_1 + F(I_0)) - (1 + r_0 - \tau_{b1})B_0^p, \quad (2)$$

where τ_{ct}, τ_{yt}, and τ_{bt} $(t = 0, 1)$ denote, respectively, the ad-valorem tax rates in period t on consumption, income, and new borrowing. In equation (1) the coefficient of C_0 indicates that the unit cost of consumption is one plus the corresponding ad-valorem tax. The coefficient of the level of income $(\bar{Y}_0 - I_0)$ is one minus the corresponding ad-valorem tax, reflecting taxes on income from existing capital and the inelastic labor supply $(\bar{Y}_0)$ and a tax rebate on negative income from current investment (I_0). This tax is a cash-flow capital income tax (with full expensing of investment, I_0). Our formulation of the tax on international borrowing assumes that the tax applies to new net private-sector borrowing—$(B_0^p - B_{-1}^p)$. This can be verified by noting that the last two terms on the right-hand side of equation (1) could also be written as $(1 - \tau_{b0})(B_0^p - B_{-1}^p) - r_{-1}B_{-1}^p$. In this formulation debt service is exempt from the tax. An analogous interpretation applies to the second budget constraint in equation (2). We note that in the second period there is negative new net borrowing (since past debt is repaid and no new debt is issued); therefore, the term $\tau_{b1} B_0^p$ corresponds to a tax rebate. As is evident from the formulation of equations (1) and (2) the three taxes are linked through an equivalence relation. This equivalence implies that the effect on the real equilibrium of any combination of the three taxes can be duplicated by a policy consisting of any two of them. Our formulation reveals that the celebrated equivalence between consumption and income tax developed in the closed-economy context (see Auerbach and Kotlikoff, 1987) does not carry over to the open-economy context.[4] In what follows we use the equivalence property to suppress the tax on international borrowing. Thus, we set $\tau_{b0} = \tau_{b1} = 0$.

With consumption and income taxes, the periodic budget constraints of the government are

$$G_0 = B_0^g + \tau_{c0} C_0 + \tau_{y0}(\bar{Y}_0 - I_0) - (1 + r_{-1})B_{-1}^g, \tag{3}$$

$$G_1 = \tau_{c1} C_1 + \tau_{y1}(\bar{Y}_1 + F(I_0)) - (1 + r_0)B_0^g. \tag{4}$$

The private-sector periodic budget constraints can be combined in order to yield the consolidated life-time budget constraint.[5] Adding equation (2), multiplied by α_1, to equation (1) and dividing and resultant equation by $(1 + \tau_{c0})$ yields

$$C_0 + \alpha_{\tau 1} C_1 = \frac{(1 - \tau_{y0})}{(1 + \tau_{c0})} \bar{Y}_0 + \frac{(1 - \tau_{y1})}{(1 + \tau_{c0})} \alpha_1 \bar{Y}_1$$

$$+ \frac{(1 - \tau_{y0})}{(1 + \tau_{c0})} [\alpha_{11} F(I_0) - I_0] - \frac{(1 + r_{-1})}{(1 + \tau_{c0})} B_{-1}^p, \tag{5}$$

where

$$\alpha_{\tau 1} = \frac{(1 + \tau_{c1})}{(1 + \tau_{c0})} \alpha_1, \qquad \alpha_{11} = \frac{(1 - \tau_{y1})}{(1 - \tau_{y0})} \alpha_1.$$

For subsequent use we recall that the world discount factor is denoted $\alpha_1 = 1/(1 + r_0)$.

Equation (5) is the private-sector consolidated budget constraint that incorporates the role of taxes. The key point to emphasize is that the discount factors applicable to future-period quantities are the tax-inclusive discount factors. These are the *effective discount factors* relevant for private-sector decisions. Accordingly, $\alpha_{\tau 1}$ measures the effective intertemporal price of C_1 in terms of C_0. This price reflects the prevailing tax structure. It is governed by the time profiles of the consumption tax (reflected by the ratio $(1 + \tau_{c1})/(1 + \tau_{c0})$).

Analogously, the effective discount factor applicable for investment decisions is α_{11}. This effective discount factor is governed by the time profiles of the taxes on capital income. It does not depend on the time profile of the tax on consumption.

This dependence of the effective discount factors on the time profiles of the various taxes reflects the non-Ricardian feature of the model. A budget deficit arising from a current tax cut must be followed by a future tax hike in order to assure government solvency. This change in the time profile of taxes alters the effective discount factors. This provides for the principal channel through which budget deficits affect the intertemporal allocation of consumption and investment.

Finally, we note that if the time profile of any given tax is flat (so that $\tau_{c0} = \tau_{c1}$ or $\tau_{y0} = \tau_{y1}$), then this tax is nondistortionary and its impact is similar to that of a lump-sum tax. This convenient property underlies our choice of the cash-flow formulation of the income tax.

9.2. Deficits with Consumption Taxes

Consider the effects of a budget deficit induced by a cut in the tax on consumption. We note in passing that this consumption tax is equivalent to a value-added tax system (VAT) under which investment and exports are exempt. In order to isolate the effect of this tax cut, we assume that all other taxes are zero. We also assume that the paths of foreign taxes are flat (so that the foreign tax system does not introduce a distortion) and that the foreign government runs a balanced budget (so that changes in the world rate of interest do not affect the foreign government's solvency).

The initial equilibrium is described in figure 9.1 by point A. The downward sloping schedules portray the desired ratio of current-period to future-period consumption. We assume that the utility functions are homothetic and therefore the desired consumption ratios depend only on the rate of interest. The world relative demand is denoted by D^w, where

$$D^w = c_0^w/c_1^w = (c_0 + c_0^*)/(c_1 + c_1^*).$$

This quantity is a weighted average of the two countries' relative demands, $D = c_0/c$ and $D^* = c_0^*/c_1^*$. Accordingly,

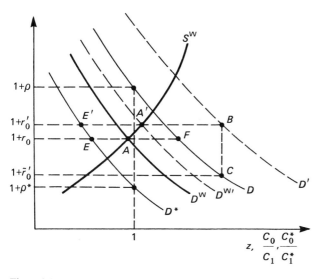

Figure 9.1
The effects of a budget deficit arising from a cut in consumption taxes.

$$D^w = \mu_d D + (1 - \mu_d)D^*,$$

where the domestic country's weight is

$$\mu_d = \frac{c_1}{c_1 + c_1^*}.$$

The upward sloping S^w schedule is the world relative supply of current- to future-period output of net investment and government spending. Its positive slope reflects the fact that investment falls when the rate of interest rises. In this figure the vertical axis measures the (tax free) world rate of interest, which is initially r_0. The schedules pertaining to the initial equilibrium (D, D^*, D^w, and S^w) are drawn for the given initial configuration of taxes. A reduction in the current tax on consumption from τ_{c0} to τ'_{c0} and a corresponding rise in the future tax from τ_{c1} to τ'_{c1} (necessary to restore government solvency) raises the effective discount factor applicable to consumption, $\alpha_{\tau 1}$ (that is, lowers the effective rate of interest) and induces a substitution toward current consumption. Thus, for each and every value of the world rate of interest, the domestic (relative) demand schedule shifts to the right from D to D'. The proportional vertical displacement of the schedule equals the proportional rise in the effective discount factor. This proportion is $[(1 + \tau'_{c1})/(1 + \tau_{c1})][(1 + \tau_{c0})/(1 + \tau'_{c0})]$. Associated with the new domestic relative demand, the new world relative demand also shifts to the right from D^w to $D^{w'}$. Furthermore, the proportional displacement of the world relative demand schedule is smaller than the corresponding displacement of the domestic relative demand schedule.[5a]

A rise in the effective discount factor applicable to consumption decisions, from $\alpha_{\tau1}$ to $\alpha'_{\tau1}$, does not affect the effective discount factor applicable to investment decisions. Therefore, the relative supply schedule in figure 9.1 remains intact. Hence the equilibrium world rate of interest rises from r_0 to r'_0. This higher world rate of interest discourages domestic investment as well as investment in the foreign country and results in a positive cross-country correlation of investment.

To determine the incidence of this change in the time-profile of taxes on the domestic effective rate of interest we recall that the percentage vertical displacement of the D schedule equals the tax-induced percentage change in the effective discount factor. This change is represented by the distance BC in figure 9.1. Accordingly, in order to determine the new equilibrium value of the domestic effective rate of interest, we subtract from $1 + r'_0$ the distance BC. This yields $1 + \tilde{r}'_0$ in figure 9.1. Evidently, the new equilibrium effective rate of interest $\tilde{r}'_0$ is lower than the initial rate r_0 since the vertical displacement of D^w is smaller than BC, and since the percentage fall in the world discount factor is even smaller than the vertical displacement of D^w.

Since in the new equilibrium world rate of interest rises, it induces intertemporal substitution in foreign consumption toward future consumption and, thereby, results in a higher growth rate of foreign consumption (represented by the move from point E to point E' in figure 9.1). By similar reasoning, the fall in the domestic effective rate of interest induces intertemporal substitution in domestic consumption toward current consumption, which lowers the growth rate of domestic consumption (represented by the move from point F to point F' in figure 9.1). Finally, we note that even though the growth rate of foreign consumption rises, the growth rate of world consumption falls (as represented by the move from point A to point A' in figure 9.1). This decline reflects the fall in world investment.

By influencing the world rate of interest the domestic budget deficit is transmitted internationally. In general, due to possible conflicts between income and substitution effects induced by the tax policy and by the interest rate changes, the effects of the budget deficit on the *levels* of consumption and the trade balance are not clear-cut. However, if the foreign economy has a flat tax profile, then, ruling out a backward bending saving function, the rise in the world rate of interest operates to reduce current foreign consumption. In this case, since world investment falls while output is unchanged, the market-clearing condition for world output implies that domestic consumption rises. We conclude that if the intertemporal elasticities of substitution between current and future consumption are relatively low, then the correlation between changes in domestic and foreign consumption consequent on the budget deficit may be positive or negative. On the other hand, if the elasticities of substitution are relatively high, then the budget deficit results in a negative correlation between domestic and foreign levels of consumption.

Finally, in the case for which the foreign saving function does not bend backward, foreign absorption (consumption plus investment) falls and, therefore, the foreign economy's trade account improves. This improvement is mirrored by a corresponding deterioration in the domestic balance of trade.

9.3.   Deficits with Income Taxes

We now consider the effects of a deficit arising from a current cut in taxes on income. Assuming that all other taxes are zero, this tax cut must be accompanied by a corresponding rise in future taxes. Accordingly, suppose that the time profile of taxes be changed from (τ_{y0}, τ_{y1}) to a steeper profile (τ'_{y0}, τ'_{y1}). The initial equilibrium is described by point A in figure 9.2. Since the taxes τ_{y0} and τ_{y1} do not influence the effective discount factor applicable to consumption decisions, $\alpha_{\tau1}$, changes in the time profile of this tax do not alter the desired ratio of intertemporal consumption. Therefore, the relative demand schedules in figure 9.2 remain intact.

Turning to the supply side, we note that, in analogy with the construction of the world relative-demand schedule, the world relative-supply schedule is also a weighted average of the two countries' schedules, S and S^*. Accordingly, $S^w = \mu_s S + (1 - \mu_s) S^*$, where the domestic-country weight is

$$\mu_s = \frac{\bar{Y}_1 + F(I_0) - G_1}{\bar{Y}_1 + F(I_0) - G_1 + \bar{Y}_1^* + F^*(I_0^*) - G_1^*} = \frac{\bar{Y}_1 + F(I_0) - G_1}{C_1 + C_1^*}.$$

By lowering the effective discount factor relevant to investment decisions, α_{11}, the budget deficit displaces the domestic relative supply schedule

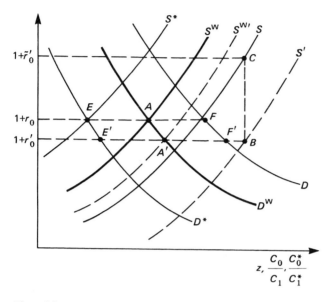

Figure 9.2
The effects of a budget deficit arising from a cut in income tax: Inelastic Labor Supply.

downward from S to S'. The proportional displacement is equal to $(1 - \tau'_{y1})(1 - \tau_{y0})/(1 - \tau_{y1})(1 - \tau'_{y0})$, which measures the percentage change in α_{11}. The proportional downward displacement of the *world* relative supply schedule can be shown to be smaller than this quantity.

The new equilibrium obtains at the intersection between the (unchanged) world relative-demand schedule, D^w, and the new world relative-supply schedule, $S^{w'}$. This equilibrium is indicated by point A', at which the world rate of interest falls, from r_0 to r'_0, and (one plus) the effective interest rate applicable to domestic investment rises by the proportion $(1 + \tilde{r}'_0)/(1 + r'_0)$. This rise is indicated by the distance BC corresponding to the vertical displacement of the domestic relative-supply schedule. In the new equilibrium the rates of growth of domestic and foreign consumption fall. This is indicated by the respective moves from points F to F' and E and E'. As a result, the rate of growth of world consumption must also fall. In view of the fall in the world rate of interest from r_0 to r'_0, foreign investment rises and, in view of the rise in the effective domestic rate of inerest from r_0 to $\tilde{r}'_0$, domestic investment falls. Thus, a deficit arising from a cut in taxes on income from capital crowds out domestic investment and crowds in foreign investment. These changes result in a negative correlation between domestic and foreign investment, and in a positive correlation between domestic and foreign rates of growth of consumption.

The effects of this cut in taxes on the level of domestic consumption are unambiguous if the initial equilibrium is undistorted (i.e., the initial tax profile is flat). The reason is that the fall in the world rate of interest raises current consumption by increasing wealth (through the increased value of the discounted sum of GDPs) and by inducing intertemporal substitution. Similarly, if the time profile of foreign taxes is also flat, the fall in the world rate of interest raises foreign consumption for the same reasons. It follows that under these circumstances the domestic budget deficits crowds in both domestic and foreign private-sector consumption and results in a positive cross-country correlation between the levels of consumption.

It is also noteworthy that, in contrast with the effects of a cut in consumption taxes, the reduction in taxes on income from capital improves the domestic-country trade balance. This improvement of the domestic balance of trade is the counterpart to the deterioration in the foreign trade account consequent on the rise in foreign absorption (consumption plus investment).

The foregoing analysis demonstrated that consumption-tax policies influence the equilibrium in the world economy by altering the relative-demand schedules whereas capital-income tax policies influence the equilibrium by altering the relative-supply schedules. With fixed labor supply, as is evident from the budget constraints (1) and (2), a tax on international borrowing is equivalent to a combination of consumption and capital-income taxes. It follows that such a tax policy influences the equilibrium by altering both the relative-demand and the relative-supply schedules. The effects of a deficit arising from a cut in taxes on international borrowing are, therefore, a combination of the effects of cuts in both consumption and capital-income taxes. Without going through the detailed derivations, we summarize the results in table 9.1.

9.4. Variable Labor Supply: The Analytical Framework

In this section we extend the stylized model to allow for a variable labor supply and focus on income taxes. We consider the effects of a budget deficit arising from a cut in current taxes on labor income. In order to

Table 9.1
The effects of domestic budget deficits arising from a cut in taxes on international borrowing, capital income, and labor income[a]

Tax cut on	g_c^w	r_0	$\tilde{r}_0$	g_c	g_c^*	I_0	I_0^*	C_0	C_0^*	$(TA)_0$
Consumption	−	+	−	−	+	−	−	+	−	−
International borrowing	+ if $\mu_s > \mu_d$									
	− + if $\mu_s < \mu_d$	+	−	−	+	+	−	?	−	−
Income	−	−	+	−	−	−	+	?	+	+

a. g_c^w, g_c, and g_c^* denote, respectively, the world, the domestic, and the foreign growth rates of consumption. $\tilde{r}_0$ denotes the effective domestic rate of interest applicable to consumption decisions (except for the case of a capital income tax for which consumption depends on the world rate r_0). This effective rate also governs domestic investment decisions (except for the case of consumption taxes for which domestic investment depends on the world rate of interest r_0). If $\mu_s > \mu_d$, then the (second-period) domestic trade account is in a surplus and vice versa. The ambiguities in the effects of taxes on domestic consumption reflect conflicting substitution and wealth effects. Domestic consumption rises if the substitution effect dominates the wealth effect. The latter depends on the initial borrowing needs position. The assumption underlying the direction of the changes in the *levels* of consumption and the trade account is the absence of backward bending saving functions.

focus on this effect, we abstract from other taxes. Further, in order to allow for endogenous labor supply and variable output, we modify the utility function and the production function.

Normalizing total endowment of time in each period t to unity, let the fraction of time spent on labor be l_t. Correspondingly, the fraction of time left for leisure is $1 - l_t$. We assume that lifetime utility is a function of four "goods": ordinary consumption, (C_0, C_1) and leisure consumption ($1 - l_0, 1 - l_1$). In order to facilitate the exposition suppose that the utility function is separable between ordinary consumption and leisure, and let each subutility be homothetic. These assumptions imply that the utility-maximizing ratio of consumption in the two consecutive periods depends only on the rate of interest; likewise, the utility-maximizing ratio of leisure in the two consecutive periods depends only on the ratio of wages (net of tax).

As in the previous sections, the individual who has access to the world capital market maximizes lifetime utility subject to the consolidated lifetime budget constraint. With variable labor supply it is convenient to include in the definition of lifetime spending the imputed spending on leisure. Correspondingly, the definition of wealth includes the imputed value of labor endowment. Thus, the lifetime budget constraint is

$$C_0 + (1 - \tau_{y0})(1 - l_0)w_{y0} + \alpha_1[C_1 + (1 - \tau_{y1})(1 - l_1)w_{y1}]$$

$$= (1 - \tau_{y0})(w_{y0} + r_{k0}K_0 - I_0) \tag{6}$$

$$+ (1 - \tau_{y1})\alpha_1[w_{y1} + r_{k1}(K_0 + K(I_0))] - (1 + r_{-1})B^p_{-1} = W_0,$$

where τ_{yt}, w_{yt}, and r_{kt} denote, respectively, the tax rates on income, the wage rate, and the rental rate on capital in period t ($t = 0, 1$), and where K_0 denotes the initial endowment of capital. As indicated in (6) the individual lifetime (full) income, that is, the individual wealth (W_0), is the discounted sum of the value of time endowment (net of taxes) and of capital income (net of initial debt committment). Capital income in the current period is the rental on existing capital, $r_{k0}K_0$, minus investment, I_0; correspondingly, the stock of capital in the subsequent period is $K_0 + K(I_0)$.

Maximization of the utility function subject to the lifetime budget constraint yields the demand functions for ordinary consumption and for leisure in each period. These demand functions depend on the three relative prices (net wages in each of the two periods and the discount factor), and on wealth. Accordingly, the labor supply functions (which are inversely related to the leisure demand functions) can be written as

$$l_0 = l_0((1 - \tau_{y0})w_{y0}, \alpha_1, \alpha_1(1 - \tau_{y1})w_{y1}; W_0), \tag{7}$$

$$l_1 = l_1((1 - \tau_{y0})w_{y0}, \alpha_1, \alpha_1(1 - \tau_{y1})w_{y1}; W_0). \tag{8}$$

The assumption that leisure is not a Giffen good implies that a rise in the current period net wage raises l_0 and a rise in the (discounted value of) future net wage raises l_1. Assuming that the amounts of leisure consumed in two consecutive periods are gross-substitutes implies that for a given level of wealth a current tax cut lowers future labor supply while a future tax cut lowers current labor supply. This specification will be useful in the subsequent analysis of the effects of changes in the time-profile of taxes on labor income.

In each period the level of outputs Y_0 and Y_1 depends on labor and capital inputs. In order to simplify the exposition we assume linear production functions. Thus, let

$$Y_0 = a_0l_0 + b_0K_0, \tag{9}$$

$$Y_1 = a_1l_1 + b_1[K_0 + K(I_0)]. \tag{10}$$

The assumption that factor markets are competitive implies that in equilibrium the wage rates and the rental rates equal the corresponding marginal productivities of labor and capital, respectively. Thus,

$$w_{y0} = a_0, \quad w_{y1} = a_1, \quad r_{k0} = b_0, \quad r_{k1} = b_1. \tag{11}$$

As usual, profit-maximizing investment implies equality between the marginal cost of capital, $(1 + r_0)$, and the marginal return on the investment, which is the product of the marginal product of investment in capital formation and the discounted sum of the rental rates on capital. Hence, in the present two-period model, profit maximization requires that

$$r_{k1} K'(I_0) = 1 + r_0. \tag{12}$$

In order to close the model we note that the present-value budget constraint of the government is

$$G_0 + \alpha_1 G_1 = \tau_{y0} w_{y0} l_0 + \alpha_1 \tau_{y1} w_{y1} l_1 - (1 + r_{-1}) B^g_{-1}. \tag{13}$$

Combining the private sector lifetime constraint (6) with the government present-value constraint (13), and making use of the supply-side equations (8)–(10), yields the economy's consolidated budget constraint, in which the discounted sum of consumption equals V_0, where

$$C_0 + \alpha_1 C_1 = [a_0 l_0 + b_0 K_0 - G_0 - I_0]$$
$$+ \alpha_1 [a_1 l_1 + b_1 (K_0 + K(I_0)) - G_1] - (1 + r_{-1}) B_{-1} \tag{14}$$
$$= V_0.$$

The right-hand side of equation (14) measures the value of the constraint, V_0, relevant for the economy as a whole. As with the previous case a key property of the specification of this constraint is that it is evaluated by using undistorted prices. Thus, in comparison with the private-sector constraint (6) the wages used in (14) for evaluating leisure and income are the tax-free wages. Obviously, the wages that appear as arguments in the consumption and leisure demand (labor supply) functions, C_0, C_1, l_0, and l_1, are the after-tax wages.

In order to analyze the equilibrium of the system we assume that the foreign economy has a similar structure of production, consumption, and taxes. The initial equilibrium of the system is described by point A in figure 9.3. As before, the downward sloping schedules D and D^* denote the domestic and foreign relative demands for (ordinary goods) consumption

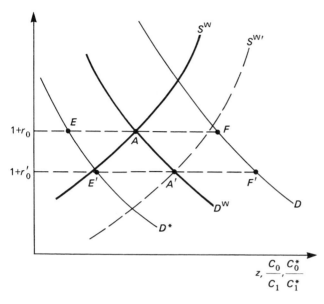

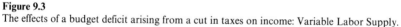

Figure 9.3
The effects of a budget deficit arising from a cut in taxes on income: Variable Labor Supply.

in the two periods, and the schedule D^w is the weighted average of the domestic and foreign relative demands. The negative slopes of the schedules reflect the intertemporal substitution arising from changes in the rate of interest. The positively sloped schedule, S^w, reflects the response of z to the rate of interest, where, as before, z measures the ratio of world GDP net of investment and government spending in the two consecutive periods. That is,

$$z = \frac{(a_0 l_0 + b_0 K_0 - I_0 - G_0) + (a_0^* l_0^* + b_0^* K_0^* - I_0^* - G_0^*)}{[a_1 l_1 + b_1 (K_0 + K(I_0)) - G_1] + [a_1^* l_1^* + b_1^* (K_0^* + K^*(I_0^*)) - G_1^*]}.$$

$$(15)$$

The S^w schedule is drawn with a positive slope for convenience. In fact changes in the rate of interest affect the intertemporal prices of leisure and of ordinary goods as well as wealth. These changes may alter the supply of labor in a way that more than offsets the effect of the induced changes in investment on z. In that case the S^w schedule is negatively sloped, but as long as it is steeper than the world relative demand schedule, our subsequent analysis remains intact.

9.5. Deficits with Variable Labor Supply

Consider the effect of a budget deficit arising from a current reduction in the tax (τ_{y0}) on income (accompanied by a future rise in the tax, τ_{y1}). The assumption that the homothetic utility functions are separable between leisure and ordinary consumption implies that for a given rate of interest the change in the time-profile of wages (net of taxes) does not alter the desired ratios of ordinary consumption in the two consecutive periods. Thus, the budget deficit does not alter the position of the relative demand schedules in figure 9.3.

On the other hand, the assumption that the amounts of leisure consumed in the two periods are gross substitutes ensures that the rise in the current net wage and the fall in the future net wage raises the current labor supply, l_0, and lowers the future labor supply, l_1. As a result, the domestic relative-supply schedule (not drawn) shifts to the right. Therefore, as seen from equation (15), this change in the time-profile of taxes raises the value of z for any given rate of interest. This is shown by the righward shift of the world relative supply schedule from S^w to $S^{w\prime}$ in figure 9.3.

The new equilibrium shifts from point A to point A', the world rate of interest falls from r_0 to r_0', and the rates of growth of domestic, foreign, and world consumption fall. The lower rate of interest induces a positive correlation between growth rates of consumption. It also stimulates investment in both countries and, therefore, induces a positive correlation between domestic and foreign rates of investment.

Finally, in the present framework the budget deficit may cause an improvement in the balance of trade. For example, if the foreign labor supply does not respond appreciably (positively) to the fall in the rate of interest, and, correspondingly, if the foreign GDP (net of government spending) does not rise much, then the rise in foreign absorption (consumption plus investment) worsens the foreign trade balance and, correspondingly, improves the domestic balance of trade. Thus, in this case, the budget deficit causes an improvement in the trade account. This improvement reflects the rise in current period output induced by the stimulative policy of the lower taxes on labor income.

9.6. Budget Deficits: Overview

The important role attached to the intertemporal substitution effects suggests that the various distortionary taxes can be usefully divided according to whether they induce excess demand for current goods or for future goods or, equivalently, whether they stimulate current external borrowing (national dissaving) or lending (national saving). Tax policy that induces an excess demand for current goods by raising current consumption or investment or by lowering current GDP relative to future GDP is classified as a *proborrowing* policy, and tax policy that creates an excess supply of current goods by discouraging current consumption or investment or by raising current GDP relative to future GDP is classified as a *prolending* policy. Alternatively, the various tax policies associated with the budget deficit can be classified into expansionary *supply-shift* policies and expansionary *demand-shift* policies. Accordingly, a deficit arising from a cut in taxes on income from capital or labor (that is, a cut in income tax) reflects supply-shift policies, whereas a deficit arising from the cut in consumption tax (valued-added tax) reflects demand-shift policy and the latter is a proborrowing policy. From this classification we note that a budget deficit arising from a cut in taxes on international borrowing contains elements of both supply- and demand-shift policies. It could be shown, however, that the demand-shift component dominates, so that a cut in the tax on international borrowing is a proborrowing policy.[6]

The results of the analysis are summarized in table 9.1. It is seen that the effects of the budget deficit on the world rate of interest, r_0, depend on whether the deficit arises from a proborrowing or a prolending tax cut. A cut in current taxes on consumption and on international borrowing is a proborrowing tax policy that raises the world rate of interest. On the other hand, a cut in current taxes on capital income and on labor income is a prolending tax policy that lowers the world rate of interest.

The table also shows that in the case of consumption and capital-income taxes domestic investment falls, while in the case of taxes on international borrowing and labor income investment rises.

The results reported in the table show that whether the tax cut is proborrowing or prolending, the budget deficit always lowers the growth rate of domestic consumption, $g_c = (C_1/C_0) - 1$. On the other hand, the international transmission of the effects of the deficit depends on whether the deficit arises from a proborrowing or prolending tax policy. If the tax policy is a proborrowing policy, then the growth rate of foreign consumption rises and foreign investment falls, and conversely if the tax policy is a prolending policy.

Table 9.1 also reports that the changes in the growth rates of world consumption g_c^w equal $(1/z) - 1$ (which is equal the growth rate of world GDP net of investment and government spending). As is seen, the direction of the change in the growth rate of world consumption depends on the characteristics of the taxes that are changed. Since the various taxes influence the levels of current and future consumption, investment, and GDP, the net effects reflect the interactions among these changes. Accordingly, the growth rate of world consumption rises if the (second-period) domestic trade account is in a surplus and the budget deficit arises from a cut in taxes on international borrowing. On the other hand, the growth rate of world consumption falls if the tax cut on international borrowing occurs in the presence of a (second-period) domestic trade-account deficit or if the budget deficit stems from a cut in the other taxes.

Expressed in terms of correlations, table 9.1 reveals that a budget deficit arising from a proborrowing tax policy results in *negative* cross-country correlations between growth rates of consumption. On the other hand, a budget deficit arising from a prolending tax policy results in *positive* cross-country correlations between the growth rates of consumption. As for the cross-country correlations between levels of investment, table 9.1 shows that this correlation is positive if the deficit arises from a cut in taxes on consumption or labor income, and that it is negative if the budget deficit stems from a cut in taxes on international borrowing and capital income.

The effects of the budget deficit on the *levels* of domestic and foreign consumption and on the balance of trade depend in general on the shape of the initial time-profile of taxes, on the initial borrowing needs of the country (being positive or negative), and on the size of the intertemporal elasticity of substitution. The signs of the effects indicated in the last three columns in table 9.1 are based on the assumption that the initial tax profile is flat and that the saving functions are not backward bending. With these assumptions a budget deficit arising from a proborrowing tax policy lowers foreign consumption and worsens the domestic balance of trade, while a budget deficit arising from a prolending tax policy raises foreign consumption and improves the domestic balance of trade.

Notes

1. Representative research emphasizing intertemporal considerations in a closed-economy framework is found in Barro (1974, 1979), Feldstein (1974), and King (1983) and Judd (1987). For recent surveys and integrations of the various issues see Aschauer and Greenwood (1985) and Auerbach and Kotlikoff (1987).

2. Examples of previous analyses of various aspects of the effects of distortionary taxes in the context of a small open economy are found in Aschauer and Greenwood (1985), Greenwood and Kimbrough (1985), and Razin and Svensson (1983). By adopting a two-country model we deal with the interdependencies within the world economy, an issue that could not be addressed in the small-country framework. Some aspects of the interdependencies are examined in van Wijnbergen (1986).

3. Elsewhere we analyzed in detail the effects of government spending on the equilibrium in the world economy and on the international transmission mechanism; see Frenkel and Razin (1985, 1986b). In Frenkel and Razin (1987b) we analyzed the international effects of revenue-neutral tax reforms.

4. In a recent tax-reform proposal Hall and Rabushka (1983) advocate the adoption of a consumption-tax system à la Fisher (1939). In specifying the implementation of the consumption tax and its virtues over the conventional income tax they use the closed-economy equivalence relation between a consumption tax and a cash-flow income tax (capital-income tax with expensing plus a labor-income tax). Being confined to a closed-economy framework, they abstract from the role that taxes on international borrowing play in this tax-equivalence relation. For a comprehensive discussion of the closed-economy tax-equivalence propositions see Auerbach and Kotlikoff (1987).

5. Our specification in equations (1)–(4) did not allow for government bond selling to the domestic private sector. This simplifying assumption was made for convenience only, without affecting the analysis. To see this point let $-B^p$ denote foreign bonds purchased by the domestic private sector, $-B^g$ denote foreign bonds purchased by the domestic government, and A^g denote domestic government bonds purchased by the domestic private sector. In the presence of a tax on international borrowing, arbitrage between government bonds and foreign bonds implies

$$\frac{1 + r_0 - \tau_{b1}}{1 - \tau_{b0}} = 1 + r_0^g, \qquad \frac{1 + r_{-1} - \tau_{b0}}{1 - \tau_{b,-1}} = 1 + r_{-1}^g,$$

where r^g is the market rate of interest on government bonds sold to the domestic private sector. Accordingly we can subtract $[A_0^g - (1 + r_{-1}^g)A_{-1}^g]$ from the right-hand side of equation (1) and add $[(1 + r_0^g)A_0^g]$ to the right-hand side of equation (2). Correspondingly, we can add the term $[A_0^g - (1 + r_{-1}^g)A_{-1}^g]$ to the right-hand side of equation (3) and subtract $[(1 + r_0^g)A_0^g]$ from the right-hand side of equation (4). The reader can check that these changes do not affect the results, and, for simplicity, henceforth we set $A_{-1}^g = A_0^g = 0$.

5a. To verify this point we note that $\hat{D}^W = [C_0/(C_0 + C_0^*)]\hat{D} + [C_0/(C_0 + C_0^*)) - (C_1/(C_1 + C_1^*))]\hat{C}_1$. Accordingly the proportional change in the world relative demand is composed of two components. The first corresponds to the proportional shift in the domestic demand. The latter reflects the difference between domestic and foreign saving propensities. If the current trade-balance deficit arises from low domestic savings, since the term $\hat{C}_1$ is negative, the displacement of D exceeds that of D^W.

6. For open-economy analyses emphasizing the pure wealth effects of lump-sum nondistortionary tax policies see Blanchard (1985), Buiter (1986), Frenkel and Razin (1986a), and Persson (1985). In these models the pure wealth effects of budget deficits arise from differences between the time horizons of individuals and of the economy at large.

References

Aschauer, David A., and Jeremy Greenwood. "Macroeconomic Effects of Fiscal Policy," in Karl Brunner and Alan Meltzer (eds.), *The New Monetary Economics: Fiscal Issues and Unemployment*, Carnegie-Rochester Conference Series on Public Policy 23, 1985, pp. 91–138.

Auerbach, Alan J., and Laurence J. Kotlikoff. *Dynamic Fiscal Policy*, New York: Cambridge University Press, 1987.

Barro, Robert J. "Are Government Bonds Net Wealth?" *Journal of Political Economy* 82 (November/December 1974): 1095–1117.

Barro, Robert J. "On the Determination of the Public Debt," *Journal of Political Economy* 87 (Part 1) (October 1979): 940–971.

Blanchard, Olivier. "Debt, Deficits and Finite Horizons," *Journal of Political Economy* 92 (April 1985): 233–247.

Buiter, Willem H. "Fiscal Policy in Open Interdependent Economies," in Assaf Razin and Efraim Sadka (eds.), *Economic Policy in Theory and Practice*, London: Macmillian, 1986.

Feldstein, Martin. "Incidence of a Capital Income Tax in a Growing Economy with Variable Savings Rates," *Review of Economic Studies* 41 (October 1974): 505–513.

Fisher, Irving. "The Double Taxation of Savings," *American Economic Review* 29 (March 1939): 16–33.

Frenkel, Jacob A., and Assaf Razin. "Government Spending, Debt, and International Economic Interdependence," *Economic Journal* 95 (September 1985): 619–636.

Frenkel, Jacob A., and Assaf Razin (1986a). "Fiscal Policies in the World Economy," *Journal of Political Economy* 94 (June 1986): 564–594.

Frenkel, Jacob A., and Assaf Razin (1986b). "Fiscal Policies and Real Exchange Rates in the World Economy," NBER Working Paper Series No. 2065, November 1986.

Frenkel, Jacob A., and Assaf Razin (1987a). *Fiscal Policies and the World Economy*, Cambridge, MA: MIT Press, 1987.

Frenkel, Jacob A., and Assaf Razin (1987b). International Effects of Tax Reforms," prepared for the NBER Summer Institute, Cambridge, MA, August 1987 (forthcoming in *Economic Journal*).

Greenwood, Jeremy and Kent P. Kimbrough. "Captial Controls and Fiscal Policy in the World Economy," *Canadian Journal of Economics* 18 (November 1985): 743–765.

Hall, Robert E., and Alvin Rabushka. *Flat Tax, Simple Tax*, New York: McGraw-Hill, 1983.

Judd, Kenneth L., "A Dynamic Theory of Factor Taxation," *American Economic Review* 77 (May 1987): 42–48.

King, Mervin A. "The Economics of Saving," NBER Working Paper, Series, No. 1247, Cambridge, MA, October 1983.

Persson, Torsten. "Deficits and Intergenerational Welfare in Open Economies," *Journal of International Economics* 19 (1985): 67–84.

Razin, Assaf, and Lars E. O. Svensson. "The Current Account and the Optimal Government Debt," *Journal of International Money and Finance* 2 (August 1983): 215–224.

van Wijnbergen, Sweder. "On Fiscal Deficits, the Real Exchange Rate, and the World Rate of Interest," *Evropean Economic Review*, 30 (October 1986): 1013–1023.

10 Optimal Time-Consistent Fiscal Policy with Finite Lifetimes: Analysis and Extensions

Guillermo A. Calvo and Maurice Obstfeld

10.1. Introduction

Since the appearance of Diamond's seminal paper on national debt (1965), theoretical studies of government budgetary policies have focused increasingly on economies with overlapping generations. With the exception of Samuelson (1967, 1968), however, there have been almost no attempts to develop intertemporal welfare criteria that would determine the best use of fiscal tools in such economies.[1] The standard optimal growth analysis developed by Cass (1965), Koopmans (1965), Ramsey (1928), and others appears inapplicable for this purpose. Its postulates seem to presuppose either a single infinitely lived household or an economy peopled by a never-ending succession of finitely lived, nonoverlapping generations.

In this chapter we show how the Cass-Koopmans-Ramsey framework can be used to evaluate paths of *aggregate* consumption even in models where different generations coexist. Our basic model of the individual is Yaari's (1965) uncertain-lifetime model.[2] For the utilitarian social welfare function we explore in section 10.2, the planning problem facing the government can be decomposed into two subproblems, a standard problem of optimal aggregate capital accumulation and a problem of distributing consumption optimally on each date among the generations alive then. A striking feature of the analysis is that the optimal aggregate growth path depends on the relative weights that the planner places on different generations, but not necessarily on the rate at which individuals themselves subjectively discount utilities accruing in the future. In particular, the optimal long-run interest rate is the planner's generational discount rate. Optimal aggregate growth has these characteristics in our setup even though the planner's own welfare criterion is a function of individuals' lifetime utilities.

In a market economy, the planner must deploy the tools of fiscal policy to place the economy on the optimal path. In section 10.3, we characterize the fiscal policy that decentralizes the optimal command allocation in

A shorter version of this chapter appears in *Econometrica* 56 (1988), under the title "Optimal Time-Consistent Fiscal Policy with Finite Lifetimes." We are grateful for extremely helpful comments from Andrew Abel and David Cass. The suggestions of Torsten Persson, Robert Townsend, Joseph Zeira, two anonymous *Econometrica* referees, and an editor of that journal are also acknowledged with thanks. Financial support was provided by the National Science Foundation and the Alfred P. Sloan Foundation.

a competitive economy with actuarially fair annuities. This optimal fiscal policy is quite complex, requiring age- and date-specific lump-sum transfer payments, but it does not require the issuance of public debt on any date. Decentralizability through lump-sum transfers is suggested, of course, by the second theorem of welfare economics.

Specification of an intertemporal social welfare function is complicated by the possibility that the planner "myopia" discussed by Strotz (1956) leads to dynamically inconsistent optimal plans. This possibility arises in any model with overlapping generations. In section 10.4 we show that some plausible social welfare functions lead to time inconsistency. If one were to insist that optimal plans should be time consistent, our findings would give some guidance regarding admissible social welfare functions.[3] Section 10.5 discusses social welfare functions (which do not respect individual preferences) whose command optima are time consistent but decentralizable only through distortionary taxation.

Even when planner preferences do not in themselves entail time-inconsistent optimal command allocations, optimal fiscal policy may be time inconsistent when the planner does not have available the full array of fiscal tools needed to attain the command optimum. This type of time inconsistency, studied by Kydland and Prescott (1977) and Calvo (1978), among others, arises through the planner's constraints rather than through his preferences (the Strotz case). Section 10.6 shows that optimal fiscal policy can be time inconsistent, even when the planner uses only lump-sum taxation, if the available lump-sum taxes do not bring the economy to the command optimum.[4] Our example of time inconsistency occurs in a finite-horizon economy where the planner must make the same transfer payment on each date to everyone then alive. It appears, however, that this fiscal-policy constraint does not lead to time inconsistency in our example if the planning horizon is infinite.[5]

10.2. An Optimal Utilitarian Allocation

In this section, we derive the optimal intertemporal allocation implied by a utilitarian social welfare function whose arguments are the expected utilities of finitely lived individuals. The aggregate planning problem reduces to the Cass-Koopmans-Ramsey problem of optimal allocation over time with a single representative infinitely lived individual.

10.2.1. The Economy's Structure

An individual born at time v (his "vintage") is uncertain about the length $\tilde{n}$ of his life. Let $F(\cdot)$ denote the cumulative distribution function of the random variable $\tilde{n}$, so that $F(n) = \text{Prob}\{\tilde{n} \leqslant n\}$. Of course, $F(0) = 0$, $\tilde{n}$ has a finite mean, and $\lim_{n \to \infty} F(n) = 1$. Implicit in our notation is the assumption that the distribution of $\tilde{n}$ does not depend on v; in addition, $F(\cdot)$ is assumed to be continuous and piecewise differentiable with an associated probability density function $f(\cdot)$ satisfying $F(n) = \int_0^n f(s)\,ds$. Individuals maximize the expected value over possible lifespans of a discounted integral of future instantaneous utilities. The time-t utility of a vintage-v individual is a function $u(\cdot)$ of consumption $c(v,t)$.[6] If $\delta > 0$ denotes the constant subjective discount rate, expected lifetime utility for an agent born on date v is, as in Yaari (1965),

$$\mu(v) = \int_v^\infty u[c(v,t)][1 - F(t - v)]e^{-\delta(t-v)}\,dt, \tag{1}$$

where $1 - F(t - v)$ is just the probability that an individual born on date v is alive on date t (when his age is $t - v$).

Define $p(n)$ to be the instantaneous death probability faced by an individual of age n:

$$p(n) = f(n)/[1 - F(n)]. \tag{2}$$

Because $f(n) = F'(n)$ and $F(0) = 0$, (2) implies

$$1 - F(n) = \exp\left[-\int_0^n p(s)\,ds \right]. \tag{3}$$

The individual's objective function (1) therefore takes the form

$$\mu(v) = \int_v^\infty u[c(v,t)]\exp\left\{ -\int_0^{t-v} [\delta + p(s)]\,ds \right\}dt. \tag{4}$$

As in Yaari's analysis, the possibility of death leads to a subjective discount rate higher than the pure time preference rate, δ.

Assume now, as in Blanchard (1985), that a new cohort of identical individuals is born each instant and that there is no *aggregate* uncertainty even though each individual's lifespan is stochastic. If the size of each newly born cohort is normalized to unity, where are exactly $1 - F(n)$ individuals of age n alive at any time and this cohort's size declines at rate $p(n)$. Total population, which equals the labor supply, is therefore constant at the level $\int_0^\infty [1 - F(n)]\,dn$ (assumed finite).

On the production side, output is given by $Y[K(t)]$, where $K(t)$ is the economy's stock of nondepreciating capital.[7] Investment $\dot{K}(t)$ is the difference between output and aggregate consumption.

10.2.2. The Planner's Objective

Our planner's objective is the sum of two components. The first is an integral of the lifetime expected utilities of representative agents from each of the generations to be born, as measured from the moment of birth. The second is an integral of the expected utilities, over the remainder of their lifetimes, of representative agents from each of those cohorts currently alive. The remaining expected utility of a surviving cohort representative is, like that of a cohort representative to be born, measured from the perspective of his birthdate. It is also assumed that the planner discounts generations at a rate $\rho > 0$. The generational discount rate ρ need not equal the pure time-preference rate δ at which individuals discount their own (certain) future utilities. Indeed, Ramsey (1928) argued that the planner should not value one generation's welfare more highly than another's; he would have set $\rho = 0$, regardless of the value of δ.

To write this social welfare function, define

$$\Delta(t - v) \equiv \exp[-\delta(t - v)], \qquad P(t - v) \equiv \exp\left[-\int_0^{t-v} p(s)\,ds \right].$$

Then welfare at time $t = 0$ is

$$W(0) = \int_0^\infty \left\{ \int_v^\infty u[c(v,t)]\,\Delta(t - v)\,P(t - v)\,dt \right\} e^{-\rho v}\,dv$$
$$+ \int_{-\infty}^0 \left\{ \int_0^\infty u[c(v,t)]\,\Delta(t - v)\,P(t - v)\,dt \right\} e^{-\rho v}\,dv.$$

$$(5)$$

It may seem unnatural to discount the utility of those already alive back to their birthdates, rather than to the present, in (5). After all, the planner is concerned with their welfare from the present (time $t = 0$) onward. This discounting scheme, however, helps ensure the time consistency of optimal intertemporal command allocations. *Unless those alive and those to be born are treated symmetrically, the planner has an incentive to change the consumption previously planned for unborn generations once they come into existence.*[8] The same consideration leads us to postulate a planner who weights the lifetime utilities of the living and the yet-unborn alike by the factor $e^{-\rho v}$.[9] We examine the time-consistency of optima generated by alternative social welfare functions in section 10.4.

After changing the order of integration, (5) may be written in the alternative form,

$$W(0) = \int_0^\infty \left\{ \int_{-\infty}^t u[c(v,t)]\,\Delta(t-v)\,P(t-v)e^{\rho(t-v)}\,dv \right\} e^{-\rho t}\,dt. \tag{6}$$

The flow of utility for the planner on any date t is the integral over all cohorts of instantaneous utilities discounted by the private discount factor, $\Delta(t-v)\,P(t-v)$, times the planner's discount factor, $e^{\rho(t-v)}$. The integral over all future t of these utility flows, discounted at rate ρ, equals $W(0)$.[10]

10.2.3. The Social Optimum: Necessary Conditions

To solve the planning problem of maximizing (6) subject to constraints, we write (6) in a slightly different form. After a change of variables from vintage v to age $n = t - v$, $W(0)$ becomes

$$W(0) = \int_0^\infty \left\{ \int_0^\infty u[c(t-n,t)]\,\Delta(n)\,P(n)e^{\rho n}\,dn \right\} e^{-\rho t}\,dt, \tag{7}$$

where $c(t-n,t)$ is the consumption of an individual of age n on date t. The planner maximizes (7) subject to the constraints

$$\dot K(t) = Y[K(t)] - \int_0^\infty c(t-n,t)P(n)\,dn, \quad K(t) \geqslant 0, \quad K(0) \text{ given.} \tag{8}$$

We are interested in solutions such that $c(v,t)$ is piecewise continuous and right-hand differentiable with respect to v and t.

The nature of the planning problem is clarified by decomposing it into two stages. Define aggregate consumption

$$C(t) \equiv \int_0^\infty c(t-n,t)P(n)\,dn.$$

Given a level of aggregate consumption on date t, $C(t)$, a maximizing planner must allocate it across individuals so as to maximize the time-t instantaneous utility flow, $\int_0^\infty u[c(t-n,t)]\,\Delta(n)\,P(n)e^{\rho n}\,dn$. We may therefore view the planner as solving this (static) problem first for given $C(t)$, and then choosing the aggregate consumption path $\{C(t)\}_{t=0}^{\infty}$ that maximizes (7) subject to (8) when consumption is allocated optimally across individuals at each point in time.

More formally, define the indirect utility function

$$U[C(t)] = \max_{\{c(t-n,t)\}_{n=0}^{\infty}} \int_0^{\infty} u[c(t-n,t)]\,\Delta(n)\,P(n)e^{\rho n}\,dn \qquad (9)$$

subject to

$$\int_0^{\infty} c(t-n,t)P(n)\,dn \leqslant C(t).$$

Then the planning problem becomes one of maximizing

$$W(0) = \int_0^{\infty} U[C(t)]e^{-\rho t}\,dt \qquad (10)$$

subject to

$$\dot{K}(t) = Y[K(t)] - C(t), \qquad K(t) \geqslant 0, \qquad K(0) \quad \text{given.} \qquad (11)$$

The function $U(\cdot)$ is obviously strictly concave, and it can be viewed as the value function for a dynamic problem in which the age index n plays the role of calendar time. The results of Benveniste and Scheinkman (1979) therefore imply that $U(\cdot)$ is continuously differentiable at $C(t)$, with

$$U'[C(t)] = u'[c(t,t)] \qquad (12)$$

at the optimum.[11] We may thus use optimal control theory to solve stage two of the planning problem, maximization of (10) subject to (11).

To solve stage one of the problem, observe that the necessary conditions for a static optimum are

$$u'[c(t-n,t)]e^{(\rho-\delta)n} = \lambda(t) \qquad (13)$$

for all $n \in [0, \infty)$, where $\lambda(t)$ is a Lagrange multiplier. Conditions (12) and (13) imply together that

$$\lambda(t) = u'[c(t,t)] = U'[C(t)] \qquad (14)$$

at the optimum. In light of (14), the necessary condition for an intertemporally optimal aggregate consumption path $\{C(t)\}_{t=0}^{\infty}$ is (see Arrow and Kurz, 1970)

$$\dot{\lambda}(t) = \lambda(t)\{\rho - Y'[K(t)]\}. \tag{15}$$

Conditions (13) and (15) yield an explicit characterization of the social optimum. By (13), consumption evolves across cohorts on a given date t according to the equation

$$\frac{\partial c(v, t)}{\partial v} = -\frac{u'[c(v, t)]}{u''[c(v, t)]}(\delta - \rho). \tag{16}$$

Condition (13) may be rewritten as $u'[c(v, t)]e^{(\rho - \delta)(t - v)} = \lambda(t)$. Differentiating this with respect to time and combining the result with (15) gives

$$\frac{\partial c(v, t)}{\partial t} = -\frac{u'[c(v, t)]}{u''[c(v, t)]}\{Y'[K(t)] - \delta\}. \tag{17}$$

What is the meaning of equation (16)? Equation (9) shows that the difference $\delta + p(t - v) - \rho$ can be viewed as the *net* rate at which the planner discounts the vintage-v cohort's utility flow $u[c(v, t)]$. If an allocation of aggregate consumption is optimal, there must be no incentive to shift a unit of consumption between cohorts at any time t. Because cohort size rises with rising v at rate $p(t - v)$, however, planner indifference requires that the rate at which the marginal utility of consumption rises as age rises (i.e., as v falls) must equal $\delta - \rho$. This is what equation (16) states. The case $\rho = \delta$ yields an "egalitarian" plan under which all individuals have the same consumption level at any point in time.

The intertemporal allocation condition (17) is identical to the condition achieved in a competitive economy with actuarially fair annuities [see Blanchard, 1985, or equation (22)]. What is the rationale for (17) in a planning context? For a representative agent of vintage v, the sum $\delta + p(t - v)$ is the instantaneous expected-utility cost, at time t, of postponing consumption. If the government shifts one unit of this cohort's consumption into the future, the instantaneous return on the investment per cohort member left alive is $Y'[K(t)] + p(t - v)$ because the proceeds are divided among a smaller group. The rate at which a cohort's marginal utility rises over time must therefore equal $\delta + p(t - v) - Y'[K(t)] - p(t - v) = \delta - Y'[K(t)]$, as specified by (17).

10.2.4. Aggregate Dynamics

If the value function $U(\cdot)$ is twice continuously differentiable for $C(t) > 0$, (14) and (15) may be combined as

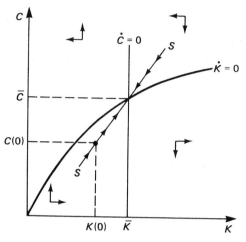

Figure 10.1
The optimal aggregate accumulation path is the convergent path SS leading to $(\bar{C}, \bar{K})$.

$$\dot{C}(t) = -\frac{U'[C(t)]}{U''[C(t)]}\{Y'[K(t)] - \rho\}. \tag{18}$$

Equation (18) and the capital accumulation equation in (11) define a differential-equation system in $C(t)$ and $K(t)$ that also governs the evolution of the economy in the standard Cass-Koopmans-Ramsey representative-agent planning model with time-preference rate ρ. Figure 10.1 shows that the system is characterized by a unique path SS converging to the steady state $(\bar{C}, \bar{K})$ defined by

$$Y'(\bar{K}) = \rho, \qquad \bar{C} = Y(\bar{K}). \tag{19}$$

SS indicates the optimal initial aggregate consumption level $C(0)$ associated with any given initial capital stock $K(0)$.

In general, the dynamic system summarizing the economy's evolution can be written in terms of the costate variable $\lambda(t)$ and $K(t)$. The resulting system is again characterized by a unique optimal saddle-path converging to the steady state specified in (19).

It is noteworthy that $Y'[K(t)]$ converges to the planner discount rate ρ regardless of the rate at which private agents discount their own utility flows (a result also found by Samuelson, 1968). The relative weight that the planner places on different generations thus determines the steady-state interest rate. If the planner placed the same welfare weight on every generation (as recommended by Ramsey), the capital stock would converge to the Golden Rule level, $Y'(\bar{K}) = \rho = 0$.

EXAMPLE   Suppose that the individual utility function $u(c)$ is of the form $u(c) = c^{1-R}/(1 - R)$, $R > 0$, $R \neq 1$. Then for all t, $U[C(t)] = \Phi \cdot C(t)^{1-R}/(1 - R)$, where $\Phi = [\int_0^\infty e^{(\rho-\delta)n/R} P(n)\, dn]^R$. The aggregate consumption path therefore maximizes $\int_0^\infty [C(t)^{1-R}/(1 - R)]e^{-\rho t}\, dt$ subject to (11). Notice that the entire aggregate optimal path is independent of private time preference.

10.3.   Optimal Fiscal Policy

This section shows how fiscal policy must be used to reproduce the optimal utilitarian allocation of section 10.2 in a competitive market economy. Only lump-sum taxes are needed to generate the optimal plan as a competitive equilibrium. The required lump-sum tax scheme is quite complex, however, because the tax an individual pays varies in general according to both his age and calendar time.

10.3.1.   The Market Economy

The market framework we assume is one in which individuals may buy actuarially fair annuities, as in Blanchard (1985).

Individuals are prohibited from dying in debt, and can borrow only if they simultaneously buy insurance against that contingency. There exist insurance companies that buy and issue annuities that pay holders the age-dependent yield $r(t) + p(t - v)$ at time t but expire in the event of the owner's death. Because there are no bequests, those with positive nonhuman wealth will choose to hold it exclusively in the form of annuities, which pay a rate exceeding the market interest rate while the owner lives. Borrowers effectively insure themselves against accidental death by issuing annuities to insurance companies. In short, insurance companies intermediate between all borrowers and lenders and also hold the private sector's net marketable assets, which in the present context will coincide with the capital stock plus any outstanding government debt. Under the assumptions of the preceding section, and with costless free entry into the insurance industry, the insurance premium $p(t - v)$ is actuarially fair and insurance companies make zero profits. The instantaneous effective interest rate faced at time t by an individual born at time v is thus $r(t) + p(t - v)$, where $r(t)$ is the "risk-free" interest rate and $p(t - v)$ is the actuarially fair insurance premium.

Define the market "risk-free" discount factor,

$$R(v, t) = \exp\left[-\int_v^t r(s)\,ds \right].$$

The lifetime problem of an individual born on date v may now be stated as follows: Choose a consumption path $\{c(v, t)\}_{t=v}^{\infty}$ so as to maximize $\int_v^{\infty} u[c(v, t)]\,\Delta(t - v)\,P(t - v)\,dt$ subject to

$$\int_v^{\infty} c(v, t) R(v, t) P(t - v)\,dt \leqslant a(v, v). \tag{20}$$

In (20), $a(v, t)$ is the overall time-t wealth of an agent of vintage v. Wealth is the sum of the present discounted value of wages, the present discounted value of expected future transfer payments from the government, bond holdings, and capital.

We assume that individuals are born holding neither capital nor bonds. Thus, $a(v, v)$ is the discounted integral of future wage payments, $w(t)$, and transfers from the government, $\tau(v, t)$:

$$a(v, v) = \int_v^{\infty} [w(t) + \tau(v, t)] R(v, t) P(t - v)\,dt. \tag{21}$$

Maximization requires individual consumption to follow the differential equation

$$\dot{c}(v, t) = -\frac{u'[c(v, t)]}{u''[c(v, t)]}[r(t) - \delta]. \tag{22}$$

An optimal individual consumption plan obeys (22) while forcing the budget constraint (20) to bind. Note that the death probabilities do not affect the time derivative of consumption along an optimal path.[12]

In a competitive equilibrium $r(t)$ must equal the marginal product of capital, $Y'[K(t)]$, so (22) is identical to (17), the first-order condition governing intertemporal allocation under the optimal plan of the last section. The equality of the two conditions is the key to decentralizing the optimal plan.

10.3.2. Decentralizing the Plan

Given an initial capital stock $K(0)$, the optimal plan generates paths $\{K(t)\}_{t=0}^{\infty}$ for capital and $\{C(t)\}_{t=0}^{\infty}$ for aggregate consumption. These in turn yield paths for the shadow real interest rate $r(t) = Y'[K(t)]$, the shadow wage $w(t) = \{Y[K(t)] - K(t)Y'[K(t)]\}/\int_0^{\infty} P(n)\,dn$, and the shadow present value of per capita wage income. To decentralize the optimal intertemporal allocation, the government must endow each agent at birth with a transfer stream inducing the desired consumption levels when the shadow price paths $\{r(t)\}_{t=0}^{\infty}$ and $\{w(t)\}_{t=0}^{\infty}$ are expected. Let $b(v,t)$ denote the present value of government transfer payments expected by an agent of vintage v at time t given the expected real-interest rate path,

$$b(v,t) \equiv \int_t^{\infty} \tau(v,s)R(t,s)[P(s-v)/P(t-v)]\,ds,$$

and define

$$h(v,t) \equiv \int_t^{\infty} w(s)R(t,s)[P(s-v)/P(t-v)]\,ds.^{13}$$

The centrally planned optimal consumption level for an individual of vintage v at time t is labeled $c^*(v,t)$.

We can write an individual's desired consumption, given his wealth and the expected future interest-rate path, as

$$\hat{c}(v,t) = c[a(v,t); \{r(s)\}_{s=t}^{\infty}], \tag{23}$$

where $a(v,t) = h(v,t) + b(v,t) + k(v,t) + d(v,t)$, the last two symbols denoting holdings of capital and debt, respectively. For a given path of interest rates, the consumption function in (23) is an invertible function of wealth $a(v,t)$ (since an increase in wealth always causes consumption to increase). (Consumption also depends on age; the notation suppresses this.)

At $t = 0$, the government must announce future paths of transfer payments for all agents alive then. These transfer paths decentralize the plan only if their present values, $b(v,0)$ ($v \leqslant 0$), satisfy,

$$c[h(0,0) + b(0,0); \{r(t)\}_{t=0}^{\infty}] = c^*(0,0) \tag{24}$$

and

$$c[h(v,0) + b(v,0) + k(v,0) + d(v,0); \{r(t)\}_{t=0}^{\infty}] = c^*(v,0) \tag{25}$$

(for all $v < 0$), where individuals use the interest-rate and wage paths associated with the plan in their calculations.

After the transfer streams for those alive at $t = 0$ are announced by the government, its only remaining choice variables are the transfer payments to be made to those born on subsequent dates. To support the optimal plan, these must be set so that their present values, $b(v, v)$ ($v > 0$), satisfy

$$c[h(v, v) + b(v, v); \{r(t)\}_{t=v}^{\infty}] = c^*(v, v).$$

The competitive equilibrium that results from the transfer scheme described replicates the optimal plan. To verify this, we must show that $\hat{c}(v, t) = c^*(v, t)$ for all $t \geqslant 0$ and $v \leqslant t$. This equality holds by construction for $t = 0$ and for $t = v$. For $v \leqslant 0$, condition (22), which follows from individual optimization, implies that

$$u'[\hat{c}(v, t)] = u'[c^*(v, 0)] \exp\left\{\int_0^t [\delta - r(s)] \, ds\right\}$$

(since $\dot{u}' = u''\dot{c}$). Optimality condition (17), however, implies that

$$u'[c^*(v, t)] = u'[c^*(v, 0)] \exp\left\{\int_0^t \{\delta - Y'[K(s)]\} \, ds\right\}$$

and because $r(s) = Y'[K(s)]$, $\hat{c}(v, t) = c^*(v, t)$. The same argument shows thatn $\hat{c}(v, t) = c^*(v, t)$ for $v > 0$.

Notice that the initial consumption choices induced by an optimal fiscal policy force the intercohort allocation condition (16) to hold automatically. For agents alive at $t = 0$, the planner chooses initial consumption levels so that $u'[c^*(v, 0)] = u'[c^*(0, 0)]e^{(\rho - \delta)v}$ [by (16)]. Therefore

$$u'[c^*(v, t)] = u'[c^*(0, 0)] \exp[(\rho - \delta)v] \exp\left\{\int_0^t [\delta - r(s)] \, ds\right\} \qquad (26)$$

for $v \leqslant 0$. For $v > 0$, $c^*(v, v)$ is chosen by (14) and (15) so that

$$u'[c^*(v, v)] = u'[c^*(0, 0)] \exp\left\{\int_0^v [\rho - r(s)] \, ds\right\}.$$

Since

$$u'[c^*(v, t)] = u'[c^*(v, v)] \exp\left\{\int_v^t [\delta - r(s)] \, ds\right\},$$

equation (26) holds for agents born after $t = 0$ as well. Differentiation of (26) with respect to v, however, gives (16).

10.3.3. The Government Budget Constraint

In the setting described above, the government can always satisfy its intertemporal budget constraint when it undertakes a fiscal policy that decentralizes the optimal allocation. This result is essentially a consequence of Walras's law: Since markets clear on each date and all private agents respect their budget constraints, the government must respect its constraint as well.

If initial government debt is assumed to be zero for simplicity, the government's budget constraint can be written

$$\int_{-\infty}^{0} b(v,0)P(-v)\,dv + \int_{0}^{\infty} b(v,v)R(0,v)\,dv = 0. \tag{27}$$

In words, (27) states that the present discounted value of transfers paid out to those alive at $t = 0$ and to those born later must be zero. Even though the interest rate faced by the government is the "risk-free" rate $r(t)$, the privately calculated present values $b(v,t)$ enter (27) because the size of a cohort of age n—and the number of its members to whom transfers must actually be paid—declines over time at a rate just equal to the insurance premium $p(n)$.

To verify (27), notice that private budget constraints imply

$$b(v,0) = \int_{0}^{\infty} c(v,t)R(0,t)[P(t-v)/P(-v)]\,dt - k(v,0) - h(v,0) \quad (v \leqslant 0),$$

$$b(v,v) = \int_{v}^{\infty} c(v,t)R(v,t)P(t-v)\,dt - h(v,v) \quad (v > 0).$$

Substitution of these expressions into (27) gives an equation that holds in equilibrium if and only if (27) does:

$$\int_{-\infty}^{0} \int_{0}^{\infty} c(v,t)R(0,t)P(t-v)\,dt\,dv + \int_{0}^{\infty} \int_{v}^{\infty} c(v,t)R(0,t)P(t-v)\,dt\,dv$$

$$= K(0) + \int_{-\infty}^{0} \int_{0}^{\infty} w(t)R(0,t)P(t-v)\,dt\,dv$$

$$+ \int_{0}^{\infty} \int_{v}^{\infty} w(t)R(0,t)P(t-v)\,dt\,dv.$$

On interchanging the order of integration, we transform this equality into

$$\int_0^\infty \left[\int_{-\infty}^t c(v,t)P(t-v)\,dv \right] R(0,t)\,dt$$

$$= \int_0^\infty C(t)R(0,t)\,dt$$

$$= K(0) + \int_0^\infty \left[w(t) \int_{-\infty}^t P(t-v)\,dv \right] R(0,t)\,dt$$

$$= K(0) + \int_0^\infty \{ Y[K(t)] - K(t)Y'[K(t)] \} R(0,t)\,dt.$$

Because $C(t) = Y[K(t)] - \dot{K}(t)$, the preceding equation reduces further to

$$\int_0^\infty K(t)Y'[K(t)]R(0,t)\,dt = K(0) + \int_0^\infty \dot{K}(t)R(0,t)\,dt.$$

Integration by parts implies, however, that

$$K(0) + \int_0^\infty \dot{K}(t)R(0,t)\,dt = \lim_{t\to\infty} K(t)R(0,t) + \int_0^\infty K(t)r(t)R(0,t)\,dt$$

$$= \int_0^\infty K(t)Y'[K(t)]R(0,t)\,dt.$$

Working backward, we see that equation (27) must also hold.[14]

There are many paths of individual lump-sum taxes producing the present-value stocks that decentralize the plan. In this sense, the optimal fiscal policy is not unique. The government can, in particular, decentralize its plan with a fiscal policy that entails a balanced budget on each date, and therefore no issue of public debt. To see why, start with an arbitrary policy that supports the plan and define the primary (or noninterest) deficit as

$$\pi(t) = \int_{-\infty}^t \tau(v,t)P(t-v)\,dv.$$

Then equation (27) states that the present discounted value of primary deficits is zero. Now add to the expected future transfer stream $\{\tau(0,t)\}_{t=0}^\infty$ of an agent born at $t=0$ the stream of stock transfers $\{-\pi(t)/P(t)\}_{t=0}^\infty$. The present discounted value of his transfers still equals the optimal value $b(0,0)$, but the government's budget now balances period by period.

An appendix gives an example characterizing optimal fiscal policy for a special case of the model.

10.4.   Social Preferences and Time Inconsistency

The social welfare function we have been studying can be written in the form (10),

$$W(0) = \int_0^\infty U[C(t)]e^{-\rho t}\, dt,$$

where the indirect utility function $U(\cdot)$ does not depend on the time elapsed since the beginning of the plan. This time independence of $U(\cdot)$ implies that $W(0)$ gives rise to time-consistent optimal command allocations. Many alternative welfare criteria, however, give rise to indirect utility functions of the form $U[C(t), t - t_0]$, where t_0 is the date on which the plan is made and $t - t_0$ therefore represents *plan* (as opposed to calendar) time. Such welfare criteria need not produce time-consistent optimal plans in general.

10.4.1.   Time Inconsistency under Some Alternative Social Welfare Functions

One alternative social welfare function would treat all people alive at $t = 0$ as if they had just been born. This treatment implies that their future utilities are discounted to $t = 0$ rather than to birth date, and that the planner applies the weight $e^{-\rho 0} = 1$ to these agents. The implied social welfare function is particularly appealing when the instantaneous death probability is a constant, p, so that all individuals are identical ex ante. We assume in this example that this constancy holds, and write the resulting welfare criterion as

$$V(0) = \int_0^\infty \left\{ \int_v^\infty u[c(v,t)]e^{-(\delta+p)(t-v)}\, dt \right\} e^{-\rho v}\, dv$$

$$+ \int_{-\infty}^0 \left\{ \int_0^\infty u[c(v,t)]e^{-(\delta+p)t}\, dt \right\} e^{pv}\, dv, \tag{28}$$

where $\rho < \delta + p$ is assumed.

To see that (28) can lead to a time-inconsistent optimum, rewrite $V(0)$ as

$$V(0) = \int_0^\infty \left\{ \int_0^t u[c(t-n,t)]e^{-(\delta+p)n}e^{\rho n}\,dn \right.$$

$$\left. + \int_t^\infty u[c(t-n,t)]e^{-(\delta+p)n}e^{-(\delta-\rho)(t-n)}e^{\rho n}\,dn \right\} e^{-\rho t}\,dt,$$

(29)

where $n = t - v$ again stands for age. Comparison of (29) with (7) shows that the former is a special case of the latter when $\delta = \rho$. In this case (as noted above), the planner treats all contemporaneous cohorts alike. Thus, no time inconsistency arises. If $\delta \neq \rho$, however, (29) and (7) are fundamentally different, since the indirect utility function associated with $V(0)$ then depends on planning time.

To be concrete, let $U_V[C(t),t]$ be the value of maximizing

$$\int_0^t \log[c(t-n,t)]\,e^{-(\delta+p)n}e^{\rho n}\,dn$$

$$+ \int_t^\infty \log[c(t-n,t)]\,e^{-(\delta+p)n}e^{-(\delta-\rho)(t-n)}e^{\rho n}\,dn$$

subject to $\int_0^\infty c(t-n,t)e^{-pn}\,dn \leqslant C(t)$. The consumption allocation that results is

$$c(t-n,t) = \begin{cases} e^{(\rho-\delta)n}C(t)/\psi(t) & (n \leqslant t) \\ e^{(\rho-\delta)t}C(t)/\psi(t) & (n > t), \end{cases}$$

where

$$\psi(t) \equiv \frac{p + (\delta - \rho)e^{-(p+\delta-\rho)t}}{p(p+\delta-\rho)}.$$

Therefore, $U_V[C(t),t] = \log[C(t)]\psi(t) + L(t)$, where $L(t)$ is a (time-dependent) constant. The key feature of this indirect utility function is that it depends not only on $C(t)$ but also on planning time.

From the perspective of the planning origin $t_0 = 0$, the marginal rate of substitution between consumption on two dates t_1 and t_2 in the future is

$$\frac{U_V'[C(t_1),t_1]e^{-\rho t_1}}{U_V'[C(t_2),t_2]e^{-\rho t_2}} = \frac{C(t_2)}{C(t_1)} \cdot \frac{\psi(t_1)}{\psi(t_2)} e^{-\rho(t_1-t_2)}.$$

If this marginal rate of substitution is recalculated using $V(t_0)$, where $t_0 > 0$ and $t_0 < t_1, t_2$, it equals

$$\frac{U_V'[C(t_1), t_1 - t_0]e^{-\rho(t_1 - t_0)}}{U_V'[C(t_2), t_2 - t_0]e^{-\rho(t_2 - t_0)}} = \frac{C(t_2)}{C(t_1)} \cdot \frac{\psi(t_1 - t_0)}{\psi(t_2 - t_0)} e^{-\rho(t_1 - t_2)}$$

at the initially chosen consumption levels. But the two marginal rates of substitution are the same only if for all t_1, t_2, and $t_0 < t_1, t_2$,

$$\frac{\psi(t_1)}{\psi(t_2)} = \frac{\psi(t_1 - t_0)}{\psi(t_2 - t_0)},$$

which is not the case (unless $\rho = \delta$). Therefore, $V(0)$ can lead to time-inconsistent plans.

Intuitively, $V(0)$ produces time-inconsistent plans for the reason noted in section 10.2: those alive at the start of the plan and those to be born are treated asymmetrically by the welfare criterion, so reoptimization after the plan's commencement leads to an allocation of aggregate consumption among cohorts different from the one initially intended.

Our example, however, shows more, namely, that the time inconsistency will apply also to the path of *aggregate* consumption $C(t)$.

Other plausible social welfare functions can also be shown to lead to time inconsistency. Suppose, for example, that the planner weighs the utilities of those alive at $t = 0$ by $e^{-\rho v}$, but discounts the utilities they enjoy to $t = 0$ rather than to birth date. This scheme is equivalent to discounting to birth date but weighing the utility of those alive at $t = 0$ by $e^{-(\rho + \delta)v}$ rather than by the factor $e^{-\rho v}$ applied to those born after $t = 0$; and this is easily seen to cause time inconsistency. Alternatively, the planner might wish to treat those alive at $t = 0$ as cohort representatives and thus drop the term $e^{\rho v}$ in the second summand in (28).[15] This again leads to time inconsistency.

An implication of our analysis is that the credibility of a planner will depend on the way he weights generations' utilities. This complication is not found in the Cass-Koopmans framework interpreted as an economy of nonoverlapping generations. There, it is a matter of indifference whether the planner discounts instantaneous utility according to the time at which it is enjoyed or the generation that enjoys it. Here the distinction is crucial.

10.4.2. Relation to Samuelson's Formulation

Samuelson (1967, 1968), building on a suggestion of Lerner (1959), was the first to study utilitarian planning in an economy with finitely lived overlapping generations. In the model of Samuelson (1968), a generation lives for two periods and a new generation is born each period until a known date T in the future. If an individual born on date t enjoys lifetime utility $u[c(t,t), c(t, t + 1)]$, Samuelson's planner maximizes

$$S(0) = \sum_{t=0}^{T-1} \beta^t u[c(t,t), c(t, t + 1)],$$

subject to constraints discussed below, on date 0. The parameter $\beta \in (0, 1]$ gives the rate at which the planner discounts future generations' utility (with $\beta = 1$ the Ramsey case). Although Samuelson assumes a finite horizon, he characterizes a hypothetical steady-state allocation satisfying first-order conditions for maximization of $S(0)$.

The welfare criterion $S(0)$ generally yields time-inconsistent programs if the planner is constrained only by the initial capital stock $K(0)$ and the saving-investment relation $K(t + 1) - K(t) = Y[K(t)] - c(t,t) - c(t - 1, t)$. The reason for this time inconsistency is that the Samuelson criterion does not attach an appropriate weight to the welfare of the old generation alive at the start of the plan. In each period s, maximization of $S(s)$ requires that consumption by the old be zero, even though this was not planned when $S(s - 1)$ was maximized. In terms of our discussion earlier in this section, the indirect utility function for a given future date maximized by the planner on the first day of the plan can differ from that maximized on a subsequent day, so the planning criterion cannot be written in a form like (10).

Samuelson (1968) in effect avoids time inconsistency by placing an additional constraint on the planner: the requirement that the consumption of the old in period s, $c(s - 1, s)$, be taken as given. If this predetermined consumption level for the old is interpreted as the level envisioned in the previous period's optimal plan, the planner is forced to pursue a time-consistent program. Samuelson does not offer this interpretation, however, and no suggestion is made regarding social institutions that might impose a time-consistency constraint.

The social welfare function proposed in Samuelson (1967) avoids time inconsistency without side constraints, but only under restrictive assumptions on social and individual preferences that mask some of the issues discussed above. [Samuelson assumes here that generations receive equal weight in plans and that $u[c(t,t), c(t, t + 1)] = v[c(t,t)] + v[c(t, t + 1)]$, so that individuals do not discount future utility.] It is noteworthy (but not surprising) that the optimal plans we explored above entail intertemporal and intergenerational allocation rules [equations (16) and (17)] that generalize those derived by Samuelson.

10.5. Social Preferences and Decentralizability

A stricter interpretation of utilitarianism than the one invoked above leads to a social welfare function whose optima, while time consistent, cannot be decentralized by lump-sum taxes alone. Distorting taxes are required for decentralization, but the optimal path of taxes is, nonetheless, time consistent. In this section we use the tools developed earlier to analyze this alternative model.

10.5.1. Stricter Utilitarianism

The welfare criterion $W(0)$ introduced in section 10.2 is a sum of the lifetime utilities of representatives from each cohort, present and future. A stricter reading of utilitarianism would suggest that instantaneous utilities be weighted, not only by the discount factors in (5) but also by the number of agents actually alive to enjoy each instantaneous utility flow. The result is the social welfare function

$$B(0) = \int_0^\infty \left\{ \int_{-\infty}^t u[c(v,t)] \Delta(t-v) P(t-v)^2 e^{\rho(t-v)} \, dv \right\} e^{-\rho t} \, dt. \tag{30}$$

Notice that we can write the planning problem as that of maximizing

$$B(0) = \int_0^\infty U_B[C(t)] e^{-\rho t} \, dt$$

subject to (11), where $U_B[C(t)]$ is the value of maximizing

$$\int_0^\infty u[c(t-n,t)] \Delta(n) P(n)^2 e^{\rho n} \, dn$$

subject to $\int_0^\infty c(t-n,t) P(n) \, dn \leqslant C(t)$. $U_B(\cdot)$ is clearly independent of planning time, implying that $B(0)$ leads to time-consistent optimal command allocations. The results of Benveniste and Scheinkman (1979) cited above again imply that $U_B(\cdot)$ is a "well-behaved" utility function with $U_B'[C(t)] = u'[c(t,t)]$ at an optimum.

10.5.2. The Social Optimum under $B(0)$

The necessary conditions for a social optimum are

$$\frac{\partial c(v,t)}{\partial v} = -\frac{u'[c(v,t)]}{u''[c(v,t)]} [\delta + p(t-v) - \rho], \tag{31}$$

$$\frac{\partial c(v,t)}{\partial t} = -\frac{u'[c(v,t)]}{u''[c(v,t)]} \{Y'[K(t)] - \delta - p(t-v)\}. \tag{32}$$

In the aggregate, the economy converges to a steady state $(\bar{C}^B, \bar{K}^B)$ defined by $Y'(\bar{K}^B) = \rho$, $\bar{C}^B = Y(\bar{K}^B)$.

EXAMPLE   As in section 10.2, let $u(c) = c^{1-R}/(1-R)$, $R > 0$, $R \neq 1$. Then for all t, $U_B[C(t)] = \Phi_B \cdot C(t)^{1-R}/(1-R)$, where

$$\Phi_B = \left[\int_0^\infty e^{(\rho-\delta)n/R} P(n)^{(1+R)/R} \, dn \right]^R.$$

Since $U_B(\cdot)$ and the indirect utility function $U(\cdot)$ associated with $W(0)$ differ only by a scalar multiple when individual utility functions are isoelastic, $B(0)$ and $W(0)$ lead to *identical* optimal paths for *aggregate* consumption in this case, given the same initial capital stock. The two criteria, however, call for different allocations of the consumption level $C(t)$ across cohorts.

10.5.3.   Decentralizability and Time Consistency

Because the first-order condition (32) entailed by maximization of $B(0)$ differs from the individual optimality condition (22), the optimal allocation under $B(0)$ cannot be replicated in a competitive economy with actuarially fair annuities unless distorting taxes are imposed. In particular, decentralization requires that each agent face an age-specific interest income tax equal to $p(t-v)$, in addition to lump-sum transfers as in section 10.3.

The plans generated by $B(0)$ are generally Pareto inefficient because this welfare criterion distorts individual preferences over consumption on different dates. This preference distortion is seen most clearly if $B(0)$ is expressed in the form

$$B(0) = \int_0^\infty \left\{ \int_v^\infty u[c(v,t)] \Delta(t-v) P(t-v)^2 \, dt \right\} e^{-\rho v} \, dv$$

$$+ \int_{-\infty}^0 \left\{ \int_0^\infty u[c(v,t)] \Delta(t-v) P(t-v)^2 \, dt \right\} e^{-\rho v} \, dv.$$

The inefficiency of these plans makes them nondecentralizable in the competitive economy without distorting taxes on capital income.

Even though distorting taxes must be used to support the planner's preferred allocation as a market outcome, fiscal policy is not time inconsistent in the present setting. The planner's preferences, as we have observed, lead to a time-consistent command optimum. Since age-dependent capital-income taxes allow the planner to attain this optimum in the market economy, the tax policies that maximize $B(0)$ will also maximize $B(t_0)$, for $t_0 > 0$, if followed from time t_0 onward.[16]

The nondecentralizability of $B(0)$ (absent distorting taxes) has an analogy in the standard Cass-Koopmans-Ramsey model when population is growing at a rate $\gamma > 0$. There, it is sometimes postulated that the planner sets everyone's consumption equal to per capita consumption, $\bar{c}(t)$, and maximizes

$$\int_0^\infty u[\bar{c}(t)]e^{-\rho t}\, dt,$$

with the result that $\bar{c}(t)$ evolves according to

$$\dot{\bar{c}}(t) = -\frac{u'[\bar{c}(t)]}{u''[\bar{c}(t)]}[r(t) - \rho - \gamma] \tag{33}$$

along the optimal trajectory. Suppose, however, that population growth is occurring because of the birth of new infinitely lived agents, each of whom maximizes

$$\int_v^\infty u[c(t)]e^{-\rho(t-v)}\, dt,$$

for some birth date v, as in Weil (1985). Each of these agents will pick a consumption path satisfying

$$\dot{c}(t) = -\frac{u'[c(t)]}{u''[c(t)]}[r(t) - \rho] \tag{34}$$

under laissez-faire, so a plan requiring (33) cannot be decentralized without a capital-income tax at the rate γ. Similarly, an infinitely lived and growing egalitarian dynasty that maximizes

$$\int_0^\infty u[\bar{c}(t)]e^{(\gamma-\rho)t}\, dt \tag{35}$$

follows (34) [for $\bar{c}(t)$] rather than (33). Koopmans (1967, p. 105) suggests that the social welfare function (35), based on a discount rate of $\rho - \gamma$, is more compatible with utilitarian principles than the one based on a discount rate of ρ. Use of the latter will also generate Pareto inefficient social optima if it distorts the underlying intertemporal preferences of the economy's agents.[17]

10.6. Implications of Instrument Insufficiency

In section 10.3 we saw that to decentralize an optimal plan, the planner must pay out lump-sum transfers that depend on an agent's vintage as well as on calendar time. The resulting fiscal policy, which is quite complex, differs from those usually studied in the macroeconomics literature. There, the usual assumption is that all agents alive on a given date face the same lump-sum tax/transfer (see, for example, Blanchard, 1985, and Weil, 1985).

We show in this section that optimal fiscal policy may be time inconsistent if the government is constrained to make the same lump-sum transfer to all individuals alive on a given date. Time inconsistency can arise in spite of the time consistency of the optimal command allocation: it arises because the government does not have enough instruments to attain the command optimum. We illustrate this by showing that the constraint on the government may not lead to time inconsistency when the government's planning horizon is infinite, so that there are, in effect, as many policy instruments as targets.

10.6.1. An Overlapping Generations Economy

To simplify the argument, we modify our earlier setup in two ways. First, we analyze an economy of two-period-lived overlapping generations that work only while young. Second, we allow the production technology to vary exogenously (but predictably) over time, so that date-t output is $Y[K(t); \theta(t)]$. Neither of these modifications is crucial for our results.

Define $c(t) \equiv c(t, t)$ and $x(t + 1) \equiv c(t, t + 1)$. Then a generation born at time t maximizes $u[c(t)] + \beta u[x(t + 1)]$ ($\beta < 1$). In the market economy this maximization is constrained by the inequality

$$c(t) + x(t + 1)/[1 + r(t + 1)] \leq w(t) + \tau(t) + \tau(t + 1)/[1 + r(t + 1)],$$

where $\tau(t)$ is the uniform government transfer made to all agents living on date t.

If the planner's discount rate equals the private rate β, social welfare is

$$W(0) = \sum_{t=0}^{T} \beta^t \{u[x(t)] + u[c(t)]\},$$

which is maximized subject to $K(t + 1) - K(t) = Y[K(t); \theta(t)] - x(t) - c(t)$ in a command economy. The planning horizon T may be infinite. Necessary conditions for the optimal command allocation include the analogues of those found in section 10.2 (cf. Samuelson, 1967, 1968):

$$u'[x(t)] = u'[c(t)] = \lambda(t),$$

$$\lambda(t) = \beta\{1 + Y'[K(t + 1); \theta(t + 1)]\}\lambda(t + 1).$$

10.6.2. Time-Inconsistent Fiscal Policy in a Three-Period Model

Assume temporarily that T runs from 0 to 2, so that the generation born in the last period (period 2) lives only one period and maximizes $u[c(2)]$. Then the planner's objective function is

$$W(0) = u[x(0)] + u[c(0)] + \beta\{u[x(1)] + u[c(1)]\}$$
$$+ \beta^2\{u[x(2)] + u[c(2)]\}.$$

Since all agents alive in any period receive the same transfer, the government's budget constraint is

$$\tau(0)[1 + r(1)][1 + r(2)] + \tau(1)[1 + r(2)] + \tau(2) = 0. \tag{36}$$

In period 0 the planner chooses $\tau(0)$, $\tau(1)$, and $\tau(2)$ to maximize $W(0)$ subject to (36), individual demand functions, and capital accumulation constraints. We are interested in seeing whether the values of $\tau(1)$ and $\tau(2)$ that maximize $W(0)$ subject to the constraints faced by the planner at $t = 0$ still maximize $W(1)$ subject to the constraints faced at $t = 1$. By (36), we need only ask whether the initially optimal $\tau(1)$ changes.

To begin, we list the budget constraints faced by private agents:

$$K(0)[1 + r(0)] + \tau(0) - x(0) \geqslant 0 \qquad \text{(old at } t = 0\text{)}, \tag{37}$$

$$w(0) + \tau(0) - c(0) + [\tau(1) - x(1)]/[1 + r(1)] \geqslant 0 \quad \text{(young at } t = 0\text{)}, \tag{38}$$

$$w(1) + \tau(1) - c(1) + [\tau(2) - x(2)]/[1 + r(2)]$$
$$= w(1) - c(1) - x(2)/[1 + r(2)] \tag{39}$$
$$- \tau(0)[1 + r(1)] \geqslant 0 \qquad \text{(young at } t = 1\text{)},$$

$$w(2) + \tau(2) - c(2) = w(2) - c(2) - \tau(0)[1 + r(1)][1 + r(2)]$$
$$- \tau(1)[1 + r(2)] \geqslant 0 \qquad \text{(young at } t = 2\text{)}. \tag{40}$$

In the last two constraints listed, we have used the government budget constraint (36) to eliminate $\tau(2)$.

We shall assume that the production technology at $t = 2$ is such that $w(2)$ and $r(2)$ are *exogenous*. Because $K(0)$ is given, $w(0)$ and $r(0)$ are also predetermined as of $t = 0$. The capital stock at $t = 1$ is given by

$$K(1) = w(0) - c(0) - \tau(0)$$

[which follows from adding gross private saving $w(0) - c(0) + \tau(0)$ to gross government saving $-2\tau(0)$], while at $t = 2$,

$$K(2) = w(1) - c(1) - \tau(1) - 2\tau(0)[1 + r(1)]$$

[the sum of $w(1) - c(1) + \tau(1)$ and $-2\tau(0)[1 + r(1)] - 2\tau(1)$].

To detect time inconsistency, we must study the planner's problem from the perspectives of both $t = 0$ and $t = 1$. Start with the later date, and consider the effect of an increase in $\tau(1)$ at the social optimum. This entails a utility gain of $u'[x(1)]\,d\tau(1)$ for the old at $t = 1$. Since $w(1)$, $r(1)$, and $\tau(0)$ are all predetermined as of $t = 1$ and $r(2)$ is fixed by assumption, (39) implies that the young at $t = 1$ (generation 1) suffer no utility change. Finally, by (40), generation 2 finds its utility decreased by $[1 + r(2)]u'[c(2)]\,d\tau(1)$. Consequently, a $\tau(1)$ level optimal from the perspective of $t = 1$ satisfies

$$u'[x(1)] - \beta[1 + r(2)]u'[c(2)] = 0. \tag{41}$$

We now study the above optimum problem from the standpoint of $t = 0$. Since we are interested in finding conditions for time consistency, we assume that (41) holds. The main difference between the present situation and the one just examined is that the members of generation 0 anticipate any change in $\tau(1)$ and are bound to change their saving in response. This will in general imply a change in $K(1)$ and the corresponding factor prices $w(1)$ and $r(1)$ (which were given for the planner at $t = 1$). We shall denote the comparative-statics derivatives by $dw(1)/d\tau(1)$ and $dr(1)/d\tau(1)$, respectively. In this connection, we notice that the factor-price frontier implies $dw(t)/d\tau(t) = -K(t)[dr(t)/d\tau(t)]$.

From the standpoint of $t = 0$, a change in $\tau(1)$ gives a utility gain for generation 0 (measured in terms of period 1 utility) of

$$u'[x(1)]\{1 + [dr(1)/d\tau(1)][x(1) - \tau(1)]/[1 + r(1)]\}\,d\tau(1),$$

where we have used (38) and the fact that we are evaluating at individually optimal solutions. By (39) and the factor-price relation, the utility change for generation 1 is

$$-u'[c(1)][K(1) + \tau(0)][dr(1)/d\tau(1)]\,d\tau(1).$$

Finally, (40) gives a utility change for generation 2 of

$$-u'[c(2)][1 + r(2)]\{1 + \tau(0)[dr(1)/d\tau(1)]\}\,d\tau(1).$$

Using the foregoing expressions and (41), we find that the first-order condition with respect to $\tau(1)$ in period 0 is

$$(u'[x(1)]\{-\tau(0) + [x(1) - \tau(1)]/[1 + r(1)]\}$$
$$- u'[c(1)][K(1) + \tau(0)])[dr(1)/d\tau(1)] = 0. \tag{42}$$

Notice that if the technology were linear at $t = 1$ (as it is assumed to be at $t = 2$), we would have $dr(1)/d\tau(1) \equiv 0$. Equation (42) is always satisfied in this case, so there is no time inconsistency. We now examine conditions under which (42) holds when $dr(1)/d\tau(1) \neq 0$.

After substitution using (38) and the relation $K(1) = w(0) - c(0) - \tau(0)$, (42) becomes

$$[w(0) - c(0)]\{u'[x(1)] - u'[c(1)]\} = 0. \tag{43}$$

Thus, time inconsistency will arise unless $w(0) = c(0)$ and/or $u'[x(1)] = u'[c(1)]$. It is straightforward, but unedifying, to check that $w(0) = c(0)$ will not hold in general at a maximum of $W(0).$[18]

The condition $u'[x(1)] = u'[c(1)]$ will not hold in general either. To see this, notice that the first-order condition with respect to $\tau(0)$ (derived as above) is

$$u'[x(0)] + u'[c(0)] = \beta[1 + r(1)]\{u'[x(1)] + u'[c(1)]\}. \tag{44}$$

If $u'[x(1)] = u'[c(1)]$, then (41), (44), and the individual Euler equations, $u'[c(t)] = \beta[1 + r(t + 1)]u'[x(t + 1)]$ $(t = 0, 1)$, imply that the economy is at the command optimum, with $c(t) = x(t)$ for $t = 0, 1, 2$. [Equation (43) thus implies, reassuringly, that fiscal policy can never be time inconsistent when the government is able to attain the command optimum for $W(0)$ using the available instruments.]

Imagine now that (43) does hold initially because $u'[x(1)] = u'[c(1)]$, but that the $t = 0$ production function is perturbed so that $K(0)[1 + r(0)]$ rises but $K(0)[1 + r(0)] + w(0)$ remains constant. It is easy to show that this change does not modify the optimal command allocation, so if $u'[x(1)] =$

$u'[c(1)]$ continues to hold, consumption levels and capital stocks for $t = 1$ and $t = 2$ are the same. Equation (37) implies, however, that $\tau(0)$ must fall to keep $x(0)$ unchanged. But since $w(1)$, $r(1)$, and $r(2)$ are also unchanged, (39) implies that $c(1)$ and $x(2)$ cannot both remain constant. This contradiction shows that (43) will not always hold and, therefore, that optimal fiscal policy can be time inconsistent in the present setting.

Our example differs considerably from the standard time-inconsistency example involving capital accumulation (see Fischer, 1980, Kydland and Prescott, 1980, Turnovsky and Brock, 1980, or Chamley, 1985). There, distorting capital-income taxes are initially set at low levels to encourage capital accumulation, but are subsequently revised upward once capital is in place and in inelastic supply. The taxes we have considered are lump-sum, however, and fall equally on the owners of capital and labor. Time inconsistency arises nonetheless because at $t = 0$, the planner is concerned about the effect of $\tau(1)$ on factor rewards in future periods. This effect operates through saving decisions at $t = 0$, which alter factor prices at $t = 1$. At $t = 1$, however, the planner no longer has the option of influencing $w(1)$ and $r(1)$ through the choice of $\tau(1)$. If the economy is not at the command optimum, the planner therefore will generally wish to move $\tau(1)$ from the level that previously seemed optimal. As we noted in discussing condition (42), policy is always time consistent if $dr(1)/d\tau(1) = 0$, so that factor prices are exogenous. In this case the planner has the same options at $t = 1$ as at $t = 0$.[19]

Our result depends heavily on the assumption that the planning horizon T is finite. When T is infinite, the planner may be able to attain the command optimum even with the constrained arsenal of fiscal instruments we have allowed. We now demonstrate this.

10.6.3. The Infinite-Horizon Case

As in section 10.3, we can write the desired first-period consumption of a member of generation t as

$$\hat{c}(t) = c\{w(t) + \tau(t) + \tau(t + 1)/[1 + r(t + 1)], r(t + 1)\}.$$

The same individual's desired second-period consumption, $\hat{x}(t + 1)$, solves

$$u'[\hat{c}(t)] = \beta[1 + r(t + 1)]u'[\hat{x}(t + 1)]. \tag{45}$$

Let $\{w(t)\}_{t=0}^{\infty}$ and $\{r(t)\}_{t=0}^{\infty}$ be the factor prices associated with the command optimum. The planner can attain the command optimum only if he sets $\tau(0)$ so that $x(0) = K(0)[1 + r(0)] + \tau(0) = x^*(0)$, where an asterisk denotes a command-optimum consumption level. The same transfer $\tau(0)$ must also be made to generation 0 in period 0; but by choice of $\tau(1)$, the planner can ensure that

$$\hat{c}(0) = c\{w(0) + \tau(0) + \tau(1)/[1 + r(1)], r(1)\} = c^*(0).$$

This equality is always possible because $\hat{c}(t)$ is monotonically increasing in $\tau(t + 1)$, given $r(t + 1)$. The first-order conditions for the command optimum automatically ensure that $\hat{x}(1) = x^*(1)$ when $\hat{x}(1)$ is generated by (45) and $\hat{c}(0) = c^*(0)$.

Generation 1 must receive the same transfer $\tau(1)$ in period 1 as generation 0 receives. But if $\tau(2)$ is chosen so that

$$c\{w(1) + \tau(1) + \tau(2)/[1 + r(2)], r(2)\} = c^*(1),$$

then $\hat{c}(1) = c^*(1)$ and $\hat{x}(2) = x^*(2)$. By choice of $\tau(3)$, the planner can now ensure that $\hat{c}(2) = c^*(2)$ and $\hat{x}(3) = x^*(3)$; and he can continue in this manner indefinitely, attaining all of the consumption levels defining the command optimum.

The present case differs from the previous finite-horizon case in that the government always has a future transfer available with which to influence the behavior of the current young. In contrast, an economy with a finite horizon admits no future transfer with which to influence the behavior of those born in the final period. As we have seen, this instrument insufficiency can push the economy away from the command optimum in every period and destroy the time consistency of the optimal fiscal policy.[20]

10.6.4. Interpreting the Government Budget Constraint with an Infinite Horizon

A problematic aspect of the time-consistent fiscal policy constructed in subsection 10.6.3 is that the size of the optimal transfer payment may eventually grow at the rate of interest, alternating in sign from period to period. This behavior is problematic because the government budget constraint as usually formulated does not hold, even though (27) does. The present value of net government transfers is a divergent sum.[21]

A simple example illustrates the problem. Assume again that the planner discount rate equals the private discount rate, β. The planner (in effect) maximizes a function

$$W(0) = \sum_{t=0}^{\infty} \beta^t U[C(t)],$$

where $C(t) = c(t) + x(t)$, and then divides optimal $C(t)$ equally between young and old.

The economy's production function is $Y[K(t)] = (1 - \beta)K(t)/\beta$; the economy starts with an initial capital stock, $K(0)$, owned entirely by the *old*. (There is no labor income.) In the finite-horizon case, the linear production function would preclude time inconsistency; but the example is meant to illustrate a separate issue, the behavior of net transfers at the infinite-horizon optimum under the fiscal restriction assumed in this section.

It is easy to see that the optimal aggregate consumption plan calls for $C^*(t) = (1 - \beta)K^*(t)/\beta$ (all t), so that $K^*(t) = K^*(t - 1) = \cdots = K(0)$. Thus, for all t,

$$x^*(t) = c^*(t) = (1 - \beta)K(0)/2\beta.$$

A difference equation for the transfer path $\{\tau(t)\}_{t=0}^{\infty}$ can be derived from the individual budget constraint:

$$\tau(t + 1) = -(1/\beta)\tau(t) + (1/\beta)[c^*(t) + \beta x^*(t + 1)]$$

$$= -(1/\beta)\tau(t) + (1 - \beta)(1 + \beta)K(0)/2\beta^2.$$

A general solution to this difference equation is

$$\tau(t) = (1 - \beta)K(0)/2\beta + m(-1/\beta)^t,$$

where m is an initial condition. The requirement that $x(0) = x^*(0) = (1 - \beta)K(0)/2\beta$ implies that $\tau(0) = x^*(0) - K(0)/\beta = -(1 + \beta)K(0)/2\beta$. So $m = -(1/\beta)K(0)$, and for all t,

$$\tau(t) = (1 - \beta)K(0)/2\beta - (-1)^t(1/\beta)^{t+1}K(0).$$

Clearly the present discounted value of net transfers, $2\sum_{t=0}^{\infty} \beta^t \tau(t)$, does not exist in the usual sense [although (27) holds].

The example shows that while the transfer scheme of subsection 10.6.3 is feasible, that scheme ceases to solve the time-inconsistency problem if one insists that the present value of net government transfers always be well defined. It is not obvious, however, that such an insistence is warranted. As Shell (1971) argues, the meaning of budget constraints is somewhat uncertain in infinite-horizon models. Wilson (1981) suggests an alternative to the usual formulation of budget constraints that is satisfied by the transfer scheme described above.

In addition, there are other examples of economies where feasible government fiscal policies violate the conventional budget constraint. One such is the dynamically inefficient case of Diamond's (1965) model, in which the government can run Ponzi schemes (see O'Connell and Zeldes, 1988). Our model motivates another example of this type, but one in which the economy is "to the left" of the Golden Rule capital-stock level.

10.7. Conclusion

This chapter has studied the idea of optimal fiscal policy in an economy where heterogeneous mortal generations coexist. A growing literature studies the effects of social security and government debt issue in economies of this type, but it stops short of describing any intertemporal social welfare function that might justify the use of fiscal tools. We examined the dynamic resource allocation chosen by a utilitarian planner who weights the welfare of both existing and future generations symmetrically, and we found that the optimal behavior of the economy's aggregates is described by the standard Cass-Koopmans-Ramsey optimal growth analysis. The relevant aggregate discount rate, however, is the rate at which the planner discounts the well-being of future generations.

The command optimum just described can be decentralized in a market economy if time-varying and age-dependent lump-sum transfer payments can be made by the government. If the government cannot distinguish among different individuals in making lump-sum transfers, however, optimal fiscal policy may be time inconsistent.[22] Some seemingly plausible social welfare functions can themselves lead to time inconsistency even when sufficient policy tools are available to the government.

Appendix

In this appendix, we analyze the fiscal policy that supports the steady state as a competitive equilibrium when $u(c) = \log(c)$ and the instantaneous death probability is a constant, denoted p. Under these assumptions, the steady state capital stock under laissez-faire, $\bar{K}^l$, is given by

$$Y'(\bar{K}^l) = \delta + p(\delta + p)\frac{\bar{K}^l}{Y(\bar{K}^l)}, \tag{A1}$$

the consumption function is $c[a(v,t); \{r(s)\}_{s=t}^{\infty}] = (\delta + p)[a(v,t)]$, and population is $1/p$ (see

Blanchard, 1985). We again denote by $\bar{K}$ the steady-state capital stock under the plan, defined by $Y'(\bar{K}) = \rho$, where ρ is the planner's discount rate.

Let us first ask why $\bar{K}$ would generally *not* be a steady-state equilibrium without government intervention. To be concrete, take the case $Y'(\bar{K}) = \rho = \delta$. If the interest rate and the wage were expected to remain constant at δ and $\bar{w}$ forever, each agent in a new cohort would be born with total wealth $\bar{w}/(\delta + p) = p[Y(\bar{K}) - Y'(\bar{K})\bar{K}]/(\delta + p)$ and his lifetime consumption path would be flat at the level $p[Y(\bar{K}) - Y'(\bar{K})\bar{K}]$. Asymptotically aggregate consumption would clearly approach labor's share in national output; and because labor's share is less than total output, this is inconsistent with goods-market equilibrium in a steady state. In the laissez-faire steady state, however, $Y'(\bar{K}^1) > \delta$. Each cohort's consumption thus rises over time [by (22)], so that aggregate consumption equals the lower level of national output and the capital stock (plus any public debt) is willingly held in private portfolios.

Return now to the decentralization problem with ρ possibly different from δ. Since we are assuming a steady state, the payment received by an individual depends on age $n = t - v$ only, and so may be written as $\tau(n)$, while the present value of these payments given the expected path of the real interest rate, $b(v, t)$, may be written as $b(n)$. The steady-state government budget constraint takes the form

$$\int_0^\infty \tau(n)P(n)\,dn = -\rho\bar{D}, \tag{A2}$$

where $\bar{D}$ is the stock of public debt and now $P(n) = e^{-pn}$.

To support the optimal steady state associated with ρ as an equilibrium, fiscal policy must confront each agent with a transfer path inducing aggregate consumption equal to $Y(\bar{K})$ when the interest rate is expected to remain at $Y'(\bar{K}) = \rho$ forever. Let $k(n)$ denote the capital held by an agent of age n [of course $k(0) = 0$]. Since all agents now have the same discounted future wage income, the consumption of an individual aged n is

$$c(n) = p(\delta + p)[Y(\bar{K}) - Y'(\bar{K})\bar{K}]/(\rho + p) + (\delta + p)[k(n) + d(n) + b(n)]. \tag{A3}$$

Integrating (A3) over the entire population, we find that aggregate consumption is

$$C(t) = (\delta + p)[Y(\bar{K}) - Y'(\bar{K})\bar{K}]/(\rho + p) + (\delta + p)\left\{\bar{K} + \bar{D} + \int_0^\infty b(n)P(n)\,dn\right\}. \tag{A4}$$

Equate the value of $C(t)$ given by (A4) to $Y(\bar{K})$ and recall the definition of $b(n)$. This yields

$$\int_0^\infty \left[\int_0^\infty \tau(n + t)e^{-(\rho + p)t}\,dt\right]e^{-pn}\,dn = [(\rho - \delta)/(\rho + p)(\delta + p)]Y(\bar{K}) - [p/(\rho + p)]\bar{K} - \bar{D}. \tag{A5}$$

To make sense of the implied fiscal policy we need to interpret the left-hand side of (A5). After changing the order of integration, this expression may be written in the form

$$\int_0^\infty \tau(n)\left[\int_0^n e^{-pt}e^{-(\rho + p)(n - t)}\,dt\right]dn = (1/p)\int_0^\infty \tau(n)e^{-(\rho + p)n}(e^{\rho n} - 1)\,dn. \tag{A6}$$

The left-hand side of (A6) is just a weighted sum of the transfer payments made at each age n. The weight given to $\tau(n)$ is in turn a sum, each term of which equals the number of agents in a cohort of age t ($n \geqslant t \geqslant 0$) times the discount factor each applies to $\tau(n)$. By the government budget constraint (A2), (A5) and (A6) can be combined to yield a formula giving the optimal present value of government transfers at birth,

$$\int_0^\infty \tau(n)e^{-(\rho + p)n}\,dn = [\rho p/(\rho + p)]\bar{K} - [\rho(\rho - \delta)/(\rho + p)(\delta + p)]Y(\bar{K}). \tag{A7}$$

Any transfer path $\{\tau(n)\}_{n=0}^{\infty}$ that simultaneously satisfies (A2) and (A7) will induce a level of aggregate consumption that is constant at $Y(\bar{K})$. In general, many such paths exist. It is noteworthy that any level of public debt $\bar{D}$ is consistent with the optimal steady state allocation. $\bar{D}$ has no effect in (A7) because at birth individuals hold no government debt; but $\bar{D}$ does influence the time path of transfers each individual faces.

Equation (A7) allows us to determine whether a newborn agent's discounted lifetime transfers $b(0)$ will be positive or negative under an optimal fiscal policy. Direct calculation shows that

$$b(0) \lessgtr 0 \qquad \text{as} \quad \rho \gtrless \delta + p(\delta + p)[\bar{K}/Y(\bar{K})]. \tag{A8}$$

According to (A1), however, the steady-state real interest rate in the absence of fiscal intervention is $Y'(\bar{K}^1) = \delta + p(\delta + p)[\bar{K}^1/Y(\bar{K}^1)]$. It follows from (A8) that the government must set $b(0)$ positive if it wishes to maintain a stationary capital stock $\bar{K}$ greater than the laissez-faire level $\bar{K}^1$, and must set $b(0)$ negative in the opposite case. In other words, additional capital accumulation requires negative (unfunded) social security, an unsurprising result in view of those obtained by Diamond (1965). Faced at birth with a declining path of transfer payments, each agent accumulates capital so as to smooth his consumption. By setting the path of transfers according to (A7), the government can equate aggregate saving to zero.

The foregoing results are underlined by considering again the special case $\rho = \delta$. Under this assumption, (A7) reduces to $b(0) = \delta p \bar{K}/(\delta + p) = p Y'(\bar{K})\bar{K}/(\delta + p)$. This equation states that the transfer system endows each agent at birth with the per capita present discounted value of capital's share in national income, so that $a(0) = h(0) + b(0) = p Y(\bar{K})/(\delta + p)$. Individual consumption is flat at $p Y(\bar{K})$, and a declining path of transfers induces a net flow demand for capital and debt just equal to the flow supply "bequeathed" to the economy by those who die.

Notes

1. Other exceptions are Phelps and Riley (1978), who study the Rawlsian "maximin" case, and Abel (1987), who uses Samuelson's utilitarian framework to evaluate steady-state welfare in overlapping-generations models with money. As is discussed in section 10.4, special assumptions made by Samuelson obscure the possibility of time inconsistency in his framework. Nonetheless, Samuelson's normative prescriptions are confirmed and generalized by those of the time-consistent utilitarian planner we study in section 10.2.

2. Recent studies of fiscal policy that emphasize lifespan uncertainty include Abel (1985), Blanchard (1985), and Eckstein, Eichenbaum, and Peled (1985). An early application of Yaari's setup is Tobin (1967). Open-economy aspects of fiscal policy with uncertain lifetimes are studied by Buiter (1984), Frenkel and Razin (1986), and Giovannini (1988). In section 10.5 (note 17), we briefly apply our framework to an economy with heterogeneous immortal individuals. Section 10.6 works with the Diamond model.

3. This position is reminiscent of that taken by Koopmans (1967). He argues that when population is growing, an infinite-horizon planner cannot reasonably base welfare judgments on an integral of all future utility flows unless he discounts future generations' utilities at a positive rate. His conclusion, which might apply also to welfare criteria implying time inconsistency, is that "ethical principles, in the subject-matter in hand, need mathematical screening to determine whether in given circumstances they are capable of implementation" (p. 125).

4. Hillier and Malcomson (1984) also give an example in which a fiscal policy based on lump-sum taxes is time inconsistent as a result of the government's failure to attain the command optimum. The example we present is more general, however, and seems (to us) to offer a clearer analytical picture of the conditions under which time inconsistency can arise.

5. Most of the apparently restrictive assumptions we make below—for example, that everyone has the same time-separable utility function and that technology is constant—could be relaxed without altering our central results. Only our particular characterizations of optimal paths would change. In section 10.6, we allow the technology to undergo foreseen exogenous shifts.

6. The function $u(\cdot)$ is bounded, strictly concave, and twice continuously differentiable. Notice that $u(\cdot)$ is assumed to be independent of v. To ensure interior solutions, the usual Inada conditions are imposed.

7. The production function is assumed (until section 10.6) to be homogeneous of degree one in capital and labor, to exhibit smoothly diminishing returns to each factor, and to obey the Inada conditions.

8. $W(0)$ has an alternative interpretation. Its first component is a weighted integral of instantaneous utilities actually enjoyed by members of future generations, discounted to the date of birth at the "risk-free" rate δ. (Recall that there is no *aggregate* uncertainty.) The second component is the weighted integral of utilities to be enjoyed by living members of the current generations, also discounted to their birth dates at rate δ. An apparent alternative to this interpretation of (5) treats current and future generations symmetrically by discounting all utility back to time 0. But this is equivalent to raising ρ to $\rho + \delta$ in (5).

9. In the context of an overlapping-generations model with both gifts to parents and bequests to children, Burbridge (1983) has pointed out a relation between the time consistency of optimal dynastic programs and "reverse discounting" of the utility of parents. The criterion $W(0)$ reverse discounts the lifetime utilities of all those currently alive.

10. By writing $W(0)$ as

$$W(0) = \int_0^\infty \left\{ \int_{-\infty}^t u[c(v,t)] P(t-v) e^{(\delta-\rho)v} \, dv \right\} e^{-\delta t} \, dt,$$

we obtain yet another interpretation of the planner's objective. $W(0)$ is just the discounted integral, over all future dates, of a weighted sum of instantaneous utilities of those then alive. The planner applies the individual subjective discount factor δ in weighting the aggregate utility enjoyed on different dates. In adding up utilities enjoyed on a given date by agents of different ages, vintage is discounted at the net rate $\delta - \rho$. Criterion (6) may therefore be viewed as a discounted sum of static "Benthamite" social welfare functions; see Samuelson (1967).

11. Benveniste and Scheinkman (1979) consider the problem of maximizing

$$\int_0^\infty \hat{u}[y(t), \dot{y}(t), t] \, dt$$

subject to $[y(t), \dot{y}(t)] \in T$, where $\hat{u}(\cdot, \cdot, t)$ is concave, T is convex, and $y(0)$ is given. To write the problem defining $U[C(t)]$ in this form, let

$$y(n) \equiv C(t) - \int_0^n c(t-m, t) P(m) \, dm,$$

so that $\dot{y}(n) = -c(t-n, t) P(n)$. Then the problem in (9) can be written as: Maximize

$$\int_0^\infty u[-\dot{y}(n)/P(n)] \Delta(n) P(n) e^{\rho n} \, dn = \int_0^\infty \hat{u}[\dot{y}(n), n] \, dn$$

subject to $y(n) \geqslant 0$, $\dot{y}(n) \leqslant 0$, for all n. The supplementary regularity conditions assumed in Benveniste and Scheinkman (1979) also hold in the case of (9), except, possibly, for one, that the optimal solution exists for every $C(t)$. Existence is guaranteed under quite general conditions when there is a finite age $\hat{n}$ such that $F(\hat{n}) = 1$ (see Yaari, 1964). Existence can also be established for standard utility functions. We therefore assume it. Note that $U[C(t)]$ may not be well-defined if the welfare weight attached to older generations grows "too quickly" relative to the rate at which members of those generations die and δ. This problem too can be avoided when there is a finite age beyond which the probability of survival is zero.

12. It is easily verified that the solution to the individual's problem is time consistent. For a detailed discussion, see Burness (1976).

13. In these expressions, $P(s - v)/P(t - v)$ (for $s \geqslant t$) is just the conditional probability that an agent of vintage v is alive on date s, given survival to date t; that is,

$$P(s - v)/P(t - v) = \exp\left[-\int_{t-v}^{s-v} p(q)\,dq\right] = \exp\left[-\int_{t}^{s} p(q - v)\,dq\right].$$

14. As conventionally stated, the government budget constraint limits the present value of net transfers (calculated using "risk-free" interest rates) to the government's initial assets [assumed to be zero in equation (27)]. To write that constraint in the form (27) in an infinite-horizon setting, however, additional constraints on the path of net transfers are needed. In particular, the present value of net transfers must be well defined. Subsections 10.6.3 and 10.6.4 describe a setting in which this convergence condition may not hold; further discussion of the issues raised is provided in those sections. Until then, we assume that the present value of net government transfers converges. (As emphasized by Wilson, 1981, Walras's law may not be valid in an infinite-horizon setup without suitable convergence conditions.)

15. In this case, existence requires a finite maximum lifespan.

16. Hillier and Malcomson (1984) give another example of a time-consistent fiscal policy requiring distortionary taxation. The economy they consider, however, is one in which consumption externalities lead to a Pareto-inefficient laissez-faire equilibrium. Distortionary taxes can therefore support efficient allocations, in contrast to our example.

17. In applying our framework to Weil's model (1985), we would write a utilitarian social welfare function (for $t_0 = 0$) as

$$\int_0^\infty u[c(0,t)]e^{-\delta t}\,dt + \int_0^\infty \left\{\gamma \int_v^\infty u[c(v,t)]e^{-\delta(t-v)}\,dt\,e^{\gamma v}\right\} e^{-\rho v}\,dv,$$

where we distinguish again between δ and ρ, the private and planner discount rates [cf. (5)]. After a change in the order of integration, this criterion becomes

$$\int_0^\infty \left\{u[c(0,t)]e^{-(\delta+\gamma-\rho)t}\,dt + \gamma \int_0^t u[c(t-n,t)]e^{-(\delta+\gamma-\rho)n}\,dn\right\} e^{(\gamma-\rho)t}\,dt,$$

where $n = t - v$ as usual [cf. (7)]. We again have a two-step maximization, where, given aggregate consumption $C(t)$, the expression in curly brackets is maximized subject to the constraint

$$c(0,t) + \gamma \int_0^t c(t-n,t)e^{\gamma(t-n)}\,dn \leqslant C(t).$$

(The resulting indirect utility function need not be independent of calendar time.) It is straightforward to verify that in the egalitarian case $\rho = \delta$, the planner sets everyone's consumption equal to $\bar{c}(t) = C(t)/e^{\gamma t}$. The social welfare function then reduces to the second formulation of Koopmans (1967), $\int_0^\infty u[\bar{c}(t)]e^{(\gamma-\rho)t}\,dt$ [equation (35)]. Notice, however, that this simplification does not occur in general unless $\rho = \delta$. As we have argued above, there is no necessity for these two discount rates to coincide.

18. Proof: Suppose that $w(0) = c(0)$ always. Then by (38), $x(1)/[1 + r(1)] = \tau(0) + \tau(1)/[1 + r(1)]$, and so by (40), $w(2) - c(2) - x(1)[1 + r(2)] = 0$. Since $w(2)$ and $r(2)$ are fixed, there is a unique value of $x(1)$, denoted $\bar{x}(1)$, simultaneously satisfying this last equation and (41). The individual Euler condition for generation 0 states that $u'[w(0)]/u'[\bar{x}(1)] = 1 + r(1)$ if $w(0) = c(0)$; so a unique interest rate $\bar{r}(1)$ is determined, along with an associated wage $\bar{w}(1)$. This interest rate of course satisfies $\bar{r}(1) = Y'[K(1); \theta(1)]$, but with $K(1) = w(0) - c(0) - \tau(0) = -\tau(0)$, we can rewrite this equality as $\bar{r}(1) = Y'[-\tau(0); \theta(1)]$ and infer the existence of a unique transfer payment $\bar{\tau}(0)$. By (39), $\bar{w}(1) - c(1) - x(2)/[1 + r(2)] - \bar{\tau}(0)[1 + \bar{r}(1)] = 0$; the key feature of this generation 1 budget constraint is that the variables under bars are functions of $w(0)$, $w(2)$, and $r(2)$ *only*. Because the budget constraint and the individual Euler equation determine $\bar{c}(1)$, $\bar{c}(1)$ is therefore *not* a function of $K(0)[1 + r(0)]$. Together with the Euler equation for generation 0, equation (44) implies that $u'[x(0)] = \beta[1 + \bar{r}(1)]u'[\bar{c}(1)]$. Using (37) we can write this as $u'\{K(0)[1 + r(0)] + \bar{\tau}(0)\} = \beta[1 + \bar{r}(1)]u'[\bar{c}(1)]$. A perturbation of the period 0 production function that changes $K(0)[1 + r(0)]$ but leaves $w(0)$ the same will cause this necessary equality to be violated, as none of the variables under bars will change. It follows that $w(0) = c(0)$ will not hold in general at an optimum.

19. By introducing a public good and constraining the government's powers of taxation further, one can devise a simpler, two-period example of time-inconsistent fiscal policy. This example is closer to the one analyzed by Hillier and Malcomson (1984). A representative of generation 0 lives two periods and maximizes $u[c(0)] + \beta\{u[x(1)] + v[G(1)]\}$, where $G(1)$ is the supply of a public good in period 1. An old generation in period 0 owns the capital stock $K(0)$ and maximizes $u[x(0)]$, while generation 1 lives only one period and maximizes $u[c(1)] + v[G(1)]$. Social welfare is $W(0) = u[x(0)] + u[c(0)] + \beta\{u[x(1)] + u[c(1)] + 2v[G(1)]\}$. The government is now allowed to make transfers *only* in the final period, which is also when it supplies the public good. The government budget constraint is therefore $2\tau(1) + G(1) \leqslant 0$, since we are still constraining the government to make the same (net) transfers to everyone alive at the time. The government has no tools with which to influence $x(0)$, so the only private budget constraints that concern us are those of generation 0 and the lamentably short-lived generation 1. These are, respectively, $w(0) - c(0) - [x(1) - \tau(1)]/[1 + r(1)] \geqslant 0$ and $w(1) - c(1) + \tau(1) \geqslant 0$. It is easy to see that once period 1 arrives, the planner will wish to set the lump-sum tax $\tau(1)$ according to the formula $u'[x(1)] + u'[c(1)] = 4v'[G(1)]$. From the perspective of time $t = 0$, however, the first-order condition for $\tau(1)$ is

$$u'[x(1)]\left[1 + \frac{x(1) - \tau(1)}{1 + r(1)}\frac{dr(1)}{d\tau(1)}\right] + u'[c(1)]\left[1 - K(1)\frac{dr(1)}{d\tau(1)}\right] = 4v'[G(1)].$$

After combining these two first-order conditions and using the relation $K(1) = w(0) - c(0)$, we see that policy will be time consistent if and only if

$$[w(0) - c(0)]\{u'[x(1)] - u'[c(1)]\}\frac{dr(1)}{d\tau(1)} = 0$$

[cf. (43)]. If $dr(1)/d\tau(1) \neq 0$, time consistency therefore requires $w(0) = c(0)$ and/or $u'[x(1)] = u'[c(1)]$ (a condition again satisfied at the command optimum). If $w(0) = c(0)$, however, $K(1) = 0$, a possibility easily ruled out if the production function obeys the restrictions listed in note 7. As in the text, $u'[x(1)] = u'[c(1)]$ can also be ruled out as a general necessary condition for maximization of $W(0)$.

20. Lucas and Stokey (1983) study a different setting in which the addition of policy instruments (in their case, the ability to manage the maturity structure of the public debt) enables the government to ensure that optimal plans are time consistent. Notice that optimal policy is time consistent in the finite-horizon economy if there is no old generation alive in period 0. In that case there are again many instruments as targets.

21. See note 14.

22. It would be interesting to study the properties of a time-consistent policy of the type constructed in Phelps and Pollak (1968). This is a subject for future research.

References

Abel, A. B. "Precautionary Saving and Accidental Bequests," *American Economic Review* 75 (1985), 777–791.

Abel, A. B. "Optimal Monetary Growth," *Journal of Monetary Economics* 19 (1987), 437–450.

Arrow, K. J., and M. Kurz. *Public Investment, the Rate of Return, and Optimal Fiscal Policy*, Baltimore: The Johns Hopkins Press, 1970.

Benveniste, L. M., and J. A. Scheinkman. "On the Differentiability of the Value Function in Dynamic Models of Economics," *Econometrica* 47 (1979), 727–732.

Blanchard, O. J. "Debts, Deficits, and Finite Horizons," *Journal of Political Economy* 93 (1985), 223–247.

Buiter, W. H. "Fiscal Policy in Open Interdependent Economies," Working Paper 1429, National Bureau of Economic Research, 1984.

Burbridge, J. B. "Government Debt in an Overlapping-Generations Model with Bequests and Gifts," *American Economic Review* 73 (1983), 222–227.

Burness, H. S. "A Note on Consistent Naive Intertemporal Decision Making and an Application to the Case of an Uncertain Lifetime," *Review of Economic Studies* 43 (1976), 547–550.

Calvo, G. A. "On the Time Consistency of Optimal Policy in a Monetary Economy," *Econometrica* 46 (1978), 1411–1428.

Cass, D. "Optimum Growth in an Aggregative Model of Capital Accumulation," *Review of Economic Studies* 32 (1965), 233–240.

Chamley, C. "Efficient Taxation in a Stylized Model of Intertemporal General Equilibrium," *International Economic Review* 26 (1985), 451–468.

Diamond, P. A. "National Debt in a Neo-classical Growth Model," *American Economic Review* 55 (1965), 1126–1150.

Eckstein, Z., M. Eichenbaum, and D. Peled. "Uncertain Lifetimes and the Welfare-Enhancing Properties of Annuity Markets and Social Security," *Journal of Public Economics* 26 (1985), 303–326.

Fischer, S. "Dynamic Consistency, Cooperation and the Benevolent Dissembling Government," *Journal of Economic Dynamics and Control* 2 (1980), 93–107.

Frenkel, J. A., and A. Razin. "Fiscal Policies in the World Economy," *Journal of Political Economy* 94 (1986), 564–594.

Giovannini, A. "The Exchange Rate, the Capital Stock, and Fiscal Policy," *European Economic Review* (1988).

Hillier, B., and J. M. Malcomson. "Dynamic Inconsistency, Rational Expectations, and Optimal Government Policy," *Econometrica* 52 (1984), 1437–1451.

Koopmans, T. C. "On the Concept of Optimal Economic Growth," in *Semaine d'Etude sur le Role de l'Analyse Econometrique dans la Formulation des Plans de Developpement*, volume I, Vatican City: Pontifical Academy of Sciences, 1965.

Koopmans, T. C. "Intertemporal Distribution and 'Optimal' Aggregate Economic Growth," in *Ten Economic Studies in the Tradition of Irving Fisher*, New York: John Wiley & Sons, 1967.

Kydland, F. E., and E. C. Prescott. "Rules Rather Than Discretion: The Inconsistency of Optimal Plans," *Journal of Political Economy* 85 (1977), 473–491.

Kydland, F. E., and E. C. Prescott. "Dynamic Optimal Taxation, Rational Expectations and Optimal Control," *Journal of Economic Dynamics and Control* 2 (1980), 79–91.

Lerner, A. P. "Consumption-Loan Interest and Money," *Journal of Political Economy* 67 (1959), 512–518.

Lucas, R. E., Jr., and N. L. Stokey. "Optimal Fiscal and Monetary Policy in an Economy without Capital," *Journal of Monetary Economics* 12 (1983), 55–93.

O'Connell, S. A., and S. P. Zeldes. "Rational Ponzi Games," *International Economic Review* (1988).

Phelps, E. S., and R. A. Pollak. "On Second-Best National Saving and Game-Equilibrium Growth," *Review of Economic Studies* 35 (1968), 185–199.

Phelps, E. S., and J. G. Riley. "Rawlsian Growth: Dynamic Programming of Capital and Wealth for Intergeneration 'Maximin' Justice," *Review of Economic Studies* 45 (1978), 103–120.

Ramsey, F. P. "A Mathematical Theory of Saving," *Economic Journal* 38 (1928), 543–559.

Samuelson, P. A. "A Turnpike Refutation of the Golden Rule in a Welfare-Maximizing Many-Year Plan," in *Essays on the Theory of Optimal Economic Growth*, K. Shell, ed., Cambridge, MA: The MIT Press, 1967.

Samuelson, P. A. "The Two-Part Golden Rule Deduced as the Asymptotic Turnpike of Catenary Motions," *Western Economic Journal* 6 (1968), 85–89.

Shell, K. "Notes on the Economics of Infinity," *Journal of Political Economy* 79 (1971), 1002–1011.

Strotz, R. H. "Myopia and Inconsistency in Dynamic Utility Maximization," *Review of Economic Studies* 23 (1956), 165–180.

Tobin, J. "Life Cycle Saving and Balanced Growth," in *Ten Economic Studies in the Tradition of Irving Fisher*, New York: John Wiley & Sons, 1967.

Turnovsky, S. J., and W. A. Brock. "Time Consistency and Optimal Government Policies in Perfect Foresight Equilibrium," *Journal of Public Economics* 13 (1980), 183–212.

Weil, P. "Overlapping Families of Infinitely Lived Agents," mimeograph, Harvard University, 1985.

Wilson, C. A. "Equilibrium in Dynamic Models with an Infinity of Agents," *Journal of Economic Theory* 24 (1981), 95–111.

Yaari, M. E. "On the Existence of an Optimal Plan in a Continuous-Time Allocation Process," *Econometrica* 32 (1964), 576–590.

Yarri, M. E. "Uncertain Lifetime, Life Insurance, and the Theory of the Consumer," *Review of Economic Studies* 32 (1965), 137–150.

11 Checks and Balances on the Government Budget

Torsten Persson and Lars E. O. Svensson

11.1. Introduction

Suppose a government currently in power knows that it will be replaced in the future by a new government with different objectives—for instance, a government that is in favor of a larger public sector. How does that affect the current government's behavior? More specifically, what are the implications for the current government's choices between distortionary taxes and borrowing? In particular, will the current government run fiscal deficits when it knows that its successor's choice of public spending will be influenced by the level of public debt that the succesor inherits? This is the first of two sets of questions we attempt to answer in this chapter.

Suppose instead that the government currently in power will remain in power in the future. The government has access to distortionary labor taxes only, and chooses, ex ante, an optimal second-best sequence of labor taxes over time and the optimal level of government expenditure. The optimal sequence of labor taxes depends on the ex ante elasticities of labor supply according to the standard formula for optimal taxes. Suppose, however, that the ex post elasticities of labor supply differ from the corresponding ex ante elasticities. This means that the optimal taxes ex post differ from the optimal taxes ex ante. Accordingly, the government has an incentive to deviate ex post from the tax policy announced ex ante. The private sector anticipates such deviations by the government, the second-best policy is not credible, and the economy ends up in a third-best optimum, rather than in a second-best optimum. How does the credible third-best policy differ from the unenforceable second-best policy? In particular, how do optimal government spending and public debt policy differ? This is the second set of questions we attempt to answer.

For the first set of questions, we can think of the two governments having time-inconsistent *preferences*, and for the second set of questions we can think of the one government having time-inconsistent *constraints*. We deal

A previous version of this chapter was presented at the Sapir Conference on Economic Effects of the Government Budget in Tel-Aviv, December 22–24, 1986. Support from NSF grant no. SES-8605871 is gratefully acknowledged. We have benefited from comments by participants in the conference, in particular the discussant Maurice Obstfeld, and by participants in seminars at the University of Rochester, the University of Pennsylvania, and Columbia University.

with these problems in turn. Thus, when dealing with time-inconsistent preferences, we make assumptions such that the problem with time-inconsistent constraints does not occur. Similarly, when dealing with time-inconsistent constraints, we assume that the problem with time-consistent preferences does not occur.

Our work in this chapter is, of course, related to the rapidly growing literature on time consistency of government policy—see Barro (1986), Cukierman (1985), Fischer (1986), and Rogoff (1987) for recent surveys. In particular, it is closely related to the papers by Lucas and Stokey (1983), Persson and Svensson (1984), and Persson, Persson, and Svensson (1987). At a specific level, these papers show that the second-best optimal fiscal and or monetary policy under commitment can be enforced under discretionary policymaking, if each government leaves its successor with a particular maturity structure of the public debt. The results also suggest a more general principle, however. As long as the current government can affect some state variable that enters (in an essential way) in its successor's decision problem, it can affect the policy carried out by the successor. In this chapter the level of public debt is the state variable that gives the current government an instrument to control the future government.[1]

The chapter has four sections. Section 11.2 deals with time-inconsistent preferences, section 11.3 deals with time-inconsistent constraints, and section 11.4 presents conclusions.

11.2. Time-Inconsistent Preferences

We assume a small open economy. There are two periods and one good. The economy can borrow and lend at a given world rate of interest equal to zero. Therefore, present-value prices of the good in the two periods are equal to unity, $p_1 = p_2 = 1$. Goods output in the two periods, y_1 and y_2, are produced with input of labor, l_1 and l_2, according to a linear technology, $y_1 = l_1$ and $y_1 = l_2$. The competitive before-tax wage rate is unity in both periods.

There is a representative consumer with a labor endowment of one unit in each period. The consumer has preferences over private consumption of goods, c_1 and c_2, and labor supply, l_1 and l_2, in the two periods given by an additively separable concave utility function, increasing in consumption and decreasing in labor supply,[2]

$$u(c_1, l_1, c_2, l_2) = f(c_1) + h_1(1 - l_1) + c_2 + h_2(1 - l_2). \tag{1}$$

Maximizing the utility function in (1) subject to the intertemporal budget constraint that the present value of consumption equals the present value of after-tax wage income gives rise to an indirect utility function $U(w_1, w_2)$ of after-tax wage rates, w_1 and w_2, and to labor supply functions, $L_1(w_1)$ and $L_2(w_2)$, in the two periods.

The additive separability, and the linearity in period 2 consumption of the utility function (1) implies that labor supply in each period depends only on the after-tax wage rate in the same period. This makes sure that ex ante and ex post labor supplies in period 2 coincide, which is necessary for the governments' constraints to be time consistent.

The government in power in period 1 is called government 1. We first look at the case when government 1 is in power in both periods 1 and 2, as a frame of reference. There is government consumption in period 2 only. Government consumption in period 1 can easily be introduced, and below we shall report results also on that case. Government 1 has preferences over government consumption in period 2, g, according to the utility function

$$U(w_1, w_2) + v^1(g), \tag{2}$$

the sum of private utility of private consumption and a concave utility function $v^1(g)$ of government consumption.

We assume that government consumption can only be financed by proportional taxes on wage income. Capital taxes are excluded to avoid more than one source of time-consistency problems. Government 1 hence faces an optimal taxation problem of maximizing (2) subject to an intertemporal budget constraint according to which the present value of government consumption equals the present value of tax revenues. This problem can be solved in two steps.

The first step is to maximizes $U(w_1, w_2)$ subject to the government's budget constraint, for given level of government consumption g. This gives rise to preferred after-tax wage functions $\bar{w}_1(g)$ and $\bar{w}_2(g)$, and a corresponding government (net) borrowing function $b(g)$. (The latter is equal to the negative of period 1 tax revenues in the case when period 1 government consumption is zero.) Substitution of the wage functions into the indirect utility function $U(w_1, w_2)$ gives a new indirect utility function of the level of government consumption, $\bar{V}(g) \equiv U(\bar{w}_1(g), \bar{w}_2(g))$. It is practical to define the ex ante marginal cost of government consumption, $\bar{\lambda}(g)$, as the negative of the derivative of the new indirect utility function, $\bar{\lambda}(g) \equiv -\bar{V}_g(g)$. The ex ante marginal cost of government consumption is a measure of the distortionary effect of taxation: it exceeds unity whenever taxes are distortionary.

The second step is to choose the level of government consumption optimally. This can now be done by equalizing the ex ante marginal cost of government consumption, $\bar{\lambda}(g)$, to the marginal utility of government consumption defined as $\mu^1(g) \equiv v_g^1(g)$,

$$\bar{\lambda}(g) = \mu^1(g). \tag{3}$$

This determines the preferred level of government consumption for government 1, $\bar{g}^1$, and the corresponding preferred debt level, $\bar{b}^1 = b(\bar{g}^1)$.

This is illustrated in figure 11.1. The preferred government consumption for government 1 is given by the intersection at point A between the upward-sloping marginal cost curve $\bar{\lambda}(g)$ and the downward-sloping marginal utility curve $\mu^1(g)$.

Let us also describe the behavior of government 1 ex post, under the assumption that it remains in power in period 2. Ex post, government 1 has to use period 2 tax revenues to finance total government expenditure in period 2, consisting of the sum of government consumption g and the predetermined borrowing $\bar{b}^1$. Default on the debt is ruled out. (For the case

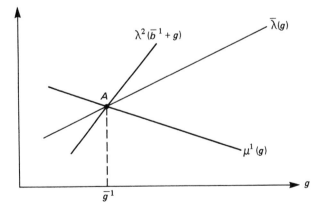

Figure 11.1

without period 1 government consumption, the debt level is negative, so there is no incentive to default.) The after-tax period 2 wage rate consistent with expenditure $\bar{b}^1 + g$ will be a function $w^2(\bar{b}^1 + g)$. As in the ex ante problem above, one can define an ex post indirect utility function for private utility of private consumption, and an ex post marginal cost of government consumption, $\lambda^2(\bar{b}^1 + g)$. Ex post, then, government 1 chooses government consumption to equalize the ex post marginal cost of government consumption to the marginal utility of government consumption.

This is also illustrated in figure 11.1. The ex post marginal cost curve is steeper than the ex ante marginal cost curve. The reason is that when government consumption increases ex post, only the period 2 tax rate is increased, since the period 1 tax rate is predetermined. This is more distortionary than when both periods' tax rates are increased as in the ex ante problem underlying the ex ante marginal cost curve. The ex post marginal cost curve intersects the marginal utility curve at point A, for the same level of government consumption as the ex ante marginal cost curve. This illustrates that the constraints of government 1 are time consistent: ex post it has incentive to pursue the same policy as it had ex ante. As further discussed in section 11.3, with a different private utility function the ex post marginal cost curve will intersect the marginal utility curve at a different level than the ex ante marginal cost curve, giving rise to a time-consistency problem even with time-consistent preferences.

Let us now consider the case when a new government, called government 2, is in power in period 2. It differs from government 1 in having a different utility function for government consumption, $v^2(g)$. This utility function differ from that of government 1 in that the marginal utility of government consumption for government 2, $\mu^2(g) \equiv v_g^2(g)$, exceeds that of government 1 for all levels of government consumption, $\mu^2(g) > \mu^1(g)$. The marginal utility curve of government 2 is illustrated in figure 11.2. Government 2 faces the same ex post optimal taxation problem as discussed for government 1 above, and hence the same ex post marginal cost curve for government consumption. Given the level of debt it inherits from government 1, it chooses the level of government consumption so as to equalize the ex post marginal cost of government consumption with its marginal utility of government consumption. If government 2 inherits the government 1 preferred debt level $\bar{b}^1$, it would choose the level of government consumption corresponding to point B, the intersection between the ex post marginal cost curve for $\bar{b}^1$ and the marginal utility curve. If government 2 were in

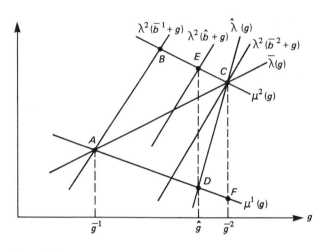

Figure 11.2

power in both periods, it would choose its preferred level of government consumption, $\bar{g}^2$, given by the intersection of the ex ante marginal cost curve and its marginal utility curve at point C. The corresponding preferred level of debt, $\bar{b}^2$, makes the ex post marginal cost curve also intersect the marginal utility curve at point C.

For an arbitrary level of debt, government 2 will hence choose a level of government consumption, $g^2(b)$, given by the intersection of the ex post marginal cost curve and the marginal utility curve,

$$\lambda^2(b + g) = \mu^2(g). \tag{4}$$

The level of government consumption will be a decreasing function of the level of debt. The inverse of that function, also a decreasing function, is denoted $\tilde{b}(g)$ and called the required debt function. It gives the debt level required to induce government 2 to choose a given level of government consumption. It summarizes the behavior of government 2.

Let us now return to the behavior of government 1, when it anticipates that it will be replaced by government 2 in period 2. The required debt function enters as an incentive-compatibility constraint in the decision problem of government 1. For each level of government consumption, the required debt level determines corresponding after-tax wage rates in the two periods, $\tilde{w}_1(g)$ and $\tilde{w}_2(g)$. Substitution of these wage functions into the indirect utility function $U(w_1, w_2)$ gives another indirect utility function

$\hat{V}(g) \equiv U(\tilde{w}_1(g), \tilde{w}_2(g))$, and its derivative defines the time-consistent marginal cost of government consumption, $\hat{\lambda}(g) \equiv -\hat{V}_g(g)$. The optimal policy for government 1 is then to equalize the time-consistent marginal cost of government consumption to its marginal utility of government consumption,

$$\hat{\lambda}(g) = \mu^1(g). \tag{5}$$

This first-order condition defines the time-consistent level of government consumption, $\hat{g}$.

The equilibrium is illustrated in figure 11.2. The time-consistent marginal cost curve intersects the marginal utility curve of government 2 at point C, because the required debt level to induce government 2 to choose its preferred level of government consumption $\bar{g}^2$, $\tilde{b}(\bar{g}^2)$, is of course equal to the preferred debt level $\bar{b}^2$ of government 2. It can be shown with some algebra that the time-consistent marginal cost curve is at least as steep as the ex post marginal cost curve (see Persson and Svensson, 1987). The time-consistent level of government consumption $\hat{g}$ corresponds to point D, and is hence a compromise between the two governments' preferred levels of government consumption,

$$\bar{g}^1 < \hat{g} < \bar{g}^2. \tag{6}$$

Government 1 induces government 2 to choose this level of government consumption by leaving it with the time-consistent debt level $\hat{b} = \tilde{b}(\hat{g})$. This is the debt level that causes the ex post marginal cost curve to intersect the marginal utility curve of government 2 at point E, vertically above point D. It follows that the time-consistent debt level is larger than the one preferred by government 2,

$$\hat{b} > \bar{b}^2. \tag{7}$$

Government 2 is forced to choose a lower level of government consumption by inheriting a larger level of debt.

But is the time-consistent level of borrowing $\hat{b}$ larger or smaller than the level of borrowing $\bar{b}^1$ that government 1 would choose if it were in power in both periods? This depends on whether the point E vertically above D is to the left or right of point B. If to the left, time-consistent borrowing is larger; if to the right, time-consistent borrowing is smaller. Numerical examples demonstrates that both cases can occur, and we cannot expect to find general global results, since the curves in figure 11.2 may have a variety of shapes.

We have, however, been able to derive a local result (for technical details, see Persson and Svensson, 1987). Suppose that points A and C in figure 11.2 are close. Then we can show that the time-consistent level of borrowing is larger or smaller depending upon whether the marginal utility curve for government 1 is steeper or flatter than the marginal utility curve for government 2. That is,

$$\hat{b} \gtrless \bar{b}^1 \qquad \text{if and only if} \qquad -\mu_g^1 \gtrless -\mu_g^2. \tag{8}$$

Let us extend on the intuition of that result. Government 1 is trading off two different distortions. One is to have too much government consumption, what we call the volume distortion. The other is to have, for given level of government consumption, relative tax rates between periods differing from the ex ante optimal taxation solution—more precisely, to have too high tax rates in period 2, what we call the intertemporal distortion. Consider again figure 11.2. Suppose government 1 would leave to government 2 the debt level $\bar{b}^2$ preferred by government 2. Then government 2 would choose its preferred level of government consumption, $\bar{g}^2$, corresponding to point C. The equilibrium would be the one government 2 would have chosen if it were in power in both periods, and there would be no distortion in relative taxes, that is, no intertemporal distortion. From the point of view of government 1, however, there would be a considerable volume distortion, namely, in the level of government consumption. The marginal cost of government consumption would be given by the distance between the horizontal axis and point C, but the marginal utility would be much less, given by the distance between the horizontal axis and point F. The optimum for government 1 is instead to decrease the volume distortion and create some intertemporal distortion, by increasing the debt level, shifting the ex post marginal utility curve to the left, and forcing government 2 to cut back on government consumption. This causes period 1 tax rates to be too low relative to period 2 tax rates, and hence creates an intertemporal distortion. If government 1 has a relatively steep marginal utility curve for government consumption, it puts relatively large weight on the volume distortion. We say that government 1 then is "stubborn." Hence, our result (8) can be interpreted as saying that if government 1 is relatively stubborn, it increases the level of borrowing so much as to shift the ex post marginal cost curve so far left as to end up to the left of the marginal utility curve for $\bar{b}^1$. Then it borrows more than it would if it had remained in power in both periods.

Let us finally comment on the situation when there is government consumption also in period 1. Let us think of government 1 as having preferences over government consumption g_1 and g_2 in period 1 and 2 according to the utility function $v_1^1(g_1) + v_2^1(g_2)$. If government 1 would be in power in both periods it would choose optimal levels of government consumption, $\bar{g}_1^1$ and $\bar{g}_2^1$, say, and an optimal level of borrowing $\bar{b}^1$. In the time-consistent equilibrium when government 1 is replaced by government 2 in period 2, would the time-consistent level of government consumption in period 1, $\hat{g}_1$, fall short of or exceed $\bar{g}_1^1$? The answer is that the time-consistent level of government consumption in period 1 is larger or smaller depending upon whether the time-consistent level of borrowing is larger or smaller than the level when government 1 is in power in both periods,

$$\hat{g}_1 \gtreqless \bar{g}_1^1 \quad \text{if and only if} \quad \hat{b} \gtreqless \bar{b}^1. \tag{9}$$

The reason is that if borrowing is larger, for a constant level of period 1 government consumption, the period 1 tax rate on labor is smaller, and the level of distortion in period 1 is lower. This makes the marginal cost of period 1 government consumption lower, and allows an expansion of period 1 government consumption. (With intertemporal distortion of relative taxes, the marginal costs of government consumption in the two periods differ.)

11.3.   Time-Inconsistent Constraints

We now consider the situation when government 1 is in power in both period, so that the problem of time-inconsistent preferences does not arise. On the other hand, we now assume that the private utility function $u(c_1, l_1, c_1, l_1)$ is not additively separable in labor supply in the two periods. Suppose, in particular, that preferences are of the form

$$u(c_1, l_1, c_2, l_2) = f(c_1) + h(1 - l_1, 1 - l_2) + c_2. \tag{10}$$

With this formulation, the ex ante labor supply functions are of the form $L_1(w_1, w_2)$ and $L_2(w_1, w_2)$, with both after-tax wage rates as arguments. The ex post period 2 labor supply function is of the form $L^2(w_2, l_1)$ with period 1 labor supply as an argument. As a consequence, ex post marginal cost of government consumption $\lambda^2(b + g, l_1)$ has period 1 labor supply as an argument, in addition to the ex post revenue requirement $b + g$. In general, then, the ex ante and ex post elasticities of labor supply (with respect to the tax rate) will differ and the government will face time-inconsistent constraints, in the sense that the ex ante marginal cost of government consumption will differ from the ex post marginal cost of government consumption.[3] This can be demonstrated in the following way.

Using the standard optimal taxation formula (see, for instance, Atkinson and Stiglitz, 1980), the ex ante and ex post marginal cost of government consumption can be written as

$$\bar{\lambda}(g) = \frac{1}{1 - \bar{e}} \quad \text{and} \quad \lambda^2(b + g, l_1) = \frac{1}{1 - e^2}, \tag{11}$$

where

$$\bar{e} = \frac{(1 - w_1)l_1}{w_2 l_2} \frac{\varepsilon L_1}{\varepsilon w_2} + \frac{1 - w_2}{w_2} \frac{\varepsilon L_2}{\varepsilon w_2} \quad \text{and} \quad e^2 = \frac{1 - w_2}{w_2} \frac{\varepsilon L^2}{\varepsilon w_2}; \tag{12}$$

here $\varepsilon L_1 / \varepsilon w_2$ denotes the partial elasticity $w_2 L_{12}/l_1$, etc. It is shown in Persson and Svensson (1987) that

$$\bar{e} \gtrless e^2 \quad \text{if and only if} \quad h_{12} \gtrless 0. \tag{13}$$

Therefore, the ex ante marginal cost of government consumption $\bar{\lambda}(g)$ is higher (lower) than the ex post marginal cost of government consumption $\lambda^2(b + g, l_1)$ if and only if the cross partial in (10) h_{12} is positive (negative).

We illustrate this in figure 11.3, for the case when $h_{12} > 0$. The ex ante marginal cost curve $\bar{\lambda}(g)$ intersects the marginal utility curve $\mu(g)$ at point A, for $g = \bar{g}$, with a corresponding preferred level of borrowing $\bar{b} = b(\bar{g})$ and a corresponding preferred period 1 labor supply $\bar{l}_1$ (we drop the superindex 1 since the same government is in power in both periods). The ex post marginal cost curve for $\bar{b}$ and $\bar{l}_1$, $\lambda^2(\bar{b} + g, \bar{l}_1)$, intersects the marginal utility curve at point B, for a level of government consumption $\tilde{g}$ larger than $\bar{g}$, since the ex post marginal cost for $\bar{g}$ is less than the ex ante marginal cost for $\bar{g}$. Ex post the government has an incentive to deviate from its announced ex ante tax policy and impose higher period 2 taxes and hence a lower period 2 after-tax wage rate, $\tilde{w}_2$, to finance the larger government consumption. That is,

$$\tilde{g} > \bar{g} \quad \text{and} \quad \tilde{w}_2 < \bar{w}_2. \tag{14}$$

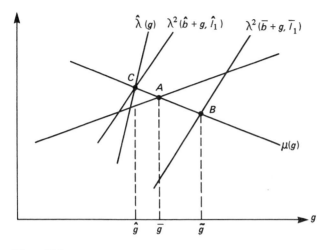

Figure 11.3

Since rational consumers would anticipate the lower period 2 wage rate, the level $\tilde{g}$ of government consumption is not a time-consistent equilibrium. When h_{12} is positive, the ex ante period 1 labor supply function is increasing in the period 2 wage rate. Hence, rational consumers would lower their period 1 labor supply, which would lead to higher borrowing. Higher borrowing shifts the ex post marginal cost curve to the left. So does the direct effect of the lower period 1 labor supply. In the time-consistent equilibrium, the ex post marginal cost curve and the ex ante time-consistent marginal cost curve $\hat{\lambda}(g)$ must intersect the marginal utility curve $\mu(g)$ at a point such as C, for a time-consistent level of government consumption $\hat{g}$, lower than $\tilde{g}$, with corresponding time-consistent borrowing $\hat{b}$ and with corresponding time-consistent period 1 labor supply $\hat{l}_1$.

At this stage, we thus know that

$$\hat{g} < \tilde{g}. \tag{15}$$

But we do not yet know whether $\hat{g} < \bar{g}$, as drawn in figure 11.3, or $\hat{g} \gtrless \bar{g}$. Neither do we know whether $\hat{b} \gtrless \bar{b}$. That is, we do not yet know the relation between third-best time-consistent government spending and public debt in the time-consistent equilibrium and second-best government spending and public debt when the government can precommit its period 2 tax rate to the level dictated by its ex ante preferred policy. We shall refer to the latter situation as policy under commitment, for short.

To obtain the time-consistent solution for government spending, we follow an approach analogous to that in section 11.2. From optimal ex post behavior in period 2, we get a required debt function $\tilde{b}(g, \tilde{l}(g))$, where $\tilde{l}(g)$ is period 1 labor supply, which is itself subject to an equilibrium constraint. Period 1 labor supply enters the required debt function because of its effect on period 2 labor supply (see Persson and Svensson, 1987, for details). There are again corresponding wage functions $\tilde{w}_1(g)$ and $\tilde{w}_2(g)$ that can be used to rewrite the private indirect utility function as $\hat{V}(g) = U(\tilde{w}_1(g), \tilde{w}_2(g))$. The time-consistent marginal cost of government consumption is $\hat{\lambda}(g) = -\hat{V}_g(g)$; $\hat{g}$ follows from the first-order condition

$$\hat{\lambda}(g) = \mu(g), \tag{16}$$

and $\hat{b}$ follows from the required debt function $\hat{b} = \tilde{b}(\hat{g}, \tilde{l}(\hat{g}))$.

It seems almost impossible to derive any general results on how the government's third-best policy, $\hat{g}$ and $\hat{b}$, differs from its second-best policy, $\bar{g}$ and $\bar{b}$, however. To get somewhere, we therefore assume a symmetric and quadratic subutility function $h(1 - l_1, 1 - l_2, \alpha)$ of the form

$$h(1 - l_1, 1 - l_2, \alpha) = -l_1^2/2 - l_2^2/2 + \alpha(1 - l_1)(1 - l_2). \tag{17}$$

Thus $\alpha > 0$ ($\alpha < 0$) corresponds to the case when h_{12} is positive (negative) in (10). With this parametrization, optimal policy under commitment, $\bar{g}(\alpha)$ and $\bar{b}(\alpha)$, as well as optimal time-consistent policy, $\hat{g}(\alpha)$ and $\hat{b}(\alpha)$, are both functions of α. Unfortunately, it turns out to be very hard to derive any definite results on how the two sets of policies differ, even under the quadratic parametrization in (17).

If we confine ourselves to a "small time-consistency problem," that is, to the neighborhood of $\alpha = 0$, we do get some definite results, however. With regard to government consumption it is demonstrated in Persson and Svensson (1987) that for small positive α

$$\hat{g}(\alpha) < \bar{g}(\alpha), \tag{18}$$

while the opposite holds for small negative α. Hence, for a small positive α optimal time-consistent government consumption is lower than optimal government consumption under commitment. The illustration drawn in figure 11.3 thus turns out to be correct. For $g = \bar{g}$, the time-consistent marginal cost curve lies above the ex ante marginal cost curve, which makes $\hat{g}(\alpha) < \bar{g}(\alpha)$.

It thus seems as if the extra distortion that the time-consistency constraint imposes, in addition to the tax distortions existing already under commitment, makes government consumption more costly to finance. Finding good intuition for the result is tricky, however. Introducing a small positive (negative) α in the subutility function (17) not only makes h_{12} positive (negative) and the ex post elasticity of labor supply lower (higher) than the ex ante elasticity. Increasing (decreasing) α from zero, *ceteris paribus*, also decreases (increases) labor supply in both periods, which clearly affects the ex ante, as well as the ex post, marginal cost of government consumption. A priori, both effects should alter the optimal solution under commitment as well as under time consistency, and could well alter the two solutions in a different way. To check which effect drives the results, we tried an alternative parametrization, namely,

$$h(1 - l_1, 1 - l_2, \alpha) = -l_1^2/2 - l_2^2/2 + \alpha l_1 l_2. \tag{19}$$

With this parametrization a positive (negative) α still corresponds to h_{12} positive (negative) in (10). But increasing (decreasing) α from zero now increases (decreases) labor supply in both periods. As discussed in Persson and Svensson (1987), with (19) in place of (17) the result in (18) is reversed. What this suggests, of course, is that it is indeed the direct effects on labor supply that drive the results, not the sign of h_{12} and the relation between the ex ante and ex post elasticities.

What is the relation between time-consistent borrowing $\hat{b}$ and borrowing under commitment $\bar{b}$? Imposing the parametrization in (17) and looking at a small positive α, we have the result (see Persson and Svensson, 1987)

$$\hat{b}(\alpha) = \bar{b}(\alpha). \tag{20}$$

Initially, we had expected that the lower level of government consumption in the time-consistent equilibrium would require the government to leave itself with a larger public debt than under commitment to "bind its own hands" in period 2—in the same way as government 1 bound government 2's hands when preferences were inconsistent by leaving government 2 with a larger debt. But what (20) says is that it is not necessary to change the debt policy, relative to the commitment equilibrium, to help enforce the lower level of government consumption in the time-consistent equilibrium. [Imposing the alternative parametrization (19) rather than (17) leads to the same result.]

Again, we need to look at the labor supply resonses to see what is going on. First, the decrease in labor supplies when we increase α from zero increases the ex post marginal cost of government consumption relative to the ex ante marginal cost. This effect should tend to decrease required debt relative to preferred debt for each level of government spending. Second, the public debt is not the only "state variable" that affects the government's ex post choices. So does period 1 labor supply, since it affects period 2 labor supply and hence the ex post marginal cost $\lambda^2(b + g, l_1, \alpha)$. Therefore a lower period 1 labor supply, as in the time-consistent equilibrium we are considering, would generally lower required debt by increasing λ^2. For the local experiment here, that effect turns out to be of second order, however (see Persson and Svensson, 1987, for details on the above argument).

Maybe our difficulty in explaining the results intuitively is not too surprising. It is often very hard to characterize the solution even to second-best optimal tax problems. Here, we add another constraint to a second-best optimal tax problem and try to explain how and why the resulting third-best solution differs from the second-best solution.

11.4. Concluding Remarks

We have shown how a government can exert some influence over the future level of government consumption when preferences over government consumption are time inconsistent. In particular, a conservative government, less expansionary than its liberal successor, will collect less taxes and leave more public debt than what the successor would want. This makes equilibrium government consumption somewhere in between what it would have been if each of the two governments had been able to commit policy. Specifically, if the conservative government is relatively stubborn, it may end up borrowing more than it would have done if it were to be in power in the future. Stubbornness here refers to the weight attached to the preferred level of government consumption relative to the welfare cost of distorted relative tax rates over time.[4]

We simplified the problem to a two-period perfect foresight framework, where the government knows with certainty that it will be succeeded by a more expansionary government. It is clearly desirable to extend the analysis to one with several periods, and to one where there is uncertainty about the nature of succeeding governments due to uncertainty about future election results. Such an analysis has been independently provided in a recent very interesting paper by Alesina and Tabellini (1987). They consider the complementary case with two political parties with different preferences such that they prefer different *kinds* of public goods, rather than different *levels* of the same public good as in our model. There is electoral uncertainty in each period about whether the current government will remain in power or will be succeded by the other party. The main result is that electoral uncertainty implies a bias toward higher debt levels for *both* governments.

We have also discussed how the time-consistent equilibrium and the commitment equilibrium differ if preferences over government consumption are time consistent but the constraints are time inconsistent. In particular, if the ex post elasticity of labor supply is lower than the ex ante elasticity, there is a temptation to deviate from the commitment equilibrium, increase taxes, and expand government consumption ex post. But when ex post optimality is imposed as an additional constraint, optimal time-consistent government consumption may be either higher or lower than optimal government consumption under commitment.

Some of the results in this chapter are no doubt specific to the simple framework that we have adopted. However, we do believe that the analysis in the paper (of time-inconsistent preferences) may shed some new light on the huge U.S. fiscal deficits under the current Republican administration. We also believe that the general idea has wider applications. The privatization policy of the current conservative governments in Britain and France and the settlements policy of the previous Likud government in Israel can both be seen as an attempt to impose a particular policy on succeding governments with different preferences by affecting future constraints on policymaking. In our view, the general idea about how governments may affect the choices of succeding governments sets an exciting agenda for new research.

Notes

1. Alesina and Tabellini (1987) have independently pursued a very interesting analysis of public debt in the complementary case when different governments have preferences for different kinds of public goods, rather than, as in our case, preferences for different volumes of the same public good. A comparison with their analysis and results is given in the concluding section.

2. We can think of each consumer as deriving utility from government consumption with government consumption entering in an additively separable way in the utility function. The different governments considered later can then be viewed as representing different parts of the population with different preferences for government consumption, but with the same preferences over private consumption of goods and labor.

3. Another way to generate a difference between ex ante and ex post labor supplies would be to specify preferences as

$$u(c_1, 1 - l_1, c_2, 1 - l_2) = f_1(c_1) + h_1(1 - l_1) + f_2(c_2) + h_2(1 - l_2).$$

Then ex post labor supply would be of the form $L^2(w_2, s_1)$, where s_1 denotes private savings in period 1.

4. Maurice Obstfeld has showed us that the following somewhat different setup leads to very similar formal results, although in a simpler way. Consider a two-period small open exchange economy. Governments have access to international capital markets, but private agents (by assumption) do not. There is one government in power in period 1, and a more expansionary government in power in period 2. Then it is easy to derive analogues to our results.

To us, the setup we use, with the distortion originating in income taxation rather than in a wedge between domestic and international interest rates, allows for a more relevant and interesting interpretation of the results.

References

Alesina, A., and G. Tabellini, 1987. "Budget Deficits and Public Debt in a Democracy," mimeo.

Atkinson, A., and J. E. Stiglitz, 1980. *Lectures on Public Economics*, McGraw-Hill: Maidenhead.

Barro, R. J., 1986. "Recent Developments in the Theory of Rules Versus Discretion," *Economic Journal* (supplement) 96, 23–37.

Cukierman, A., 1985. "Central Bank Behavior and Credibility—Some Recent Developments," mimeo, Tel-Aviv University.

Fischer, S., 1986. "Time-Consistent Monetary and Fiscal Policies: A Survey," mimeo, MIT.

Lucas, R. E., and N. L. Stokey, 1983. "Optimal Fiscal and Monetary Policy in an Economy without Capital," *Journal of Monetary Economics* 12, 55–93.

Persson, M., T. Persson, and L. E. O. Svensson, 1987. "Time Consistency of Fiscal and Monetary Policy," *Econometrica* 55, 1419–1431.

Persson, T., and L. E. O. Svensson, 1984. "Time-Consistent Fiscal Policy and Government Cash-Flow," *Journal of Monetary Economics* 14, 365–374.

Persson, T., and L. E. O. Svensson, 1987. "Checks and Balances on the Government Budget," Seminar Paper No. 380, IIES.

Rogoff, K., 1987. "Reputational Constraints on Monetary Policy," *Carnegie-Rochester Conference Series* 26, 141–181.

IV INFLATION

12 World Inflation Revisited

Arnold C. Harberger

12.1. Introduction

The occasion of the 1986 Pinhas Sapir Conference presented me with a rare opportunity to return to a line of investigation that I had earlier pursued for several years on the topic of world inflation. Coincidentally, one of my first major reports on this topic was presented at the 1979 Pinhas Sapir Conference, and was published in its proceedings volume.[1] The coincidence led me to the decision to make this chapter, which is based on a paper presented at the 1986 conference, to a considerable degree the "twin" of its predecessor—using, however, entirely new data. This idea might not have worked, but luck was with me. In only the seven years since the 1979 conference, a whole new generation of inflationary episodes of different types has been spawned—4 new episodes of acute inflation, 15 new cases of chronic inflation, 18 new cases of devaluation crisis. All this new evidence brings interest to the question of whether the new data support the principal conclusions of the earlier exercise.

12.2. The Key Variables Examined

The exercise is relevant for the present volume, since variables representing fiscal pressure play an important role. While the earlier study took it for granted that monetary expansion was an essential ingredient of the inflation process, its main focus was on *why* such expansion took place.

What I had in mind was a sort of "canonical inflation scenario" in which a fiscal deficit lay at the root of the inflationary process. The deficit is linked to inflation via monetary expansion only when the government turns to the banking system for financing its deficit are inflationary troubles engendered. One measure of the "pressure" that is put on the banking system by the need to finance the government is

$\beta = (\Delta$ banking system credit to the public sector) $\div$ GDP.

The data on banking system credit to the public sector are derived from the consolidated accounts of the banking system, as given in the monetary survey of *International Financial Statistics* (*IFS*, lines 32an, 32b, 32c). In calculating β, the increase in these items over the course of a year (i.e., from December to December) is expressed as a fraction of the nominal GDP of that year; β is thus the fraction of total GDP that the public sector siphons out of the banking system.

A second measure of the pressure put on the banking system by the government is

γ = (banking system credit to the public sector) $\div$ total bank credit.

Whereas β is a flow variable reflecting concurrent *action* by the public sector, γ deals with stocks and reflects the cumulative result of past actions. In the "canonical inflation scenario," the government might draw new credit from the banking system, and the banking system then curtail private sector credit by a like amount, thus "sterilizing" the effect on β on the money supply. Such sterilization might be easy in the first stages of an inflationary surge, if γ started at very low levels. But if sterilization continues, γ will rise, at each step squeezing private sector credit still further. Because the resistance against further squeezing of the share of the private sector will grow at each step, as will the true social cost thereof, we can expect that the higher is the level of γ, the less likely it is that new advances to the government will be offset through "sterilizing" reductions in private sector credit.[2]

Note that neither β nor γ alone has any direct mechanical connection to the increase in the money supply. As already shown, it is possible up to a point for the government to borrow from the banking system without the latter, in turn, increasing the money supply (M). But under a typical inflationary scenario we would expect that a high β would sooner or later lead to increases in M, especially when γ is itself already relatively high.

The choice of the third variable was similarly governed by a desire to avoid a "money supply identity." That variable is

λ = (Δ bank credit during year t) $\div$ (total bank credit at end of $t - 1$).

Obviously, there is more of a connection between the rate of increase in money (μ) and λ than between μ and β or γ, for domestic credit is usually the largest single item on the asset side of the banking system's consolidated balance sheet, while money is the largest single item on the liability side. The degree of connection between λ and μ is not complete, however. In a country with a fixed exchange rate, for example, the money supply is *not* a policy variable, but is endogenously determined by the tastes of the public for holding money. However, the distribution of the assets of the banking system between domestic credit and net foreign assets *is* subject to policy control by the Central Bank and the natural instrument for exercising this control is the volume of domestic credit, with the Central Bank easing credit when it wants to get rid of international reserves and tightening credit when it wants to draw them in.

Thus one can at least say that the volume of credit *is* a policy variable and that it is *distinct from* the quantity of money. The volume of credit retains its identity as a policy variable even when the quantity of money is beyond the control of the Central Bank, as in a fixed exchange rate system, or one with a pre-fixed crawling peg. Nonetheless, when the rate of inflation gets to be high, it is most often driven by the domestic credit component of the asset side. (Only in rare cases does one witness a major price inflation that is simply fueled by a huge inflow of reserves.)

12.3. The Four Categories of Countries

All of the data used in the exercises presented here are drawn from *International Financial Statistics* (Washington, D.C.: International Monetary Fund, various issues and tapes). The objective was to place countries in groups according to the nature and severity of their inflationary processes. The countries in each group represent a virtual enumeration of the *IFS* data available for the category in question. Once a country met the criteria, it was left out only for lack of adequate data from *IFS*.[3] Apart from missing data, only small size (population less than 2 million) could cause a country to be left out.

There follows a listing of the groupings into which country-episodes were placed. In each case the criteria for a country's entering that particular classification are specified.

12.3.1. Acute Inflation

The annual average rate of inflation reported in *IFS* is the average level of the consumer price index (CPI) for one year minus the same index for the previous year. It can also be thought of as the average of twelve consecutive yearly inflation rates, each comparing one month of year t with the corresponding month of year $t - 1$. If the rate of inflation, π, defined in this way exceeds 80% for two or more consecutive years, the span of time for which it remains greater than or equal to 80% is considered to be an episode of acute inflation.

12.3.2. Chronic Inflation

The annual average rate of CPI inflation reported in *IFS* had to equal or exceed 20% for four or more consecutive years. The episode of chronic inflation was defined as the period of years of consecutive inflations of greater than or equal to 20%. In order to preserve the separation between the data here analyzed and those dealt with in previous work, the new episode treated in this study began one year after the terminal year covered in the previous study. Thus, in the present case, the episodes of chronic inflation in Iceland, Ghana, Zaire, and Peru all have a starting date of 1980. This is because in a previous study data on these countries up to and including 1979 were analyzed.[4] In addition, small and short lapses below the 20% rate were not permitted to exempt a country from the chronic inflation category. Thus, Uruguay's inflation rate of 19% in 1982 did not prevent it from being characterized as a chronic inflation country for the full period 1976–85. Also in the case of Greece one year with 19% inflation was included.

12.3.3. Devaluation Crises

The basic principle underlying the definition of a devaluation crisis was quite clear: the crisis was an event that broke sharply with a history characterized by stable exchange rates. In previous work the specific definition said that the country's exchange rate vis-à-vis the dollar should have been stable for a period of at least four years, with the crisis being signaled by a devaluation of at least 20% in the lapse of a single year. But the tumultuous movements of relative exchange rates among the major currencies rendered the above criterion obsolete in the 1970s and 1980s, when not even the Deutschmark or the Swiss franc could have been classified as "stable" vis-à-vis the dollar over a four-year period.

In place of stability over a four-year period, the new definition required that the exchange rate with the dollar not exhibit much depreciation over a four-year period. In order for an episode to be characterized as an exchange-rate crisis the devaluation in a single year had to exceed 25% plus the particular country's range of variation vis-à-vis the dollar during the previous four years. Thus, if a currency had varied over an 8% range, vis-à-vis the dollar, in the four years prior to a devaluation episode, the amount of the devaluation in a single year would have to be 33% before the episode would be classified as a devaluation crisis.

A further complication with respect to devaluation crises concerns how to date them. *IFS* gives exchange rate data of two kinds, at the end of the period (ae) and average rate over the period (rf). In present paper, the choice was made to rely mainly on the rf series. This leads to the curiosity that a discrete devaluation of nearly 100% occurring in Sri Lanka in December 1977 is carried in this study with a 1978 date. This is because the average exchange rate of 1977 was only 5% higher than that for 1976, not enough to trigger our criterion for a devaluation crisis. This occurred in 1978, when all twelve months of data reflected the higher rate, and Sri Lanka's average (rf) exchange rate stood at 15,661 compared with 8,873 for 1977 and 8,412 for 1976.

The nature of the criterion for a devaluation crisis also led to other anomalies. For example, Ghana's currency was devalued by 139% (from 1.15 to 2.75 cedis to the dollar) toward the end of 1978. Its average exchange rate moved up by 32% in 1978, and by 83% in 1979. There was a strong temptation to date he devaluation in 1979, when the biggest change in the average occurred, but our criterion required it to be placed in 1978, and so it was.

The dating of the devaluation crises is relevant, because we shall end up making comparisons between data for the year of devaluation, for the year prior to devaluation, and for a period that preceded the devaluation by four years. The criterion followed in dating the crises obviously also has a bearing on those comparisons. So far as I can tell, however, it is not in any way critical; the broad conclusions of this chapter are sufficiently robust to survive any plausible change in the choice of periods (e.g., four years of exchange stability), levels (e.g., an increase of at least 25% to define a devaluation crisis), or criteria to fix the dating of a crises.

12.3.4. Control Group—"Stable" Exchange Rate Countries

Just as in the case of devaluation crises, the criteria for choosing a set of "stable" exchange rate countries to serve as a control group is influenced by the more flexible exchange rate system of the 1970s and 1980s. In the predecessor to this chapter and in other earlier work, the control group consisted of countries that had successfully maintained a fixed exchange rate for a relatively long period. Under the Bretton Woods system, a peg to any major currency was pretty much a peg to them all. After that system broke up, the only exchange rates that remained fixed to the dollar were those that were explicitly pegged to it.

To choose the control group a preliminary filter was imposed: a country had to exhibit an inflation rate of less than 10.5% per year for the 1970–82 period. To guard against the inclusion of crippled or totally stagnant economies, a minimum growth rate of 3% per year for total (not per capita) real GDP over the 1970–82 period was also imposed. Both these preliminary figures appeared in the World Bank's *World Development Report 1984*, so the filter was easy to apply.

The next step was to examine the 1970–80 exchange rate experience of twelve countries surviving the filtering process. They fell into four groups. Three (Dominican Republic, Guatemala, and Panama) met the old criterion of strict fixity vis-à-vis the dollar. Six (Jordan, Malawi, Morocco, Thailand, Togo, and Tunisia) experienced appreciations vis-à-vis the U.S. dollar. Two (Kenya and India) depreciated very slightly vis-à-vis the dollar, while one (Singapore) appreciated vis-à-vis both the dollar and the SDR.

12.4.   On Chronic and Acute Inflations

In table 12.1 are presented the basic data for the cases of chronic and acute inflation that were identified in the course of the present study, as well as for the control group. Each data point in the table is itself the median value of that particular variable for the period specified.

Table 12.2 summarizes the results of the comparison of chronic and acute inflations with each other and with the control group. The picture emerging from this table is exceedingly clear. Inflationary countries siphon more resources out of their banking systems to finance their public sectors than do noninflationary countries. Similarly, countries where the inflation disease is acute do so in a more exaggerated way than do countries where the disease takes on the more sustainable "chronic" form.

These are exactly the conclusions that emerged from the predecessor study. Table 12.3 makes the comparison of the results of the two studies just for the medians of the three policy variables. The general hierarchical pattern—acute dominating chronic, chronic dominating control group— is apparent in both studies. This hierarchy also prevails when other parameters (quartiles, means, etc.) of the frequency distributions of β, γ, and λ are examined. Conclusion: fiscal deficits financed at the banking system, high government claims on the available supply of bank credit, and general lack of credit restraint on the part of monetary authorities play an impor-

Table 12.1
The new evidence: acute and chronic inflation episodes, plus control group[a]

Variable		π	β	γ	λ
Acute inflation cases					
Argentina	(1982–84)	2.546	.125	.325	3.123
Bolivia	(1982–84)	2.690	.142	.600	3.432
Brazil	(1980–85)	1.230	.015	.283	1.421
Israel	(1980–85)	1.383	.275	.363	1.631
Chronic inflation cases					
Iceland	1980–85	.499	.009	.053	.671
Ghana	1980–85	.500	.047	.894	.549
Sudan	1979–84	.281	.045	.656	.222
Tanzania	1980–84	.290	.078	.936	.216
Zaire	1980–84	.421	.062	.806	.471
Greece	1979–85	.203	.073	.408	.219
Portugal	1974–84	.228	.064	.162	.256
Turkey	1977–85	.450	.068	.466	.491
Yugoslavia	1979–84	.360	.003	.057	.282
Chile	1977–81	.351	.005	.282	.474
Mexico	1980–85	.583	.077	.613	.500
Nicaragua	1979–85	.353	.083	.345	.200
Peru	1980–85	.928	.033	.380	.853
Uruguay	1976–85	.531	.016	.140	.652
Control group: "stable" exchange rates (1970–1980)					
Dominican Republic		.092	.012	.287	.160
Guatemala		.109	.004	.186	.148
India		.056	.019	.449	.171
Jordan		.111	.032	.240	.293
Kenya		.114	.014	.252	.257
Malawi		.086	.018	.425	.287
Morocco		.083	.031	.517	.177
Panama		.052	.009	.087	.238
Singapore		.032	<0	<0	.201
Thailand		.075	.023	.251	.225
Togo		.076	.005	.035	.282
Tunisia		.053	.003	.140	.146

Source: International Monetary Fund, *International Financial Statistics*, various issues and tapes.
a. Data are median observations of the indicated variables during the period specified.

Table 12.2
Comparison of inflationary countries with control group[a]

	Acute inflation countries		Chronic inflation countries		Control group of stable LDCs
β = net increase in banking system credit to public sector expressed as a percentage of GDP					
First quartile	.070	>	.016	>	.004
Median	.133	>	.054	>	.013
Third quartile	.208	>	.073	>	.021
γ = public sector bank credit/total bank credit					
First quartile	.304	>	.162	>	.114
Median	.344	~	.394	>	.245
Third quartile	.481	<	.656	>	.356
λ = percent increase in total bank credit					
First quartile	1.526		.222		.166
Median	2.377		.472	>	.213
Third quartile	3.277		.549	>	.270
π = percent increase in consumer price index					
First quartile	1.307		.290		.054
Median	1.965		.390		.080
Third quartile	2.618		.500		.101

a. Criterion for approximate equality designation (~): Difference should be less than .01 for β, less than .10 for γ and λ. Diagonal arrows indicate first quartile of one comparison group exceeds third quartile of the other.

tant role in causing the major inflationary episodes that we observe in the real world, period after period. The connection is not myth, but reality.

12.5. On Devaluation Crises

The devaluation crisis became a subject of our study many years ago. It was apparent that the inflation disease took on forms other than the ones we had defined as chronic and acute. That is, there were many countries that had undeniably suffered from the disease (above and beyond the "world inflation" shared by nearly everybody), yet which were not identified as inflationary countries by the criteria adopted for the terms "chronic" and "acute" to be applied. Additional classifications were required to pick up some or all of these remaining cases of the inflation syndrome. It should come as no surprise that the devaluation crisis seemed a very natural category to add.

Table 12.4 gives the basic data for the new cases of devaluation crisis

Table 12.3
Comparison of present with previous results[a]

	Acute inflation countries		Chronic inflation countries		Control group of stable LDCs
Median values for β					
Old study	.037	>	.023	>	.005
New study	.133	>	.054	>	.013
Median values for γ					
Old study	.467	>	.316	~	.247
New study	.344	~	.394	>	.245
Median values for λ					
Old study	1.20	>	.34	>	.13
New study	2.377	>	.472	>	.213

a. Criterion for approximate equality designation ($\sim$): Difference should be less than .01 for β, less than .10 for γ and λ.

that are being reported on for the first time in this chapter. In previous work, data for the year of devaluation were first reported, then compared with data for the year prior to devaluation. The basic conclusions were that devaluation crisis countries looked much like chronic inflation countries, in terms of the variables, β, γ, and λ. Moreover, this similarity was also true the year before the devaluation, indicating that policy weaknesses (as reflected in high values of β, λ, and γ) probably played a significant role in bringing on the crises.

These conclusions from earlier work are borne out in the new data analyzed for the first time here. The conclusions of the previous work are all repeated here (see table 12.5). If anything, the present chapter shows that the policy behavior of the devaluation crisis countries was a little more dangerous (with β, γ, and λ a little higher) one year before the devaluation than in the year of devaluation itself.

In the present chapter a new element is added: we also present data for the year $t - 4$ where the devaluation is dated at t. This enables us to check (in table 12.6) on two matters: (a) whether the similarity of behavior between year t and year $t - 1$ carries all the way back to $t - 4$ and (b) whether (if behavior in $t - 4$ is in fact more moderate than in $t - 1$ and t) that behavior comes close to approximating the norm given by the control group of stable countries. The answer to (a) is negative, with the policy signs in $t - 4$ being substantially more moderate than in t or $t - 1$. On the other hand, the answer to (b) is also negative. Though the devaluation crises countries have

Table 12.4
Devaluation countries: key variables in year of devaluation (t), in year before devaluation (t − 1), and 4 years before devaluation (t − 4)[a]

Country (year of devaluation)	β Δ public sector credit as percent of GDP			γ public sector credit/total bank credit			λ % increase total credit		
	t	(t − 1)	(t − 4)	t	(t − 1)	(t − 4)	t	(t − 1)	(t − 4)
Bangladesh (1975)	.004	.168	n.a.	.409	.427	n.a.	.122	n.a.	n.a.
Costa Rica (1981)	.011	.060	.036	.346	.359	.214	.119	.272	.309
Ecuador (1982)	.012	<0	<0	<0	<0	<0	.388	.304	.110
Egypt (1979)	.109	.265	.180	.732	.743	.707	.253	.572	.505
Ghana (1978)	.083	.108	.045	.701	.722	.466	.677	.584	.487
Ghana (1983)	.079	.005	.013	.865	.587	.662	.722	.216	.148
Italy (1981)	.042	.046	.072	.402	.397	.380	.127	.166	.163
Indonesia (1979)	<0	<0	.027	<0	<0	.066	.044	.382	.958
Indonesia (1983)	<0	<0		<0	<0	<0	.187	.500	.044
Jamaica (1978)	.069	.080	<0	.603	.585	.151	.287	.120	.087
Jamaica (1984)	.034	.132	<0	.611	.631	.632	.120	.305	.049
Mexico (1982)	.179	.055	.027	.582	.446	.468	1.131	.495	.314
Paraguay (1984)	.007	.021	<0	.143	.121	<0	.215	.205	.525
Peru (1976)	.057	.024	.019	.326	.235	.301	.543	.412	.265
Sierra Leone (1983)	.086	.109	.068	.855	.844	.771	.247	.329	.293
Sri Lanka (1978)	<0	.030	<0	.343	.458	.413	.250	.380	.203
Zaire (1976)	.127	.063	.022	.678	.582	.642	.564	.369	.302
Zambia (1983)	.072	.135	.032	.685	.683	.710	.150	.280	.095
First quartile	.011	.021	<0	.326	.235	.108	.127	.244	.102
Median	.050	.058	.022	.494	.452	.413	.249	.329	.265
Third quartile	.083	.109	.041	.685	.631	.652	.543	.453	.400

Source: International Monetary Fund, *International Financial Statistics*, various issues.
a. Data are observations for the year in question.

Table 12.5
Comparison of devaluation crisis countries with chronic and acute inflation episodes[a]

	Acute inflation countries		Devaluation crisis countries year $t-1$		Devaluation crisis countries year t		Chronic inflation countries
β = net increase in banking system credit to public sector expressed as a percentage of GDP							
First quartile	.070	>	0.021	>	.011	~	.016
Median	.133	>	.058	>	.050	~	.054
Third quartile	.208	>	.109	>	.083	>	.073
γ = public sector bank credit/total bank credit							
First quartile	.304	~	.235	~	.326	>	.162
Median	.344	<	.452	~	.494	>	.394
Third quartile	.481	<	.631	~	.685	~	.656
λ = percent increase in total bank credit							
First quartile	1.526	>	.244	>	.127	~	.222
Median	2.377	>	.329	~	.249	<	.472
Third quartile	3.277	>	.453	~	.543	~	.549

a. Criterion for approximate equality designation ($\sim$): Difference should be less than .01 for β, less than .10 for γ and λ.

more moderate policy behavior four years earlier than in years t and $t-1$, they do not come close to the degree of moderation exhibited by the control group. This confirms another conclusion from earlier work: that the basic policy stance of the exchange rate crisis countries seems to exhibit greater willingness to run inflation risks than is the case in the stable countries. This was found to be true in terms of the distributions of the ratio of international reserves (R) to domestic credit (D) of the banking system,[5] where the devaluation crisis countries kept systematically lower international reserves (even in noncrisis years) than did the successful countries. It was also true that in the successful countries, policies of defending international reserves (by reducing credit when international reserves were falling) were triggered at higher levels of $[R/(R+D)]$ than was the case for the crisis countries (see table 14 in the work cited in note 4). Finally, a much higher fraction of the stable countries shifted to a reserve-defending monetary policy when international reserves fell into operationally defined danger zones.[6]

In short, the evidence examined in earlier work led to the conclusion that the countries that ended up having devaluation crises played riskier policy games than the stable countries, even in years when no crisis was im-

Table 12.6
Comparison of devaluation crisis countries with control group[a]

	Devaluation countries year t		Chronic inflation countries		Devaluation countries year $t-4$		Control groups of stable LDCs
β = net increase in banking system credit to the public sector, expressed as a percentage of GDP							
First quartile	.011	~	.016	>	<0	~	.004
Median	.050	~	.054	>	.023	>	.013
Third quartile	.083	>	.073	>	.041	>	.021
γ = public sector bank credit/total bank credit							
First quartile	.326	>	.162	~	.108	~	.114
Median	.494	>	.394	~	.413	>	.245
Third quartile	.685	~	.656	~	.652	>	.356
λ = percent increase in total bank credit							
First quartile	.127	~	.222	>	.102	~	.166
Median	.249	<	.472	>	.265	~	.213
Third quartile	.543	~	.549	>	.400	>	.270

a. Criterion for approximate equality designation (~): Difference should be less than .01 for β, less than .10 for γ and λ.

pending. To determine whether this sort of behavior was also reflected in the new evidence of the present chapter, a simple test would compare the devaluation crisis countries, four years before their respective devaluations, with the control group. This is done in table 12.7, which also shows the other relevant comparisons. It is shown therein that for every comparison made, the crisis countries revealed either greater riskiness (>) or approximately equal riskiness (~). There were no cases at all of lower riskiness. Even assuming a probability as low as one-third to the (<) category, the change of getting no observations of this kind in nine tries is less than .03.

12.6.   On Major Disinflations

A final message concerns the experience of countries with major disinflations. In earlier work (see note 4), Edwards and myself reported on ten major disinflations. In each of them we calculated the average rate of growth of real GDP as the rate of CPI inflation was rising, and compared it (in table 19 of the work cited in note 4) to the average growth rate of GDP during the period of disinflation. At the same time we compared (in table 20 of the work cited in note 4) the growth rate of GDP in the year of peak inflation to the growth rate in the year immediately following the peak. These two sets of comparisons gave the following results, considering approximate equality ($\sim$) to prevail in cases where the difference in GDP growth rates was less than 1%. Comparing the period of rising with the period of declining inflation, the average rate of GDP growth was greater in the period of falling inflation rates in seven out of ten comparisons. Approximate equality prevailed in two cases. Only Israel revealed a greater GDP growth during rising inflation (13.6%, 1951–52) than during declining inflation (10.6%, 1952–55). When the single peak year of inflation is compared with the first year of disinflation, the disinflation year showed the higher rate of growth in five out of nine cases, approximate equality held in three, and the peak inflation year (1974) exhibited higher real growth than the first disinflation year (1975) only in one case (Chile).[7]

In preparing this chapter we encountered five additional cases, which are reported in table 12.7. In this instance the verdict is unanimous. In each of the five countries, the GDP growth rate was higher on the way down from the inflationary peak than it was on the way up. This evidence may be surprising to some, but it simply replicates what we have found in earlier work.

I do not believe that this evidence is sufficient to provide a total challenge to conventional wisdom concerning the high net costs of disinflation, the big trade-off between inflation and growth. However, I would rather limit my comment to cases where the brakes are applied only after inflation has reached the 80–100% range or higher. My own guess is that when inflation gets this high, it is because policymakers have caved in to pressures of many kinds. Doing so typically affects not only the inflationary aspect but also many other facets of policy. Thus, when the government gathers the necessary courage, or has the necessary luck, or when the various groups in the population have been sufficiently worn down by inflationary experience to permit a genuine disinflationary policy to be imposed, many other improvements in economic policy are carried out at the same time. Thus, according to my interpretation, what we are seeing in this repeated evidence is the reflection of a generalized deterioration of policy in the stage where the inflation rate is rising, and a generalized improvement in the stage where that rate is falling. The low growth rates while inflation rises are thus attributed to the general deterioration of the policy package, and the higher growth rates under disinflation to a general policy improvement. But nonetheless—and this is extremely important—let no one scare you away

Table 12.7
Basic data and major disinflations[a]

| Country | Period | Annual rate of growth of real GDP (IFS) | | Annual rate of inflation | | |
		Rising inflation (%/annum)	Declining inflation (%/annum)	Average (%/annum)	Maximum (%/annum)	Minimum (%/annum)
Turkey	1976–80–82	1.4	4.0	51.4	110.2	27.1
Zaire	1975–79–82	−2.4	0.7	58.1	108.6	29.0
Ghana	1975–77–80	−0.7	1.7	68.4	116.5	29.8
Uruguay	1971–73–76	−0.6	4.3	51.6	97.0	24.0
Costa Rica	1980–82–84	−4.8	5.1	40.2	90.1	11.9

a. Average rates over periods are compound growth rates between the terminal values of the variable in question (real GDP or CPI). Basic data from *International Financial Statistics*.

from a serious disinflationary effort, on grounds of its high cost, in cases where the inflation disease is already acute. In such cases the evidence from the past loudly proclaims the compatibility of "disinflation plus growth."

12.7. Some Reflections on Methodology

In this section I attempt to articulate some of the considerations that motivated the approach taken in this chapter. Certainly I do not regard it as a mere whim or caprice. On the contrary, I take it quite seriously—not pompously so, I hope, but seriously enough to encourage others to follow related approaches in their own work.

12.7.1. Setting the Limits That Define Categories

I am fully aware that many of the choices involved in this sort of work reflect a professional "feel" acquired as a result of extensive work with real numbers over a long period of time. Decisions as to how to define a category like chronic or acute inflation were, so to speak, pulled out of the air, not at random, but neither after any significant process of search. Rather they were boundaries that "made sense" to me in the light of years of observation and experience. But the sense they make is rough, not at all fine-tuned or otherwise refined. For example, when I choose 80% as a criterion level for acute inflation, I do so because it makes sense to me; it "feels right." But so, too, do 75 or 85 or 90%. Pushing it up to 250% would be "wrong," because I have the sense that 90% inflations and 80% inflations share similar attributes—belong to the same class, as it were—with inflation at much higher rates. I would not want to exclude quite a few truly acute inflations by setting the boundary line as high as, say, 150%. One the other hand, 30 or 40% per annum is too low for acute inflation. Too many countries have lived "reasonably well" with such rates of inflation for quite extended periods of time—30 and 40% are rates that are properly chronic; they can be adapted to and lived with, much as many people do with conditions like diabetes or heart arrhythmia.

Of course, man's ingenuity with respect to living with inflation may have raised the threshold of what can be tolerated. My own appreciation is that the substantial spates of inflation in excess of 100% that have been experienced—for example, by Argentina, say, during the ministry of Martinez de Hoz, and by Brazil and Israel over the last several years— would not have been so long sustained in the 1950s or 1960s. The techniques of adaptation were not yet sufficiently developed then. But I have not allowed this particular judgment to cause me to alter the numerical limits placed on the categories of chronic and acute. Rather, I take this greater ease of adaptation as one of several reasons why we have recently had more "outbreaks" of both kinds of inflation per quinquennium or per decade, say, than we had in earlier times.

12.7.2. Avoiding Cross-Country Regressions

I am very troubled by the amount of work I see using cross-country regression analysis. To me, the ideal regression equation is a behavior or technical relation—like the demand for sugar, the supply of wheat, or the production function for cigarettes. These relations typically hold for given sets of demanders, of farmers, of producers. Even here we often have to allow for changes in tastes and technology, but on the whole we can point to a fair number of more than modest successes with the time-series analysis of behavior relations.

As we move away from demand and supply relations to policy relations, I am already worried, even by time-series analyses following the history of a particular country. Why? Because I have watched too many changes of government, even of key ministers within a given government, which have entailed very major changes in policy behavior—in terms of the objectives pursued, the instruments used, and the manner of use of given instruments. So I am even leery of doing time-series regressions explaining policy behavior for a single country, except where I feel that there was substantial continuity of the same basic policy processes and norms.

You can imagine how much worse I feel about a cross-section regression that throws into the same hopper the policymakers of Switzerland and Iceland, of Indonesia and India, of Argentina and Australia, of Ghana and the Ivory Coast, and of Burma and Thailand. I do not believe for a minute that the same regression could summarize the policy behavior of all these countries, or even of the two countries that constitute each of the listed pairs.

But lots of cross-country policy regressions do throw together, hence imputing similar behavior patterns to, countries as dissimilar as these. I find that to be of the same order of mistake as, say, lumping India and Pakistan together in a cross-section study of the demand for beef. In fact, most cross-sectional policy regressions are easy to pull apart. Where good

R^2s are present, they are usually determined by a few outlier observations. Get rid of the outliers, and what remains is usually a shapeless blob of data points.

Conclusion: Be wary of policy regressions over time, even in a single country. Be doubly or triply wary of regressions that in effect presume the existence of similar behavior parameters across countries.

12.7.3. Policy Triggers versus Policy Parameters

Even from economic theory alone, we should not expect most economic policy actions to be well described by standard-looking regressions. In a Central Bank a reduction of foreign exchange reserves from 80% to 40% of assets may be treated with utter indifference, while a reduction of reserves from 15% to 10% of total assets may trigger something close to panic. The solution is not to be found in artful choice of equation forms. The solution lies instead in recognizing the relevance of the idea of a perceived "danger zone" for the ratio of foreign reserves to assets. When we do so, and look at the data of many countries, we begin to perceive the reality of the notion of a danger zone. In a word, the data "confirm" the usefulness of the concept of danger zone, a policy trigger.

12.7.4. Policy Responses Are Often Not "Mechanical"

I think of a "mechanical" response as a movement along some sort of function: linear, logarithmic, quadratic, etc. There are lots of problems for which the mechanical response might not be the relevant one. As people move their hands across a line near a fire, a certain fraction will draw them back. As the fire gets a bit hotter, the fraction of people drawing back their hands will (I would assert) increase—not necessarily (or equally predict-ably) the distance to which they draw their hands away.

So it is with, say, international reserves. Probably at any one time each central banker has a critical trigger, which could move him to constrict credit in order to defend or rebuild his international reserves. But the same banker may change his mind from time to time, and his successor may think differently from him. So, too, central bankers in other countries may have different levels of $[R/(R + D)]$ that trigger reserves-defending responses.

Beyond this, when a policymaker decides he is going to defend reserves by constricting credit, he may one time be moved to slam on the brakes, another time to apply them slowly. And there is no reason at all why central bankers in different countries should all have the same "style" of credit restrictions—some may opt quite regularly for sharp curbs, others for more gradual tightening.

Now the type of behavior just described can very easily create havoc with a standard regression. This is just the type of circumstance where a couple of outliers can dominate the entire picture. But with a different procedure—at least in some ways more sensitive and more subtle—one can get the data to tell a coherent (and robust) story: The lower we set the critical value of $[R/(R + D)]$, the greater will be the fraction of central bankers undertaking to restrict credit. And if, of two identifiable sets of central bankers, one set has a consistently lower fraction of response, we can conclude certainly that there is a systematic difference in behavior between these groups. Most probably this would be due to a greater propensity to run "risks," though we cannot totally ignore the possibility that some of the nonresponders face objectively lower risks, hence have less "need" for reserves.

This is the sort of contrast that we found between the devaluation crisis countries and the control groups in our earlier study, and that I confidently expect to hold for the new groups emerging in the present chapter. Meanwhile, the tests reported in table 12.6 bear out in a different vein the hypothesis that the devaluation crisis countries seem to follow, certainly one year before the crisis, but even as much as four years ahead, policies that are riskier (as measured by β, γ, and λ) than those of their control-group counterparts.

12.7.5. Probabilistic Connections between Risk and Reward

The human behavior we see around us would be a lot different if there were a mechanical link between smoking and dying of cancer or between drinking and dropping dead of a heart attack or of cirrhosis (i.e., if, for example, cigarette smokers could expect to drop dead after half a million cigarettes, with, say, a coefficient of variation of 10 or 20%). But it is not that way. Nature has been more insidious, more cruel, in providing the temptation without a ready and clear perception of the risk. People with the habit are soothed and calmed by smoking, made to feel pleasantly at ease by drinking. They also see around them many who live to a ripe old age, both unsullied by their addiction and unrepentant in it. It is "natural" for many of them to proceed as if unmindful of the risks they run. And self-selection works to make us see these very people: the truly risk-perceptive and risk-averse probably never started the habit in the first place; others may have started once or twice, but quit early.

So it is with the policies that lead to inflation. Financing government deficits by the banking system (β) feels good to begin with; so also does generalized credit expansion (λ). Increasing the share of total bank credit going to the government (γ) may also be a temporary palliative, though in the end a high γ, like sedimentary rock, imbeds in layers the record of successive policy erosions in the past.

I think the analogy with addictions of various kinds is quite apt. Those who fall prey are succumbing to temptation; those who resist (or who, once victims, return to surmount their nemesis) reveal character. Governments, as well as presidents and ministers and central bankers, reflect these characteristics on the policy scene. The relatively weak ones are swayed by temptation, and end up letting themselves be convinced by one or another "plausible excuse" for taking the route that is momentarily easy and painless. Only later do they *sometimes* pay the price.

Sometimes is an important word here, for the fact is that those who indulge do not always pay a price (at least not always a heavy one). This leads the vulnerable to succumb to temptation that much more easily. Note how, in table 12.2, the distributions of β, γ, and λ for the chronic inflation countries overlap those for the control group, and how, in table 12.6, the same applies between the devaluation crisis countries and the control group. This overlap permits people to get the idea that one can get away with pretty high values of β, γ, and λ, both adding to the temptation to run the risk and weakening resistance to it.

12.8. Conclusion

Policymakers, like individuals, are often tempted to follow the path of least resistance—the easy way. When they do so, it is easy for them to select out precedents where one country or another followed this path with apparent impunity. The connection between risky or "wrong" policies and their consequences is, unfortunately, probabilistic rather than mechanical, and the probability distributions of the outcomes of bad and better policies have the unfortunate habit of overlapping. They are not disjoint.

This chapter is one of a series attempting to link policy actions to their consequences in ways that are less mechanical, less parametric than usual. Since several years have passed since the predecessor studies; we here employ fresh data on new cases.

Applying to these new cases the same procedures used in previous studies gave results that were essentially "the same" as those obtained before. There are no surprises here, just confirmations of what "good economists" and "wise policymakers" knew all along.

Running a modest fiscal deficit does not create problems, but running big deficits financed at the banking system (or by printing money) is a dangerous step, linked to symptoms of the inflation disease in much the same way as smoking is linked to cancer. The same is true for letting the public sector absorb "too high" a fraction of bank credit, or allowing total bank credit to expand too rapidly.

This chapter totally confirms previous work in demonstrating the link between these risky policies on the one hand and inflationary consequences on the other. The procedure does not deny—on the contrary, it quite explicitly accepts—the familiar link between excessive monetary expansion and inflation. Rather, what it tries to do is "go behind the money supply" to other, perhaps more fundamental, causes.

In addition to giving empirical underpinning to some inherited canons of prudent policy behavior, this chapter examines new cases for evidence on the link between inflation and growth. Here again the new evidence confirms earlier conclusions: countries experiencing inflations peaking at 80 or 90 or 100% or more, and then successfully disinflating, reveal significantly higher growth rates of real GDP "on the way down" than "on the way up." This evidence surprised me when I first uncovered it, mainly because our profession has paid so much lip service to the great "costs of disinflation." These costs are hard to find among the sets of cases examined here and in earlier work.

This does not mean that conventional wisdom and conventional characterizations are just a myth. Rather I reach the more modest interpretation that countries work up to inflation rates of near 100% not out of conscious desire but out of policy weakness. I believe that policy weakness on the inflation front is usually accompanied by policy weakness on many other fronts as well. I also believe that when, finally, the upsurge of inflation rates is stopped, and actual reduction sets in, this usually comes as part of a broad reform, a rather general correction of policy mistakes, an overall improvement of the quality of the economic policy package.

In particular, I do not want to assert that reducing inflation from 10% to 0% comes without important costs of the type traditionally implied. But there is no doubt concerning the lessons of experience that in actual fact disinflations from peaks of 80, 90, 100% and more have, on the whole, been accompanied by greater prosperity. It is here, in this subset of our experience, that one finds it hard to document the traditional view of the "high costs of disinflation."

Notes

1. See Arnold C. Harberger, "In Step and Out of Step with World Inflation: A Summary History of Countries, 1952–1976," in *Development in an Inflationary World*, edited by Assaf Razin and June M. Flanders (New York: Academic Press, 1981), pp. 35–46.

2. But bear in mind that rises in γ can act to absorb inflationary pressure. Therefore and quite clearly, the relevant variable is γ (a pure stock variable) rather than $\Delta\gamma$ (a flow variable).

3. Since the data used for individual observations on β, λ, γ, and π are median observations over the years contained in each given period, it was possible to handle cases where observations were missing for a small fraction of the years. But there were a few cases of countries for which data on GDP were not available for any of the relevant years. This precluded β being calculated, and thus caused the elimination of the country observation. Similarly, when all but one or two years of data were missing for a country during a given episode, that episode was left out.

4. The previous study in this case was Arnold C. Harberger and Sebastian Edwards, "Causes of Inflation in Developing Countries: Some New Evidence," a paper presented at the annual meeting of the American Economic Association in New York, December 1982.

5. See Harberger and Edwards, op. cit., table 13 and the surrounding text. That table presents data on 932 quarters of observation for 18 devaluation crisis countries and a 1,123 quarters of observation for 23 successful (control group) countries. The data on $R/(R + D)$ were grouped into five classes (less than 0.1, 0.1–0.2, 0.2–0.3, 0.3–0.5 and over). The crisis countries exhibited systematically lower reserves ratios than the control group, having twice as high a fraction of cases with $R/(R + D)$ less than 0.1 and less than a fifth as high a fraction of cases with $R/(R + D)$ at 0.5 or above. A χ^2-test with ten cells (five classes × two groups) yielded $\chi^2(4) = 263.36$. The critical comparison level was $\chi^2_{.001}(4) = 18.47$.

6. The danger zones were $[R/(R + D)]$ below 0.1 and falling ("serious danger") and $[R/(R + D)]$ between 0.1 and 0.2 and falling ("moderate danger"). A reserves target policy was indicated by a contraction of credit, a monetary-target policy by an expansion (so as to help keep the quantity of money constant in the face of falling reserves). While monetary target policies were more frequent for both the crisis countries and the control group, the latter group pursued reserve-targets with more than ten times the frequency of the crisis countries in situations of "serious danger" and more than three times the frequency of the crisis countries in cases of "moderate danger." The $\chi^2(1)$ covering 224 quarterly observations of crisis countries and 150 observations of successful (control group) countries was 29.76 for situations of "serious danger," and that for 115 observations of crisis countries and 184 of successful countries was 12.33. In comparison, $\chi^2_{.001}(1)$ is 10.83. See Harberger and Edwards, op. cit., table 15.

7. The ten episodes covered here include Argentina I (1958–59–60), Argentina II (1970–73–74), Bolivia I (1953–56–58), Bolivia II (1969–70–76), Brazil (1961–64–68), Chile I (1962–64–67), Chile II (1972–74–78), Paraguay (1951–52–56), Uruguay (1963–69–70), and Israel (1951–52–55). Here the span between the first two dates in each triad represents the period of rising inflation, while the period of falling inflation goes from the second to the third dates. The middle date is obviously the year of peak inflation. Data reported here are drawn from *International Financial Statistics*. Parallel series of real GDP drawn from United Nations/World Bank sources lead to similar results.

13 Inflation, Deficit, and Seignorage with Expected Stabilization

Benjamin Bental and Zvi Eckstein

13.1. Introduction

There is a general agreement among economists that observed trends and correlations between government deficits, revenues derived from money creation (seignorage), and inflation depend on expectations concerning future government deficits and their financing. Still, many were surprised by the Sargent and Wallace (1981) result that it is possible to get high inflation in periods of zero seignorage if inflation is expected to rise in the future because of money-financed deficits.[1] We argue here that inflation can be obtained in periods of positive but constant seignorage levels, even if the government deficit is expected to be eliminated in the future.

In the Sargent and Wallace (1981) model a constant deficit financed only by money creation has two rational expectations steady state equilibria. The low inflation equilibrium is efficient but dynamically unstable, and the high inflation is inefficient but stable. On this basis Sargent and Wallace (1986) developed a stochastic "sunspot equilibrium" version of the model, where the "sunspots" are typically associated with the high inflation solution, in order to explain phenomena in hyperinflationary episodes. The phenomena Sargent and Wallace point out are that inflation rates are increasing, that inflation rates exceed the money growth rates, and that seignorage is constant and lower than the maximum feasible seignorage level. These facts seem to hold in most of the recent inflationary episodes, including the case of Israel (see Dornbusch and Fischer, 1986, Bruno, 1986, and the appendix to this chapter). Bruno (1986, p. 19) claims that an explanation of the runaway inflation in Israel in 1984–1985, a period characterized by a constant deficit and constant revenues from money printing, lies in the theory of dual inflationary equilibria.[2] We claim that the inflationary episode is due to the public's expectation that the government is about to stabilize the economy by reducing the budget deficit through tax increases.

To establish our claim, we use a rational expectations version of Cagan's (1956) money demand equation (presented also by Sargent and Wallace,

We would like to thank Leo Leiderman and participants of the Pinhas Sapir Conference on Economic Effects of the Government Budget for a lively discussion of an earlier version of this chapter. Carmela Edelstein ably computed the data presented here.

1981) to analyze the relationship between deficit financing and inflation when stabilization is expected to occur. We focus on an economy in which there is a constant deficit prior to stabilization. In this respect, our analysis is compatible with that of Sargent and Wallace (1981, 1986), Bruno and Fisher (1986), and Bruno (1986). We show that as long as a perpetual balanced budget yields a fixed price level, the equilibrium path of an economy in which the poststabilization deficits are zero is *unique* and *stable*. Furthermore, the inflation rate converges to the steady state *low* rate that is necessary to finance the prestabilization deficit at steady state. Hence, expected stabilization eliminates the *bad* equilibrium even if the date of the stabilization is expected to be far in the future. We show further that whether inflation is predicted to rise or to fall toward stabilization depends on three components of the model. First, the size of the deficit prior to stabilization: If the deficit is "too large," i.e., larger than the maximum feasible at steady state, then inflation is necessarily decreasing toward stabilization. Hence, increasing inflation toward stabilization is consistent *only* with lower than maximum feasible stationary seignorage.[3] Second, the components of the stabilization program: We find that high taxes (as opposed to reduction in expenditures) tend to decrease demand for money at the stabilization. The result of this change in money demand may be increasing inflation rates toward stabilization. Third, the share of money creation versus net increases of the internal debt: A high share of (liquid) debt financing just before stabilization makes it more likely that inflation will rise toward stabilization due to an asset substitution effect between money and liquid debt.

The evidence on the behavior of the deficit seignorage and inflation in many high inflation episodes, including the recent Israeli experience, seems to correspond to the model's predictions. The appendix to this chapter presents half-year monthly averages from 1981:1 to 1986:9 of Israeli data. Quite consistently with other observers (e.g., Bruno, 1986), we identify particular trends in the data that the model mimics. In particular, table 13.1 indicates that the primary deficit during the inflationary period prior to July 1985 is a positive constant (zero trend), and zero ever since. Inflation is rising toward the stabilization date (July 1985) and is very close to zero after July 1985. There is almost no trend in seignorage that financed only about 20% of the deficit. The other part of the deficit is financed with very liquid government debt in the form of foreign exchange, and other governmental real debt. Furthermore, we point out the fact that immediately after stabilization there is an increase in the money stock that does not affect prices because it is offset by government purchases of real debt. These facts are, in general, consistent with the phenomena associated with the inflationary episodes in Europe in the 1920s (see Sargent, 1982). The main difference is the significant role of the internal indexed debt in the Israeli case. Our model accommodates this feature and shows how the existence of indexed debt affects both the budget financing and the demand for money.[4]

Section 13.2 describes the model. In section 13.3 we characterize the equilibrium in the prestabilization period and in section 13.4 we demonstrate that after stabilization open market operations are neutral. Section 13.5 relates, in some detail, the model's predictions to the actual trends observed in the Israeli data.

13.2. The Model

The economy is populated by two-period-lived overlapping generations. All members of a given generation are identical, and every generation is an exact replication of its predecessor. In particular, the size of all generations remains fixed at N. Agents are endowed with y_1 units of a single, nonstorable good when young and y_2 units of the same good when old. Agents derive utility only from consumption in both periods of their lives.

The government in the model consumes resources and engages in transfer payments. Its deficit may be financed using three instruments. The government can create money, borrow at home, or borrow abroad. Local borrowing is done is the form of one-period real bonds, or any other form of indexed asset (e.g., "Patam" accounts that are indexed to an exchange rate). The government sets the real rate of return on the bonds by specifying their selling price (in terms of current goods). We normalize this price to be 1. In addition, the government chooses the amount of bonds it sells each period. Foreign borrowing is also assumed to be in the form of one-period real bonds that the government sells to foreigners at the internationally set interest rate.[5] The government's budget constraint takes the following form:

$$\bar{G}_t = G_t + V_t - F_t + xF_{t-1} = \frac{M_t - M_{t-1}}{P_t} + B_t - zB_{t-1}, \tag{1}$$

where $\bar{G}_t$ = domestic deficit at period t, G_t = government consumption at period t, V_t = tax/transfers at period t imposed on the young, F_t = foreign government debt incurred at period t, x = gross rate of return on foreign debt, B_t = real government domestic debt incurrent at period t, z = gross rate of return on domestic debt, M_t = nominal money supply at period t, and P_t = price level at period t.

Let the young agents preferences be represented by

$$u(c_{1t}, c_{2t}) = \ln c_{1t} + \ln c_{2t}, \tag{2}$$

where c_{it} = consumption of an agent born at t at this ith period of his life, $i = 1, 2$.

We assume that private agents have no access to the international capital market, so that their portfolio can consist only of money and government bonds. Accordingly, a young agent's budget constraints are given by

$$c_{1t} + m_t + b_t \leqslant y_1 + \tau_t, \tag{3}$$

$$c_{2t} \leqslant y_2 + m_t/\pi_{t+1} + zb_t, \tag{4}$$

where

m_t = real balances held at t, b_t = real bonds at t, π_{t+1} = gross inflation between period $t + 1$ and t ($\equiv P_{t+1}/P_t$), and τ_t = tax/transfers imposed on an agent born at t.

The agent maximizes (2) subject to (3) and (4) by choosing c_{1t}, c_{2t}, m_t, and b_t, taking π_{t+1} and z as given. At date 1 there are N old agents who hold money and government bonds and who maximize their consumption by supplying all their money at any price.

An *equilibrium* consists of a sequence $\{m_t, b_t, \pi_{t+1}\}_{t=1}^{\infty}$ such that for a given policy sequence $\{G_t, V_t, F_t, M_t, B_t\}_{t=1}^{\infty}$, initial values M_0 and B_0, and for given x and z

i. agents optimize,

ii. the money market clears at any t,

iii. the bond market clears at any t, and

iv. perfect foresight prevails.

For simplicity of notation we assume that each generation consists of a single representative agent. Accordingly, $V_t = \tau_t$ and conditions (ii) and (iii) imply

$$m_t = \frac{M_t}{P_t} \tag{5}$$

and

$$b_t = B_t. \tag{6}$$

We restrict our attention to equilibria in which bonds dominate money in return, i.e., $z \geqslant 1/\pi_{t+1}$ with strict inequality for some t. Accordingly, agents purchase as many bonds as they can. Incorporating (6), their optimal real money balances are given by

$$m_t = \tfrac{1}{2}[(y_1 + \tau_t - b_t) - \pi_{t+1}(y_2 + zb_t)]. \tag{7}$$

We simplify further by setting $z = 1.$[6] We now substitute (7) for m_t and m_{t-1} in the government budget constraint (1), and let $\bar{g}_t = \bar{G}_t$, to obtain

$$\pi_t = \frac{y_1 + \tau_{t-1} - b_{t-1}}{y_1 + \tau_t - b_{t-1} + y_2 + b_t - 2\bar{g}_t - \pi_{t+1}(y_2 + b_t)}. \tag{8}$$

It is clear from (8) that the composition of the government deficit except for τ_t is immaterial. In particular, the domestic population does not distinguish between government consumption and net foreign borrowing. Accordingly, we can treat $G_t - F_t + xF_{t-1}$ as one term. Any change in foreign borrowing is therefore equivalent to changes in government consumption.

Equation (8) is written as a forward looking difference equation. This formulation facilitates a backward solution from a point in time in which some policy changes take place.

13.3. Inflation Paths

Equation (8) summarizes all possible inflation paths for a given sequence of policies that set values to $\{\tau_t, b_{t-1}, \bar{g}_t\}_{t=1}^{\infty}$. Our goal in this section is to analyze possible inflation paths under restrictions on the time path of the above policy variables. In particular, we focus on the effects an expected stabilization program has on the time path of inflation prior to the implementation of this program. We define the stabilization policy at date T as a program that sets the above variables at constant values so that $\pi_{t+1} = 1$ ($P_t = P > 0$) for $t \geqslant T$. Let $b_t = \bar{b}$, $\tau_t = \bar{\tau}$, for $t \geqslant T$, and as implied by equation (8), $\bar{g}_t = 0$ for $t \geqslant T$. That is, there is no inflation in the economy

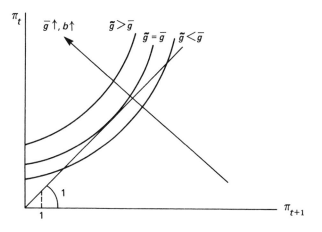

Figure 13.1
The $H_t(\cdot)$ function.

when no money is printed. This assumption corresponds to the observation that economies in which the government does not use money creation in order to finance its activities have a stable value of money. Given that $\pi_t = 1$ for $t \geq T + 1$ we can solve for π_t backward using equation (8).

It is clear that the path of π_t for $t \leq T$ is uniquely determined. To facilitate the characterization of the path of π_t prior to stabilization ($t \leq T$) under different policies prior to and at the date of stabilization, let the right-hand side of (8) be called $H_t(\pi_{t+1})$. We get that for $\pi_{t+1} > 1$ and $\bar{g}_t > 0$, $\partial H_t / \partial b_t > 0$ and $\partial H_t / \partial b_{t-1} > 0$. This fact implies that for a given $\bar{g} > 0$, any given future inflation is associated with higher current inflation as the level of domestic debt increases. Figure 13.1 summarizes this result for fixed levels of $\bar{g}$, τ, and for an increasing sequence of b_t.

In order to study the sequence of inflation prior to stabilization it is useful, as we show later, to investigate whether given $\bar{g}$ and τ, $H_t(\cdot)$ has any fixed points. To do so, we solve $\pi = H_t(\pi)$, and obtain

$$\bar{\pi}_{1,2} = \frac{y_1 + \tau - b_{t-1} + y_2 + b_t - 2\bar{g}_t \pm D_t^{1/2}}{2(y_2 + b_t)}, \tag{9}$$

where

$$D_t = (y_1 + \tau - b_{t-1} - (y_2 + b_t))^2 - 4\bar{g}(y_1 + \tau - b_{t-1} + y_2 + b_t)$$
$$+ 4\bar{g}^2. \tag{10}$$

Clearly, if $D_t < 0$, H_t does not have a (real) fixed point (see figure 13.1). For any given values of b_t and b_{t-1}, we can find, using (10), the value of the deficit $\bar{g}$ for which $D_t = 0$. Let this value of $\bar{g}_t$ be defined as $\tilde{g}_t$. Now we obtain as the feasible root of (10)[7]

$$\tilde{g}_t = \tfrac{1}{2}[(y_1 + \tau - b_{t-1})^{1/2} - (y_2 + b_t)^{1/2}]^2. \tag{11}$$

For a given feasible sequence of b_t, $\tilde{g}_t$ defines the sequence of maximum feasible deficits such that no stabilization policy is required. These $\tilde{g}_t$ make $H_t(\cdot)$ tangent to the 45° line in figure 13.1 and they define a unique sequence of inflation rates. Observe that from (11) we get the fact that $\partial \tilde{g}_t / \partial b_t < 0$ and $\partial \tilde{g}_t / \partial b_{t-1} < 0$. This fact implies that for a given $\bar{g}$, sufficiently large b_t imply that $H_t(\cdot)$ has no fixed point. Figure 13.1 displays this feature when $H_t(\cdot)$ is above the 45° line.

Suppose that for a while the actual prestabilization deficit $\bar{g}$ is higher than the feasible long run deficit $\tilde{g}_t$. What are the consequences for inflation? Claim 1 answers this question.

CLAIM 1   Suppose that there exists a $t_0 \leqslant T - 1$ such that $\bar{g} > \tilde{g}_t$ and b_t is not decreasing for all $t \in [t_0, T - 1]$. Then $\pi_t < \pi_{t-1}$ (inflation is decreasing toward stabilization for all $t_0 \leqslant t \leqslant T - 1$).

Proof   Since $\tilde{g}_{T-1} < \bar{g}$, $H_{T-1}(\cdot)$ has no fixed point. Therefore, for any π_T, $\pi_{T-1} = H_{T-1}(\pi_T) > \pi_T$. The fact that b_t is not decreasing implies that for any π, $H_t(\pi) > H_{t-1}(\pi)$ for all $t \in [t_0, T - 1]$. Hence, we get that $\pi_{t_0} > \pi_{t_0+1} > \cdots > \pi_T$ (see also figure 13.2).   QED

Since $\tilde{g}_t$ decreases as b increases, for sufficiently high b we get $\tilde{g}_t < \bar{g}$. In this case stabilization *must* occur within finite time and inflation must be decreasing toward stabilization. Furthermore, even if $b_t = b_{t-1} = b$, the government may want to finance for a short period a deficit that exceeds the maximum money-financed feasible steady state deficit, i.e., $\bar{g} > \tilde{g}(b)$. In this case too stabilization must occur to guarantee the feasibility of this regime.

CLAIM 2   Let $b_t = b$ for all $t \geqslant 1$. Further, let $\tau_t = \tau$ for all $t \geqslant 1$. Then $1 = \pi_T < \pi_{t-1} < \cdots < \pi_1$.

Proof   When τ does not change at T, $H_{T-1}(\cdot) = H_{T-2}(\cdot) = H(\cdot)$. Accordingly, the fixed points of H, $\bar{\pi}_1$ and $\bar{\pi}_2$ (if they exist), remain the same. Since $\pi_{T+1} = 1$, we get form (8) that $\pi_T = 1$. Clearly, $\pi_{T-1} = H(1) > 1$. Furthermore if $\bar{\pi}_1$ exists, $H(1) < H(\bar{\pi}_1) = \bar{\pi}_1$ (with $\bar{\pi}_1 < \bar{\pi}_2$). Accordingly,

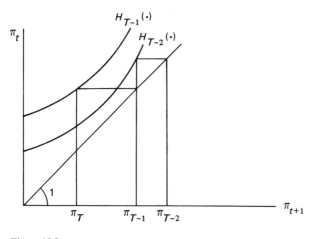

Figure 13.2
Inflation when $\tilde{g} > \bar{g}$.

$\pi_{T-1} > \pi_T$. If $\bar{\pi}_1$ and $\bar{\pi}_2$ do not exist, it is necessarily true that $\pi_{T-1} > \pi_T$. Repeated application of this argument complete the proof (see figure 13.3).

QED

Claims 1 and 2 identify two conditions that are necessary to have inflation that increases prior to stabilization. First, there must exist $t_0 \leqslant T$ such that $\bar{g} < \tilde{g}_t$ for $t < t_0$ assuming that b_t is a nondecreasing sequence. This condition is necessary for inflation to increase at least for part of the period prior to stabilization. Accordingly, $\bar{g} < \tilde{g}_t$ for all $t \leqslant T - 1$ is a necessary condition for inflation to increase during the entire period prior to T. In addition, if domestic debt remains unchanged prior to T, stabilization must involve changes in the tax/transfer schemes. More specifically, we have the following result.

CLAIM 3   Let $\bar{\pi}_{it}$ be the real fixed points of $H_t(\cdot)$, $i = 1, 2$. Then, if $H_t(\bar{\pi}_{1t}) < \pi_{t+1} < H_t(\bar{\pi}_{2t})$, we have (i) $\pi_t < \pi_{t+1}$ and (ii) $H_{t-1}(\bar{\pi}_{1t-1}) < \pi_t < H_{t-1}(\bar{\pi}_{2t-1})$.

Proof   Result (i) follows from the fact that for any $\pi_{t+1} \in (\bar{\pi}_{1t}, \bar{\pi}_{2t})$, $H_t(\pi_{t+1}) < \pi_{t+1}$ (see figure 13.1). Result (ii) follows the fact that $b_{t-1} \leqslant b_t$ and $b_{t-2} \leqslant b_{t-1}$ imply $H_{t-1}(\cdot) < H_t(\cdot)$. Therefore, $\bar{\pi}_{1t-1} < \bar{\pi}_{1t}$ and $\bar{\pi}_{2t-1} > \bar{\pi}_{2t}$. Thus $\pi_t \in (\bar{\pi}_{1t-1}, \bar{\pi}_{2t-1})$ as claimed.   QED

According to claim 3, if inflation increases from some date t to $t + 1$, it must have increased for every date prior to t.

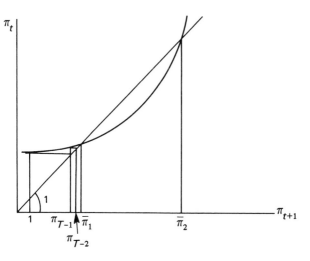

Figure 13.3
Inflation with fixed τ and b.

As stated above, $\pi_T = 1$ if $\tau_t = \tau$ for all $t \geqslant 1$. Therefore, inflation can rise up to $T - 1$ only if the government increases the domestic debt at $T - 1$, so that $H_{T-2}(\bar{\pi}_{1T-2}) < \pi_{T-1} < H_{T-2}(\bar{\pi}_{2T-2})$. In fact it is possible to get a sequence of increasing inflation if $b_t - b_{t-1} > 0$ for all $t \leqslant T$ and the above condition on H_{T-2} holds. Figure 13.2 depicts a simple case where $\bar{g} < \tilde{g}_t$. If, on the other hand, the domestic debt remains unchanged throughout the inflationary period, increasing inflation rates can be explained only if $H(\bar{\pi}_1) < \pi_T < H(\bar{\pi}_2)$. As $H(\bar{\pi}_{T+1} = 1) > 1$, clearly we require $\pi_T > 1$ despite the fact that $\bar{g} = 0$ and $\pi_{t+1} = 1$ for $t \geqslant T$ and $b_T = b_{T-1}$. From equation (8) we observe that this condition can hold only if the poststabilization $\hat{\tau}$ is less than the prestabilization τ. The increase in taxes decreases the poststabilization demand for money. Therefore, the post-stabilization price level increases so that $P_T/P_{T-1} > 1$.

Finally we state the following result. Suppose that $b_t = b$, $\bar{g} < \tilde{g}$, and $\tau_t = \tau$ for all $t \geqslant t_0$, where t_0 is the date at which stabilization is announced. Then $\lim \pi_{t_0}$ as $T \to \infty$ equals to $\bar{\pi}_1$.

This result states that as the stabilization date is moved further into the future, the announcement date $(t = t_0)$ inflation rate gets closer to $\bar{\pi}_1$, which is the lower steady state inflation that is associated with a deficit $\bar{g}$. This is true regardless of whether inflation is increasing or decreasing between $t = t_0$ and $t = T$. Thus, the certainty of the future stabilization rules out the "bad" (high inflation) path. The economy converges backward toward the lowest inflation rate that is consistent with $\bar{g}$. The fact that inflation is expected to end reverses completely the result in Sargent and Wallace (1986). The stable root of the inflation path is the lower inflation rate, rather than the higher one.

13.4. Poststabilization Policies

After stabilization the government budget (1) takes the following form:

$$0 = \frac{M_t - M_{t-1}}{P_t} + B_t - B_{t-1}. \tag{12}$$

Equation (12) states that every change in the money supply is exactly offset by changes in the domestic debt. In other words, the Central Bank engages in open market operations exchanging one form of government liability (money) against another (bonds) at market prices. The neutrality of such open market operations has been established by Peled (1985) and others in much more complicated environments. Nevertheless, it is helpful to have the following result.

CLAIM 4 An equilibrium allocation generated by $\{G_t, V_t, F_t, M_t, B_t\}_{t=1}^{\infty}$ with $G_t = 0$ and $\pi_{t+1} = 1$ for $t \geq T$ is identical to the allocation generated by $\{G_t, V_t, F_t, \overline{M}_t, \overline{B}_t\}_{t=1}^{\infty}$ where $\overline{M}_t = M_t$, $\overline{B}_t = B_t$ for $t \leq T - 1$ and

$$\frac{\overline{M}_t - \overline{M}_{t-1}}{P_t} + \overline{B}_t - \overline{B}_{t-1} = \frac{M_t - M_{t-1}}{P_t} + B_t - B_{t-1} \qquad \text{for} \quad t \geq T.$$

Proof From equation (8) it is clear that subject to (12) $\pi_t = 1$ for all $t \geq T + 1$ regardless of the values of b_t, $t \geq T$. It remains to be shown that consumption allocations are identical. To show this, it suffices to demonstrate that $m_t + b_t$ is independent of m_t. Using (7), we obtain

$$m_t + b_t = \tfrac{1}{2}(y_1 + \hat{t} - b_t - (y_t + b_t)) + b_t = \tfrac{1}{2}(y_1 + \hat{t} - y_2). \tag{13}$$

Equation (13) establishes the desired fact.   QED

Note that the assumptions that $z = 1$ and $\pi_{t+1} = 1$ for $t \geq T$ are crucial for the result in claim 4. That is, there is no rate of return dominance in the poststabilization period. Hence, an increase in M and a decrease in B have no effect on inflation, or/and any other real part of the allocation.

13.5. A Discussion of the Model and the Israeli Case

We showed that in an inflationary economy, an expected stabilization that reduces inflation to zero through a balanced budget may cause inflation to increase prior to the stabilization date even if the deficit is constant. In the appendix to this chapter we provide some evidence that shows that inflation in Israel was on average rising toward the stabilization while the deficit was constant. Next, the model implies that this deficit cannot be larger than the maximum steady state deficit. The annual deficit in Israel during the eight years prior to stabilization (July 1, 1985) was about 9–10% of GNP. Seignorage was also fairly constant and amounted only to 2.0–2.5% of GNP.[8] It has been claimed that these deficits are smaller than the feasible maximum (see a discussion in Bruno, 1986). Therefore our result is consistent with these claims. However, this very observation was used in order to discredit the conventional model of government deficit induced inflation while here we argue just the opposite. Indeed, the relatively small seignorage is a necessary condition for inflation to be rising.

The model provides the result that given a constant (less than maximum) deficit and constant taxes prior to stabilization, two policy measures make rising inflation most likely. The first is that balancing the budget is achieved by an increase in taxes so that lower disposable income causes a lower demand for money at the stabilization date. The second is that shortly before stabilization a larger part of the deficit is financed by liquid assets that substitute money in the public's portfolio.

The Israeli case is consistent with all the aforementioned conditions. The reduction in the deficit was entirely due to higher real tax revenues obtained directly by the indexation of tax liabilities and indirectly by a sharp reduction in subsidies to consumption and capital goods. As for the role of debt, table 13.1 shows that a large and increasing part of the deficit was financed by real debt. Table 13.2 indicates that sales of foreign currency to the public were heavily used. We view these sales as being equivalent to other forms of government debt. The exchange rate followed (more or less) the inflation, so that the gross return on foreign exchange was roughly 1. Furthermore, in accordance with note 5, the government facilitated the conversion of foreign exchange into goods by running a large current account deficit. In addition, more and more transactions and savings were done using U.S. dollars, thus reducing the demand for shekel denominated assets.

After stabilization we observe a large open market operation increasing

Table 13.1
Semiannual monthly averages of several monetary indicators

Semiannual	(1) ΔM/P (Constant shekels)	Index	(2) Δb (Constant shekels)	Index	(3) = (1) + (2) Deficit (Constant shekels)	Index	(4) M/P Index	(5) π 1 + inflation
81:1	0.087	100	0.363	100	0.450	100	100	1.050
81:2	0.197	226	1.193	329	1.390	309	109	1.063
82:1	0.066	76	1.551	427	1.828	406	106	1.070
82:2	0.278	320	0.380	105	0.657	146	114	1.075
83:1	0.385	443	0.814	224	1.199	266	135	1.071
83:2	0.076	87	1.767	487	1.842	409	96	1.117
84:1	0.147	169	1.016	280	1.164	259	91	1.143
84:2	0.456	524	1.236	340	1.691	376	90	1.163
85:1[b]	0.249	286	0.944	260	1.193	265	104	1.142
85:2	0.979	1125	−0.984	−271	−0.006	−1	254	1.027
86:1	0.024	28	0.174	48	0.198	44	219	1.014
86:2[c]	0.556	639	0.934	257	−0.378	−84	288	1.010
81:1–85:1	.239		1.029		1.268			

Source: Bank of Israel, *Main Economic Indicators*, various reports.
a. The columns of constant shekels refer to actual value in millions of new shekels in 1980 prices.
b. Includes July 1985.
c. The data are up to September 1986.

Table 13.2[a]
Semiannual monthly averages of the components of Δb

	Real revenue from sales of foreign exchange	Real change in PATAM accounts	Real net change in government bonds transactions
81:1	−0.041	0.011	0.394
81:2	0.424	0.108	0.662
82:1	0.617	0.413	0.520
82:2	0.138	0.001	0.516
83:1	0.367	0.356	0.091
83:2	0.931	0.819	0.016
84:1	0.764	0.526	−0.273
84:2	1.009	−0.084	0.143
85:1	0.760	0.088	0.096
85:2	0.197	−0.958	−0.224
86:1	0.228	−0.154	0.100
86.2[b]	0.354	−0.406	−0.882

Source: Bank of Israel, *Main Economic Indicators*, various reports. All numbers are in millions of new shekels, 1980 prices.
a. The sum of the three separate columns gives the value of Δb_t in column (2) of table 13.1.
b. 1986:2 is only for three months (until September).

the monetary base through an equivalent decrease in real debt, while the deficit remained zero (see table 13.1, 1985:2). The model predicts that this open market operation would have *no* effect on the price level (a Modigliani-Miller theorem for open market operations).

Finally, our results indicate that as long as we assume that credible policies maintaining balanced budget yield zero inflation (as the facts show with no exception), an expected stabilization is incompatible with a view that the economy tends to be at a neighborhood of the high and inefficient inflation rate. Therefore, it seems that the only alternative to explain the Israeli (and for that matter, any other) episode would be to that the observed path as belonging to two, unrelated, regimes. The inflationary period would correspond to the phase in which the economy somehow "slips" from the unstable low inflation path to the dynamically stable but inefficient high inflation that corresponds to a given constant government deficit.[9] The second phase is the poststabilization equilibrium, in which the deficit (and the attendant inflation) is zero. However, this view requires that the stabilization should come as a complete surprise, an idea that anybody living through an actual inflationary episode would find hard to entertain.

Appendix: Deficit Financing and Inflation, Israel 1981–1986

We collected monthly data published by the Bank of Israel to construct a time series of local government deficit and the components of the financing regime. We define the government deficit in this chapter to be the difference between expenditure and direct taxes. We do not include the interest payments on the government debts in the expenditures. This definition corresponds to McCallum's (1984) primary deficit. We calculated the nominal deficit by adding the nominal changes in the monetary base to the Bank of Israel's net cash flow stemming from transactions in interest bearing internal indexed debt and domestic transactions in foreign exchange (see tables 13.1 and 13.2). The net cash flows on indexed government bonds represent the difference between the value of sales of new bonds and the principal and interest payments on existing debt. We included in this government debt also the PATAM accounts. These accounts are (indirectly) government issued assets indexed to foreign currencies. Table 13.2 gives the real values of the three components of debt. To get real values we divide by the CPI. We summarize our results in semiannual average in table 13.1 in order to net out fluctuation and to get a view on the trends of these variables. It is clear that there is no upward trend in the real primary deficit up to 1985:2. The stabilization program was enacted on July 1, 1985. The deficit is very close to zero during the fifteen months following the stabilization. On the other hand, inflation is constantly rising up to the last half-year prior to stabilization. The monthly inflation rate increases from 5 to 16% before the stabilization and it goes down to 2.1%, 1.4%, and 1% per month afterward. During the second half of 1985 (the first half-year of the stabilization) the deficit is zero. Concurrently, there is a very significant activity reducing the government debt and increasing the money supply. Clearly, this activity has no significant effect on the inflation rate. Prior to stabilization there is a positive real growth in government debt that covers about 80% of the primary deficit while money creation covers only 20% of the deficit. These monthly averages are consistent with other methods of calculating the deficit published in the Bank of Israel's annual reports as well as the data presented by Bruno (1986) and Dornbusch and Fischer (1986).

The trends in seignorage or in the change in real debt in table 13.1 are hardly significant. At most one can argue that there is a low positive trend in the value of revenue derived from money creation and a slight negative trend in the revenue derived from real bonds and foreign exchange that finance the deficit. Somewhat surprisingly, we do not observe much of a down trend in real balances prior to stabilization. The most striking feature of the real balance index is its high increase after stabilization. Using the same index, real balances in 1977 were at about 550, declining mainly in 1979 and 1980. The upsurges in 1982:2 and 1983:1, and then in 1985:1, were due to temporary government measures (the Aridor plan and a wage-price-tax freeze package, respectively). The six-months averages are obviously not sufficient to capture price expectations (which determine money demand) during these periods. Despite the less-than-perfect correspondence of the real balances sequence to the theoretical prediction, there is an overall agreement between the data and the theory. In particular, poststabilization real balances do not return to their original high level, a phenomenon observed in most other inflationary episodes that corresponds to our model's requirement that money demand decrease at the stabilization date.

Notes

1. Liviatan (1984) and Drazen (1985) replicated the Sargent and Wallace result in a Sidrauski type monetary model. Drazen and Helpman (July 1985 and September 1985) extended this result to the case of uncertain date and uncertain programs of stabilization. Their results indicate very clearly that inflation trends and correlations among various macroeconomic variables depend crucially on the stabilization policy, despite the fact that government deficit stays constant in the prestabilization period.

2. Notice that the higher inflation solution predicts that higher seignorage is associated with a lower inflation rate. Therefore, zero deficit cannot (by itself) set inflation to zero. Bruno (1986) concludes that some additional administrative measures are necessary to shift expectations toward the low inflation solution. The fact is that no such measures were undertaken in any of the successful stabilization programs in Europe, but inflation rate was immediately reduced to zero (Sargent, 1982). Hence, the poststabilization phenomena in Europe are inconsistent with the explanation that hyperinflation is associated with the inefficient high inflation equilibrium.

3. Notice that in our model low seignorage is a condition for obtaining rising inflation rates. Others regard the fact that actual seignorage levels seem to be low in inflationary episodes as a puzzle. See, for example, the introduction to Sargent and Wallace (1986).

4. In the episodes of the 1920s internal debt (which was nominal) was no longer used as inflation became significant, but played an important role in government finances before. In Germany, for example, debt was used in 1920–1922, but not in 1923. In the Hungarian 1946 episode, on the other hand, the government did not use any money creation, but issued indexed debt to finance its deficit (the tax-pengo). The result was the worst inflation in recorded history.

5. Equivalently, we may think of the government as the sole importer and exporter of the economy, where F_t represents imports and xF_{t-1} exports. This interpretation follows from the national accounts of this economy, whereby

$$Nc_{1t} + Nc_{2t-1} + G_t = Ny_1 + Ny_2 + F_t - xF_{t-1}.$$

6. This assumption guarantees that our results do not stem from the fact that the real interest rate is always greater than the economy's growth rate. Assuming that the real interest is zero is reasonable keeping in mind that the real rate of return on money is so highly negative in inflationary economies.

7. The other root of (10) is given by $\frac{1}{2}[(y_1 + \tau - b_{-1})^{1/2} + (y_t + b_7)^{1/2}]^2$. It is easy to verify from (9) that this root implies $\bar{\pi} < 0$, whereas the root given in (11) implies $\bar{\pi} > 1$.

8. These numbers are for annual averages, and are consistent with the data presented in the appendix to this chapter.

9. This move from the low to the high inflation rate must be accompanied by decreasing real balances. The data indicate that the main decline of real balances occurred in 1979, prior to the date most observers associate with the "slippage."

References

Bruno, Michael, "Israel's Stabilization: The End of the 'Lost Decade'?" unpublished, The Hebrew University (June 1986).

Bruno, Michael, and S. Fisher, "The Inflationary Process: Shocks and Accommodation," Chap. 17 in Y. Ben-Porth (ed.), *The Israeli Economy: Maturing through Crisis*, Cambridge, MA: Harvard University Press (1986).

Cagan, Phillip, "The Monetary Dynamics of Inflation," in Milton Friedman (ed.), *Studies in the Quantity Theory of Money*, Chicago: Chicago University Press (1956).

Dornbusch, R., and S. Fischer, "Stopping Hyperinflations Past and Present," NBER Working Paper No. 1810 (1986).

Drazen, Alan, "Tight Money and Inflation: Further Results," *Journal of Monetary Economics* 15 (1985), 113–120.

Drazen, Alan, and Elhanan Helpman, "Inflationary Consequences of Uncertain Macroeconomic Policies," Tel-Aviv University Working Paper No. 21–85 (July 1985).

Drazen, Alan, and Elhanan Helpman, "Inflationary Consequences of Uncertain Macroeconomic Policies Part II: Budget Cuts" (September 1985).

Liviatan, N., "Tight Money and Inflation," *Journal of Monetary Economics* 13 (1984), 5–15.

McCallum, Bennet T., "Are Bond-Financed Deficits Inflationary? A Ricardian Analysis," *Journal of Political Economy* 92 (1984), 123–135.

Peled, D., "Stochastic Inflation and Government Provision of Indexed Bonds," *Journal of Monetary Economics* 14 (1985), 291–307.

Sargent, Thomas J., "The Ends of Four Big Inflations," in Robert E. Hall (ed.), *Inflation Causes and Effects*, Chicago: Chicago University Press (1982).

Sargent, Thomas J., and Neil Wallace, "Some Unpleasant Monetarist Arithmetics," *Federal Reserve Bank of Minneapolis Quarterly Review* (1981).

Sargent, Thomas J., and Neil Wallace, "Identification and Estimation of a Model of Hyperinflation with a Continuum of 'Sunspot' Equilibria," in A. Razin and E. Sadka (eds.), *Economics in Theory and Practice*, London: McMillan Press (1986).

V STABILIZATION IN OPEN ECONOMIES

14 The Economic Consequences of the Franc Poincaré

Barry Eichengreen and Charles Wyplosz

In this chapter we reassess the cyclical performance of the French economy in the 1920s, focusing in particular on the period 1926–1931 and on France's resistance to the Great Depression. France expanded rapidly after 1926 and, unlike the other leading industrial economies, resisted the onset of the Depression until 1931. We find strikingly little support for the conventional explanation for these events, which emphasizes an undervalued French franc and an export-led boom. While French exports as a share of GDP turned down as early as 1928, the economy continued to expand for several years. Investment, not exports, emerges as the proximate source of the French economy's resistance to the Great Depression, and fiscal policy emerges as the major determinant of the surge in French investment spending. Previous accounts have emphasized the role of monetary policy in determining the real and nominal exchange rates ostensibly responsible for French economic fluctuations in the decade after 1921. In contrast, we argue here for a more balanced view of the roles of monetary and fiscal policies in French macroeconomic fluctuations over that critical decade.

14.1. Introduction

The macroeconomic performance of the French economy in the 1920s contrasts sharply with cyclical experience in the rest of the industralized world. French gross domestic product and industrial output grew with exceptional vigor over the first half of the 1920s (see table 14.1).[1] After a recession in 1926–1927 and despite a noticeable deceleration in the rate of economic growth, through the end of the decade the French economy continued to expand at a rate significantly in excess of the international average. Well into calendar year 1930, France remained immune to the effects of the Great Depression, and even in 1931 the downturn remained moderate compared to other parts of the world. But once the full effects of the Depression were felt, its impact in France was exceptionally severe; as late as 1938 gross domestic product had not recovered to 1931 levels.

Accounts of the interwar period attach more weight to the exchange rate than to any other variable affecting the French economy's macroeconomic performance. Histories of the period 1919–1926 are dominated by "the

Work on this chapter was begun during Eichengreen's visit to the Institut National de la Statistique et des Etudes Economiques. A fellowship from the French Ministry of External Affairs and a Fulbright Grant made this visit possible. We are grateful to INSEAD for financial support, to Robert Levy for exceptionally capable assistance, and to Bradford Lee and participants in the Harvard Economic History Workshop for comments.

Table 14.1
Interwar growth rates

	France	U.S.	U.K.	Italy	Germany	"World"
Average annual rates of growth of real GDP						
1921–26	10.2	8.4	2.3	2.8	15.1	5.8
1927–30	5.0	−0.9	1.3	1.4	−2.4	−0.3
1930–31	−4.3	−7.7	−5.1	−2.2	−10.9	−7.0
1931–38	−1.6	2.3	3.1	2.8	8.9	−2.8
1921–1938	2.8	2.8	2.3	2.0	7.9	2.8
Average annual rates of growth of industrial production						
1921–26	18.9	10.0	6.2	9.1	6.7	9.4
1927–30	8.7	−0.6	−0.7	2.2	−3.8	−1.0
1930–31	−14.8	−19.2	−6.4	−9.4	−18.8	−18.5
1931–38	1.2	7.7	6.1	4.6	14.9	6.9

Source: Eichengreen and Wyplosz (1986), appendix A.

battle of the franc," when financial difficulties culminating in the loss of 80% of the currency's external value greatly stimulated the export industries and macroeconomy. The period 1926–1931 is characterized as the golden era of the "franc Poincaré," when exchange-rate stabilization at an undervalued parity enhanced the competitiveness of French exports, stimulating growth through the end of the decade and insulating the economy from the onset of the Great Depression. Then successive devaluations of other major currencies starting in 1931 rendered the franc overvalued and greatly exacerbated the impact of the slump on French industry and trade, largely accounting for the singular depth and long duration of the French Depression.

Typically monetary policy is credited with driving the exchange rate and the French economy over the decade ending in 1930. Fiscal policy plays a role only insofar as it influences money supply. In conventional accounts, the period through the summer of 1926 is marked by real and nominal exchange rate depreciation due to excessive money creation. Real depreciation stimulated the French economy for reasons related to both aggregate demand and aggregate supply. On the supply side, the rise in producer prices exceeded the rate of wage inflation, reducing unit labor costs and thereby encouraging firms to increase employment and production. On the demand side, the rate of exchange-rate depreciation exceeded the rate of domestic inflation, enhancing the competitiveness of exports and switching expenditure toward French goods. The period after 1926 is marked by stabilization of the franc at an undervalued rate. Monetary stabilization, by eliminating inflation and reducing nominal interest rates, increased the demand for money, which, under France's gold standard rules, could only be obtained by running a balance-of-payments surplus and importing reserves.[2] Hence the franc's undervaluation continued to stimulate exports after 1926. In this conventional view, the French economy's expansion in the decade ending in 1930 is a classic instance of export-led growth.

In this chapter we reassess the cyclical performance of the French economy in the 1920s, focusing particularly on the period 1926–1931 and on France's resistance to the Great Depression. We find strikingly little support for the export-based explanation of French economic growth after 1926. While French exports as a share of GDP turn down as early as 1928, the economy continues to expand for several subsequent years. Investment, not exports, emerges as the proximate source of the French economy's resistance to the Great Depression. And fiscal stabilization emerges as the major determinant of French investment spending. In effect, we argue for a more balanced view of the roles of monetary and fiscal policies in French macroeconomic fluctuations over the decade 1921–1930.

While our discussion of the links between fiscal policy and investment stresses the resource flow or classic crowding-in effects of budget deficit reductions, an alternative explanation emphasizes instead Poincaré's reputation for financial orthodoxy: Poincaré's return to power removed the specter of financial uncertainty, prospective future budget deficits and large-scale capital levies, igniting a massive capital inflow that reduced the required rate of return on capital and stimulated investment. In fact, the two hypotheses are compatible, as we explain below. Our empirical analysis suggests, however, that classic crowding-in due to current budgetary measures, rather than confidence-induced capital inflows due in part to expected future budgetary measures, was the critical determinant of the French investment boom.

In the course of challenging the traditional interpretation of French macroeconomic trends in the 1920s, we touch on several issues of more general interest relevant to contemporary experiences with fiscal stabilization. We provide an explicit analysis of the effects of a fiscal contraction in a perfect-foresight model of an open economy in which the government budget is linked to stocks of productive capital and foreign debt, and in which fiscal policy has an impact on employment due to inertia in labor markets. Previous investigators have studied fiscal policy in the presence of wage and price rigidities but in static models without public sector and economy-wide budget constraints (Mundell, 1963; Fleming, 1962; Sachs, 1980). Dynamic models have been developed but without capital accumulation (Branson and Buiter, 1983; Sachs and Wyplosz, 1984; Cuddington and Viñals, 1986). Investigators working in the disequilibrium tradition combine wage and price rigidities with capital accumulation, but only under restrictive assumptions about dynamics (Neary and Stiglitz, 1983). In these pages, we integrate the essential features of these models into a more general framework.

14.2. French Economic Performance, 1921–1931

Historical accounts of the French economy in the years 1921–1930 typically divide the decade into three segments: the period of inflation from 1921 through mid-1926, the period of stabilization from Poincaré's return to power in July 1926 through the 1927 recession, and the period of renewed growth through the end of 1930. The decline of the franc in the first half of the twenties is credited with subsidizing exports and promoting investment by lightening the burden of fixed charges (Kemp, 1972, p. 97; Bernard, 1975, p. 180; Jackson, 1985, p. 11). Establishment of the franc Poincaré in the second half of the decade, "by slightly undervaluing the currency," is credited with stimulating "an export-led boom to round off the period of postwar prosperity" (Kemp, 1972, p. 84). The Great Depression has relatively little impact on France as late as 1930 chiefly because of exchange-rate undervaluation (Kemp, 1971, p. 89; 1972, p. 100).[3]

To assess the role of the exchange rate in these developments, it is first necessary to have an adequate measure of its movement. We therefore construct quarterly time series for the real and nominal effective exchange rates for the period 1922–1937.[4] The nominal effective exchange rate is a weighted average of bilateral rates against France's trading partners, with trade shares serving as weights. The real effective exchange rate is the product of the nominal effective rate and the ratio of foreign to domestic prices. Both effective exchange rates are displayed in figure 14.1 along with exports in constant 1929 prices.[5] Clearly the real exchange rate had powerful demand-side effects.[6] But although persistent real depreciation was accompanied by steady export growth through 1926, post-1927 experience is inconsistent with the export-based interpretation of the French economy's subsequent expansion. Despite the real exchange rate's maintenance at

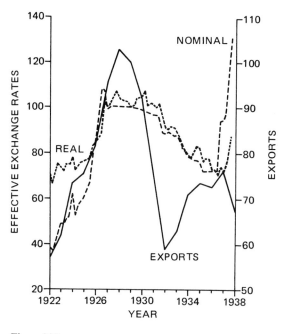

Figure 14.1
Effective exchange rates and exports (1929 = 100).

peak levels through 1930, export volume fell in 1929, reflecting the decline in world incomes due to the onset of the Depression followed by imposition of trade restrictions abroad.[7] The export share of GDP fell even earlier, in calendar year 1928. While exchange-rate depreciation may have prevented exports from declining even more rapidly than this, the extent and the very fact of their decline suggests that the impact of real depreciation on export demand cannot by itself account for the persistence of French economic growth after 1928.[8]

To see whether these demand-side effects were accompanied by supply-side stimuli, we consider in figure 14.2 two measures of real labor costs: the nominal wage deflated by wholesale and retail price indices, labeled, respectively, the real producer and real consumer wage. While each index includes both traded and nontraded goods, the wholesale price index places a heavier weight on traded-goods prices.[9] Since the profitability of traded goods production is particularly relevant to the export-led interpretation of the French economy's growth, we focus on money wages relative to

Figure 14.2
Real consumer and producer wages and unemployment.

wholesale prices as a measure of the real wage. Although figure 14.2 confirms that nominal wages lagged wholesale prices during the 1922–1926 inflation, it indicates also that much of this reduction in real producer wages was eroded within a year of stabilization.[10] Once inflation was halted in 1926, the franc appreciated over the second half of the year and prices declined, albeit more slowly than the exchange rate recovered. As prices fell, money wages lagged behind, and by 1927:III the relationship between wages and wholesale prices had been restored to 1923 levels. By 1928 the franc no longer provided the producers of traded goods an incentive to expand export supplies. It does not appear, therefore, that the franc's depreciation had long-lived supply-side effects.

This emphasis on supply-side considerations is predicated on the notion that the real producer wage influenced the level of employment, because employers adjusted hiring to equate the cost of labor and the value of its marginal product. As evidence on this relationship, figure 14.2 also presents Galenson and Zellner's (1957) estimate of French unemployment. While this estimate of the unemployment rate is far from definitive, even with a generous margin for error it would appear that the real producer wage and unemployment tended to move in the same direction. Although the 1927 recession, when firms apparently were demand constrained, is a notable exception, the correspondence between the real producer wage and unemployment is generally consistent with our interpretation.

The finding that the franc's depreciation failed to have long-lived supply-side effects contrasts with experience elsewhere in Europe both in the first half of the 1920s and after 1931. In both instances, nominal depreciation tended to reduce real wages and have a sustained impact on unit labor costs.[11] Only in France in the mid-1920s was the impact of nominal depreciation on real wages not sustained. The reason for the contrast, figure 14.2 suggests, is not necessarily any exceptional flexibility of the French labor market, but that the Poincaré stabilization initiated a large fall in the nominal exchange rate and prices that largely neutralized the implications for aggregate supply of the preceding depreciation. Thus, if the franc Poincaré insulated France from the initial effects of the Depression, it must have worked through different channels than those emphasized in simple aggregate-supply/aggregate-demand analyses.[12]

To shed further light on the behavior of investment-goods industries, table 14.2 decomposes GNP into consumption, investment, government spending, and the current account of the balance of payments. The share of investment in GNP rises rapidly toward the end of the 1920s, from 14% in 1927 to nearly 21% in 1930 and 19% in 1931. In comparison, the current account moves only slightly, from a surplus of 3% of GNP in 1926 to balance in 1930. Clearly, the "French boom" of the second half of the 1920s was investment-led expansion, not export-led growth. Insofar as France resisted the onset of the Depression, credit lies with the buoyancy of investment rather than with exports.

The shifts in the composition of demand between exports, investment, and government spending emerge as a key feature of the period. Figure 14.3 further documents the dramatic evolution of the government budget. It moves from substantial deficit in the immediate postwar years to balance by 1925–1926 and then into surplus, which peaks as a share of GNP in 1929. These shifts should have been promoted by the changes in relative prices displayed in figure 14.4 (and implicit in figure 14.2). The rise in the ratio of retail to wholesale prices after 1927 implies an increase in the relative price of nontraded goods that should have shifted resources

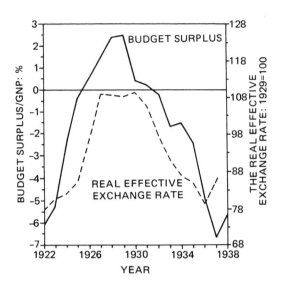

Figure 14.3
The budget surplus and the real effective exchange rate.

Table 14.2
Decomposition of national income (as percentage of GNP)

	Consumption	Investment	Government spending	Current account
1922	.533	.139	.312	.016
1923	.606	.140	.240	.014
1924	.599	.167	.216	.019
1925	.648	.152	.176	.023
1926	.645	.174	.152	.029
1927	.670	.143	.163	.023
1928	.643	.180	.159	.017
1929	.658	.183	.147	.013
1930	.608	.209	.182	.001
1931	.629	.193	.190	−.012
1932	.645	.165	.214	−.023
1933	.646	.156	.213	−.015
1934	.656	.146	.205	−.007
1935	.631	.147	.225	−.004
1936	.634	.153	.230	−.016
1937	.634	.156	.232	−.022
1938	.637	.141	.221	.001

Source: calculated from Carré, Dubois, and Malinvaud (1975).

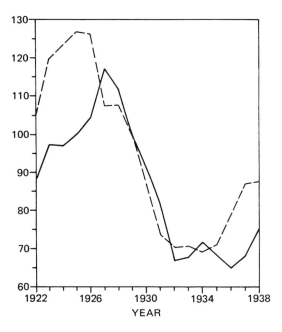

Figure 14.4
Export performance and relative prices (1929 = 100). Key: solid line, share of exports/GNP; dashed line, wholesale/retail prices.

out of the production of exportables and into the home goods sector. This explains how the French economy accommodated the fall in export demand associated with the onset of the Depression abroad without significantly reducing the level of economic activity. At approximately the same time the onset of the Depression was reducing foreign demand for French exports, the rise in the relative price of nontraded goods at home was transferring resources out of the production of exportables and into the production of nontradables.

This reallocation of resources cannot be viewed simply as a response to the Depression, however. Were this the case, one would expect the traded-nontraded goods price ratio to move concurrently with or to follow the decline in export demand. In fact figure 14.4 shows that the fall in the relative price of traded goods led by a year the decline in the export share of French GNP. This suggests the need to analyze supply conditions at a more disaggregated level.

This review of French economic performance in the 1920s identifies two central questions. First, why did the price and production of French exports fall after 1927 despite the maintenance of a depreciated exchange rate? Second, what accounts for the surge in domestic investment? We take up these questions one at a time in the next two sections.

14.3.   Export Growth and Stabilization: A Franco-Scandinavian Model

Clearly, a one-sector model that fails to distinguish between the production of traded and nontraded goods is incapable of capturing key aspects of French economic performance in this period.[13] The distinction between traded and nontraded goods has been popularized by Scandinavian economists (e.g., Aukrust, 1977; Edgren, Faxen, and Odhner, 1969). In the Scandinavian model, wages are tied to the prices of traded goods.[14] Figure 14.2 suggests, however, that in the 1920s French wages were more closely linked to the cost of living inclusive of the prices of nontraded goods. Our model therefore departs from the Scandinavian approach in its specification of wage determination, and in addition by allowing the level of employment to be endogenously determined.[15]

We start with the small country assumption, which implies that rest-of-world prices of traded goods P^* together with the exchange rate determine the domestic price of traded goods P_T (we relax the assumption of parametric export prices in the next section):

$$P_T = eP^*, \tag{1}$$

where the exchange rate e is the domestic price of one unit of foreign currency. P^* is normalized to unity. Throughout, T and N subscripts denote traded and nontraded goods, respectively.

We assume that the production of nontraded goods is less capital intensive than the production of tradables. For simplicity, nontraded goods are characterized as Ricardian commodities, requiring inputs of labor alone. (All our conclusions carry over to the general case, so long as nontraded goods remain labor intensive.) Perfect competition, constant returns to scale, and marginal cost pricing together imply that the price of nontraded goods is proportional to the wage W. Normalizing labor productivity to unity gives

$$W = P_N. \tag{2}$$

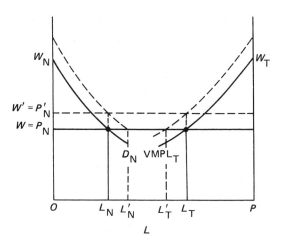

Figure 14.5

Traded goods, in contrast, are Heckscher-Ohlin commodities, produced using both labor and an exogenously fixed stock of capital. (We relax the assumption of a fixed capital stock in the next section.) Given a production function $f(L, K)$ and the assumption of perfect competition, employment in the traded goods sector is adjusted to equate the wage with the value marginal product of labor ($VMPL_T$):

$$W = P_T f_L(L) = e f_L(L), \qquad f_L < 0, \tag{3}$$

where $f_L = \partial f / \partial L$. Inverting (3) yields the derived demand for labor in the traded goods sector:

$$L_T = f(W/e), \qquad f' < 0. \tag{4}$$

Under the small country assumption, domestic producers of traded goods are not constrained in the quantities they sell: while domestic demand depends on relative prices and income, any excess of domestic supply over demand can be exported to foreign markets. Domestic producers adjust production and hiring to be on their labor demand curves. In figure 14.5, employment in the production of traded goods is the distance PL_T. This distance is determined by the intersection of the employment schedule $VMPL_T$ with the wage.

In contrast to the demand for traded goods, which is perfectly elastic at world prices, the demand for nontraded goods depends on domestic income (which is proportional to total employment L_T and L_N) and on their relative price P_N/P_T. The (uncompensated) price elasticity of demand for nontraded goods appears in figure 14.5 as the D_N schedule, which (under the Ricardian assumption) is also the derived demand for labor in the nontraded goods sector. Employment in the production of nontraded goods is the distance OL_N:

$$L_N = g(P_N/P_T) = g(W/e), \qquad g' < 0. \tag{5}$$

Aggregate labor supply is constant and represented in figure 14.5 by the length OP. Unemployment is the distance $L_T L_N$. Taking the exchange rate as exogenous, the model is closed by a wage determination rule. We assume that labor mobility equates wages across sectors and, as suggested by figure 14.2, that economy-wide wages respond with a lag to the cost of living:[16]

$$W_t = \gamma e_{t-1} + (1 - \gamma) P_{N,t-1}. \tag{6}$$

We can use this model to analyze the effects of a permanent, unanticipated depreciation of the exchange rate.[17] Depreciation raises the $VMPL_T$ schedule in figure 14.5. Given the lagged response of nominal wages to the cost of living, the real producer wage in the traded goods (W/e) sector falls, and employment in that sector expands to OL'_T. Since $W/e = P_N/P_T$ [from equations (1) and (2)], depreciation switches domestic demand toward nontraded goods. Both the relative price and the income effects shift the D_N schedule upward, increasing the demand for labor in the nontraded goods sector. In the period of the depreciation, unemployment falls from $L_T L_N$ to $L'_T L'_N$. In the subsequent period, wages respond to the initial rise in the cost of living, restoring the equality $W = P_N = P_T = e$ and returning employment to its initial level. In figure 14.5 this is shown as an upward shift in the $W = P_N$ schedule.

These dynamics are depicted in figure 14.6. A one-time depreciation moves the system from α to 1; with the economy to the right of the 45° line, the real wage has been reduced and the level of employment has been correspondingly increased. With no further change in the exchange rate, the wage rises in the next period to α', restoring employment to its initial level. The model can be used to interpret several macroeconomic features of the 1920s. According to leading accounts of the period (e.g., Sauvy, 1984), the years 1921–1926 were dominated by a series of unanticipated depreciations.[18] Each time the exchange rate depreciated, domestic prices initially lagged behind. Prices and wages subsequently responded, however, to

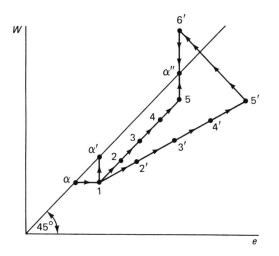

Figure 14.6

increases in the exchange rate. In figure 14.6, the path α-1-2-3-4-5 is meant
to capture these aspects of French experience. As in figure 14.2, the real
wage (nominal wage deflated by the cost of living) initially falls but remains
stable in the face of successive depreciations. (In contrast, the path α-1'-2'-
3'-4'-5' shows the effects of accelerating depreciation.) As in figure 14.4, the
CPI falls relative to the WPI, and depreciation is associated with a decline
in unemployment. As in figure 14.1, depreciation is accompanied by a rise
in exports.

The effects of terminating inflation and permitting the exchange rate to
appreciate before returning the franc to the gold standard (the course of
events between Poincaré's return to power in the summer of 1926 and the
de facto stabilization at the end of the year) are depicted in figure 14.6 by
the path 5'-6'-α''. Due to the response of wages to lagged prices, real wages
rise above their initial level following stabilization, and employment temporarily falls. As in figure 14.2, stabilization is associated with transitional
unemployment, and, as in figure 14.1, the volume of exports falls.

Thus, a simple model provides a coherent explanation for many of the
dominant macroeconomic characteristics of the French economy in the
1920s, including the declining role of exports in French economy following
the Poincaré stabilization. What remains to be explained is the buoyancy
of investment in the poststabilization era.

Table 14.3
The model

$Y = Y^E + \lambda^N Y^N$	(9)
$D = D(Y - T, \Omega), \qquad D_1, D_2 > 0$	(10)
$\Omega = B + \lambda B^* = qK$	(11)
Nontraded goods sector	
$\quad Y^N = D^N + G^N$	(12)
$\quad D^N = \alpha_N D / \lambda_N$	(13)
$\quad G^N = \alpha^N G / \lambda_N$	(14)
$\quad \lambda_{N,t+1} = \lambda_{N,t} + \gamma[Y_t^N - f^N(\lambda_N)], \qquad f_{\lambda_N}^N < 0$	(15)
Exportables sector	
$\quad Y^E = f^E(K, \lambda_N), \qquad f_K^E > 0, \quad f_{\lambda_N}^E < 0$	(16)
$\quad Y^E = D^E + G^E + I + X$	(17)
$\quad D^E = \alpha^E D$	(18)
$\quad G^E = \alpha^E G$	(19)
$\quad X = X(\lambda), \qquad X_\lambda > 0$	(20)
Investment	
$\quad K_{t+1} - K_t = \psi(q_t), \qquad \psi_q > 0$	(21)
$\quad I_t = K_{t+1} - K_t + \delta K_t$	(22)
$\quad r_t = (q_{t+1} - q_t)/q_t + f_{K,t}^E$	(23)
Portfolio balance	
$\quad r_t = r^* + (\lambda_{t+1} - \lambda_t)/\lambda_t + \theta(B_t + q_t K_t, \lambda_t B_t^*), \qquad \theta_1 > 0 \qquad \theta_2 > 0$	(24)
Government budget	
$\quad G_t = T_t - r_t B_t + (B_{t+1} - B_t)$	(25)

14.4. Investment and Fiscal Stabilization: A Dynamic Model

In this section, we explore the links between the 1926 stabilization, the subsequent decline in the export share of GNP, and the surge in investment spending that was the proximate source of the French economy's resistance to the onset of the Great Depression. The previous section explains the decline in the export share as a delayed effect of exchange-rate stabilization. In this section, we integrate that explanation with an analysis of the investment response.

The model providing the basis for the analysis is summarized in table 14.3. As in our Franco-Scandinavian model, the domestic economy produces both traded and nontraded goods, traded goods using capital and labor, nontraded goods using labor alone, with price of nontraded goods proportional to the wage. But in contrast to that model, three distinct commodities are consumed: importables, exportables, and nontraded goods (with the domestic economy specialized in the production of the last two).

Demands depend on two relative prices, the price of nontradables relative to exports (P_N/P_E), and the price of imports relative to exports (eP^*/P_E). (Exportables are the numeraire throughout.) We adopt the semi-small-country assumption that the world price of imports is given exogenously, but that domestic supplies are capable of influencing the world price of exports. We define the real exchange rate as

$$\lambda = eP^*/P_E \tag{7}$$

and the relative price of nontraded goods as

$$\lambda_N = P_N/P_E. \tag{8}$$

The real exchange rate, investment, and the adjustment of government spending are now endogenously determined. Real GDP is given by (9) in table 14.3. Real expenditure, given by (10), is a function of real disposable income and real wealth Ω. Disposable income as a determinant of expenditure can be justified on the basis of liquidity constraints; thus, our expenditure function incorporates both Keynesian and permanent income features.[19] As in the previous section, the supply of traded goods is perfectly elastic at the prevailing wage (12), with the wage adjusting gradually to eliminate excess supply or demand in the labor market (15). Domestic expenditure is the sum of the demands of the private (13) and public (14) sectors, whose allocations across commodities are derived from instantaneous Cobb-Douglas utility functions.

The real exchange rate λ adjusts instaneously to clear the market for exportables (17). The demand for exportables is the sum of private (18), public (19), and foreign (20) consumption plus domestic investment (17). Capital accumulation is a function of Tobin's q (21). Gross investment spending differs from capital accumulation by an allowance for capital depreciation at rate δ (22).

Domestic debt and equity are assumed to be perfect substitutes for one another but imperfect substitutes for foreign assets. Foreigners do not hold domestic assets. These assumptions highlight the role of the (exchange) risk premium in rendering domestic residents willing to hold increasing quantities of domestic assets. They are designed to capture the idea that increases in public debt raise the danger of a capital levy on all domestic assets, a policy option much discussed in France in the 1920s. Portfolio balance determines the relationship between the domestic real interest rate, foreign real interest rate, and real exchange rate (23), where B_t is the real value of public debt (in units of exportables) and B_t^* the net real value of foreign assets held by domestic residents. We assume perfect foresight regarding the evolution of the real exchange rate λ and equity prices q. The perfect substitutability of domestic debt and equity implies that the real yield on one-period bonds r_t equals dividends plus capital gains on shares. This arbitrage condition is given by (24) with dividends assumed to equal the marginal productivity of capital.

Equation (25) is the government budget constraint. The growth of public debt equals the excess of government spending G over the sum of net taxes T and debt service rB. Changes in fiscal policy take the form of changes in government spending, holding taxes constant.

Our neglect of the monetary sector in general, and of money financing of the deficit in particular, in our analysis of the post-1926 situation can be justified on two grounds. First, under the gold standard the supply of money was determined in principle exclusively by money demand. Given a credibly pegged exchange rate, nominal interest rates were determined exclusively by interest rates in the rest of the world; changes in the domestic credit component of the monetary base therefore should have had no implications for total money supply. Second, after 1926 the Bank of France functioned under new regulations, which prohibited it from monetizing government budget deficits.

To analyze the post-1926 situation in France, we perform the following experiment. Starting from steady-state equilibrium in period zero, we cut government spending so as to reduce the steady state value of public debt from B_0 to $\bar{B}$. The real debt is assumed to evolve according to

$$B_t = B_{t-1} + \mu(\bar{B} - B_{t-1}). \tag{26}$$

Since taxes are held constant, (25) and (26) together determine the path of public spending.[20]

Given its size, the model in table 14.3 cannot be solved analytically. Instead, we calibrate it using data for the 1920s, linearize it around the steady state, and simulate it under the assumption of perfect foresight. Parameter values and initial conditions for endogenous variables are given in tables 14.3 and 14.4. While we have attempted to use historical data to guide the selection of parameter values, any attempt at calibration can only approximate the properties of the economy being modeled. The simula-

Table 14.4
Simulation results $(B_0 = 800, \bar{B} = 700)^a$

	B	λ	λ_N	q	I	G	X	Y
Initial steady state	800	100.0	100.0	1.0	9.5	38.0	25.1	145.0
Period 1	800	109.1	100.0	1.026	10.8	23.8	26.8	137.9
Period 2	781	108.3	99.4	1.018	10.4	29.0	26.7	141.6
Period 3	773	108.2	99.1	1.017	10.4	30.1	26.7	142.7
Period 4	766	108.2	99.0	1.016	10.3	30.7	26.6	143.3
Period 5	759	108.1	98.9	1.014	10.2	31.3	26.6	143.8
Period 10	735	108.3	98.6	1.011	10.1	33.3	26.7	145.4
Period 20	712	109.2	98.2	1.008	10.0	35.4	26.8	147.4
Period 30	704	110.3	97.9	1.005	9.8	36.0	27.0	148.3

a. Initial values:

$Y_0 = 145$, $Y_0^N = 69$, $Y_0^E = 76$, $G_0 = 38$, $I_0 = 9.5$, $D_0 = 100$, $X_0 = 25.1$,

$B_0 = 800$, $B_0^* = 500$, $K_0 = 1900$, $q_0 = \lambda_0 = \lambda_{N0} = 1$, $r_0 = 0.01$.

Parameter values:

$\alpha^E = 0.3$, $\alpha^N = 0.5$, $\delta = 0.1$, $\mu = 0.1$, $r^* = 0.05$.

Production functions: exportables, Cobb-Douglas with share of capital $= 0.25$; nontraded goods, $(\partial Y^N/\partial\lambda)(\lambda/Y^N) = 0.2$.

Consumption function marginal propensities to spend: out of income, 0.9; out of wealth, 0.1.

Portfolio balance: $\partial r/\partial(B + \cdots/\lambda B^*) = 0.001$.

Investment function: $\partial(K_{t+1} - K_t)/\partial q_t = 4$.

tion results only illustrate the properties of the model and indicate the general orders of magnitude of the result of our fiscal policy experiment.

The simulation generates a real depreciation on impact followed by a relatively flat real exchange rate path, both of which resemble figure 14.1. As the fiscal contraction reduces domestic demand, an incipient excess supply of exportables develops and is eliminated through a fall in their relative price, which increases export sales. The brevity of the 1927 recession may be explicable in part on the basis of this expenditure-switching effect.

Thus, we find that not only monetary policy but fiscal policy as well are critical for understanding the post-1926 real exchange rate path. Had the real depreciation of the period 1922–1926, so prominent in figure 14.1, resulted simply from nominal exchange rate overshooting in response to monetary expansion and inflation prior to the Poincaré stabilization (the Dornbusch, 1976, mechanism), one would expect the real exchange rate to recover following monetary stabilization; instead, the real exchange rate remains high, suggesting that the domestic expenditure effects of fiscal contraction played a dominant role in its post-1926 path. (The correlation between the government budget deficit and the real exchange rate is evident in figure 14.3.) Thus, the real depreciation of the franc, rather than a clever ploy by French monetary policymakers, should be seen as a consequence of the fiscal reforms which eliminated the budget deficit.

The simulation also generates a surge in investment as a result of a jump in Tobin's q.[21] Following its initial rise, q declines continuously toward its steady-state level, and investment falls gradually. The behavior of q is a consequence of the public debt reduction. The real exchange rate depreciates on impact, after which it rises slowly; so long as it is rising the domestic interest rate must fall relative to the yield on foreign assets. Over time, a fall in the outstanding stock of domestic debt reduces the interest rate domestic residents require in order to hold that debt, reinforcing this effect. Since arbitrage equalizes the rates of return on domestic debt and equity, the lower interest rate on debt implies capital losses on equity, causing q to fall over time. For q to fall over time, it must rise on impact, providing the initial stimulus to investment. Thus our model exhibits the crowding-in effect of fiscal stabilization familiar from simple income-expenditure models. But there are two important differences. First the short-run crowding-in results from the relationship between real interest rates, real exchange rates, and Tobin's q. Second, while the fiscal multiplier is positive in the short run, leading to a contraction following stabilization, it is negative in the long run, leading to more real growth. This is because the larger capital stock, which results from higher investment, sustains an increased volume of production. Over the span of time of concern to us here, 1926 to 1931, the reduction in government spending probably remained contractionary, reducing the rate of growth of the French economy. This is consistent with the deceleration in the rate of French economic growth between 1921–1926 and 1927–1930. At the same time, the fiscal stabilization switched demand toward domestic sources, namely, investment, reducing the economy's dependence on foreign demand and insulating the economy from the initial effects of the Great Depression.

The one aspect of the simulation at variance with historical experience is the simulated decline in the price of nontraded goods relative to the price of exports. The reason for this result is our assumption that investment spending falls exclusively on exportables while government spending is distributed among exportables, importables, and nontraded goods. In the simulation, as government spending falls and investment rises, expenditure tends to be switched away from nontraded goods, resulting in a modest decline in their relative price. It would be straightforward to alter the specification of the composition of investment spending to track better this aspect of historical experience.

14.5.   Further Evidence

Our specification of investment in section 14.4 highlights the role of Tobin's q. Figure 14.7 illustrates the close correlation between q and French investment during the interwar years, but suggests that investment depended not on current but on lagged real share prices.[22] This is inconsistent with early formulations of the q theory of investment, as proposed by Tobin (1969)

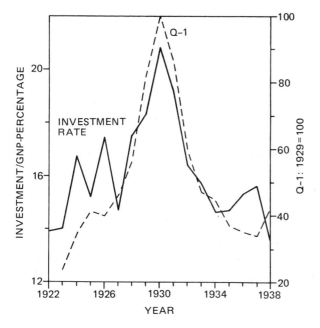

Figure 14.7
Investment and Q_{-1}.

Table 14.5
Investment function[a]

	Constant	q	q_{-1}	dY/Y	Capital inflows	RHO	SEE
1	0.66	−0.08	0.52	0.53		−0.55	0.049
	(27.58)	(−0.79)	(5.22)	(2.31)		(−1.93)	
2	0.66		0.45	0.41		−0.52	0.048
	(28.02)		(10.77)	(2.41)		(−1.90)	
3	0.67		0.43			−0.43	0.056
	(24.47)		(8.56)			(−1.58)	
4	0.63		0.49	0.31	−0.36	−0.56	0.047
	(21.74)		(9.74)	(1.80)	(−1.34)	(−2.17)	

Source: Sauvy (1984), *Statistique Générale de la France* (various issues).
a. Annual data: 1923–1938. Dependent variable: I/Y.

and developed by Abel (1980) and Hayashi (1982), in which current q encapsulates all relevant information about the current and expected future profitability of additions to the capital stock. However, a variety of studies of the postwar period have found, as in figure 14.7, that lagged q has more explanatory power than current q, leading Fischer (1983), Kydland and Prescott (1982), and Veda and Yoshikawa (1986) to incorporate order and delivery lags into the q theory of investment and to derive estimating equations in which current investment depends on lagged q. Empirical versions of our investment equation appear in table 14.5. The results confirm that lagged q dominates current q as a determinant of investment.[23]

Lagged q plays a central role in our interpretation of French macroeconomic performance on the eve of the Great Depression. The buoyancy of the French economy in calendar year 1930 is primarily a buoyancy of investment spending, which remains high in 1930 because q was high in 1929. The investment boom continued into 1930 because of lags in the ability of firms to order, receive, and install capital goods and equipment that they would have wished to obtain in 1929 when stock prices peaked. The French economy was exceptionally resistant to the onset of the Depression because demand had been switched toward this domestic source—investment—and away from foreign sources precisely when foreign markets collapsed.

How general was this surge in investment spending? Table 14.6 displays investment trends in agriculture, three leading manufacturing industries,

Table 14.6
Real investment-growth rates (annual averages)

	1922–1926	1922–1927	1928	1929	1930	1931	1928–1931	1932–1938
Total economy	7.8	3.9	23.4	18.7	9.3	−15.0	9.1	−3.6
Agriculture	4.0	3.2	9.2	23.5	−0.8	−8.9	5.8	−1.2
Metallurgy	24.9	18.9	24.6	21.9	4.2	−30.3	5.1	−3.5
Chemical industry	18.4	11.1	37.9	29.8	4.6	−19.7	13.1	−0.9
Textile industry	5.9	3.5	12.0	7.8	−2.1	−28.5	−2.7	−5.1
Buildings	58.2	42.4	43.1	28.2	4.9	−17.1	14.8	−8.9
Transport	−9.2	−9.4	23.5	12.9	44.6	11.5	23.1	−3.9
Services	6.9	1.5	25.2	15.0	7.8	−8.9	9.8	−4.3
Commerce	14.2	8.7	21.5	14.0	−0.5	−13.0	5.5	−8.2

Source: INSEE.

construction, transportation, services, and commerce. Investment rose in all sectors but transportation in 1927 and across the board in 1928 and 1929. In 1930 investment fell significantly only in the textile industry (which produced luxury goods for export and therefore was overwhelmed by the onset of Depression abroad), declining marginally in agriculture and commerce as well. In 1931, in contrast, there was a dramatic fall in investment in every sector except transportation, which was dominated by the relative stability of government spending. Thus, the investment surge highlighted in our account of post-1926 French macroeconomic trends is impossible to explain in terms of shocks to particular sectors, and surely resulted from economy-wide developments such as changes in the stance of fiscal policy.

In our model, investment is linked to fiscal policy via Tobin's q. Table 14.7 documents the linkage. In the first two equations, q (and, according to table 14.5, investment) responds positively to the budget surplus. Evidence of serial correlation led us to add additional regressors. Neither the money supply nor its rate of growth (in real or nominal terms) significantly influenced real share prices or reduced the autocorrelation. In contrast, the real exchange rate was statistically significant, reduced the autocorrelation, and dominated the fiscal policy measure, as shown in the third line of table 14.7. The close correlation between Tobin's q and the real exchange rate is evident in figure 14.8. Yet this correlation is evidence against the fiscal policy-q relationship only if the real exchange rate is not itself a function

Table 14.7
q and the government budget (annual data, 1922–1937; dependent variable, q)[a]

Constant	Budget surplus	λ	Capital inflows	RHO	SEE
0.57	0.10			0.63	0.117
(6.88)	(2.33)			(3.25)	
−0.54	0.02	1.25		0.40	0.104
(−1.20)	(0.54)	(2.51)		(1.63)	
0.57	0.10		0.15	0.62	0.121
(6.72)	(2.25)		(0.17)	(3.08)	

Source: see Eichengreen and Wyplosz (1986), Appendix A.
a. t-statistics in parentheses. The budget surplus variable is defined as the ratio of the surplus to GNP.

of fiscal variables. Our model predicts that Tobin's q and the real exchange rate should be jointly determined by fiscal policy. Table 14.8 confirms that this was the case, that fiscal contraction led to real exchange rate depreciation. We enter as additional regressors the rate of real money growth and the rate of real money growth interacted with a dummy variable for the fixed exchange rate period to allow the real exchange rate to respond to both monetary and fiscal policies. Adding monetary policy confirms that both monetary and fiscal policies influenced the path of the real exchange rate, but does nothing to undermine the real exchange rate's dependence on the budget surplus.

Finally, we attempt to test our explanation for the post-1926 investment surge against a competing interpretation. While our explanation for the investment boom stresses observed reductions in the budget deficit and the classic crowding-in effects of contractionary fiscal policy, the alternative emphasizes the impact on confidence of Poincaré's reputation for financial orthodoxy. According to the reputational argument, Poincaré's return to power removed the specter of continued financial uncertainty, future budget deficits, and capital levies. Once confidence was restored, capital flight came to end, reducing the required rate of return on capital and stimulating investment. Thus, confidence—in particular, confidence-induced capital inflows—rather than the resource flow or classic crowding-in effects of contractionary fiscal policy explains the investment boom. Since Tobin's q captures market expectations, the confidence interpretation is not incompatible with ours; it differs by asserting that the rise in stock prices cannot be explained solely by contemporary observable policy measures.

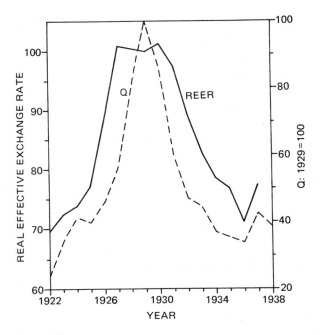

Figure 14.8
Q and the real effective exchange rate.

Table 14.8
The real exchange rate (annual data, 1922–1937)[a]

Constant	Budget surplus	Real money growth	Real money growth times FIX	Capital inflows	RHO	SEE	DW
0.88	0.058	—	—	—	0.64	0.054	—
(22.65)	(2.96)				(3.37)		
0.87	0.045	0.17)	—	—	0.64	0.052	—
(22.18)	(2.14)	(1.37)			(3.03)		
0.83	0.066	−0.28	0.90	—	—	0.039	1.66
(47.62)	(5.21)	(−1.67)	(4.18)				
0.84	0.066	−0.30	0.88	0.11	—	0.040	1.63
(40.28)	(5.03)	(−1.65)	(3.88)	(0.39)			

a. See table 14.3. FIX is a dummy variable that takes a value of unity during the fixed exchange rate period (1927–1935), and zero elsewhere. Money supply is from Saint-Etienne (1983).

Attempts to test the confidence argument lend it little support. Capital inflows, under the alternative view, should be comprised of both a component reflecting observed policy measures and a residual component reflecting confidence. Since the equations estimated in tables 14.7 and 14.8 include both observed policy measures and capital inflows, the confidence argument can be tested by examining the coefficient on the capital inflows variable.[24] In both tables, the capital inflows proxy uniformly enters insignificantly. Thus, we find no support for the alternative view.

14.6. Conclusion

In this chapter we have critiqued the standard view that the undervalued franc Poincaré, by boosting exports, succeeded initially in insulating France from the Great Depression. Our own explanation emphasizes instead the role of investment growth as the proximate source of France's resistance to the onset of the slump. The traditional interpretation has also tended to stress monetary factors, attributing undervaluation of the franc even after 1929 to a sustained period of inflation terminated by an abrupt monetary stabilization in 1926. We consider such a long-lasting monetary non-neutrality unplausible and focus instead on fiscal stabilization, which transformed the government budget from large deficit in the early 1920s to surplus after 1926. Real depreciation, the surge in stock prices, and the attendant crowding-in of investment spending are all shown to follow from fiscal stabilization. We do not intend to belittle the role either of monetary factors in the nominal depreciation or of monetary finance of budget deficits. But we wish to emphasize that the independent effects of fiscal policy have not been adequately acknowledged.

These effects are analyzed here using a model relevant to current policy discussions in countries attempting to curb their government deficits and reduce their public debts in the course of stabilization. While we have not estimated the model, its key assumptions are supported by the data. In particular, the links between fiscal policy, the real exchange rate, and Tobin's q are sufficiently well established that we see no need to invoke the purely psychological effects of Poincaré return to power when attempting to understand the macroeconomic sequel to that event. What mattered were Poincaré's policies, not just his reputation.

Appendix: Nominal and Real Effective Exchange Rates (1929:1 = 100)

Table 14.9

	Nominal	Real		Nominal	Real
1921:4	41.1	75.3	1930:1	98.6	103.4
1922:1	38.3	71.2	1930:2	98.3	107.5
1922:2	37.3	66.4	1930:3	97.5	100.3
1922:3	41.1	71.4	1930:4	97.1	102.1
1922:4	45.1	75.2	1931:1	96.5	100.5
1923:1	49.8	73.7	1931:2	96.5	99.9
1923:2	48.0	71.8	1931:3	94.8	101.6
1923:3	51.4	75.6	1931:4	88.6	96.4
1923:4	53.0	75.1	1932:1	88.3	91.2
1924:1	62.2	78.3	1932:2	89.4	90.4
1924:2	52.6	72.1	1932:3	88.6	92.1
1924:3	57.6	75.2	1932:4	87.6	91.4
1924:4	59.0	75.8	1933:1	87.8	89.7
1925:1	60.6	76.9	1933:2	85.9	86.5
1925:2	63.6	77.0	1933:3	82.9	81.7
1925:3	67.3	77.6	1933:4	81.2	80.7
1925:4	79.1	83.6	1934:1	79.0	78.3
1926:1	88.5	84.2	1934:2	77.7	78.6
1926:2	96.0	87.0	1934:3	77.1	80.7
1926:3	108.2	88.7	1934:4	77.1	83.3
1926:4	107.3	102.1	1935:1	76.1	82.3
1927:1	98.8	100.1	1935:2	72.1	75.9
1927:2	100.3	101.0	1935:3	72.1	78.3
1927:3	100.4	104.2	1935:4	72.1	77.3
1927:4	100.3	107.1	1936:1	72.1	72.9
1928:1	100.1	103.8	1936:2	72.4	72.9
1928:2	100.2	102.5	1936:3	72.6	70.4
1928:3	100.3	102.5	1936:4	94.4	74.5
1928:4	100.2	102.1	1937:1	94.3	71.5
1929:1	100.0	100.0	1937:2	97.8	74.8
1929:2	99.6	100.4	1937:3	118.3	81.6
1929:3	99.5	103.6	1937:4	131.2	88.2
1929:4	99.2	104.6			

Notes

1. Data sources and variable definitions are provided in appendix A of Eichengreen and Wyplosz (1986). The country data and weights used to construct "world GDP" in table 14.1 are the same as in the effective exchange rate calculations described below.

2. Domestic credit creation was effectively precluded by prohibiting the Bank of France from engaging in expansionary open market operations or monetizing government budget deficits. See Eichengreen (1986a).

3. These conclusions are representative of an extensive and growing literature. Surveys of the period, such as Fohlen (1966) and Ambrosi et al. (1984), convey the same impression of the exchange rate's central role. Kindleberger (1973, p. 63) argues that what he refers to as the "French boom" of the second half of the 1920s—an upswing that raised production to impressive levels compared to previous business cycle peaks and did not turn down until the second half of 1931—was fed by undervaluation of the franc. Even Sargent (1983), not one normally inclined toward nominal variables as explanations for real economic trends, suggests that France remained prosperous in the wake of the Poincaré stabilization partially because of the undervaluation of the franc.

4. This is not the first nominal effective rate calculated for the interwar years. Redmond (1980) has constructed a nominal effective exchange rate for sterling in the 1930s, while Redmond (1981) presents nominal effective rates for several currencies, including the franc, for the period from 1929. However, his series for the franc is annual rather than quarterly and does not cover the portion of the twenties of particular interest here. We know of no previous attempt to calculate a real effective exchange rate for this period.

5. Detailed descriptions of the data are provided in the data appendix to Eichengreen and Wyplosz (1986). In the appendix we present the effective exchange rate series.

6. With both series measured on an annual average basis, an ordinary least squares regression corrected for first-order serial correlation yields:

$$\text{EXPORTS} = -2.17 + 0.74\,\text{REER} + 0.62Y^*, \qquad \rho = 0.48, \qquad \bar{R}^2 = 0.83, \qquad \text{DW} = 1.60,$$
$$\phantom{\text{EXPORTS} = -2.17 + }(3.89)\ (3.12)\phantom{\text{REER} + }(3.68)(1.63)$$

where EXPORTS is Commerce Spécial (in millions of tons) from Sauvy (1984, p. 338, col. 8), REER is the real effective exchange rate (calculated as in figure 14.1, so that a rise denotes real depreciation), and Y^* is the index of world industrial production (from London and Cambridge Economic Service, 1970), shown in table 14.1. The data are annual and the estimation period is 1922–1938. In the regression, all variables are entered in logs, with t-statistics in parentheses. ρ is the first-order autocorrelation coefficient.

7. The pattern we describe in the text holds for exports of foodstuffs, raw materials and manufactured goods alike, except that raw materials exports fall in 1928, foodstuffs in 1929, and manufactures in 1930. The early downturn in exports of materials reflects the worldwide slump in primary commodity markets (Lewis, 1949), which even an "undervalued franc" was apparently unable to overcome.

8. Another channel through which the exchange rate conceivably might have influenced demand was import substitution. Even if the volume of exports fell after 1928 and the export/GNP ratio fell after 1927, depreciation could have stimulated domestic demand had expenditure on imports been switched toward home goods at an even faster rate. In fact, the trade balance deteriorates rather than improving over the period, indicating that imports declined less quickly than exports, casting doubt on the import-substitution hypothesis.

9. For example, such nontraded goods as housing, the prices of which moved in a very different fashion due to rent control (Hawtrey, 1931), are included only in the retail price index. On the construction of these indices, see INSEE (1966).

10. The one exception to the general erosion of real wages during the inflationary era—the rise in real wages between the first and second quarters of 1924—is itself explicable in terms of wage lag: the exceptional real wage increase of early 1924 took place in a period when the authorities succeeded in temporarily stabilizing the franc and actually engineering a price decline.

11. On the early 1920s in Europe, North America, Japan, and the Antipodes, see Eichengreen (1987). On European experience in the 1930s, see Eichengreen and Sachs (1985).

12. One possibility is that it had major sectoral effects. It is true that all sectors of the economy did not share equally in France's initial immunity to the Great Depression. Textiles and autos did relatively poorly while engineering machinery did relatively well. The general pattern seems to favor investment-goods over consumer-goods industries. (We used here industrial production indices from various issues of League of Nations.) Existing accounts provide no guidance, however, as to why exchange-rate changes should have had such differential effects.

13. The importance of this distinction did not escape contemporary French economists such as Dessirier (1935), who calculated indices of profitability separately for industries producing traded and nontraded goods. (In addition, Dessirier distinguished a third sector comprised of firms engaged in the provision of public services.)

14. It is this focus on wage formation that leads us to emphasize our model's resemblance to the Scandinavian Model rather than the Dependent Economy Model of Salter (1959), which also distinguishes traded and nontraded goods.

15. The only other model incorporating both these features is, to the best of our knowledge, in Obstfeld (1986). Related models are those of Dornbusch (1974; 1980, pp. 97–115), and Frenkel and Rodriguez (1982). Dornbusch's Dependent Economy Model implicitly maintains the assumption of full employment, however, while in Frenkel and Rodriguez (1982) output depends only on relative commodity prices.

16. Equation (6) is a linear approximation around an initial position in which W, e, and P_N all equal unity and γ is the share of traded goods in consumption.

17. In the absence of explicit treatment of the monetary sector, depreciation of the exchange rate must be taken as exogenous.

18. The lack of foresight regarding the evolution of the exchange rate, inflation, and the money supply can be justified on the grounds that changes in the rate of money growth were related to unanticipated changes in governments and Ministers of Finance. There were 11 cabinets in the period 1921–1926 (Sauvy, 1984, vol. I, pp. 388–392).

19. In the interest of simplicity, we suppress the Laursen-Metzler effect. However, permitting saving to be positively related to λ would have no effect on our simulation results.

20. Alternative deficit closing rules are discussed in Sachs and Wyplosz (1984). Nothing of importance hinges on the particular specification adopted here since it is assumed that government spending falls on exportables, nontradables, and imported goods in the same proportions as private spending.

21. By specifying investment solely as a function of q and eliminating any accelerator mechanism, we reduce the danger that an investment response to an autonomous recovery could be misconstrued as a cause of that recovery.

22. Note that the dependence of investment on real equity prices need not suggest that the stock market was a significant source of liquidity for firms wishing to fund investment. (In fact, this was generally not the case in interwar France.) Rather, it reflects the impact on investment of assessments of the current and future profitability of additions to the capital stock relative to the cost of those additions, assuming only that the expectations of stock market participants are positively correlated if not necessarily representative of the expectations of investors as a whole.

23. Our preferred specification, equation (2), provides support for a hybrid investment equation that combines the q theory with the accelerator. Such equations are sometimes justified on the grounds that some firms are liquidity constrained and able to increase investment only when profits rise as a result of increased output.

24. Alternatively, we included a dummy variable for the years of Poincaré's government to proxy for confidence effects. This variable failed to undermine the significance of the fiscal policy measure, was itself statistically insignificant, and generally entered with a negative sign.

References

Abel, A. B. (1980), "Empirical Investment Equations: An Integrative Framework," *Carnegie Rochester Conference Series* 12, pp. 39–91.

Ambrosi, C., M. Baleste, and M. Tagel (1984), *Economie Contemporaine*, Paris: Delgrave.

Aukrust, D. (1977), "Inflation in the Open Economy: A Norwegian Model," in L. B. Krause and W. S. Salant (eds.), *Worldwide Inflation*, Washington, D.C.: Brookings Institution.

Bernard, P. (1975), *La Fin d'un Monde, 1914–1929*, Paris: Sevil.

Branson, W., and W. Buiter (1983), "Monetary and Fiscal Policy with Flexible Exchange Rates," in J. Bhandari and B. Putnam (eds.), *The International Transmission of Economic Disturbances*, Cambridge, MA: MIT Press.

Carré, J. J., P. Dubois, and E. Malinvaud (1975), *French Economic Growth*, Stanford: Stanford University Press.

Cuddington, J. T., and J. M. Viñals (1986), "Budget Deficits and the Current Account: An Intertemporal Disequilibrium Approach," *Journal of International Economics* 21, pp. 1–24.

Dessirier, J. (1935), "'Secteurs abrités' et 'non abrités' dans le Déséquilibre Actuel de l'Economie Française," *Revue d'Economie Politique* (July–August), pp. 1330–1361.

Dornbusch, R. (1974), "Real and Monetary Aspects of the Effects of Exchange Rate Changes," in R. Z. Aliber (ed.), *National Monetary Policies and the International Financial System*, Chicago: University of Chicago Press.

Dornbusch, R. (1976), "Expectations and Exchange Rate Dynamics," *Journal of Political Economy* 84, pp. 1161–1176.

Dornbusch, R. (1980), *Open Economy Macroeconomics*, New York: Basic Books.

Edgen, G., K. O. Faxen, and C. E. Odhner (1969), "Wages, Growth and the Distribution of Income," *Swedish Journal of Economics* 71, pp. 133–160.

Eichengreen, B. (1986a), "The Bank of France and the Sterilization of Gold, 1926–31," *Explorations in Economic History* 23, pp. 56–84.

Eichengreen, B. (1986b), "The Australian Economic Recovery in International Comparative Perspective," in N. G. Butlin and R. G. Gregory (eds.), *Economic Recovery in Australia in the 1930s*, Cambridge: Cambridge University Press, forthcoming.

Eichengreen, B. (1987), "Understanding 1921–1927 (Inflation and Economic Growth in the 1920s)," *Rivista di Storia Economica* 3, pp. 34–66.

Eichengreen, B., and J. Sachs (1985), "Exchange Rates and Economic Recovery in the 1930s," *Journal of Economic History* XLV, pp. 925–946.

Eichengreen, B., and C. Wyplosz (1986), "The Economic Consequences of the Franc Poincaré," NBER Working Paper 2064, November.

Fischer, Stanley (1983), "A Note on Investment and Lagged Q," unpublished manuscript, MIT.

Fleming, J. M. (1962), "Domestic Financial Policies under Fixed and under Flexible Exchange Rates," *IMF Staff Papers* 9, pp. 369–380.

Fohlen, C., (1966), *La France de l'Entre-Deux-Guerres, 1917–1939*, Paris: Casterman.

Frenkel, J., and C. A. Rodriguez (1982), "Exchange Rate Dynamics and the Overshooting Hypothesis," *IMF Staff Papers* 29 (March), pp. 1–30.

Galenson, W., and A. Zellner (1957), "International Comparisons of Unemployment Rates," in National Bureau of Economic Research, *The Measurement and Behavior of Unemployment*, Princeton: Princeton University Press, pp. 439–580.

Hawtrey, Ralph (1931), "French Monetary Policy," in Ralph Hawtrey, *The Art of Central Banking*, London: Macmillan.

Hayashi, F. (1982), "Tobin's Marginal q and Average q: A Neoclassical Interpretation," *Econometrica*, 50, pp. 213–224.

INSEE (1966), *Annuaire Statistique de la France: résumé retrospectif*, Paris: INSEE.

Jackson, Julian (1985), *The Politics of Depression in France, 1932–1936*, Cambridge: Cambridge University Press.

Kemp, T. (1971), "The French Economy under the Franc Poincaré," *Economic History Review* (2nd ser.) XXIV, pp. 82–99.

Kemp, T. (1972), *The French Economy, 1913–39*, London: Longmans.

Kindleberger, C. (1973), *The World in Depression, 1929–39*, Berkeley: University of California Press.

Kydland, F. E., and E. C. Prescott (1982), "Time to Build and Aggregate Fluctuations," *Econometrica* 50, pp. 1345–1370.

League of Nations (various issues), *International Statistical Yearbook*, Geneva: League of Nations.

Lewis, W. A. (1949), *Economic Survey 1919–1939*, London: Allen and Unwin.

London and Cambridge Economic Service (1970), *The British Economy: Key Statistics, 1900–1970*, London: Times Newspapers Ltd.

Mitchell, B. R. (1975), *European Historical Statistics 1750–1970*, London: Macmillan.

Mundell, R. A. (1963), "Capital Mobility and Stabilization Policy under Fixed and Flexible Exchange Rates," *Canadian Journal of Economics* 29, pp. 475–485.

Neary, P., and J. Stiglitz (1983), "Toward a Reconstruction of Keynesian Economics: Expectations and Constrained Equilibria," *Quarterly Journal of Economics* 98, pp. 199–228.

Obstfeld, M. (1986), "Capital Flows, the Current Account, and the Real Exchange Rate: Some Consequence of Stabilization and Liberalization," in S. Edwards and L. Ahmed (eds.), *Economic Adjustment and Exchange Rates in Developing Countries*, Chicago: University of Chicago Press, pp. 201–229.

Redmond, J. (1980), "An Indicator of the Effective Exchange Rate of the Pound in the 1930s," *Economic History Review* XXXIII, pp. 83–91.

Redmond, J. (1981), "More Effective Exchange Rates in the 1930s: North America and the Gold Bloc," University of Birmingham, Faculty of Commerce and Social Science Discussion Paper D8.

Sachs, J. (1980), "Wages, Flexible Exchange Rates and Macroeconomic Policy," *Quarterly Journal of Economics* 94, pp. 737–747.

Sachs, J., and C. Wyplosz (1984), "Real Exchange Rate Effects of Fiscal Policy," Harvard Institute of Economic Research Discussion Paper 1050 (April).

Saint-Etienne, C. (1983), "L'Offre et la demande de monnaie dans la France de l'Entre-Deux-Guerres (1920–1939)," *Revue Economique* 34, pp. 344–367.

Salter, W. (1959), "Internal and External Balance: The Role of Price and Expenditure Effects," *Economic Record* 35, pp. 226–228.

Sargent, T. (1983), "Stopping Moderate Inflations: The Methods of Poincaré and Thatcher," in R. Dornbusch and M. H. Simonsen (eds.), *Inflation, Debt, and Indexation*, Cambridge, MA: MIT Press, pp. 54–98.

Sauvy, A. (1984), *Histoire Economique de la France entre les deux guerres*, Paris: PUF.

Tobin, J. (1969), "A General Equilibrium Approach to Monetary Theory," *Journal of Money, Credit and Banking* 1, pp. 15–29.

Veda, K., and H. Yoshikawa (1986), "Financial Volatility and the q Theory of Investment," *Economica* 53, p. 11–28.

15 Inflation, Balance of Payments Crises, and Public Sector Deficits

Sweder van Wijnbergen

The analysis focuses on the government budget constraint and the resolution of inconsistent implications of different policy instruments under that constraint. We show that, to achieve a sustainable reduction in inflation, an exchange rate freeze or crawling peg requires restrictions not only on domestic credit growth but also on the rate of increase in interest-bearing public debt. We endogenize regime collapse by introducing rational speculation against the Central Bank, and show that if an exchange rate freeze collapses, postcollapse inflation will exceed the rate prevailing before the freeze started.

15.1. Introduction

This chapter deals with inflation, fiscal deficits, and exchange rate policy in high-inflation countries. In particular we focus on the unhappy experience of countries attempting to stabilize inflation through an exchange rate freeze or, similarly, a preannounced slowdown in the rate of change.

Not only did the experiments along those lines in Latin America in the late seventies and in Israel in 1982–1983 end in failure, but all countries involved saw inflation accelerate after the collapse of the experiment to levels well above those observed before the stabilization program started. A case in point is the Israeli experience in 1982–1984. Inflation before the initiation of the exchange rate freeze was 7% per month (125% annually, continuously compounded). Then, in September 1982, a preannounced crawling peg policy was instituted, under which the nominal exchange rate was devalued at a rate of 5% per month independent of domestic price developments. The stabilization program collapsed in October 1983, after which the inflation rate rapidly increased to reach 12–15% per month (15% per month implies a 435% annual rate!).

A related puzzle concerns the relation between upward jumps in inflation and balance of payment (BoP) crises. Liviatan and Piterman (1984) have drawn attention to the fact that in Israel each jump in the inflation rate was preceded by a BoP crisis, often forcing a change in exchange rate policy. This relation is a puzzle, since a BoP crisis can explain a price level

This chapter was written during a visit to Tel-Aviv University in November 1985. Helpful discussions with Willem Buiter, Homi Kharas, Elhanan Helpman, Torsten Persson, and Assaf Razin and comments from seminar participants at the Bank of Israel, Princeton University, MIT, and the NBER Summer Institute for International Economic Studies, 1986, are gratefully acknowledged.

shift where it resulted in a large devaluation, but not a sustained increase in inflation rates.

In this chapter we suggest an explanation for these phenomena drawing on the "public finance approach" to inflation introduced by Phelps (1973). Our approach draws on several strands in the recent literature that have until now remained separate. First of all, several closed-economy applications of the Phelps approach to inflation have analyzed the effects of unsustainable monetary policies under the assumption of an exogenous future regime switch, restoring consistency between fiscal and monetary policy (Sargent and Wallace, 1982; Liviatan, 1984; Bental and Eckstein, 1985). Drazen and Helpman (1985a,b) extend this literature by introducing uncertainty with respect to both the timing and nature of the regime switch; both remain exogenous, however. We introduce open economy considerations to study exchange rate policy and, in a departure from this literature, we endogenize the regime switch by linking it to rational speculative behavior.

The introduction of rational speculators forcing a regime switch in our chapter draws on the literature on speculative attacks on Central Bank foreign reserves: Krugman (1979), Flood and Garber (1984), and Bianco and Garber (1986). They, in turn, build on an earlier analysis of the sustainability of commodity price stabilization schemes (Salant and Henderson, 1978; Salant, 1983; see also Flood and Garber, 1980). However, that literature typically ignores the intertemporal budget constraint faced by the public sector, a constraint that plays a crucial role in our analysis.

Finally, since we analyze a switch to a fixed exchange rate (or preannounced crawling peg) regime, one should mention the "crawling peg" literature instigated by Diaz Alejandro's description of the Southern Cone experience (Diaz Alejandro, 1979; Calvo, 1980; Dornbusch, 1980; Obstfeld, 1985; van Wijnbergen, 1979, 1986; and many others). That literature, in a step back from Krugman (1979), invariably assumes an exogenous switching point if consistency between different policy instruments is analyzed at all.

We present a simple open economy model to analyze the transition to a fixed exchange rate regime, discuss sustainability, and demonstrate what happens when policy measures are inconsistent and the fixed regime unsustainable. We analyze conditions under which a collapse will occur and show that, if a collapse occurs, postcollapse inflation will exceed the inflation rate that obtained just before the start of the stabilization experiment.

We also show that restricting domestic credit growth to a rate that will prevent reserve outflows during a freeze is not sufficient to prevent a speculative attack, contrary to suggestions in Krugman (1979) and Flood and Garber (1984). In fact we demonstrate that the postcollapse inflation will be even higher when the public sector follows such a credit policy, covering the remainder of the deficit by public debt issue—higher, that is, than the postcollapse inflation rate that obtains after a policy of covering the deficit through credit creation alone.

15.2. Model Structure

There is only one good whose world price is normalized to one. The domestic price therefore equals e (=the nominal exchange rate, units of local per unit of foreign currency). Home output is exogenous and constant over time; asset choice for domestic residents is restricted to domestic money $m = M/e$ and foreign bonds b, yielding an instantaneous rate of return r; and accumulation of physical capital is ignored.

Consumers derive instantaneous welfare $\tilde{u}$ from consumption of goods c, and from real money holdings m:

$$\tilde{u} = \log u(c,m),$$

where u is homogeneous of degree one. The form of $\tilde{u}$ implies an *intertemporal* substitution elasticity equal to one. We furthermore assume that $u_{cm} = 0$. Note that this implies

$$\tilde{u}_{cm} = \frac{-u_c u_m}{u(c,m)^2} < 0.$$

It is possible to construct transaction technologies that are equivalent to this money in the utility function approach (Chamley, 1985; Feenstra, 1985).

We follow Blanchard (1985) in assuming a simple overlapping generations structure where each individual alive today faces a time and age independent instantaneous probability of death p.[1] This implies an unconditional rate of time preference $\rho + p$, where ρ is the rate of time preference conditional on staying alive (Blanchard, 1985). We furthermore follow Blanchard (1985) in assuming that consumers annuitize their nonhuman wealth at actuarily fair rates.

Consumers maximize the integral of current and discounted future welfare subject to the savings identity, the condition that holdings of money and foreign bonds cannot exceed wealth (of course equality always obtains) and the intertemporal budget constraint. The latter plus the savings identity is equivalent to that savings condition and a limiting condition on wealth w:

$$\lim_{t \to \infty} e^{-(r+p)t} w(t) = 0.$$

The maximization problem then becomes

$$\max_{c,m,b} \int_0^\infty e^{-(\rho+p)t} \log u(c,m) \tag{1}$$

subject to

a. $\dot{w} = rb + pw + y - \tau - \pi m - c = (r + p)w + y - \tau - c - im.$

b. $w = m + b.$

c. $\lim_{t \to \infty} e^{-(r+p)t} w(t) = 0.$

Here i is the nominal interest rate and π the inflation rate (note that $\pi = \hat{e}$, the rate of change in the exchange rate e). Thus, $i = r + \pi$.

The first-order conditions to (1) yield, after routine manipulation, the following expressions describing consumer behavior:

$$\frac{u_m(m)}{u_c(c)} = i, \tag{2}$$

$$c + im = (\rho + p)\left(w + \frac{(y - \tau)}{r + p}\right), \tag{3}$$

$$\dot{w} = (r + p)w + y - \tau - c - im, \tag{4}$$

where τ represents tax payments, assumed constant over time. Aggregation over all individuals alive yields

$$\dot{V} = (r - \rho)\frac{(y - \tau)}{r + p} + (r - \rho - p)V \tag{5}$$

where convergence of the integral defining $\dot{V}$ requires $r < \rho + p$ (Blanchard, 1985). Equations (2), (3), and (5) completely describe private behavior. There remains the introduction of the government budget constraint and the description of government policies.

The public sector consists of a government proper and a Central Bank. The Central Bank implements the exchange rate policy decreed by the government; under a floating regime it does not intervene in foreign exchange markets, and it buys and sells foreign exchange as needed under any other regime. Furthermore, it incurs no administrative costs and transfers its profits to the government. Its profits equal rR with R the level of foreign reserves measured in foreign currency terms. The Central Bank earns the same rate on its foreign assets as the private sector. (Obstfeld, 1981, stresses the importance of properly keeping track of Central Bank interest earnings.)

The government budget constraint equals

$$g + r(d - R) - \tau = \dot{d} + \dot{m} + \pi m. \tag{6}$$

g is real government expenditure and τ real tax revenue, both of which are constant in all policy experiments discussed in this chapter.[2] Under floating rates, R is constant; d is the foreign debt of the government. We assume, for simplicity only, that the government issues no domestic interest bearing liabilities. As in Drazen and Helpman (1985a,b), there is a maximum level of government debt that can be supported in steady state since g cannot fall below zero and there are limits to the revenues that can be raised through τ and the inflation tax in steady state. Call this level d^*. We shall assume, following Drazen and Helpman (1985a,b) and Kharas (1984), that no rational lender will lend beyond d^*. The intertemporal budget constraint for the government will thus always be satisfied [that constraint implies $\lim_{t \to \infty} e^{-rt} d(t) = 0$].

We can analyze the working of the model once we have specified the funding policy of the government. Throughout this chapter we shall assume that g and τ remain constant. Government policy within the context of the floating rate regime therefore implies a choice of $\dot{d}$. Consider first the case of $\dot{d} = 0$, i.e., full monetary financing of the "basic" deficit $g - \tau + r(d - R)$.

In that case the model under floating exchange rates boils down to

$$u_m(m)/u_c(c) = r + \pi, \tag{7a}$$

$$c + im = (\rho + p)(V + (y - \tau)/(r + p)), \tag{7b}$$

and the two dynamic equations

$$\dot{V} = (r - \rho)\frac{(y - \tau)}{r + p} + (r - \rho - p)V, \tag{8}$$

$$\dot{m} = g - \tau + r(d - R) - \pi m. \tag{9}$$

Equations (7a) and (7b) can be used to derive expressions for c and π conditional on m, V, and r:[3]

$$c = c(m, V; r) \qquad \text{and} \qquad \pi = \pi(m, V; r).$$
$$\pm \; + \; - \qquad\qquad\qquad\qquad - \; + \; -$$

"+" or "−" indicates the sign of the corresponding partial derivatives. Analytical expressions are in the appendix.

Insertion of (7a) and (7b) into (8) and (9) yields two dynamic equations:

$$\dot{V} = \dot{V}(m, V; r), \tag{10}$$
$$0 \; - \; +$$

$$\dot{m} = \dot{m}(m, V; r). \tag{11}$$
$$\pm \; - \; +$$

Once again, analytical expressions are in the appendix; but note from those expressions that

$$\dot{m}_m \propto (1 - \varepsilon_\pi^m)$$

with ε_π^m the general equilibrium elasticity of real money demand with respect to π. Here we only discuss the equilibrium where $\varepsilon_\pi^m < 1$ and $\dot{m}_m > 0$, i.e., where the economy operates on the upward part of the inflation tax Laffer curve.

Consider equations (10) and (11) around the equilibrium where $\varepsilon_\pi^m < 1$. Equation (10) represents a vertical curve in (m, V) space (locus VV in figure 15.1); steady state nonhuman wealth $\bar{V}$ depends exclusively on human wealth $y - \tau$, the real interest rate r, the rate of time preference ρ, and the decay parameter p. $\bar{V}$ may be negative; $\bar{V} < 0$ corresponds to external debt in excess of the real value of the monetary base. Since $\dot{V}_V < 0$ unambiguously, V is falling to the right of the VV locus and rising to the left of it (see figure 15.1).

The slope of the MM curve (along which $\dot{m} = 0$) is unambiguously positive as long as $\varepsilon_\pi^m < 1$:

$$\left. \frac{\partial m}{\partial V} \right|_{MM} = \frac{-\dot{m}_V}{\dot{m}_m} \tag{12}$$

$$= \frac{-\pi_V}{\pi_m}(1 - \varepsilon_\pi^m)^{-1}. \tag{13}$$

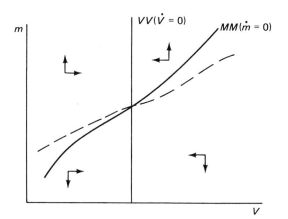

Figure 15.1
Dynamics of the model under floating exchange rates.

Also, as long as $\varepsilon_\pi^m < 1$, $\dot{m}_m > 0$ and MM therefore slopes up. In that case real money balances will be rising above and falling below MM (see figure 15.1). The system is thus saddlepoint stable around the equilibrium E (see appendix A of van Wijnbergen, 1986b, for a formal analysis.)

Standard techniques show that the slope of the saddle path is positive and less than the slope of MM around E. The slope will be less than one for $\varepsilon_i^m < 1$, a slightly stronger condition than $\varepsilon_\pi^m < 1$.

If we could ignore sustainability issues (and of course we cannot; that is the subject of section 15.3), the model equations would need only minor adjustment to describe developments under a fixed exchange rate regime. This is because we use a competitive framework where consumers are price takers; whether prices are supported by one or another type of exchange rate regime is of no importance. Sustainability introduces Krugman (1979)-type speculative attack issues and the regime switch such attacks force. In this section we shall show how to check whether such attacks will take place or not, but not yet introduce the attack itself in the analysis; that will be done in section 15.3, where we discuss the use of an exchange rate freeze as an antiinflation device.

Since consumers are price takers, (7a), (7b), and (8) will continue to describe private behavior. Note that now (7a), for any given value of consumption c, determines the equilibrium moneystock m. This is because

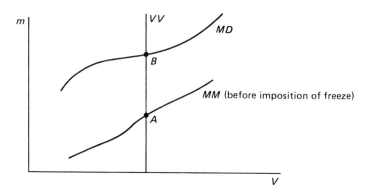

Figure 15.2
The fixed exchange rate regime.

under a fixed exchange rate regime, π is exogenous (under a preannounced crawling peg regime it might be nonzero, but the point is that it is predetermined). Hence we can use (7b) to substitute out c from (7a) and obtain an equilibrium relation between m and V that has to hold for the value of π implied by the choice of exchange regime:

$$\frac{u_m(m)}{u_c((\rho + p)(V + (y - \tau)/(r + p)) - im)} = r + \pi. \tag{14}$$

Equation (14) defines the MD locus in figure 15.2; as long as the fixed exchange regime lasts, the economy has to be on that locus. The slope of that locus equals the marginal propensity to hold money out of wealth:

$$\frac{\partial m}{\partial V}\bigg|_{MD} = \frac{(\rho + p)u_{cc}/u_c}{(r + \pi)(u_{cc}/u_c) + (u_{mm}/u_m)} > 0, \tag{15}$$

where we repeatedly used $u_m/u_c = r + \pi$.

Of course, the location of the curve shifts if the preannounced rate of crawl is changed, changing π one for one:

$$\frac{\partial m}{\partial \pi}\bigg|_{V=\bar{V}}^{MD} = \frac{-[(r + \pi)Am + 1]}{[(r + \pi)(A(r + \pi) - u_{mm}/u_m)]} < 0, \tag{16}$$

with $A = -u_{cc}/u_c > 0$. Note that (16) is simply the inverse of the expression for π_m derived in section A.1 of the appendix.

As to the intersection of MD and VV, let us anticipate the experiment performed in section 15.3, a transition from a high inflation floating regime to a low inflation (say zero) fixed rate regime. In that case (14) will not be satisfied at the old equilibrium values for m and V (see point A in figure 15.2). At A, $u_m(m_A)/u_c(c(m_A, V_A)) = r + \pi_A$, but during the freeze $\pi = 0 < \pi_A$. Accordingly, for given V, m will increase as π decreases (section A.1). Hence after a freeze reducing π to zero instantaneously, MD shifts up from A to, say, B in figure 15.2.

The government budget constraint will tell us whether the exchange rate freeze is feasible or not. It needs a minor amendment, since under fixed exchange rates the issue of new noninterest bearing government liabilities does not necessarily equal the increase in the nominal moneystock anymore. Central Bank foreign assets may change and so drive a wedge between changes in nominal money and changes in credit to the government.

Call the stock of noninterest bearing domestic government liabilities C. The government budget constraint then becomes

$$g - \tau + r(d - R) = \dot{d} + \frac{\dot{C}}{e}. \tag{17}$$

Note that R now may vary over time.

Equations (7a), (7b), and (8) fully specify the dynamic path of m under this exchange rate regime. The desired (and actual, given our assumptions of perfect capital mobility and, in this section, predetermined exchange rates) nominal increase in money hence equals

$$\frac{\dot{M}}{e} = \dot{m} + \pi m, \tag{18}$$

with $\dot{m}$ and πm determined from (7a), (7b), and (8) and the policy choice of the rate of crawl.

Reserve changes equal the difference between $\dot{M}$ and $\dot{C}$ given in (17) and (18):

$$\dot{R} = \frac{\dot{M}}{e} - \frac{\dot{C}}{e}. \tag{19}$$

A fixed exchange rate regime needs to pass two tests of sustainability. The first test follows from the fact that for any debt policy defining a time path for $\dot{d}$ and thus d, reserve losses cannot continue indefinitely. Although a Central Bank can borrow, it too will face a debt ceiling for the same reason that d cannot exceed d^* (see section 15.2).

The second test is that even where the time path of R satisfies the first test, the time path of $\dot{d}$ and d that supports it should not imply that d will eventually exceed d^*. In the next section we shall consider both types of sustainability failures and show that they lead to different postcollapse inflation rates; both, however, will be in excess of the inflation rate prevailing before the collapse.

15.3. An Exchange Rate Freeze, Speculative Attacks, and the Postcollapse Inflation Rate

Consider now the effects of freezing the exchange rate. We shall do so under two alternative assumptions about the mix of interest bearing debt and noninterest bearing liabilities the public sector uses to fund its "basic deficit" $g - \tau + r(d - R)$. Under the first assumption, no further increase in external public debt is allowed ($\dot{d} = 0$); the entire basic budget deficit is funded through issuing domestic credit. In the second case we assume that domestic credit policy is designed to avoid gradual reserve losses during the period that the freeze is operating, rather along the lines of a standard IMF program. External borrowing is used to fill the gap. We show that the two strategies lead to different postcollapse equilibria: the tight-credit approach will lead to higher inflation eventually, through the eroding effect of higher external debt on the basic budget balance of the public sector.

15.3.1. An Exchange Rate Freeze with $\dot{d} = 0$ Imposed

An exchange rate freeze (or a preannounced crawling peg at a rate below the prestabilization program inflation rate) shifts up the MD locus, say from A to B in figures 15.3A and 15.3B. e is fixed by assumption, so Central Bank reserves are not necessarily constant anymore. Discrete changes are effected through one for one swaps between m and b: the public can buy discrete quantities of foreign exchange from the Central Bank in order to purchase foreign assets, with the CB losing an equivalent amount of foreign reserves; or, in the other direction, the public will deposit foreign currency obtained from the sale of units of b in the banking system to require domestic money, so increasing the CB's foreign assets and the monetary base m. Hence under fixed rates jumps take place vertically maintaining V while m changes, and with reserves R going through a matching stock adjustment during the jump.

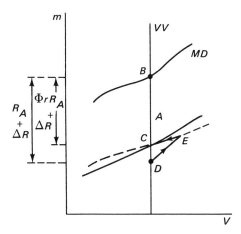

Figure 15.3A
Transition to fixed rate regime followed by an instantaneous speculative attack.

Call the level of CB reserves available at the moment of the announcement of the stabilization program R_A. After the start of the program, a vertical jump to move to the MD curve will bring the economy from A to B (figures 15.3A and 15.3B): a discrete inflow of Central Bank reserves (the counterpart of which is a private sale of foreign assets or increase in foreign borrowing) expands the money supply from m_A to m_B, where it is in line with the new lower inflation rate π_B (π_B equals zero in the case of an actual "freeze"). To see whether a fixed rate regime at B is sustainable, we need to inspect the government budget constraint and check whether the implied rate of domestic credit issue is compatible with the increase in nominal money demand that arises when the economy stays at B.

Consider therefore (17) and (18). We know that, since the economy was in equilibrium at A,

$$g_A - \tau_A + r(d_A - R_A) = \pi_A m_A. \tag{20}$$

Also, between A and B, a reserve inflow of $\Delta R = m_B - m_A$ has taken place, so at B profit transfers by the CB into the government budget have increased by $r\Delta R$. On the other hand, the private sector will absorb domestic credit at the rate $\pi_B m_B$; anything higher will cause unsustainable reserve losses.

The issue therefore is whether

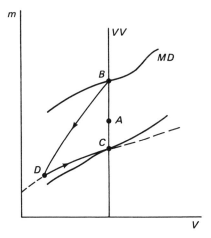

Figure 15.3B
Transition to fixed rate regime followed by a regime switch after gradual reserve losses
have exhausted CB foreign reserves.

$$g_A - \tau_A + r(d_A - R_A - \Delta R) \gtreqless \pi_B m_B.$$

Using (20) we get

$$
\begin{aligned}
g_A - \tau_A + r(d_A - R_A - \Delta R) - \pi_B m_B &= \pi_A m_A - r\,\Delta R - \pi_B m_B \\
&= \pi_A m_A - r(m_B - m_A) - \pi_B m_B \\
&= i_A m_A - i_B m_B \\
&> 0
\end{aligned}
\tag{21}
$$

since $\varepsilon_i^m < 1$ around A and more so around B (see the discussion of the slope of the saddle path in secton A.3).

Hence the situation at B is not sustainable; the initial reserve inflow will be followed by a period of reserve losses for $t > 0$ until the regime collapses:

$$\dot{R}(t) = i_B m_B - i_A m_A < 0. \tag{22}$$

Krugman (1979) shows that such a situation leads to a speculative attack on the exchange rate regime, exhausting the Central Bank's foreign exchange reserves, thus forcing a return to floating exchange rates. We can use our diagrammatic framework to analyze the timing of the attack and the postattack equilibrium.

Before doing that, however, we draw attention to an important issue not covered in the speculative attack literature: a speculative attack will exhaust the Central Bank's reserves and thus reduce its postcollapse profits from interest earnings on foreign assets to zero; as a consequence, this positive contribution to the government budget comes to an end after the collapse and the government's basic budget balance deteriorates not only with respect to B but even with respect to the prestabilization situation at A. Call the postcollapse situation C; then

$$g_c - \tau_c + r(d_c - R_c) = g_A - \tau_A + rd_A$$
$$> g_A - \tau_A + r(d_A - R_A). \tag{23}$$

The first equality obtains because a speculative attack exhausts the CB's reserves; hence $R_c = 0$.[4] Therefore, the postcollapse equilibrium will not be at A but lower, since the basic budget deficit has deteriorated by rR_A. Hence a shift down from A to C is equal to

$$\Delta|_{\dot{d}=0} = rR_A \frac{\partial m}{\partial(rR)}\bigg|_{V=\bar{V}}^{MM}$$
$$= rR_A \dot{m}_m^{-1}$$
$$= rR_A \varepsilon_\pi^m/(\pi_A(1 - \varepsilon_\pi^m)) \tag{24}$$
$$= \Phi rR_A,$$

where Φ is a positive constant defined for later use. The postcollapse equilibrium will be at C, below the prestabilization equilibrium at A. This is important because at C inflation will be higher than at A:

$$\pi_C = \pi(m_C, V_C)$$
$$= \pi(m_C, V_A) \quad \text{(since } V_A = V_C\text{)} \tag{25}$$
$$> \pi(m_A, V_A) \quad \text{(since } m_A > m_C, \pi_m < 0\text{)}.$$

This establishes an important result: *If the crawling peg or exchange rate freeze ends through a speculative attack à la Krugman (1979), the postcollapse inflation rate will exceed the inflation rate that prevailed before the start of the stabilization program.*

Consider finally the timing of the speculative attack. Figures 15.3A and 15.3B consider two extremes. At the one end is the case where no attack takes place and the regime changes when CB reserves have been exhausted through the gradual outflow given in (22) (figure 15.3B). In that case, $R = 0$ at the time of the regime change, so no outflow takes place and on impact no vertical jump takes place. However, in the postcollapse float, the economy will need to remain on the saddle path passing through C. Hence immediately after R reaches zero and the CB abandons the fixed rate regime, a discrete devaluation takes place, taking the economy from B to D in figure 15.3B. However, such a devaluation would inflict capital losses at an infinite rate on holders of domestic money. Rational speculators will therefore bring down the regime before that occurs (Krugman, 1979).

On the other extreme is a speculative attack at the very beginning of the freeze, immediately after the economy has jumped to B. That is the case depicted in figure 15.3A. Such a speculative attack will exhaust Central Bank reserves and therefore instantaneously reduce the money stock by an equal amount. Since R_A is positive, the attack at that time will move the economy down below A. What we do not know is whether it will move below C. The downward shift equals $R_A + \Delta R$, while the distance $B - C$ equals

$$\Phi r R_A + \Delta R.$$

Therefore the attack will take the economy below C if $\Phi < r^{-1}$ (figure 15.3A). Consider that case first.

After the attack the economy moves below C since by assumption $\Phi < r^{-1}$. Hence, after the float starts, the economy is below the saddle path on which it should be. Accordingly the exchange rate will immediately appreciate, moving the economy from D to E. It will then gradually depreciate back down to C. This scenario would also be incompatible, however, with rational competitive speculative behavior: speculators would have moved out of domestic currency at the very moment holding on would have yielded capital gains at an infinite rate during the jump. Instead, forcing the jump from D to E implies losses at an infinite rate.

The existence of competitive rational speculators will lead to a speculative attack timed to fall in between these two extremes, in such a way that no discrete depreciation will take place and therefore no infinite rate of capital gain will occur.

We can easily calculate the timing of the attack. The only way such a discrete change could be avoided is if the economy is forced to jump to C in the process of exhausting the CB's foreign reserves. That suggests that the time of the attack is determined by the following equation [where

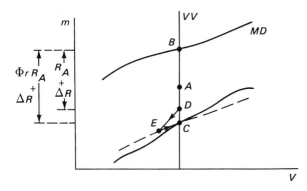

Figure 15.3C
$\Phi > r^{-1}$; the speculative attack occurs immediately after the initiation of the freeze.

$\{\dot{R}\}$ is the time path of reserve losses implied by (22)]:

$$R(T) = R_A + \Delta R + \int_0^T \{\dot{R}(t)\}\, dt$$

$$= \Delta R + \Phi r R_A \tag{26}$$

$$= m_A - m_C.$$

Equation (26) is an implicit equation in T, the time of the attack.

It is possible that (26) has no solution for positive T; then

$$R_A + \Delta R < \Phi r R_A + \Delta R \qquad \text{or} \qquad \Phi > r^{-1}. \tag{27}$$

In that case an initial jump at $t = 0$ would fall short of C and also produce a depreciation, as in figure 15.3B, although a smaller one (see figure 15.3C). In that case a speculative attack will abort the freeze straight at the beginning.

15.3.2.   An Exchange Rate Freeze with d Set to Avoid Gradual Reserve Losses While the Freeze Operates

Consider finally a freeze backed up by a domestic credit policy designed to avoid reserve losses, i.e., a time path of $\dot{C}$ that would keep $\dot{R} = 0$ in (22). This is very much the type of credit policy imposed during IMF administered adjustment programs.

From (21) we can immediately derive that such a policy implies

$$\dot{d} = i_A m_A - i_B m_B > 0 \tag{28}$$

for as long as the freeze lasts. This in turn will, in the absence of a speculative attack, lead to a steady increase in external debt until the maximum level $d*$ is reached. Then the policy will need to be discontinued and, if there still is no speculative attack, the economy is back to the situation analyzed in subsection 15.3.1. An attack will then bring the regime down in the manner discribed in that subsection.

There is, however, one important difference. In the process, public sector external debt has increased from d_A to $d*$. Hence the downward shift of MM from A to C is larger and will now equal

$$\Delta|_{\dot{d}>0} = \Phi r R_A + \Phi r(d* - d_A) \tag{29}$$

$$= \Delta|_{\dot{d}=0} + \Phi r(d* - d_A) \tag{30}$$

$$> \Delta|_{\dot{d}=0}.$$

We shall not take the reader through the mechanics of calculating the timing of the attack, but point out that the above relations imply that the postcollapse equilibrium with a tighter domestic credit policy before, and hence a higher public interest bearing debt afterward, will be below C, say, at F, and will therefore be characterized by an even higher inflation rate:

$$\pi_F = \pi(m_F, V_F) = \pi(m_F, V_B)$$

$$> \pi(m_B, V_B) \tag{31}$$

$$> \pi(m_A, V_A).$$

We leave it to the reader to show that that attack can take place before $d*$ will have been reached.[5] As a final observation, note that if it takes place before $d*$ is reached, the speculative attack will take place without any gradual loss of Central Bank foreign reserves. The conditions that will prevent an attack, derived in Krugman (1979) and Flood and Garber (1984), are, therefore, necessary but not sufficient. In addition conditions need to be satisfied on the growth rate of interest bearing public sector debt.

One qualifying remark is in order, however. The internal logic of this chapter suggests that, in a crisis, a Central Bank should be able to obtain foreign loans equal to $d* - d$ (note that R disappears during the crisis). This opportunity, if used, would make the postcollapse public sector debt equal to $d*$ irrespective of the domestic credit policy followed prior to the collapse. In that case the dependence of the postcollapse inflation rate on the precollapse domestic credit policy would disappear (Calvo, 1986, and Drazen and Helpman, 1986, use such an approach).

This assumption on foreign lenders' behavior, while appealing in its symmetry, seems counterfactual. Recent exchange rate crises in Latin America strongly suggest that no additional foreign loans will be available at all during a crisis—this in spite of the fact that lenders might have been willing to lend more before the crisis atmosphere took hold, and have been observed to lend more afterward. The implication of such behavior is that the maximum reserve loss during a crisis equals gross reserves of the Central Bank. Since we assume that the fiscal authorities conduct all public sector foreign borrowing, gross reserves of the CB equal its net foreign reserves—hence our assumption that R is reduced to zero during a speculative attack.

15.3.3. Conclusions

In the introduction we pointed out puzzles in the recent inflationary experience of high inflation countries and stabilization failures in countries such as Israel, Brazil, and Argentina. We present an analysis that explains these puzzles within the context of a model with rational, optimizing, and forward looking consumers endowed with perfect foresight. The government budget constraint and the resolution of inconsistencies between the implications of different policy instruments for that constraint are at the core of our analysis.

In doing so this chapter is in the spirit of the "public finance approach" to macroeconomics popularized by Phelps (1973). Several authors have recently used this approach to analyze current effects of future policy changes (Sargent and Wallace, 1982; Liviatan, 1984; Drazen and Helpman, 1985a,b; Bental and Eckstein, 1985). In a departure from those papers, we endogenize the regime switch by linking it to rational speculative behavior. Furthermore, we extend this approach to an open economy framework, which enables us to analyze exchange rate policy and changes in an exchange rate regime.

We introduce a fixed exchange rate version of the model and analyze the use of an exchange rate freeze (or preannounced crawling peg) in an attempt to reduce the rate of inflation, as was done in Israel from October 1982 and Argentina from December 1978 onward. We derive conditions that need to be satisfied for such an experiment to be sustainable. These conditions are derived from the government budget constraint. In particular, we show that a domestic credit issuance policy designed to offset loss of international reserves while the fixed regime lasts is necessary but not sufficient to prevent speculative attacks in fixed exchange rate regimes (Krugman, 1979, and Flood and Garber, 1984, focus on reserve losses only). The difference arises because we explicitly incorporate the government budget constraint. We show that speculative attacks will also take place if such a domestic credit policy implies unsustainable increases in interest bearing (nonmonetary) government debt.

We show that, if a collapse occurs, the postcollapse inflation rate is higher than the inflation rate that prevailed prior to the stabilization experiment. This accords well with Argentine and Israeli experience. The explanation is rather subtle and is related to the loss of interest earnings on the foreign assets of the Central Bank that are lost during the speculative attack, and the ensuing decline in profit transfers from the Central Bank into the government budget.

This result also sheds light on another puzzle brought up in the introduction: the link between jumps in inflation and BoP crises. Increases in inflation will follow the exchange rate crisis because of the underlying deterioration of the government budget constraint. Both the crisis and the subsequent increase in inflation are triggered by basic fiscal policy inconsistencies; their simultaneous occurrence is therefore not necessarily an argument against the theory linking inflation to fiscal policy.

We then endogenize such speculative attacks following Krugman (1979). We show that if a collapse occurs after a domestic credit policy, designed to prevent reserve losses while the freeze lasts, such a policy will lead to a higher postcollapse inflation rate than will prevail when domestic credit issuance is higher during the freeze period—high enough to keep external public debt at the prefreeze level. The explanation is the postcollapse deterioration in the basic government budget because of higher real interest payments on the extra external debt accumulated under the first policy. Moreover, under the first, restrictive domestic credit policy, a speculative attack will take place without any Central Bank foreign reserve losses *prior* to the attack (there will be such losses *during* the attack of course). This ultimately inflationary effect of restrictive credit policies under an unsustainable fixed exchange rate regime is related to the Sargent-Wallace (1982) result of high inflation in response to temporary tight money in a closed economy.

Most of these results are of course conditional on the government not undertaking the reform in government expenditure and (noninflation) taxes necessary to make the fixed regime feasible. However, it is important to realize that, even where the government intends to undertake such reforms in the future, private doubts on whether these reforms will in fact be implemented will lead to similar results. This point is made in Drazen and Helpman (1985b) in a discussion of monetary policy in a closed economy context. The policy conclusion is clear: fiscal reform is not only necessary for the success of antiinflation programs, but should come up front.

Appendix

A.1.   Derivation of $\pi(m, V; r)$ and $C(m, V, r)$

Total differentiation of (7a) and (7b) yields

$$
\begin{pmatrix} (r + \pi)A & -1 \\ 1 & m \end{pmatrix} \begin{pmatrix} dc \\ d\pi \end{pmatrix} = dr^* - U_{mm}/U_c\, dm
$$

$$
- \left(m + \frac{\rho + p}{(r + p)^2}(y - \tau) \right) dr^* \tag{A1}
$$

$$
- (r + \pi)\, dm + (\rho + p)\, dV,
$$

with $A = -U_{cc}/U_c$ the coefficient of absolute risk aversion. Define the determinant of the matrix on the left-hand side as Δ:

$$
\Delta = (r + \pi)Am + 1 > 0.
$$

Hence

$$
\pi_m = -\Delta^{-1}(r + \pi)(A(r + \pi) - U_{mm}/U_m)) < 0,
$$

$$
\pi_V = \Delta^{-1}(r + \pi)A(\rho + p) > 0,
$$

$$
\pi_r = -\Delta^{-1}\left((r + \pi)Am + 1 + \frac{(\rho + p)}{(r + p)^2}(y - \tau) \right) < 0,
$$

$$
c_m = -\Delta^{-1}(r + \pi)(1 + mU_{mm}/U_m) \gtrless 0,
$$

$$
c_V = \Delta^{-1}(\rho + p) > 0,
$$

$$
c_r = -\Delta^{-1}\frac{(\rho + p)}{(r + p)^2}(y - \tau) < 0,
$$

with repeated use of $U_c^{-1} = (U_m/U_c)U_m^{-1} = (r + \pi)U_m^{-1}$. Two terms involving $\Delta^{-1}m$ cancel in c_r. The necessary condition referred to in subsection 15.3.1 is

$$
\pi_m + \pi_V < 0,
$$

or

$$
\pi > \rho + p - r + U_{mm}/(U_m A).
$$

A.2. Derivation of $\dot{m}(m, V; r)$ and $\dot{V}(m, V; r)$

Differentiation of (8) and (9) yields

$$\dot{V}_m = 0,$$

$$\dot{V}_V = (r - \rho - p) < 0,$$

$$\dot{V}_r = \left(V + \frac{(y - \tau)}{(r + p)}\right) - \frac{(r - \rho)(y - \tau)}{(r + p)^2}$$

$$= -\frac{y - \tau}{r + p} \frac{p(\rho + p) + (r - \rho)^2}{(r + p)(r - \rho - p)} > 0.$$

The second expression for $\dot{V}_r$ uses the fact that at $V = \bar{V}$ (steady state value),

$$(r - \rho)\frac{y - \tau}{r + p} + (r - \rho - p)V = 0.$$

It therefore holds exactly when evaluated at $\bar{V}$, but only approximately around $\bar{V}$:

$$\dot{m}_m = -(\pi + m\pi_m)$$

$$= -m\pi_m(1 - \varepsilon_\pi^m) \gtrless 0 \rightleftarrows \varepsilon_\pi^m \lessgtr 1,$$

$$\dot{m}_V = -m\pi_V < 0,$$

$$\dot{m}_r = d - m\pi_r > 0.$$

A.3. Stability of (11), (12), and the Slope of the Saddle Path around E

The characteristic equation of the matrix of partial derivatives of $\dot{m}$ and $\dot{V}$ [(11) and (12)] with respect to m, V is

$$(\lambda + m\pi_m(1 - \varepsilon_\pi^m))(\lambda - (r - \rho - p)) = 0. \tag{A2}$$

Around E, $\varepsilon_\pi^m < 1$; hence the negative root is $\lambda^- = r - \rho - p$. The other root λ^+ is $-m\pi_m(1 - \varepsilon_\pi^m) > 0$ around E, so the system is saddlepoint stable around E.

Straightforward calculation shows that the eigenvector corresponding to λ^- equals

$$(m, V) = \left(\frac{Z}{Z + Z_1}, 1\right),$$

where

$$Z = m(r + \pi)A(\rho + p) > 0$$

and

$$Z_1 = -m\pi_m(1 - \varepsilon_\pi^m) - r$$

$$= \frac{\pi}{\varepsilon_\pi^m}(1 - \varepsilon_\pi^m) - r.$$

Clearly, the slope of the saddle path equals $Z/(Z + Z_1)$, so that the slope is smaller than one if $Z_1 > 0$. That in turn implies

$$\frac{\pi}{\varepsilon_\pi^m}(1 - \varepsilon_\pi^m) > r,$$

or

$$\varepsilon_i^m < 1,$$

or

$$\varepsilon_\pi^m < \frac{\pi}{r + \pi},$$

a slightly stronger condition than $\varepsilon_\pi^m < 1$, which we shall assume to hold.

Notes

1. This structure is used to guarantee existence of a steady state without having to impose the arbitrary assumption of $r = \rho$ (r is the foreign real rate and ρ the domestic rate of time preference). See also Frenkel and Razin (1985) and Buiter (1984) for open economy applications of the Blanchard (1985) framework.

2. Helpman and Razin (1987) discuss the transition from a floating to a fixed rate exchange regime in a policy setting where taxes τ are varied to insure sustainability of the fixed rate regime. This leads to a set of issues entirely different from the one discussed in this chapter.

3. Plus other variables and parameters that will not be varied in this chapter and are therefore dropped from the argument list.

4. In fact the Central Bank might abandon the fixed rate regime before R has reached zero, say at $R_c > 0$. Clearly $R_c < R_A$, since R_A was considered sufficiently high to actually start the fixed rate regime. We shall assume $R_c = 0$, but all results carry through as long as $R_c < R_A$. See Calvo (1986) and Drazen and Helpman (1986) for alternative restrictions on the Central Bank.

5. The attack takes place before d^* has been reached if an attack at the moment d^* is reached would result in an immediate depreciation after the attack forced a transition to the floating rate regime. This will happen if

$$R_A + \Delta R < \Phi r R_A + \Phi r(d^* - d_A) + \Delta R.$$

If an attack ends the freeze before d^* is reached, the new equilibrium will be between C and F. This is because $d(T) < d^*$, although $d(T) > d_A$ (unless the attack takes place immediately after the announcement of the freeze, in which case the new equilibrium is at C again).

References

Bental, B., and Z. Eckstein (1985), "Inflation Deficit and Seignorage with Expected Stabilization," in Elhanan Helpman, Assaf Razin, and Efraim Sadka (eds.), *Economic Effects of the Government Budget*, Cambridge, MA: The MIT Press.

Bianco, H., and P. Garber (1986), "Recurrent Devaluation and Speculative Attacks on the Mexican Peso," *Journal of Political Economy.*

Blanchard, O. (1985), "Debt, Deficits and Finite Horizons," *Journal of Political Economy.*

Boskin, M., and Kotlikoff (1985), "Public Debt and U.S. Saving: A New Test of the Neutrality Hypothesis," prepared for Carnegie-Rochester Conference.

Bruno, M. (1984), "External Shocks and Domestic Response: Israel's Macroeconomic Performance (1965–1982)," Jerusalem, Falk Institute Discussion Paper No. 84.01.

Buiter, W. (1984), "Comment on T. J. Sargent and N. Wallace: Some Unpleasant Monetarist Arithmetic," in eds. B. Griffiths and G. Wood (eds.), *Monetarism in the United Kingdom*, London: McMillan, pp. 42–60.

Buiter, W. (1986), "Borrowing to Defend the Exchange Rate and the Timing and Magnitude of Speculative Attacks," *Journal of International Economics*.

Calvo, G. (1981), "Trying to Stabilize," in P. Aspe and R. Dornbusch (eds.), *Financial Policies and World Capital Markets: the Problem of Latin American Countries*, Chicago: University of Chicago Press.

Calvo, G. (1986), "Balance of Payments Crises in a Cash-in-Advance Economy," *Journal of Money*, 19.

Cardoso, E. (1985), *Economia Brasileira ao Alcance de Todos*, Sao Paulo: Editora Brasiliense S.A.

Chamley, C. (1985), "On a Simple Rule for the Optimal Inflation Rate in Second Best Taxation," *Journal of Public Economics*.

Diaz Alejandro, C. (1979), "Southern Cone Stabilization Plans," mimeo, Yale University.

Dornbusch, R. (1980), *Open Economy Macroeconomics*, New York: Basic Books, Chap. 11.

Dornbusch, R., and S. Fischer (1985), "Stopping Hyperinflation Past and Present," *Weltwirtschatf-liches Archiv*.

Drazen, A. (1985), "Tight Money and Inflation: Further Results," *Journal of Monetary Economics*.

Drazen, A., and E. Helpman (1985a), "Inflationary Consequences of Uncertain Macroeconomic Policies," mimeo, Tel-Aviv University.

Drazen, A., and E. Helpman (1985b), "Inflationary Consequences of Anticipated Macroeconomic Policies. Part II: Budget Cuts," mimeo, Tel-Aviv University.

Drazen, A., and E. Helpman (1986), "Stabilization with Exchange Rate Management under Uncertainty," in Elhanan Helpman, Assaf Razin, and Efraim Sadka (eds.), *Economic Effects of the Government Budget*, Cambridge, MA: The MIT Press.

Feenstra, R. (1985), "Functional Equivalence between Liquidity Costs and the Utility of Money," *Journal of Monetary Economics*.

Flood, R., and P. Garber (1980), "An Economic Theory of Monetary Reform," *Journal of Economy*.

Flood, R., and P. Garber (1984), "Collapsing Exchange Rate Regimes: Some Linear Examples," *Journal of International Economics*.

Frenkel, J., and A. Razin (1985), "Fiscal Expenditure and International Economic Interdependence," in W. Buiter and R. Marston (eds.), *International Economic Policy Coordination*, Cambridge: Cambridge University Press.

Helpman, E., and A. Razin (1987), "Exchange Rate Management: Intertemporal Tradeoffs," *American Economic Review*.

Kharas, H. (1984), "The Long-Run Creditworthiness of Developing Countries: Theory and Practice," *Quarterly Journal of Economics*.

Krugman, P. (1979), "A Model of Balance of Payments Crises," *Journal of Money, Credit and Banking*.

Liviatan, N. (1984), "Tight Money and Inflation," *Journal of Monetary Economics*.

Liviatan, N., and S. Piterman (1984), "Acceleration Inflation and Balance of Payments Crises: Israel 1973–1984," Bank of Israel, Discussion Paper Series 84-6.

Obstfeld, M. (1981), "Macroeconomic Policy, Exchange Rate Dynamics and Optimal Asset Accumulation," *Journal of Political Economy.*

Obstfeld, M. (1985), "The Capital Inflows Problem Revisited," *Review of Economic Studies.*

Phelps, E. (1973), "Inflation in the Theory of Public Finance," *Swedish Journal of Economics.*

Salant, S. (1983), "The Vulnerability of Price Stabilization Schemes to Speculative Attack," *Journal of Political Economy.*

Salant, S., and D. Henderson (1978), "Market Anticipations of Government Policies and the Price of Gold," *Journal of Political Economy.*

Sargent, T., and N. Wallace (1982), "Some Unpleasant Monetarist Arithmetic," *Federal Reserve Bank of Minneapolis Quarterly Review.*

van Wijnbergen, S. (1979), "Capital Inflows, the Real Exchange Rate and the Crawling Peg," mimeo, World Bank.

van Wijnbergen, S. (1986a), "Exchange Rate Management and Stabilization Policy in Developing Countries," *Journal of Development Economics.*

van Wijnbergen, S. (1986b), "Fiscal Deficits, Exchange Rate Crises and Inflation," NBER Working Paper No. 2130.

16 Stabilization with Exchange Rate Management under Uncertainty

Allan Drazen and Elhanan Helpman

16.1. Introduction

Several countries have attempted to reduce inflation via exchange rate management. Sometimes it was the main instrument, as in the case of Argentina and Chile in the late seventies; sometimes it was part of a comprehensive policy package, as in the case of Argentina and Israel in 1985. However, in all these cases exchange rate management was attempted without an immediate balancing of the government's budget that would make the policy sustainable over the long run. Expectations of a future policy change were therefore engendered. One may therefore think about such policies as two-stage programs, where in the first stage the exchange rate is frozen or the rate of currency devaluation is substantially reduced, while in the second stage the budget deficit is eliminated or exchange rate management is abandoned. In Drazen and Helpman (1987) we studied such programs for economic environments with complete certainty, including certainty about timing of the second-stage policy adjustment. Here we extend the analysis to an environment in which there is uncertainty about the timing of the second-stage change.

The introduction of uncertainty helps to explain certain observed phenomena that cannot be explained in its absence. These include discrete devaluations upon the abandoning of exchange rate management and runs on reserves that are not associated with the abandoning of exchange rate management. Our work is in the spirit of Krugman (1979) and elaborations that followed, such as Flood and Garber (1984).

Our basic model is described in section 16.2. In section 16.3 we discuss the certainty case in order to set the stage for a discussion of the role of uncertainty. Finally, in section 16.4 we discuss stabilization under timing uncertainty.

16.2. The Basic Model

We consider a simple open economy model identical to that in Drazen and Helpman (1987). There are two consumption goods, traded and nontraded.

For helpful comments we wish to thank seminar participants at the Institute for International Economic Studies, Stockholm, the Hebrew University, and Tel-Aviv University and participants of the Sapir Center Conference on Economic Effects of the Government Budget. Financial support from the Bank of Israel is gratefully acknowledged.

Current macroeconomic policy, consisting of a fixed level of public spending on traded and on nontraded goods, fixed taxes in terms of traded goods, and a fixed exchange rate, is infeasible in the long run. The precise nature of this infeasibility will be spelled out later. There are no restrictions on international capital movements, which, combined with the exchange rate policy, means that the government has no direct control over the money supply. Stabilization is effected by a change in at least one policy variable that is under direct control of the government.

The utility of the representative individual is assumed to depend on consumption of the two goods and real money balances, where the instantaneous utility function is assumed separable across consumption and real balances. This is represented by

$$u(c(t), c_N(t)) + v(M(t)/Q(t)),$$

where t is a time index, and c, c_N, and M, are real consumption of traded goods, nontraded goods, and nominal domestic currency balances. Q, the domestic currency price index of the two goods, is defined by $Q(t) = Q(\varepsilon(t), P_N(t))$, where ε is the exchange rate (the domestic currency price of foreign exchange), the foreign currency price of traded goods is constant and equal to one, and P_N is the domestic currency price of nontraded goods. The functions $u(\cdot)$ and $v(\cdot)$ are increasing and concave, and the function $Q(\cdot)$ is increasing and positively linear homogeneous.

The individual may hold domestic currency or bonds denominated in foreign currency, denoted b, with the latter paying the exogenously fixed world interest rate r. We assume that the individual's subjective discount rate equals r and that he receives fixed income of y in terms of traded goods plus y_N in terms of nontraded goods. The assumption of constant output levels eliminates employment considerations, while the equality of the subjective discount rate to the real interest rate in terms of traded goods eliminates secular trends in the trade account. This allows us to focus attention on the speculative aspects of stabilization.

We consider the case where the timing of a stabilization is not known ex ante. We assume that the switch may occur at any time between 0 and some T_{max}, where the cumulative distribution of a switch occuring until T is $F(T)$. Clearly $F(0) = 0$ and $F(T_{max}) = 1$. We consider the case where only one switch takes place.

The individual maximizes expected discounted utility over his horizon subject to his budget constraints, the expectation taken over $dF(T)$. It will be useful to write the individual's present discounted utility if a switch occurs with certainty at T as follows. Let $V^s(\cdot)$ be the present discounted value of maximized utility from T onward. It will be a function of the real value of an individual's assets at T, and perhaps of T as well. The present discounted utility from 0 to infinity if a switch occurs at T is then (using the instantaneous utility function from above)

$$\int_0^T e^{-rt}[u(c(t), c_N(t)) + v(M(t)/Q(t))]\, dt \tag{1}$$

$$+ e^{-rT}V^s[b(T) + m(T); T],$$

where $b(T)$ is the stock of private bond holding at the time of stabilization and $m(T)$ is the stock of real balances. Expected welfare is then the expected value of (1) taken over all possible realizations of T. The individual can switch between money and bonds at any instant of time. Using traded goods as the numeraire, his budget constraint may be written as

$$\int_0^\infty e^{-rt}\left[c(t) + \frac{P_N(t)}{\varepsilon(t)}c_N(t) + \frac{z(t)}{\varepsilon(t)} + \tau(t) - y - \frac{P_N(t)}{\varepsilon(t)}y_N \right] dt \tag{2}$$

$$+ \sum_{t_i} e^{-rt_i}\frac{\Delta M(t_i)}{\varepsilon(t_i)} \leqslant b_0,$$

where $z(t)$ is the flow addition to nominal balances, $\tau(t)$ is the level of nondistortionary taxes in terms of traded goods, $\Delta M(t_i)$ is the *stock* increase in domestic currency holdings resulting from sale of foreign currency to the monetary authority, and b_0 is the initial stock of bonds. All variables in these equations represent values conditional on no policy switch taking place before t. Asset swaps take place at discrete points in time t_i. The evolution of the stock of private bond holdings $b(t)$ is given by

$$\dot b = rb - c - \frac{P_N}{\varepsilon}c_N - \tau + y + \frac{P_N}{\varepsilon}y_N - \frac{z}{\varepsilon} \qquad \text{for} \quad t \neq t_i, \tag{2'}$$

$$b(t_i) - b(t_i^-) = -\Delta M(t_i)/\varepsilon(t_i).$$

Nominal domestic balances at t are related to z and ΔM via

$$M(t) = M_0 + \int_0^t z(x)\, dx + \sum_{t_i \leqslant t} \Delta M(t_i) \qquad \text{for all} \quad t, \tag{3}$$

where M_0 is the initial stock of money holdings.

The individual chooses the functions $c(t)$, $c_N(t)$, $M(t)$, $z(t)$, the timing of stock adjustments t_i, and their size $\Delta M(t_i)$ to maximize the expected value of the objective function given in (1) under constraints (2) and (3). (The reader may refer to the appendix for the exact mathematical formulation.)

Using the clearing condition in the market for nontraded goods

$$c_N(t) + g_N(t) = y_N,$$ (4)

where $g_N(t)$ is government purchase of nontraded goods, the first-order conditions of this problem imply (see the appendix)

$$\theta(t) = \int_t^{T_{\max}} \theta^s(T) \frac{dF(T)}{1 - F(t)} \quad \text{for} \quad t < T_{\max},$$ (5)

$$p[c(t), y_N - g_N(t)] \equiv \frac{u_2'[c(t), y_N - g_N(t)]}{u_1'[c(t), y_N - g_N(t)]} = \frac{P_N(t)}{\varepsilon(t)} \quad \text{for all} \quad t,$$ (6)

$$\frac{1}{\varepsilon(t)} = \frac{1}{\theta(t)} \int_t^{T_{\max}} \left[e^{-r(T-t)} \frac{\theta^s(T)}{\varepsilon^s(T)} \right.$$

$$\left. + \int_t^T e^{-r(x-t)} \frac{v'(x)}{Q(x)} dx \right] \frac{dF(T)}{1 - F(t)} \quad \text{for} \quad t < T_{\max},$$ (7)

where a superscript s indicates the value of a variable after stabilization. Thus, $\theta^s(T)$ is the marginal utility of consumption of traded goods at time T provided stabilization takes place at time T and $\varepsilon^s(T)$ is the exchange rate at time T provided stabilization takes place at time T. The value of $T_{\max}$ is smaller than or equal to the point in time at which the government reaches the limit of its ability to finance the budget without further growth of net debt. We shall say more about this point in due course.

Equation (5) says that traded goods consumption is chosen at each point before a stabilization to equalize current marginal utility of consumption to conditional expected future poststabilization marginal utility (that is, conditional on no stabilization before t). This condition allows for the fact that the marginal utility of consumption after a stabilization may depend on the timing of the stabilization. Equation (6) represents the standard equality of the marginal rate of substitution to relative prices. The marginal rate of substitution $p(\cdot)$ is equal to the inverse of the real exchange rate, where the real exchange rate is defined as the price of nontradables in terms of tradables. Equation (7) is an asset pricing equation of money balances, with the return on the asset being uncertain. The left-hand side is the real value in terms of traded goods of one unit of nominal balances at t. On the right-hand side, the term inside square brackets is the sum of the present discounted value of the resale value of one unit of money at T (in marginal utility terms) and the discounted value of the flow of utility from money holdings from t until T. Taking the expectation over all possible switch time gives expected returns, which, on division by $\theta(t)$, is in the same units as the left-hand side.

The government, which consists of a fiscal and monetary authority, faces the following consolidated budget constraint:

$$\int_0^\infty e^{-rt} \left[g(t) + \frac{P_N(t)}{\varepsilon(t)} g_N(t) - \tau(t) - z(t)/\varepsilon(t) \right] dt$$
$$- \sum_{t_i} e^{-rt_i} \Delta M(t_i)/\varepsilon(t) + b_0^G = 0, \tag{8}$$

where $g(t)$ is purchases of traded goods, $g_N(t)$ is purchases of nontraded goods, and b_0^G is initial net debt in terms of traded goods. Net government debt equals outstanding debt minus reserve holdings, where outstanding debt is denominated in terms of foreign currency. Implicit in (8) is the assumption that foreign exchange reserves, like all other foreign currency denominated assets, bear interest at the rate r.

The evolution of the government's net debt $b^G(t)$ is given by

$$\dot{b}^G = rb^G + g + pg_N - \tau - \dot{M}/\varepsilon \qquad \text{for} \quad t \neq t_i,$$
$$b^G(t_i) - b^G(t_i^-) = -\Delta M(t_i)/\varepsilon(t_i), \tag{8'}$$

where use has been made of (3) to derive $\dot{M} = z$ for $t \neq t_i$, since the stock of money is not under the government's direct control when it controls the exchange rate.

The difference between government net debt b^G and private holding of interest-bearing assets b is net foreign indebtedness, which we denote $\bar{b} = b^G - b$. Using (2'), (8'), and the clearing condition in the market for nontraded goods (4), we obtain

$$\dot{\bar{b}} = r\bar{b} + g + c - y \qquad \text{for all} \quad t, \tag{9}$$

where the right-hand side represents the deficit on current account.

It is clear that if (2) and (8) hold, meaning the private and government sectors are intertemporally balanced, then the present value of net external debt is nonpositive (i.e., $\lim_{t \to \infty} e^{-rt}\bar{b}(t) \leqslant 0$), and the economy is also intertemporally balanced.

16.3. Stabilization under Certainty

We consider a situation where the government fixes the exchange rate ε without eliminating the budget deficit, implying growing government debt. In addition, the spending levels g and g_N and the tax level τ are maintained constant before stabilization. Stabilization takes place at a point in time T at which the government changes its policy instruments to new constant levels so as to freeze its net debt at its then current level $b^G(T)$.

The case of certainty about the timing of a stabilization may be seen as a special case of this formulation, where the probability distribution has all its mass at a single T. This case, which is discussed in greater detail in Drazen and Helpman (1986, 1987), is meant to set the stage for the uncertainty results. In the certainty case equation (5) would imply constancy of θ over time. This implies that private consumption of tradables and nontradables is also constant before T, as well as being constant after T, although not necessarily at the same level. Then (6) implies constancy of the real exchange rate. Moreover, given the fixed exchange rate before T, (6) implies a constant price of nontraded goods P_N and a constant price level Q before T. In the steady state that is reached after stabilization, the triple (ε, P_N, Q) is rising at the rate of money growth μ. When the marginal utility of consumption θ is constant, (7) implies that the exchange rate ε is continuous even at T. Under these circumstances differentiation of the first-order conditions yields (see the appendix)

$$\frac{v'(m/q)}{\theta q} = r + \mu \qquad \text{for} \quad t \geqslant T \tag{10}$$

(with $\mu = 0$ for $t < T$ under certainty), where $q = Q/\varepsilon$ and real balances m are defined as M/ε. The variable q is an alternative representation of (the inverse of) a real exchange rate, with the real exchange rate here defined as the price of traded goods in terms of a domestic basket of goods. In what follows we use the earlier definition of the real exchange rate as the price of traded goods in terms of nontraded, that is [by (6)], the inverse of $p(\cdot)$. q is an increasing function of p (or a declining function of the real exchange rate), since the price index function $Q(\varepsilon, P_N)$ is positively linear homogeneous, so that $q \equiv q[p(\cdot)] = Q(1, P_N/\varepsilon) = Q[1, p(\cdot)]$.

Equation (10) implies constant nominal money balances before T (since the exchange rate is fixed). Hence,

$$z = \dot{M} = 0 \quad \text{and} \quad \Delta M = 0 \quad \text{for} \quad t, t_i < T, \tag{11}$$

and, from (8),

$$\dot{b}^G = rb^G + g + pg_N - \tau - \mu m \quad \text{for} \quad t \geqslant T, \tag{12}$$

with $\mu = 0$ for $t < T$. Our primary interest in these equations is to derive the poststabilization terminal surfaces, which are relevant also in the case of timing uncertainty. We shall simply describe the characteristics of the dynamic paths prior to stabilization, referring readers to our earlier papers for more precise details.

When the stabilization date is known, some qualitative characteristics of the dynamic path before a stabilization takes place do not depend on the instruments that are used to stabilize. For every value of b^G larger than $\underline{b}^G = -(g + pg_N - \tau)/r$ government net debt will grow without bound for unchanged policy parameters. At all $t < T$ money balances are constant, as is private consumption of traded and nontraded goods.

In the case of stabilizations effected by an increase in taxes, τ, or a cut in government consumption of traded goods, g, with no reliance on money growth, real balances before T will be identical to those held after T, so there will be no need for an asset swap. In this case the locus of $m - b^G$ combinations described by (10) and (12) is simply a horizontal line at the prestabilization level of m, as in figure 16.1.

The anticipation of a g-based stabilization brings about an increase in net external debt for $t < T$, but a constant level of private bond holdings. Since more resources will become available for private consumption after the budget cut, the private sector's consumption of traded goods prior to T is larger than income from traded goods and foreign asset holdings, generating a deficit on current account prior to stabilization. The resources released by the spending cut at T will be just sufficient to pay for the extra interest on the additional foreign debt, by which the deficit on current account has been financed. Constant private bond holdings and rising net government debt imply that all increases in net government debt result from foreign borrowing, budget deficits being financed by external debt. The consumption of tradables is $c = rb_0 + y - \tau + pg_N$, which is independent of T (see Drazen and Helpman, 1987).

A stabilization via an increase in taxes with no reliance on monetary injections has similar implications for growth in the government's net debt and constant money balances. However, unlike the case of a g-based

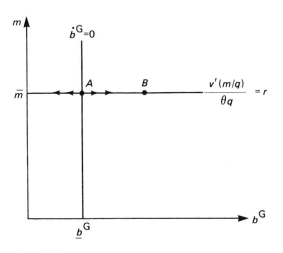

Figure 16.1

stabilization, a tax-based stabilization brings about a balanced current account, which means that prior to T consumption is equal to income from traded goods and foreign asset holdings. Constant private consumption and net wealth are maintained by rising bond holdings, which compensates for the rising present value of tax obligations, with the reverse taking place within the government sector. This means that the increase in government net debt is held entirely by domestic residents, budget deficits being financed by internal debt. Moreover, there is a unique value of c that will bring about this outcome, namely, $c = y - g - r\bar{b}_0$. As in the earlier case, this consumption level does not depend on the timing of stabilization. This observation will prove useful at a later stage (see Drazen and Helpman, 1987).

A third case is a stabilization via a reduction in government spending on nontradables with no reliance on money financing. It is straightforward to show that a reduction in g_N (implying an increase in c_N at T) reduces the relative price of nontraded goods p and q, and that it increases private consumption of tradables if and only if $u_{12}(\cdot) > 0$. This means that at the moment of stabilization there is a real exchange rate devaluation resulting from a downward jump in the price of nontradables P_N; the nominal exchange rate remains constant. Prior to stabilization, consumption of tradables has to be sufficiently low so that the implied current account

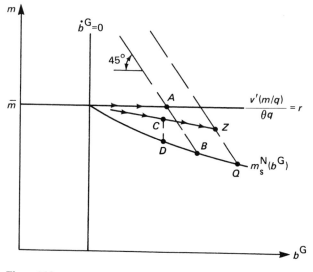

Figure 16.2

surplus and foreign asset accumulation generate enough interest earnings to cover the costs of the increased consumption of traded goods.

Since the budget cut reduces aggregate government spending in terms of tradables (which is helped by the real devaluation), the $\dot{b}^G = 0$ line in figure 16.1 moves to the right. The fall in q implies a fall in the value of m that satisfies (10) when the elasticity of $v'(\cdot)$ is larger than one in absolute value. (See Drazen and Helpman, 1986, for a discussion of both this and the alternative case.) Since the elasticity of the demand for money with respect to the interest rate is equal to the inverse of the elasticity of $v'(\cdot)$, this implies that m declines as a result of a cut in g_N if and only if the elasticity of money demand is smaller than one. Thus, the curve $m_s^N(b^G)$ in figure 16.2 describes all steady state points that can by attained by means of a cut in g_N with an interest inelastic demand function for money. The fall in m at the time of stabilization will clearly come about via an asset swap in the certainty case (see Drazen and Helpman, 1987).

In the previously discussed cases stabilization at T did not require abandoning the fixed exchange rate. When stabilization is effected via an increase in the rate of monetary growth μ, it must be abandoned. An increase in the rate of monetary growth does not change private consumption levels and the real exchange rate, but it nevertheless affects

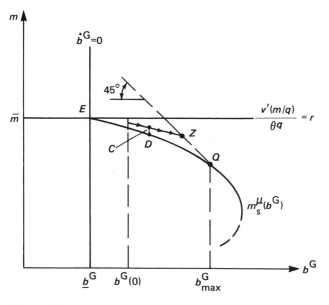

Figure 16.3

both of the steady state loci. After T the rate of depreciation $\dot{\varepsilon}/\varepsilon$ must
equal μ, and (10) implies that an increase in μ shifts down the steady state
value of m. A positive value of μ means that the line $\dot{b}^G = 0$ will be upward
sloping rather than vertical [see (12)], increases in μ shifting the line down.
Therefore, as long as increases in μ increase seignorage the new steady state
point will lie to the southeast of the original point, as does point D relative
to point E in figure 16.3. The locus of steady state combinations can be
represented by the curve $m_s^\mu(b^G)$. We assume that the government chooses
the lowest possible rate of money growth whenever there is more than one
value that can finance the budget deficit. As in the previous case, under
certainty the fall in m at the time of stabilization is brought about via
a run on foreign exchange reserves.

Since a money-based stabilization relies on the collection of an inflation
tax, it will have identical consequences to a tax-based stabilization for consumption, the current account, and debt prior to T as long as preferences
are additively separable between consumption and real money balances.
A difference emerges at T because in anticipation of an inflation tax there
is a run on reserves and a drop in money holdings, while no run takes place
in anticipation of a lump-sum tax (see Drazen and Helpman, 1987).

To summarize the results under certainty, current account developments provide information about what type of stabilization is expected. There will be a deficit on current account when a budget cut on traded goods is expected, a surplus when the expected change is a budget cut on nontraded goods, and a balanced current account when a tax-based or money-based stabilization is expected. Until the point of stabilization money balances are constant, implying no loss of reserves. At the point of stabilization there will be a discrete change in money demand, and hence a run on reserves, in two cases, those of a g_N-based and a money-based stabilization. The first is due to the real exchange rate change that accompanies the stabilization, the second to the accompanying increase in the nominal interest rate. In all cases the path of the nominal exchange rate is continuous not only before a stabilization, but at the point of stabilization as well. In no case is a stabilization whose timing is certain accompanied by a discrete devaluation.

In actual practice, however, a policy of fixing the exchange rate without balancing the budget often puts continual pressure on foreign exchange reserves, causing partial runs that do not imply immediate abandonment of the given policy. Even in the absence of discrete runs, fixing the exchange rate in a way known to be unsustainable in the long run usually causes a continuous loss of reserves. When the policy is abandoned, a discrete nominal devaluation often takes place (see Helpman and Leiderman, 1987). None of these observed phenomena can be explained by the certainty model, but, as will be shown below, can arise when there is uncertainty about the timing of a stabilization.

16.4. The Importance of Timing Uncertainty

We now return to the more general formulation to show how timing uncertainty can explain the above phenomena. Under uncertainty, the first-order conditions (5)–(7) have a number of implications. First, as t approaches $T_{\max}$, they imply

$$\theta^s(T_{\max}) = \theta(T_{\max}) \tag{13}$$

and

$$\varepsilon^s(T_{\max}) = \varepsilon(T_{\max}). \tag{14}$$

That is, at the moment at which stabilization is sure to take place if it did not take place before, there can be no jump in the marginal utility of consumption of tradables or in the exchange rate. This stems from the fact that at $T_{\max}^-$ there is no residual uncertainty, so that we obtain the same results as in the case of certainty.

Differentiation of the first-order conditions with respect to t, taking into account the fact that the exchange rate is fixed prior to stabilization and assuming that $F(T)$ is differentiable for $T < T_{\max}$, yields

$$\frac{\dot{\theta}}{\theta} = \frac{f}{1 - F}\left(1 - \frac{\theta^s}{\theta}\right) \qquad \text{for} \quad t < T_{\max} \tag{15}$$

and

$$\frac{v'}{\theta q} = r + \frac{f}{1 - F}\frac{\theta^s}{\theta}\left[1 - \frac{\varepsilon}{\varepsilon^s}\right] \qquad \text{for} \quad t < T_{\max}, \tag{16}$$

where f is the density function of F, and t has been suppressed in these equations. The right-hand side of (16) represents the nominal interest rate, which equals the interest on foreign currency denominated assets plus a term reflecting the expected capital gain or loss on nominal balance holdings as a result of a possible exchange rate jump. This last term is the product of the density of a stabilization at t conditional on no stabilization having occurred until t (the hazard rate), the change in the marginal utility of consumption, and the percentage change in the foreign currency value of nominal balances due to an exchange rate jump.

Given the available financing instruments of the government's consolidated budget, there is a maximum level of debt consistent with a stabilization. Therefore, one expects that if no stabilization has occurred before debt hits some $b_{\max}^G$, then a regime switch must occur at that point in time. More generally, one may argue that the probability of a stabilization grows as $b^G(t)$ approaches $b_{\max}^G$, with a stabilization occurring with certainty sometime between time 0 and the time that $b^G(t)$ hits $b_{\max}^G$. We therefore assume that the conditional density of a stabilization can be expressed as a nondecreasing function of the level of net government debt, namely,

$$\frac{f(t)}{1 - F(t)} = \phi(b^G(t)) \qquad \text{for} \quad t < T_{\max}. \tag{17}$$

The restriction that $F(T_{max}) = 1$ will imply that $\phi(\cdot)$ becomes infinite as debt approaches b^G_{max}, unless the distribution has a mass point at T_{max}.

For τ-based and g-based stabilizations, equilibrium time paths have the same characteristics as in the certainty case, because under certainty the trajectories did not depend on T, the date of stabilization (see Drazen and Helpman, 1986). When stabilization is effected by changes in μ or g_N, however, uncertainty about timing does have an effect.

Consider first a stabilization effected by an increase in the rate of monetary growth, so that (12) is satisfied with $\dot{b}^G = 0$ at the level of government debt attained at the date of stabilization. To analyze this path recall first that since consumption of traded goods is independent of T in the certainty case, it will also be constant over time in this case. The locus of steady state points (the terminal surface) is $m^\mu_s(b^G)$, as in the certainty case, and it is described in figure 16.3. With constant consumption of traded goods the marginal utility of consumption of traded goods is constant before and after a switch, so that, taking account of (17), (16) becomes

$$\frac{v'(m/q)}{\theta q} = r + \phi(b^G)\left[1 - \frac{m^\mu_s(b^G)}{m}\right] \qquad \text{for} \quad t < T_{max}, \tag{16'}$$

where use has been made of the fact that $M^s(t) = M(t)$ for $t < T_{max}$. Since in this case stabilization also implies the abandoning of the fixed exchange rate, there can be no jump in the quantity of money after stabilization. Condition (16') describes a curve in (b^G, m) space on which the system has to be prior to stabilization. The direction of its movement is determined by (8'), which can be reproduced here as

$$\dot{b}^G + \dot{m} = rb^G + g + pg_N - \tau \qquad \text{for} \quad t < T_{max}. \tag{8'}$$

Our assumption is that at time zero the right-hand side of (8') is positive. Therefore, it remains positive if net government debt is rising over time.

The downward-sloping arrow curve in figure 16.3 describes the direction of the system's movement. (See Drazen and Helpman, 1986, for a proof.) On this trajectory net government debt is rising and money holdings are declining. The decline in money holdings results in reserve losses. If a policy switch takes place before point Z is reached, the system jumps downward to the terminal surface, as from C to D. This jump cannot involve a discrete change in money holdings, because the policy switch brings to an end exchange rate stabilization. Hence, the jump results from an unexpected discrete exchange rate devaluation. The figure is drawn on the assumption that $F(\cdot)$ has a mass point at $T_{\max}$. (See Drazen and Helpman, 1986, for details.) Therefore, if no policy switch takes place before the system reaches point Z, then when it reaches this point at $t = T_{\max}^-$, there is a run on reserves that brings it to Q. The exchange rate does not jump at this last moment. Point Z is defined by the intersection of the curve that satisfies (16′) and a 45° line that passes through Q (Q is the point on the terminal surface that corresponds to $b_{\max}^G$).

Our analysis implies that expectations of a money-financed stabilization lead to the same consumption levels and the same evolution of debt as expectations of a tax-based stabilization, but that in the presence of uncertainty they generate different expectations of exchange rate movements and therefore also different trajectories of money holdings. In the latter case no exchange rate jump is expected, while in the former case a devaluation is expected to follow a policy switch at $t < T_{\max}$. Consequently, in the former case there are no changes in the nominal interest rate and money holdings, while in the latter the nominal interest rate rises and money holdings decline over time.

We now consider a stabilization via a cut in expenditures on nontraded goods. For the discussion that follows it is assumed for simplicity that $u(c, c_N)$ is additively separable. In this case c is constant over time and the same as the consumption level for a tax-based and a money-based stabilization, so that the current account is balanced. This stems from the fact that in the certainty case this property of the utility function implies a consumption level that is independent of the timing of stabilization (see Drazen and Helpman, 1986).

When stabilization includes the abandoning of exchange rate management, the dynamic path is once again described by (16′) with the terminal surface for changes in g_N, namely, $m_s^N(b^G)$, replacing $m_s^\mu(b^G)$ on the right-hand side. The system must be on this curve and its direction of movement is given by (8′). The path therefore depends on the characteristics of the terminal surface $m_s^N(b^G)$. As in the previously discussed case, where the interest elasticity of money demand is smaller than one and the terminal surface is falling, the dynamic path will be monotonically falling until the policy switch takes place, as depicted by the downward-sloping arrow path in figure 16.2. At $T_{\max}$ the system reaches point Z if no policy switch took place before that, and then jumps to Q via a run on reserves. If a policy switch takes place before point Z is reached, the system jumps down to the terminal surface, as from point C to point D. This jump results from an unexpected devaluation. The real exchange rate also depreciates.

If the government were to maintain the fixed exchange rate also after stabilization, then an unexpected policy switch would not result in an exchange rate jump, but rather in a run on reserves that would bring the system instantaneously to the terminal surface. In this case (16) implies that prior to stabilization the system moves on the horizontal line in figure 16.2, as in the certainty case, and if an unexpected policy switch takes place when it reaches point A, it jumps instantaneously to point B. Point B is the intersection point between the terminal surface and a 45° line that passes through A.

Hence, if the fixed exchange rate is not maintained after stabilization, the dynamic trajectory prior to stabilization is characterized by a rising nominal interest rate and a continuous reserve loss as a result of the decline in money holdings, followed by a surprise devaluation if the policy switch occurs before $T_{\max}$. If, on the other hand, the fixed exchange rate is maintained after the policy switch, there is no reserve loss on account of changes in the demand for money, but there is a run on reserves immediately following the policy switch.

To summarize, the above analysis demonstrates a number of effects of timing uncertainty for the non-traded-goods and money-based stabilizations. Before a stabilization there will be a gradual decline in money holdings brought about by a continuous loss of reserves. This arises from the nominal interest rate rising over time, reflecting a rising risk premium (which in turn reflects our assumption about the conditional probability of a switch being an increasing function of government debt). Moreover, a discrete jump in the nominal exchange rate will accompany a stabilization whenever exchange rate management is abandoned (except when there is no residual uncertainty about its timing). These characteristics are consistent with actually observed episodes, such as those discussed in Helpman and Leiderman (1987).

Timing uncertainty may generate even richer time paths, a few examples of which we now quickly discuss. In the case of a stabilization expected to be effected by a budget cut on nontraded goods, the slope of the terminal surface $m_s^N(b^G)$ will be positive when the interest elasticity of money demand is larger than one, and will change sign if money demand is neither everywhere elastic nor everywhere inelastic. In the first case the time path for real balances may be nonmonotonic, while in the second case it must be nonmonotonic, as inspection of (16′) indicates when $m_s^N(b^G)$ replaces $m_s^u(b^G)$. Nonmonotonicity means we will have alternating periods of reserve gains and losses even with no money financing of the budget.

The above discussion on nontraded goods relied on the assumption that $u(\cdot)$ is additively separable; that is, $u_{12} = 0$. Nonseparability makes things more complicated. For u_{12} positive but small one can show that the qualitative features of the dynamics described above will not change, except that the current account will be at least initially in surplus rather than being balanced. (A fuller discussion of this and the above extensions may be found in Drazen and Helpman, 1986.)

Finally, the observed phenomenon of partial runs on reserves not necessarily associated with a breakdown of fixed exchange rates arises in our model when the density function associated with $F(\cdot)$ is not continuous (see also Drazen and Helpman, 1986, for a discussion of mass points). For example, suppose that $F(\cdot)$ is continuous, but the density function $f(\cdot)$ has one point of discontinuity at which it jumps up. The economic interpretation of this is that if a particular point in time is reached and a policy change has not taken place so far, then the chances of a policy change in the near future increase discretely. This point in time may be associated with political or other relevant events. Clearly, the upward jump in $f(\cdot)$ induces an upward jump in the hazard-rate function $\phi(\cdot)$. Now suppose that stabilization is expected to be effected by money financing and hence the abandonment of the fixed exchange rate. Then it is clear from (16′) that in this case the downward sloping arrow path in figure 16.3 is discontinuous at the debt level at which $\phi(\cdot)$ is discontinuous. In particular, it consists of two parts, with the part further to the right being lower. The discontinuity reflects a downward jump in the demand for money that results from an upward jump of the interest rate. In turn, the upward jump in the interest rate is caused by an upward jump of the risk premium reflecting the jump in the conditional density $\phi(\cdot)$. Since these jumps are fully expected once this point in time is reached, the discrete adjustment of money balances will be effected by a run on reserves that will shift the system from the higher to the lower branch of the adjustment path. If no regime switch takes place at this point in time, the economy moves on the lower branch. Hence, the model explains runs on reserves that are not associated with a collapse of the exchange rate policy.

Appendix

In this appendix, we derive the first-order conditions when the date T of a switch is unknown. These will also apply to the certainty case when the probability distribution has all its mass at a single T. When the cumulative distribution of a switch occurring until T is $F(T)$, maximization of the expected value of (1) subject to constraints (2′) and (3) may be written [where $b(T)$ has been calculated by integrating (2′)]

$$
\begin{aligned}
\max_{\{c(t),c_N(t),M(t),z(t),\Delta M(t_i)\}} & \int_0^{T_{max}} \left[\int_0^T e^{-rt}\left[u(c(t),c_N(t)) + v\left(\frac{M(t)}{Q(t)}\right)\right] dt \right. \\
& + e^{-rT}V^s\left(e^{rT}b_0 - \int_0^T e^{r(T-t)}\left[c(t) + \frac{P_N(t)}{\varepsilon(t)}c_N(t) + \frac{z(t)}{\varepsilon(t)} + \tau(t) - y \right.\right. \\
& \left. - \frac{P_N(t)}{\varepsilon(t)}y_N\right] dt - \sum_{t_i \leqslant T} e^{r(T-t_i)}\frac{\Delta M(t_i)}{\varepsilon(t_i)} + \frac{M_0 + \int_0^T z(x)\,dx + \sum_{t_i \leqslant T}\Delta M(t_i)}{\varepsilon(T)}; T\bigg) \\
& \left. + \int_0^T \gamma(t)\left[M_0 + \int_0^T z(x)\,dx + \sum_{t_i \leqslant t}\Delta M(t_i) - M(t)\right]\right] dF(T),
\end{aligned}
$$

(A1)

where $\gamma(t)$ is the multiplier on constraint (3) in the text. Maximization of (A1) with respect to each of the $c(t)$, $c_N(t)$, $M(t)$, and $z(t)$ yields [where $\theta(t)$ is the marginal utility of traded goods at time t, $u_2(t)$ is the marginal utility of nontraded goods, and where superscript s indicates the variable after stabilization]

$$
\int_t^{T_{max}} e^{-rt}\theta(t)\,dF(T) = \int_t^{T_{max}} e^{-rt}\theta^s(T)\,dF(T),
$$

(A2)

$$
\int_t^{T_{max}} e^{-rt}u_2(t)\,dF(T) = \int_t^{T_{max}} e^{-rt}\theta^s(T)\frac{P_N(t)}{\varepsilon(t)}\,dF(T),
$$

(A3)

$$
\int_t^{T_{max}} e^{-rt}v'(t)\frac{1}{Q(t)}\,dF(T) = \int_t^{T_{max}} \gamma(t)\,dF(T),
$$

(A4)

$$
\int_t^{T_{max}} \left[e^{-rT}\theta^s(T)\left(-\frac{e^{r(T-t)}}{\varepsilon(t)} + \frac{1}{\varepsilon^s(T)}\right) + \int_t^T \gamma(x)\,dx\right] dF(T) = 0.
$$

(A5)

Maximization with respect to $\Delta M(t_i)$ yields a condition identical to (A5) for $t = t_i$. (A2) simplifies to

$$
\theta(t) = \int_t^{T_{max}} \theta^s(T)\frac{dF(T)}{1 - F(t)}.
$$

(A6)

(A3) then yields equation (6). Since (A4) implies $\gamma(t) = e^{-rt}v'(t)[1/Q(t)]$, (A5) becomes

$$
\frac{1}{\varepsilon(t)} = \frac{1}{\theta(t)}\int_t^{T_{max}} \left[e^{-r(T-t)}\frac{\theta^s(T)}{\varepsilon^s(T)} + \int_t^T e^{-r(x-t)}\frac{v'(x)}{Q(x)}\,dx\right]\frac{dF(T)}{1 - F(t)}.
$$

(A7)

As t approaches T_{max}, (A2) implies that $\theta(T_{max}) = \theta^s(T_{max})$, while (A6) implies that $\varepsilon(T_{max}) = \varepsilon^s(T_{max})$. Differentiation of (A6) when $F(T)$ is differentiable yields equation (15), while differentiation of (A7) when ε is constant, taking account of (15), yields equation (16).

References

Drazen, Allan, and Elhanan Helpman, "Stabilization with Exchange Rate Management," Working Paper No. 41-86, Foerder Institute for Economic Research, Tel Aviv University (November 1986).

Drazen, Allan, and Elhanan Helpman, "Stabilization with Exchange Rate Management," *Quarterly Journal of Economics* 11 (1987), 835–855.

Flood, Robert D., and Peter M. Garber, "Collapsing Exchange Rate Regimes: Some Linear Examples," *Journal of International Economics* 17 (1984), 1–13.

Helpman, Elhanan, and Leonardo Leiderman, "Slowdown of Devaluations, Monetary Accommodation, and Inflation: A Comparison of Argentina, Chile and Israel," *The Economic Quarterly* 38 (1987), 19–33 (Hebrew).

Krugman, Paul R., "A Model of Balance-of-Payments Crises," *Journal of Money, Credit and Banking* 11 (1979), 311–325.

17 The Irrelevance of Government Foreign Exchange Operations

Thomas J. Sargent and Bruce D. Smith

Introduction

Governments sometimes intervene in foreign exchange markets to influence exchange rates. Often these interventions are thought of as pure open market operations, and have been modeled by having one government exchange domestic currency for foreign currencies, with own-country fiscal policy being held fixed and with other governments holding both their monetary and their fiscal policies fixed.

This chapter analyzes the effects of such open market exchanges in the context of a model in which there obtains a version of the monetary approach to exchange rate determination. We find that with own-country fiscal policy held fixed, open market exchanges in foreign currency leave the equilibrium exchange rate unaltered. This result, which is a version of a Modigliani-Miller theorem for government finance,[1] holds even though the equilibrium being studied is one in which government currency is dominated in rate of return by other assets, possibly including the currencies of other governments.

Our model also has implications about the endogeneity of the domestic money supply under a fixed exchange rate regime. Under the monetary theory of the exchange rate, it is often asserted that if a small country chooses to peg its exchange rate, it must as a consequence accept an endogenously and uniquely determined money supply. Given a fixed fiscal policy, the currency stock of a small country is said to be determined by the requirement to peg its exchange rate. Contrary to this assertion, our model has the property that the currency stock of a small country pegging its exchange rate is not pinned down. This is simply another aspect of a general Modigliani-Miller theorem for government finance that asserts the indeterminacy of the gross government portfolio under a fixed fiscal policy.

Modigliani-Miller theorems for exchanges in foreign currencies can be attained by extending the analysis of Wallace (1981) to a multicountry context, but retaining Wallace's specifications leads to an absence of rate

The views expressed in this chapter are solely those of the authors and do not necessarily reflect the views of the staff, officers, or Board of Overseers of the Hoover Institution. Sargent's research was supported by a grant from the National Science Foundation to the University of Minnesota, NSF SES 8508935.

of return dominance (see Manuelli and Sargent, 1987). In multiple-country models, absence of rate of return dominance implies exchange rate indeterminacy (see Kareken and Wallace, 1981). The purpose of this chapter is to show that Modigliani-Miller theorems for government foreign exchange operations also obtain in environments in which government currencies are dominated in rate of return.[2] Equilibria in which government issued currencies are dominated in rate of return underlie the monetary approach to exchange rate determination.

In order to obtain an environment in which government currency is potentially dominated in rate of return in equilibrium, we use a two-country version of the economy studied by Sargent and Smith (1987). Their economy modifies the one originally studied by Wallace (1981) by imposing a set of legal restrictions on private agents' portfolios that have the purpose of separating markets for country-specific currencies from markets for credit. The legal restrictions that we impose deliver a captive demand for the currency of at least one government, shielding it from potentially annihilating competition with higher yielding assets. After the economy and its equilibrium have been described, we shall proceed to characterize an equivalence class of policies for a single government that support a given equilibrium allocation of goods. We find that this equivalence class is nonsingular, and contains policies that can be interpreted as open market exchanges in foreign currencies. Choices from among these policies leave both the nominal exchange rate and the real allocation of goods unaltered.

17.1. The Model

17.1.1. Physical Environment and Markets

In this section we lay out the physical environment and the structure of markets in which agents operate. At each date $t = 1, 2, \ldots$, there is born a set $H(t)$ of two period lived agents. Members of $H(t)$ are indexed by h. Agent $h \in H(t)$ faces an endowment stream of the single consumption good given by $[y_t^h(t), y_{ti}^h(t + 1)]$, where the second period endowment may be contingent on the realization of a random variable $x(t + 1)$. The random variable $x(t + 1)$ can take on the values $\{x_1, x_2, \ldots, x_I\}$. We let $f_i = \text{prob}\{x(t) = x_i\}$, so that the stochastic process $x(t)$ is independently and identically distributed through time. We let $y_t^h(t)$ and $y_{ti}^h(t + 1)$ refer to gross of tax endowments. We let $[w_t^h(t), w_{ti}^h(t + 1)]$ denote the net of tax endowment stream of agent h. Also, we let $\underline{w}_t^h(t + 1) \equiv [w_{t1}^h(t + 1), \ldots, w_{tI}^h(t + 1)]$.

The random variable $x(t + 1)$ governs the return to physical storage of the good. We let $k^h(t)$ denote the storage of agent $h \in H(t)$. Storage of $k^h(t)$ units returns $x(t + 1)k^h(t)$ at $t + 1$. We assume $x_i > 0 \: \forall i$.

In addition to storage, there are two other kinds of assets that are traded in the model. There is a market for state contingent claims, a market that is international in scope. Let $d_i^h(t)$ be the number of claims for delivery of one unit of the good in state i at time $t + 1$ bought by $h \in H(t)$. We assume that $x(t)$ is realized before economic decisions are made at t. Hence members of $H(t)$ do not trade claims for state contingent delivery at t. State contingent claims for delivery of one unit in state i at time $t + 1$ trade for $s_i(t)$ units of the time t consumption good, which is the numeraire. We let $\underline{s}(t) = [s_1(t), \ldots, s_I(t)]$.

The third type of asset that is traded is fiat currency. We restrict consideration to a two-country world.[3] Let q index countries; $q = 1, 2$. The government of country q has $M^q(t)$ units of its currency outstanding at t. The price of country q's currency in terms of the date t consumption good (the inverse price level) is $p_i^q(t)$ if $x(t) = x_i$. We will often suppress the subscript and denote the inverse price level by $p^q(t)$.

We let $c_t^h(t)$ denote the consumption of $h \in H(t)$, and $c_{ti}^h(t + 1)$ denote the old age consumption of agent h in state i. Agent $h \in H(t)$ has preferences over non-negative vectors $[c_t^h(t), \underline{c}_t^h(t + 1)]$ that are represented by $\sum f_i u^h[c_t^h(t), c_{ti}^h(t + 1)]$, where $u^h(\cdot)$ is strictly increasing in each argument, is concave, and is twice continuously differentiable, and $\underline{c}_t^h(t + 1) = [c_{t1}^h(t + 1), \ldots, c_{tI}^h(t + 1)]$.

In addition to the agents described above, there is a set of initial old agents at $t = 1$, who are members of $H(0)$. For simplicity we let $k^h(0) = 0 \: \forall h \in H(0)$. Agent $h \in H(0)$ has an after tax endowment $w_0^h(1)$, and an endowment $m^{hq}(0)$ of the currency of country q. Then $c_0^h(1) = w_0^h(1) + \sum_q p^q(1)m^{hq}(0)$. Agent $h \in H(0)$ supplies his currency holdings inelastically at $t = 1$.

The final aspects of the environment to be discussed are the legal restrictions that we impose on private agents. The restrictions are motivated by Sargent and Wallace (1982), and are meant to separate "money" from "credit" markets. In particular, we partition $H(t)$ into four groups. Two of these groups we denote $H^{p1}(t)$ and $H^{p2}(t)$. Following Sargent and Wallace (1982) we refer to these agents as "the poor." For $h \in H^{pq}(t)$, agent h is a resident of country q, and is precluded from storing the good, trading state contingent claims, or holding the currency of country $\bar{q}$ (where $\bar{q}$

means "the other" country). Thus for $h \in H^{pq}(t)$, our legal restrictions are of the form $k^h(t) = d_i^h(t) = m^{h\bar{q}}(t) = 0$. We let $H^p(t) \equiv H^{p1}(t) \cup H^{p2}(t)$, and $H^{p1}(t) \cap H^{p2}(t) = \varnothing$ (poor agents are immobile across countries). In addition, there are groups $H^{R1}(t)$ and $H^{R2}(t)$, the so-called "rich." Members of $H^{Rq}(t)$ may trade any assets and may trade internationally. The only restriction they face is that $\forall h \in H^{Rq}(t)$, $m^{hq}(t) \geqslant 0 \; \forall q$. This restriction prevents "the rich" from arbitraging between money and credit markets. Again $H^R(t) \equiv H^{R1}(t) \cup H^{R2}(t)$ and $H^{R1}(t) \cap H^{R2}(t) = \varnothing$. Also $H^R(t) \cap H^p(t) = \varnothing$, $H^R(t) \cup H^p(t) = H(t)$.

17.1.2. Behavior of Agents

i. *"Rich" Agents* As in Sargent and Smith (1987), rich agents choose $c_t^h(t)$, $c_{ti}^h(t + 1)$, $k^h(t)$, $m^{h1}(t)$, $m^{h2}(t)$, and $\underline{d}^h(t) \equiv [d_1^h(t), \ldots, d_I^h(t)]$ to maximize

$$\sum_i f_i u^h[c_t^h(t), c_{ti}^h(t + 1)]$$

subject to

$$c_t^h(t) + k^h(t) + \sum_q m^{hq}(t)p^q(t) + \sum_i s_i(t)d_i^h(t) \leqslant w_t^h(t), \tag{1}$$

$$c_{ti}^h(t + 1) \leqslant w_{ti}^h(t + 1) + x_i k^h(t)$$
$$+ d_i^h(t) + \sum_q p_i^q(t + 1)m^{hq}(t), \qquad i = 1, \ldots, I, \tag{2}$$

$$k^h(t) \geqslant 0, \qquad m^{hq}(t) \geqslant 0. \tag{3}$$

Computations described in Sargent-Smith (1987) permit one to show that an absence of arbitrage opportunities for rich agents requires

$$\sum_i s_i(t)x_i \leqslant 1 \qquad \forall t \geqslant 1, \tag{4}$$

$$\sum_i s_i(t)p_i^q(t + 1) \leqslant p_j^q(t) \qquad \forall j, \forall t \geqslant 1, \; \forall q. \tag{5}$$

If (5) holds with strict inequality for some q, the currency of country q is dominated in rate of return. We henceforth focus on situations for which (4) holds with equality.

Since $m^{hq}(t) \geqslant 0 \; \forall h \in H^R(t)$, (4) and (5) and computations described by Sargent and Smith (1987) serve to reduce (1) and (2) to

$$c_t^h(t) + \underline{s}(t)\underline{c}_t^h(t + 1) \leqslant w_t^h(t) + \underline{s}(t)\underline{w}_t^h(t + 1), \tag{6}$$

where $\underline{c}_t^h(t + 1) \equiv [c_{t1}^h(t + 1), \ldots, c_{tI}^h(t + 1)]$. Agents with $h \in H^R(t)$ maxi-

mize $\sum_i f_i u^h [c_t^h(t), c_{ti}^h(t + 1)]$ subject to (6). This maximization gives rise
to the demand functions

$$c_t^h(t) = q^h [\underline{s}(t), w_t^h(t), \underline{w}_t^h(t + 1)], \tag{7a}$$

$$c_{ti}^h(t + 1) = q_i^h [\underline{s}(t), w_t^h(t), \underline{w}_t^h(t + 1)], \qquad i = 1, \ldots, I. \tag{7b}$$

ii. *"Poor" Agents*   Poor agents with $h \in H^{pq}(t)$ choose $c_t^h(t)$, $c_{ti}^h(t + 1)$, and
$m^{hq}(t)$ to maximize

$$\sum_i f_i u^h [c_t^h(t), c_{ti}^h(t + 1)]$$

subject to

$$c_t^h(t) + p^q(t) m^{hq}(t) \leqslant w_t^h(t), \tag{8a}$$

$$c_{ti}^h(t + 1) \leqslant w_{ti}^h(t + 1) + p_i^q(t + 1) m^{hq}(t), \qquad i = 1, \ldots, I. \tag{8b}$$

Equation (8) implies the sequence of budget constraints

$$c_t^h(t) + \frac{p^q(t)}{p_i^q(t + 1)} c_{ti}^h(t + 1)$$

$$\leqslant w_t^h(t) + \frac{p^q(t)}{p_i^q(t + 1)} w_{ti}^h(t + 1), \qquad i = 1, \ldots, I. \tag{9}$$

Agents with $h \in H^{pq}(t)$ can be viewed as choosing $c_t^h(t)$ and $c_{ti}^h(t + 1)$ to
maximize $\sum_i f_i u^h [c_t^h(t), c_{ti}^h(t + 1)]$ subject to (9). This maximization problem
gives rise to the following demand functions for young period consumption
and real balances for $h \in H^{pq}(t)$:

$$c_t^h(t) = g^h [p^q(t), \underline{p}^q(t + 1), w_t^h(t), \underline{w}_t^h(t + 1)], \tag{10}$$

$$p^q(t) m^{hq}(t) = w_t^h(t) - c_t^h(t). \tag{11}$$

The implied values for $c_{ti}^h(t + 1)$ are

$$c_{ti}^h(t + 1) = w_{ti}^h(t + 1) + \frac{p_i^q(t + 1)}{p^q(t)} p^q(t) m^{hq}(t), \qquad i = 1, \ldots, I. \tag{12}$$

iii. *Governments*   The government of country q stores $K^q(t)$, purchases
$G_i^q(t)$ units of the good for government consumption (which does not con-
tribute to future stocks), collects taxes $T_{t-1,i}^{hq}(t)$ from old agent $h \in H(t - 1)$
and $T_t^{hq}(t)$ from young agent $h \in H(t)$, and circulates $M^q(t)$ units of fiat
currency. In addition, the government of country q holds $M_{\bar{g}}^{\bar{q}}(t)$ units of

the country $\bar{q}$ (other country's) currency as a foreign exchange reserve. Notice that we permit each government to tax (or make transfers to) residents of other countries. It is important that this assumption can be dispensed with. In Sargent and Smith (1987) we show that if the government is permitted to trade a sufficiently rich set of state contingent securities, then fiscal policy can be held constant in the manner required by our theorem without governments having to alter taxes and transfers. That result means that in the present context we need only assume that the government of country q can engage in asset exchanges with residents of all countries, and need not literally require that it have the ability to levy taxes or transfers on foreign residents.

The choices of government policy sequences are required to satisfy the following sequence of government budget constraints:

$$K^q(t) + G_i^q(t) = \sum_{H(t-1)} T_{t-1,i}^{hq}(t) + \sum_{H(t)} T_t^{hq}(t) + x_i K^q(t-1)$$

$$+ p^q(t)[M^q(t) - M^q(t-1)] - p^{\bar{q}}(t)[M_g^{\bar{q}}(t) \tag{13}$$

$$- M_g^{\bar{q}}(t-1)], \qquad i = 1, \ldots, I, \quad t \geqslant 1.$$

Also, notice that

$$w_t^h(t) = y_t^h(t) - T_t^{h1}(t) - T_t^{h2}(t), \tag{14}$$

$$w_{ti}^h(t+1) = y_{ti}^h(t+1) - T_{ti}^{h1}(t+1) - T_{ti}^{h2}(t+1), \qquad i = 1, \ldots, I. \tag{15}$$

The quantities $w_0^h(1)$, $h \in H(0)$, $M^q(0)$, $M_g^q(0)$, and $K^q(0)$, $q = 1, 2$, are given as initial conditions. As an auxiliary assumption, we henceforth assume that

$$\sum_{H(t)} y_t^h(t) + \sum_{H(t-1)} y_{t-1,i}^h(t) = Y(t), \tag{16}$$

where $Y(t)$ is an exogeneous positive and nonstochastic sequence.

17.2. Equilibrium with Both Currencies Dominated in Rate of Return

Since we wish to avoid exchange rate indeterminacy, we require the currency of at least one country to be dominated in rate of return. Our results need to be stated somewhat differently depending on whether only one currency is dominated in return or both are dominated. We begin with the simplest case, which is the one where both currencies are dominated. A sufficient condition for both currencies to be inferior in rate of return (see Sargent–Smith, 1987) is

$$x_i \geq \frac{p_i^q(t+1)}{p_j^q(t)} \qquad \forall i, j, t, q, \tag{17}$$

with strict inequality for some i, $\forall j, t, q$.

Using this assumption, $m^{hq}(t) = 0 \ \forall h \in H^R(t)$, $\forall q$. Hence equilibrium in currency markets requires

$$\sum_{H^{pq}(t)} m^{hq}(t) + M_g^q(t) = M^q(t), \qquad q = 1, 2, \quad \forall t \geq 1,$$

or using (11),[4]

$$\sum_{H^{pq}(t)} [w_t^h(t) - c_t^h(t)] = p^q(t)[M^q(t) - M_g^q(t)], \qquad q = 1, 2. \tag{18}$$

Equilibrium in markets for state contingent claims requires that

$$\sum_{H(t)} d_i^h(t) = 0 \qquad \forall i, t. \tag{19}$$

This condition may be expressed more conveniently as follows. Sum (2) over $H^R(t)$, use $m^{hq}(t) = 0 \ \forall h \in H^R(t)$ and $d_i^h(t) = 0 \ \forall h \in H^P(t)$, and note (19) to obtain

$$\sum_{H^R(t)} c_{ti}^h(t+1) = \sum_{H^R(t)} w_{ti}^h(t+1) + x_i \sum_{H^R(t)} k^h(t), \qquad i = 1, \dots, I, \tag{20}$$

with $c_{ti}^h(t+1)$ given by (7b). Equations (20) are goods market equilibrium conditions.

We now define the following terms. The *government policy* of country q consists of the sequences $\{K^q(t)\}$, $\{G_i^q(t)\}$, $\{T_{t-1,i}^{hq}(t)\}$, $\{T_t^{hq}(t)\}$, $\{M^q(t)\}$, and $\{M_g^{\bar{q}}(t)\}$, which are chosen subject to (13). An *allocation* consists of a set of values $c_0^h(1)$, $h \in H(0)$; a set of sequences $\{G_i^q(t)\}$, $\{c_t^h(t)\}$, $\{c_{ti}^h(t+1)\}$, $h \in H(t)$, $i = 1, \dots, I$; and a sequence $\{K(t)\}$, where we define

$$K(t) \equiv \sum_{H^R(t)} k^h(t) + \sum_q K^q(t).$$

A *price system* is a set of sequences $\{\underline{s}(t)\}$, $\{p^q(t)\}$, $q = 1, 2$. Given a sequence $\{Y(t)\}$ and a stochastic process $x(t)$, an *equilibrium* (with both currencies dominated in rate of return) is a pair of government policies, an allocation, and a price system that together satisfy (4), (7), (10)–(12), (17) (with strict inequality for some i, $\forall j$, t), (18), and (20).

Our definition of equilibrium is agnostic with respect to what are "endogenous" and what are "exogenous" variables. For instance, if government policies are exogenous and the sequences $\{p^q(t)\}$ are endogenous, then the exchange rate sequence $\{e(t)\} = \{p^1(t)/p^2(t)\}$ is endogenous, which is to say that we have a flexible exchange rate regime. If, on the other hand, the sequence $\{e(t)\}$ is exogenously given, then government policy choices may be viewed as being endogenous and restricted by the requirements of adhering to fixed exchange rates. The agnosticism of our definition permits us to study fixed, flexible, and intermediate exchange rate regimes.

17.3. An Irrelevance Theorem

The structure of our irrelevance theorem takes the following form. Suppose there exist equilibrium sequences of government policies, allocations, and prices. Denote these sequences the $(\bar{\ })$ equilibrium. Our theorem describes an equivalence class of government policies that support the $(\bar{\ })$ allocation and the $(\bar{\ })$ price system as an equilibrium. We denote the new equilibrium the $(\hat{\ })$ equilibrium. We shall describe a $(\hat{\ })$ equilibrium consistent with

$$\hat{c}_t^h(t) = \bar{c}_t^h(t), \qquad \forall t \geqslant 1, \quad \forall h \in H(t), \tag{21}$$

$$\hat{c}_{ti}^h(t+1) = \bar{c}_{ti}^h(t+1), \qquad \forall t \geqslant 1, \quad \forall h \in H(t), \quad \forall i, \tag{22}$$

$$\hat{s}_i(t) = \bar{s}_i(t), \qquad \forall i, t \geqslant 1, \tag{23}$$

$$\hat{p}_i^q(t) = \bar{p}_i^q(t), \qquad \forall i, t, q, \tag{24}$$

$$\hat{K}(t) = \hat{K}^1(t) + \hat{K}^2(t) + \sum_{H^R(t)} \hat{k}^h(t)$$

$$= \bar{K}^1(t) + \bar{K}^2(t) + \sum_{H^R(t)} \bar{k}^h(t) \tag{25}$$

$$= \bar{K}(t), \qquad \forall t \geqslant 1.$$

We now assert the following:

THEOREM Suppose the existence of an initial $(\bar{\ })$ equilibrium. Consider a set of government policies satisfying (14), (15), $\bar{G}_i^q(t) = \hat{G}_i^q(t)$ $\forall i, t, q$,

$$\hat{w}_t^h(t) + \underline{s}(t)\hat{w}_t^h(t+1) = \bar{w}_t^h(t) + \underline{s}(t)\underline{w}_t^h(t+1), \qquad h \in H^R(t), \tag{26}$$

$$\hat{w}_t^h(t) + \frac{\bar{p}^q(t)}{\bar{p}_i^q(t+1)} \hat{w}_{ti}^h(t+1)$$

$$= \bar{w}_t^h(t) + \frac{\bar{p}^q(t)}{\bar{p}_i^q(t+1)} \bar{w}_{ti}^h(t+1), \qquad \forall i, \quad \forall h \in H^{pq}(t), \quad \forall q,$$

(27)

$$\sum_{H^{pq}(t)} [\hat{w}_t^h(t) - \bar{w}_t^h(t)]$$

$$= \bar{p}^q(t)[\hat{M}^q(t) - \overline{M}^q(t)] - \bar{p}^q(t)[\hat{M}_g^q(t) - \overline{M}_g^q(t)], \qquad q = 1, 2,$$

(28)

$$\sum_{H^R(t)} [\hat{w}_{ti}^h(t+1) - \bar{w}_{ti}^h(t+1)] = x_i[\hat{K}^1(t) + \hat{K}^2(t) - \bar{K}^1(t) - \bar{K}^2(t)], \qquad (29)$$

and such that the policies of one government are fixed at their levels in the $(^-)$ equilibrium. All such $(^\wedge)$ policies support the $(^-)$ allocation and price system as an equilibrium.

In order to interpret the theorem in terms of government asset exchanges, it is useful to fix the policy sequences of one government (say, $q = 2$), and use (26), (28), and (29) to obtain

$$\bar{p}^1(t)[\hat{M}^1(t) - \overline{M}^1(t)] = [\hat{K}^1(t) - \bar{K}^1(t)] + \bar{p}^2(t)[\hat{M}_g^2(t) - \overline{M}_g^2(t)]$$

$$+ \sum_{H(t)} [\hat{w}_t^h(t) - \bar{w}_t^h(t)].$$

(30)

In the special case that $\sum [\hat{w}_t^h(t) - \bar{w}_t^h(t)] = 0 \ \forall t$, equation (30) describes a set of asset exchanges by government 1. If $\hat{K}^1(t) = \bar{K}^1(t) \ \forall t$ as well, (30) describes a sequence of open market exchanges of currencies. The theorem implies that under a flexible exchange rate regime such exchanges leave the stochastic process for the exchange rate unaffected.[5] The theorem also implies that under a fixed exchange rate regime, with a given price system and a given government policy for country 2, the currency supply process for country 1 is not uniquely determined. Conditions (26)–(29) can be given an interpretation in terms of "holding fiscal policy constant" as in Wallace (1981) or Sargent and Smith (1987).

The theorem just stated can be proved by construction by extending in minor ways the proof given by Sargent and Smith (1987). Here we briefly present a quicker (but less informative) proof. First note that (23) and (26) imply that (21) and (22) satisfy (7) $\forall h \in H^R(t)$. In addition (24) and (27) imply that optimizing consumption choices for all $h \in H^p(t)$ satisfy (21) and (22). Since $w_0^h(1)$ is fixed $\forall h \in H(0)$ and $\hat{p}^q(1) = \bar{p}^q(1)$, $\hat{c}_0^h(1) = \bar{c}_0^h(1) \ \forall h \in H(0)$. Thus the optimizing choices of consumption values are unchanged for private agents. Second, (28), (21), (11), and (18) imply that the sequences $\{\bar{p}_i^q(t)\}$ continue to be market clearing sequences, $q = 1, 2$.

Third, to see that state contingent claims markets clear if (21)–(23) and (25) hold, sum (2) over $H^R(t)$ for both the $(\hat{})$ and $(\bar{})$ equilibria, and subtract to obtain

$$\sum_{H^R(t)} [\hat{w}_{ti}^h(t + 1) - \bar{w}_{ti}^h(t + 1)] + x_i \sum_{H^R(t)} [\hat{k}^h(t) - \bar{k}^h(t)]$$

$$+ \sum_{H^R(t)} [\hat{d}_i^h(t) - \bar{d}_i^h(t)] = 0 \qquad \forall i, \tag{31}$$

where (22) has been used to obtain (31). Now substitute (25) and (29) into (31) and use $\sum_{H^R(t)} \bar{d}_i^h(t) = 0$ to get $\sum_{H^R(t)} \hat{d}_i^h(t) = 0$. Hence, state contingent claims markets clear when (21)–(29) are satisfied.

It remains to show that the $(\hat{})$ equilibrium satisfies (13) $\forall q$. This is immediate, however, since the $(\hat{})$ equilibrium has been shown to satisfy the budget constraints of all private agents and all market clearing conditions. Moreover, the policy of one government has been fixed, and hence by (24) that government's budget constraint is satisfied. Thus, by Walras's Law, the budget constraint of the remaining agent (the remaining government) must be satisfied. Therefore we have established that the $(\hat{})$ allocation, the $(\hat{})$ price system, and the $(\hat{})$ policies do, in fact, constitute an equilibrium.

It is straightforward to take an initial $(\bar{})$ equilibrium and construct alternative $(\hat{})$ equilibrium sequences. Evidently, then, there are nontrivial equivalence classes of government policy choices supporting given allocations and price systems. These include foreign exchange operations.

As indicated above, conditions (26)–(29) can be given an interpretation in terms of constancy of fiscal policy. Fix the policy of one country (say $q = 2$). Then, following an argument given in Sargent and Smith (1987), equations (26)–(29), (21), (22), and the budget constraint of government 1 can be used to derive

$$\sum_{H(t)} [\hat{w}_{ti}^h(t + 1) - \bar{w}_{ti}^h(t + 1)]$$

$$= x_i [\hat{K}^1(t) - \bar{K}^1(t)] - \frac{\bar{p}_i^1(t + 1)}{\bar{p}^1(t)} \bar{p}^1(t) [\hat{M}^1(t) - \overline{M}^1(t)] \tag{32}$$

$$+ \frac{\bar{p}_i^2(t + 1)}{\bar{p}^2(t)} \bar{p}^2(t) [\hat{M}_g^2(t) - \overline{M}_g^2(t)], \qquad t \geq 1.$$

This is a version of Wallace's (1981) condition requiring the government of country 1 to hold constant the retained earnings on its portfolio across the ($\hat{\ }$) and the ($^-$) equilibria. Equation (32) and equations (26) and (27), which preserve income distributions across individuals [and across states for agents with $h \in H^p(t)$], give the precise sense in which fiscal policy is being held constant across the ($\hat{\ }$) and the ($^-$) equilibria.

Condition (24) precludes the kind of irrelevance theorems described by Chamley and Polemarchakis (1984) in the context of a single-country model. To see why one cannot expect theorems like theirs to hold in two-country environments like ours, note that Chamley and Polemarchakis's scheme for paying out altered earnings on one government's portfolio would require that government to alter its portfolio policy in the face of a fixed policy on the part of the other government. Except under special circumstances, this fixed policy will not remain feasible unless (24) is imposed. It is not generally feasible for the government to engage in foreign exchange operations that simultaneously alter the sequence $\{e(t)\} = \{p^1(t)/p^2(t)\}$, hold fiscal policy constant in the sense described, and do not force the government of the other country to alter its policy.

17.4. An Example

This example parallels that of Sargent and Smith (1987). We let $H^{R1}(t) = H^{R1}$, $H^{R2}(t) = H^{R2}$, $H^{p1}(t) = H^{p1}$, and $H^{p2}(t) = H^{p2}$ $\forall t$. For all h we assume that $u^h[c_t^h(t), c_{ti}^h(t+1)] = \ln c_t^h(t) + \beta \ln c_{ti}^h(t+1)$. We also suppose that $w_{ti}^h(t+1) = w_{tj}^h(t+1)$ $\forall i, j, \forall h \in H^p(t)$, and focus on equilibria satisfying $p_i^q(t) = p_j^q(t)$ $\forall i, j, t, q$. Then, assuming (17) holds $\forall q$ (with strict inequality for some i, $\forall t$) we have the following demand functions:

$$c_t^h(t) = \left(\frac{1}{1 + \beta}\right)[w_t^h(t) + \underline{s}(t)\underline{w}_t^h(t + 1)], \tag{33}$$

$$c_{ti}^h(t + 1) = \left(\frac{\beta}{1 + \beta}\right)\left[\frac{f_i}{s_i(t)}\right]$$
$$\times [w_t^h(t) + \underline{s}(t)\underline{w}_t^h(t + 1)], \qquad i = 1, \dots, I, \quad h \in H^R, \tag{34}$$

$$c_t^h(t) = \left(\frac{1}{1 + \beta}\right)\left[w_t^h(t) + \frac{p^q(t)}{p^q(t + 1)}w_t^h(t + 1)\right], \qquad h \in H^{pq}, \tag{35}$$

$$p^q(t)m^{hq}(t) = \left(\frac{\beta}{1 + \beta}\right)w_t^h(t) - \left(\frac{1}{1 + \beta}\right)\frac{p^q(t)}{p^q(t + 1)}$$
$$\times w_t^h(t + 1), \qquad h \in H^{pq}. \tag{36}$$

Summing (36) over H^{pq} and using the equilibrium condition (18) gives

$$p^q(t)[M^q(t) - M_g^q(t)] = \left(\frac{\beta}{1+\beta}\right) \sum_{H^{pq}} w_t^h(t) - \left(\frac{1}{1+\beta}\right)$$

$$\times \left[\frac{p^q(t)}{p^q(t+1)}\right] \sum_{H^{pq}} w_t^h(t+1), \qquad q = 1, 2. \tag{37}$$

Summing (34) over H^R and using equilibrium condition (20) gives

$$\sum_{H^R} w_{ti}^h(t+1) + x_i \sum_{H^R} \left\{\left(\frac{\beta}{1+\beta}\right) w_t^h(t) - \left(\frac{1}{1+\beta}\right) \underline{s}(t) \underline{w}_t^h(t+1)\right\}$$

$$= \left(\frac{\beta}{1+\beta}\right)\left[\frac{f_i}{\underline{s}_i(t)}\right] \sum_{H^R} [w_t^h(t) + \underline{s}(t)\underline{w}_t^h(t+1)], \quad i = 1, \dots, I, \quad t \geqslant 1. \tag{38}$$

Finally, we assume that gross of tax endowment sequences are given by $y_t^h(t) = y^h \ \forall t, \ y_{ti}^h(t+1) = 0 \ \forall h, i, t.$

17.4.1. Equilibrium ($^-$)

Consider the policy settings $K^q(t) = 0$, $G_i^q(t) = 0$, $w_t^h(t) = y^h$, $w_{ti}^h(t+1) = 0$, $M^q(t) = \overline{M}^q$, $M_g^q(t) = \overline{M}_g^q < \overline{M}^q \ \forall i, t, h, q$. Then the equilibrium for this economy (which operates under a flexible exchange rate regime) is

$$\overline{p}^q(t)(\overline{M}^q - \overline{M}_g^q) = \left(\frac{\beta}{1+\beta}\right) \sum_{H^{pq}} y^h, \qquad q = 1, 2,$$

$$K(t) = \left(\frac{\beta}{1+\beta}\right) \sum_{H^R} y^h,$$

$$\overline{s}_i(t) = \frac{f_i}{x_i}.$$

Notice that $\overline{s}_i(t)$ satisfies (4). Consumption allocations can be found using (33)–(36) and $c_t^h(t+1) = \overline{p}^q(t+1)m^{hq}(t), h \in H^{pq}$.

17.4.2. Equilibrium ($^\wedge$)

Fix all policy settings at their values in the ($^-$) equilibrium, except that $M^1(t) = \hat{M}^1 \neq \overline{M}^1$, $\hat{M}_g^1 = \overline{M}_g^1 + (\overline{p}^1/\overline{p}^2)(\hat{M}^1 - \overline{M}^1)$,

$$\hat{w}_t^h(t) = y^h + [\#H^{p1}]^{-1} \overline{p}^1(\hat{M}^1 - \overline{M}^1), \qquad h \in H^{p1}, \tag{39}$$

$$\hat{w}_t^h(t+1) = -[\#H^{p1}]^{-1} \overline{p}^1(\hat{M}^1 - \overline{M}^1), \qquad h \in H^{p1}, \tag{40}$$

$$\hat{w}_t^h(t) = y^h - [\#H^{p2}]^{-1}\bar{p}^2(\hat{M}_g^1 - \overline{M}_g^1), \qquad h \in H^{p2}, \tag{41}$$

$$\hat{w}_t^h(t + 1) = [\#H^{p2}]^{-1}\bar{p}^2(\hat{M}_g^1 - \overline{M}_g^1), \qquad h \in H^{p2}. \tag{42}$$

Here $\#H^{pq}$ denotes the number of poor agents in country q. Notice that (39)–(42) hold $T_t^{h2}(t)$ and $T_{t-1}^{h2}(t)$ fixed at their initial levels. It can be verified directly that $\hat{p}^q(t) = \bar{p}^q(t) \forall q, t, \hat{s}_i(t) = \bar{s}_i(t) \forall i, t$, that $\hat{K}(t) = \overline{K}(t) \forall t$, and that the remainder of the ($\hat{\ }$) and ($\bar{\ }$) allocations are identical. Thus the once-and-for-all open market exchange of currencies contemplated in moving from the ($\bar{\ }$) to the ($\hat{\ }$) equilibrium has no affects, even on the (constant) exchange rate $e = \bar{p}^1/\bar{p}^2$.

17.5. Equilibrium and Irrelevance with One Currency Dominated in Rate of Return

Nothing in our reasoning requires that both currencies be dominated in rate of return. In this section we examine how our results differ when only one currency is dominated in rate of return. Without loss of generality we let

$$x_i \geqslant \frac{\bar{p}_i^2(t + 1)}{\bar{p}_j^2(t)} \qquad \forall i, j, t, \tag{43}$$

with strict inequality for some $i, \forall j, t$. Since the currency of country 1 is not dominated, (5) implies that

$$\sum_i s_i(t)p_i^1(t + 1) = p_j^1(t) \qquad \forall j, \quad \forall t \geqslant 1. \tag{44}$$

The description of individuals' behavior is unaltered, except that now $m^{h1}(t) > 0$ can hold for $h \in H^R(t)$. Thus the equilibrium conditions are as before, except that (18) is replaced by

$$\sum_{H^R(t)} m^{h1}(t) + \sum_{H^{P1}(t)} m^{h1}(t) + M_g^1(t) = M^1(t) \qquad \forall t \tag{45}$$

[while (18) continues to be the equilibrium condition in the market for country 2 currency], and (20) is replaced by

$$\sum_{H^R(t)} c_{ti}^h(t + 1) = \sum_{H^R(t)} w_{ti}^h(t + 1) + x_i \sum_{H^R(t)} k^h(t)$$

$$+ p_i^1(t + 1) \sum_{H^R(t)} m^{h1}(t), \qquad i = 1, \dots, I. \tag{46}$$

Condition (17) continues to hold (for country 2 only), while (17) for country 1 is replaced by (44).

As before, we assume the existence of an initial ($^-$) equilibrium, and explore alternative ($\hat{}$) equilibrium sequences satisfying (21)–(25) and $\bar{G}_i^q(t) = \hat{G}_i^q(t)$ $\forall i$, q, t, i.e., that preserve the allocation and price system of the initial equilibrium. We prove a result analogous to that stated in section 17.3. The method of proof is to proceed from (21)–(25), to use the equilibrium conditions (4) (with equality), (18) (for country 2), (45), (46), and the demand functions of individual agents to construct an equivalence class of government policies.

First, note that (21)–(24) along with equations (6) and (9) (for each i) imply that the ($\hat{}$) sequences must satisfy

$$\hat{w}_t^h(t) + \underline{s}(t)\hat{w}_t^h(t+1) = \bar{w}_t^h(t) + \underline{s}(t)\bar{w}_t^h(t+1), \qquad h \in H^R(t), \tag{47}$$

$$\hat{w}_t^h(t) + \frac{\bar{p}^q(t)}{\bar{p}_i^q(t+1)}\hat{w}_{ti}^h(t+1)$$

$$= \bar{w}_t^h(t) + \frac{\bar{p}^q(t)}{\bar{p}_i^q(t+1)}\bar{w}_{ti}^h(t+1), \qquad h \in H^{pq}(t). \tag{48}$$

Second, use (25),

$$\sum_{H^R(t)} [\hat{k}^h(t) - \bar{k}^h(t)] = \sum_{H^R(t)} [\hat{w}_t^h(t) - \bar{w}_t^h(t)]$$

$$- \bar{p}^1(t) \sum_{H^R(t)} [\hat{m}^{h1}(t) - \bar{m}^{h1}(t)], \tag{49}$$

$$\sum_{H^R(t)} [\hat{m}^{h1}(t) - \bar{m}^{h1}(t)]$$

$$= \hat{M}^1(t) - \bar{M}^1(t) - [\hat{M}_g^1(t) - \bar{M}_g^1(t)] - \sum_{H^{p1}(t)} [\hat{m}^{h1}(t) - \bar{m}^{h1}(t)], \tag{50}$$

and (11) to obtain

$$[\bar{K}^1(t) + \bar{K}^2(t)] - [\hat{K}^1(t) - \hat{K}^2(t)]$$

$$= \sum_{H^R(t)} [\hat{w}_t^h(t) - \bar{w}_t^h(t)]$$

$$+ \sum_{H^{p1}(t)} [\hat{w}_t^h(t) - \bar{w}_t^h(t)] - p^1(t)[\hat{M}^1(t) - \bar{M}^1(t)]$$

$$+ \bar{p}^1(t)[\hat{M}_g^1(t) - \bar{M}_g^1(t)] \qquad \forall t \geqslant 1. \tag{51}$$

Equation (49) is obtained by summing (1) over $H^R(t)$ and using $\sum_{H^R(t)} d_i^h(t) = 0$ $\forall i$ and (21), while (50) is the market clearing condition for country 1 currency. Equation (51) then describes a relation between policy choices in the ($\hat{\ }$) and ($\bar{\ }$) equilibria.

Third, (24) for country 2 requires (as before) that

$$\bar{p}^2(t)[\hat{M}^2(t) - \overline{M}^2(t)] = \bar{p}^2(t)[\hat{M}_g^2(t) - \overline{M}_g^2(t)]$$
$$+ \sum_{H^{p2}(t)} [\hat{w}_t^h(t) - \overline{w}_t^h(t)], \qquad t \geqslant 1. \tag{52}$$

Equation (52) is obtained by using (18) for $q = 2$ along with (21) for $h \in H^{p2}(t)$. Condition (24) for country 1 requires that

$$\sum_{H^{p1}(t)} [\hat{w}_t^h(t) - \overline{w}_t^h(t)] + \sum_{H^R(t)} [\hat{w}_t^h(t) - \overline{w}_t^h(t)]$$
$$+ \bar{p}^1(t)[\hat{M}_g^1(t) - \overline{M}_g^1(t)]$$
$$= \bar{p}^1(t)[\hat{M}^1(t) - \overline{M}^1(t)] + [\overline{K}^1(t) + \overline{K}^2(t)]$$
$$- [\hat{K}^1(t) + \hat{K}^2(t)], \qquad t \geqslant 1. \tag{53}$$

Equation (53) is obtained by using (45), (11) for $h \in H^{p1}(t)$, (49), and (25). Thus ($\hat{\ }$) policy sequences constructed from (52) and (53) will satisfy (24).

Fourth, in order for the market clearing conditions (46) to be satisfied along with (21)–(25), it is necessary that

$$\sum_{H^R(t)} [\hat{w}_{ti}^h(t+1) - \overline{w}_{ti}^h(t+1)] + x_i \sum_{H^R(t)} [\hat{k}^h(t) - \overline{k}^h(t)]$$
$$+ \frac{\bar{p}_i^1(t+1)}{\bar{p}^1(t)} \bar{p}^1(t) \sum_{H^R(t)} [\hat{m}^{h1}(t) - \overline{m}^{h1}(t)] = 0 \qquad \forall i, t. \tag{54}$$

Equation (54) is obtained by subtracting (46) for the ($\bar{\ }$) equilibrium from (46) for the ($\hat{\ }$) equilibrium and using (22). Substituting (25) into (54), using (50) and (11) for $h \in H^{p1}(t)$, and rearranging gives

$$\sum_{H^R(t)} [\hat{w}_{ti}^h(t+1) - \overline{w}_{ti}^h(t+1)] + \sum_{H^{p1}(t)} [\hat{w}_{ti}^h(t+1) - \overline{w}_{ti}^h(t+1)]$$
$$+ \frac{\bar{p}_i^1(t+1)}{\bar{p}^1(t)} \{\bar{p}^1(t)[\hat{M}^1(t) - \overline{M}^1(t)] - \bar{p}^1(t)[\hat{M}_g^1(t) - \overline{M}_g^1(t)]\} \tag{55}$$
$$= x_i\{[\hat{K}^1(t) + \hat{K}^2(t)] - [\overline{K}^1(t) + \overline{K}^2(t)]\} \qquad \forall i, t.$$

This condition again requires governments to rebate earnings resulting from changes in their portfolios in a particular way.

As a final point, if we multiply both sides of (55) by $s_i(t)$ and sum over i we obtain (53). Hence, (47), (48) (for $i = 1, \ldots, I$), (51), (52), and (55) summarize the restrictions relating the ($^-$) policy choices to the ($^\wedge$) policy choices that support the ($^-$) allocations and ($^-$) price system as an equilibrium.

We are now prepared to state the following.

THEOREM Suppose an initial equilibrium ($^-$) exists. Hold the policy of government $\bar{q}$ fixed at its value for the ($^-$) equilibrium. Consider the class of policies for government $q \neq \bar{q}$ that satisfy (47), (48), (51), (52), (55), and $\bar{G}_i^q(t) = \hat{G}_i^q(t)$. All such policies support the ($^-$) equilibrium allocation and price system.

We have essentially proved the theorem by construction. It only remains to note that the ($^-$) price system continues to satisfy (17) (for $q = 2$) and (44) (for $q = 1$), and that under (24), since the policy of government $\bar{q}$ is fixed, the budget constraint for that government is satisfied $\forall t$. Moreover, all private agents' budget constraints are satisfied by construction, as are all market clearing conditions. Hence, by Walras's Law, the budget constraint of the remaining agent (the government of country q) is satisfied $\forall t$. Thus, all such policies satisfy the complete set of equilibrium conditions, proving the desired result.

17.6. Conclusion

We have described a multicountry model in which government issued currencies are dominated in rate of return in equilibrium. As in Sargent and Wallace (1982), a version of the quantity theory of money holds, and in the present model so does a version of the monetary theory of exchange rates. The model is also characterized by a Modigliani-Miller theorem for government finance. Under a flexible exchange rate regime, this theorem implies that government open market exchanges in foreign currencies are irrelevant in the sense that they leave unaltered an initial equilibrium sequence of prices, exchange rates, and real allocations. Under a fixed exchange rate regime, the theorem implies that a government's gross portfolio, and in particular its currency supply, is not uniquely determined by the requirements of supporting its fixed exchange rate.

Our model does not deny the feasibility of government interventions designed to manage an exchange rate, but it does assert that fiscal policy is required to support successful exchange rate management.

Notes

1. Modigliani-Miller theorems for government asset exchanges describe an equivalence class of government policies, all of which support particular resource allocations as equilibria. Certain versions of these theorems also describe an equivalence class of government policies that leave equilibrium price processes unaltered. Examples of various types of Modigliani-Miller theorems appear in Wallace (1981), Peled (1985), and Chamley and Polemarchakis (1984). The underlying similarity of these theorems is discussed in Sargent (1987).

2. Our desire to do this is motivated in part by the observations cited in Sargent (1983) and Smith (1985a,b), which appear to be consistent with the predictions of the Modigliani-Miller theorem we describe below.

3. In general, these kinds of restrictions simplify exposition, and can readily be relaxed, as can the assumptions of a single good and two-period-lived agents.

4. Notice that condition (18) is of the form of standard money market equilibrium conditions posited in "monetary theories" of exchange rate determination.

5. Alternatively, one could impose $\sum [\hat{w}_i^h(t) - \overline{w}_i^h(t)] = 0$ and $\hat{M}^1(t) = \overline{M}^1(t) \; \forall t \geq 1$, in which case (30) describes a "sterlized intervention" in foreign exchange markets. Such an intervention is irrelevant so long as (26)–(29) are satisfied.

References

Barro, Robert J., "Are Government Bonds Net Wealth?" *Journal of Political* Economy, 82:6, Nov.–Dec. 1974, 1095–1117.

Chamley, Christophe, and Heraklis Polemarchakis, "Assets, General Equilibrium, and the Neutrality of Money," *Review of Economic Studies*, 51:1, Jan. 1984, 129–138.

Kareken, John, and Neil Wallace, "On the Indeterminacy of Equilibrium Exchange Rates," *Quarterly Journal of Economics*, 96:2, May 1981, 207–222.

Manuelli, Rodolfo, and Thomas J. Sargent, *Exercises in Dynamic Macroeconomic Theory*, Harvard Univ. Press, Cambridge, MA, 1987.

Modigliani, Franco, and Merton Miller, "The Cost of Capital, Corporation Finance, and the Theory of Investment," *American Economic Review*, 48:3, June 1958, 261–297.

Peled, Dan, "Stochastic Inflation and Government Provision of Indexed Bonds," *Journal of Monetary Economics*, 15:3, May 1985, 291–308.

Sargent, Thomas J., "The Ends of Four Big Inflations," in *Inflation: Causes and Effects*, Robert Hall, ed., University of Chicago Press, for the NBER, 1983.

Sargent, Thomas J., *Dynamic Macroeconomic Theory*, Harvard University Press, 1987.

Sargent, Thomas J., and Bruce D. Smith, "Irrelevance of Open-Market Operations in Some Economies with Government Currency Being Dominated in Rate of Return," *American Economic Review*, 77:1, March 1987, 78–92.

Sargent, Thomas J., and Neil Wallace, "The Real Bills Doctrine vs. the Quantity Theory: A Reconsideration," *Journal of Political Economy*, 90:6, Dec. 1982, 1212–1236.

Sargent, Thomas J., and Neil Wallace, "A Model of Commodity Money," *Journal of Monetary Economics*, 12:1, July 1983, 163–187.

Smith Bruce D., "Some Colonial Evidence on Two Theories of Money: Maryland and the Carolinas," *Journal of Political Economy*, 93:6, Dec. 1985(a), 1178–1211.

Smith, Bruce D., "American Colonial Monetary Regimes: The Failure of the Quantity Theory and Some Evidence in Favour of an Alternate View," *Canadian Journal of Economics*, 18:3, August 1985(b), 531–565.

Wallace, Neil, "A Modigliani-Miller Theorem for Open-Market Operations," *American Economic Review*, 71:3, June 1981, 267–274.

Name Index

Subject Index

Page numbers in *italics* refer to figures.